CHOICES: AN AMERICAN GOVERNMENT READER

A CUSTOMIZED AMERICAN GOVERNMENT READER

COMPILED BY

American Politics, 2004-2005 Edition
SS202 Reader
Custom Edition for the United States Military Academy at West Point

Editors:
ıvid P. Filer, Joanne C. Moore, John Gossart, Celestino Perez, Jr., Kyle F. Jette

PEARSON CUSTOM PUBLISHING

Director of Database Publishing: Michael Payne
Sponsoring Editor: Karen Usdan
Development Editor: Colby R. Lawrence
Marketing: Kathleen Kourian
Operations Manager: Eric M. Kenney

Proofreader: Amy Krammes (Paperback Writer Communications)
Keyer: Carole Chu
Designer: Julie Gecha
Cover Design: Seamus Culligan
Composition and Layout: Lorraine M. Hamwey

Cover Art: Courtesy of Michael Simpson/FPG.

Printed in the United States of America

10 9 8 7 6 5 4 3 2 1

ISBN 0536834466

PEARSON CUSTOM PUBLISHING
75 Arlington Street, Suite #300/ Boston, MA 02116
Pearson Education Group

Contents

☆ ☆ ☆

How Democratic Is America?

Howard Zinn

How Democratic is America? Liberal historian and philosopher Howard Zinn proposes that to answer this question we must first define democracy and then measure our society against the criteria included in our definition. Zinn's criteria include participation in decisions, access to information, equal protection of the laws, equality before the law, equitable distribution of resources, access to education, freedom of expression, freedom for individuality, a spirit of cooperation, and opportunity to protest. Zinn finds American democracy deficient in some way with respect to all of these criteria and that democracy exists primarily for the rich.

To give a sensible answer to the question "How democratic is America?" I find it necessary to make three clarifying preliminary statements. First, I want to define "democracy," not conclusively, but operationally, so we can know what we are arguing about or at least what I am talking about. Second, I want to state what my criteria are for measuring the "how" in the question. And third, I think it necessary to issue a warning about how a certain source of bias (although not the only source) is likely to distort our judgments.

Our definition is crucial. This becomes clear if we note how relatively easy is the answer to our question when we define democracy as a set of formal institutions and let it go at that. If we describe as "democratic" a country that has a representative system of government, with universal suffrage, a bill of rights, and party competition for office, it becomes easy to answer the question "how" with the enthusiastic reply, "Very!" . . .

☆ ☆ ☆ ☆ ☆ ☆

I propose a set of criteria for the description "democratic" which goes beyond formal political institutions, to the quality of life in the society (economic, social, psychological), beyond majority rule to a concern for minorities, and beyond national boundaries to a global view of what is meant by "the people," in that rough, but essentially correct view of democrat as "government of, by, and for the people."

Let me list these criteria quickly, because I will go on to discuss them in some detail later:

1. To what extent can various people in the society participate in those decisions which affect their lives: decisions in the political process and decisions in the economic structure?
2. As a corollary of the above: do people have equal access to the information which they need to make important decisions?
3. Are the members of the society equally protected on matters of life and death—in the most literal sense of that phrase?
4. Is there equality before the law: police, courts, the judicial process—as well as equality with the law-enforcing institutions, so as to safeguard equally everyone's person, and his freedom from interference by others, and by the government?
5. Is there equality in the distribution of available resources: those economic goods necessary for health, life, recreation, leisure, growth?
6. Is there equal access to education, to knowledge and training, so as to enable persons in the society to live their lives as fully as possible, to enlarge their range of possibilities?
7. Is there freedom of expression on all matters, and equally for all, to communicate with other members of the society?
8. Is there freedom for individuality in private life, in sexual relations, family relations, the right of privacy?
9. To minimize regulation: do education and the culture in general foster a spirit of cooperation and amity to sustain the above conditions?
10. As a final safety feature: is there opportunity to protest, to disobey the laws, when the foregoing objectives are being lost—as a way of restoring them? . . .

Two historical facts support my enlarged definition of democracy. One is that the industrialized Western societies have outgrown the original notions which accompanied their early development: that constitutional and procedural tests sufficed for the "democracy" that overthrew the old order;

that democracy was quite adequately fulfilled by the Bill of Rights in England at the time of the Glorious Revolution, the Constitution of the United States, and the declaration of the Rights of Man in France. It came to be acknowledged that the rhetoric of these revolutions was not matched by their real achievements. In other words, the limitations of that "democracy" led to the reformist and radical movements that grew up in the West in the middle and late nineteenth century. The other historical note is that the new revolutions in our century, in Africa, Asia, Latin America, while rejecting either in whole or in part the earlier revolutions, profess a similar democratic aim, but with an even broader rhetoric. . . .

My second preliminary point is on standards. By this I mean that we can judge in several ways the fulfillment of these ten criteria I have listed. We can measure the present against the past, so that if we find that in 1997 we are doing better in these matters than we were doing in 1860 or 1910, the society will get a good grade for its "democracy." I would adjure such an approach because it supports complacency. With such a standard, Russians in 1910 could point with pride to how much progress they had made toward parliamentary democracy; as Russians in 1985 could point to their post-Stalin progress away from the gulag; as Americans could point in 1939 to how far they had come toward solving the problem of economic equality; as Americans in the South could point in 1950 to the progress of the southern African-American. Indeed, the American government has given military aid to brutal regimes in Latin America on the ground that a decrease in the murders by semiofficial death squads is a sign of progress.

Or, we could measure our democracy against other places in the world. Given the high incidence of tyranny in the world, polarization of wealth, and lack of freedom of expression, the United States, even with very serious defects, could declare itself successful. Again, the result is to let us all off easily; some of our most enthusiastic self-congratulation is based on such a standard.

On the other hand, we could measure our democracy against an ideal (even if admittedly unachievable) standard. I would argue for such an approach, because, in what may seem to some a paradox, the ideal standard is the pragmatic one; it affects what we do. To grade a student on the basis of an improvement over past performance is justifiable if the intention is to encourage someone discouraged about his ability. But if he is rather pompous about his superiority in relation to other students (and I suggest this is frequently true of Americans evaluating American "democracy"), and if in addition he is a medical student about to graduate into a world ridden with disease, it would be best to judge him by an ideal standard. That might spur him to an improvement fast enough to save lives. . . .

My third preliminary point is a caution based on the obvious fact that we make our appraisals through the prism of our own status in society. This is particularly important in assessing democracy, because if "democracy" refers to the condition of masses of people, and if we as the assessors belong to a number of elites, we will tend (and I am not declaring an inevitability, just warning of a tendency) to see the present situation in America more benignly than it deserves. To be more specific, if democracy requires a keen awareness of the condition of black people, of poor people, of young people, of that majority of the world who are not American—and we are white, prosperous, beyond draft age, and American—then we have a number of pressures tending to dull our sense of inequity. We are, if not doomed to err, likely to err on the side of complacency—and we should try to take this into account in making our judgments.

★ 1. Participation in Decisions

We need to recognize first, that whatever decisions are made politically are made by representatives of one sort or another: state legislators, congressmen, senators, and other elected officials, governors and presidents; also by those appointed by elected officials, like Supreme Court justices. These are important decisions, affecting our lives, liberties, and ability to pursue happiness. Congress and the president decide on the tax structure, which affects the distribution of resources. They decide how to spend the monies received; whether or not we go to war; who serves in the armed forces; what behavior is considered a crime; which crimes are prosecuted and which are not. They decide what limitations there should be on our travel, or on our right to speak freely. They decide on the availability of education and health services.

If representation by its very nature is undemocratic, as I would argue, this is an important fact for our evaluation. Representative government is *closer* to democracy than monarchy, and for this reason it has been hailed as one of the great political advances of modern times; yet, it is only a step in the direction of democracy, at its best. It has certain inherent flaws—pointed out by Rousseau in the eighteenth century, Victor Considerant in the nineteenth century, Robert Michels in the beginning of the twentieth century, Hannah Arendt in our own time. No representative can adequately represent another's needs; the representative tends to become a member of a special elite; he has privileges which weaken his sense of concern at others' grievances; the passions of the troubled lose force (as Madison noted in *The Federalist 10*) as they are filtered through the representative system; the elected official develops an expertise which tends toward its own perpetuation.

Leaders develop what Michels called "a mutual insurance contract" against the rest of society. . . .

If only radicals pointed to the inadequacy of the political processes in the United States, we might be suspicious. But established political scientists of a moderate bent talk quite bluntly of the limitations of the voting system in the United States. Robert Dahl, in *A Preface to Democratic Theory,* drawing on the voting studies of American political scientists, concludes that "political activity, at least in the United States, is positively associated to a significant extent with such variables as income, socio-economic status, and education." He says:

> By their propensity for political passivity the poor and uneducated disfranchise themselves. . . . Since they also have less access than the wealthy to the organizational, financial, and propaganda resources that weigh so heavily in campaigns, elections, legislative, and executive decisions, anything like equal control over government policy is triply barred to the members of Madison's unpropertied masses. They are barred by their relatively greater inactivity, by their relatively limited access to resources, and by Madison's nicely contrived system of constitutional checks.1

Dahl thinks that our society is essentially democratic, but this is because he expects very little. (His book was written in the 1950s, when lack of commotion in the society might well have persuaded him that no one else expected much more than he did.) Even if democracy were to be superficially defined as "majority rule," the United States would not fulfill that, according to Dahl, who says that "on matters of specific policy, the majority rarely rules."[2] After noting that "the election is the critical technique for insuring that governmental leaders will be relatively responsive to nonleaders," he goes on to say that "it is important to notice how little a national election tells us about the preferences of majorities. Strictly speaking, all an election reveals is the first preferences of some citizens among the candidates standing for office."[3] About 45 percent of the potential voters in national elections, and about 60 percent of the voters in local elections do not vote, and this cannot be attributed, Dahl says, simply to indifference. And if, as Dahl points out, "in no large nation state can elections tell us much about the preferences of majorities and minorities," this is "even more true of the interelection period." . . .

Dahl goes on to assert that the election process and interelection activity "are crucial processes for insuring that political leaders will be *somewhat* responsive to the preferences of *some* ordinary citizens."[4] I submit (the emphasized words are mine) that if an admirer of democracy in America can say no more than this, democracy is not doing very well.

Dahl tells us the election process is one of "two fundamental methods of social control which, operating together, make governmental leaders so responsive to nonreaders that the distinction between democracy and dictatorship still makes sense." Since his description of the election process leaves that dubious, let's look at his second requirement for distinguishing democracy: "The other method of social control is continuous political competition among individuals, parties, or both." What it comes down to is "not minority rule but minorities rule."[5]

If it turns out that this—like the election process—also has little democratic content, we will not be left with very much difference—by Dahl's own admission—between "dictatorship" and the "democracy" practiced in the United States. Indeed, there is much evidence on this: the lack of democracy within the major political parties, the vastly disproportionate influence of wealthy groups over poorer ones. What antismoking consumer group in the election year of 1996 could match the five million dollars donated to the Republican Party by the tobacco interests? What ordinary citizen could have the access to President Bill Clinton that a group of bankers had in May of that election year when they were invited to the White House?[6] All of this, and more, supports the idea of a "decline of American pluralism" that Henry Kariel has written about. What Dahl's democrat comes down to is "the steady appeasement of relatively small groups."[7] If these relatively small groups turn out to be the aircraft industry far more than the aged, the space industry far more than the poor, the Pentagon far more than the college youth—what is left of democracy?

Sometimes the elitism of decision-making is defended (by Dahl and by others) on the ground that the elite is enacting decisions passively supported by the mass, whose tolerance is proof of an underlying consensus in society. But Murray Levin's studies in *The Alienated Voter* indicate how much nonparticipation in elections is a result of hopelessness rather than approval. And Robert Wiebe, a historian at Northwestern University, talks of "consensus" becoming a "new stereotype." He approaches the question historically.

> Industrialization arrived so peacefully not because all Americans secretly shared the same values or implicitly willed its success but because its millions of bitter enemies lacked the mentality and the means to organize an effective counterattack.[8]

Wiebe's point is that the passivity of most Americans in the face of elitist decision making has not been due to acquiescence but to the lack of resources for effective combat, as well as a gulf so wide between the haves and have-nots that there was no ground on which to dispute. Americans neither revolted violently nor reacted at the polls; instead they were subservient, or else worked out their hostilities in personal ways. . . .

Presidential nominations and elections are more democratic than monarchical rule or the procedures of totalitarian states, but they are far from some reasonable expectation of democracy. The two major parties have a monopoly of presidential power, taking turns in the White House. The candidates of minority parties don't have a chance. They do not have access to the financial backing of the major parties, and there is not the semblance of equal attention in the mass media; it is only the two major candidates who have free access to prime time on national television.

More important, both parties almost always agree on the fundamentals of domestic and foreign policy, despite the election-year rhetoric which attempts to find important differences. Both parties arranged for United States intervention in Vietnam in the 1950s and 1960s, and both, when public opinion changed, promised to get out (note the Humphrey-Nixon contest of 1968). In 1984, Democratic candidate Walter Mondale agreed with Republican candidate Ronald Reagan that the United States (which had ten thousand thermonuclear warheads) needed to continue increasing its arms budget, although he asked for a smaller increase than the Republicans. Such a position left Mondale unable to promise representatives of the black community (where unemployment was over 20 percent) that he would spend even a few billion dollars for a jobs program. Meanwhile, Democrats and Republicans in Congress were agreeing on a $297 billion arms bill for the 1985 fiscal year.[9]

I have been talking so far about democracy in the political process. But there is another serious weakness that I will only mention here, although it is of enormous importance: the powerlessness of the American to participate in economic decisionmaking, which affects his life at every moment. As a consumer, that is, as the person whom the economy is presumably intended to serve, he has virtually nothing to say about what is produced for him. The corporations make what is profitable; the advertising industry persuades him to buy what the corporations produce. He becomes the passive victim of the misallocation of resources, the production of dangerous commodities, the spoiling of his air, water, forests, beaches, cities.

★ 2. Access to Information

Adequate information for the electorate is a precondition for any kind of action (whether electoral or demonstrative) to affect national policy. As for the voting process, Berelson, Lazarsfeld, and McPhee tell us (in their book, *Voting*) after extensive empirical research: "One persistent conclusion is that the public is not particularly well informed about the specific issues of the day." . . .

Furthermore, there are certain issues which never even reach the public because they are decided behind the scenes. . . .

Consider the information available to voters on two major kinds of issues. One of them is the tax structure, so bewilderingly complex that the corporation, with its corps of accountants and financial experts, can prime itself for lobbying activities, while the average voter, hardly able to comprehend his own income tax, stands by helplessly as the president, the Office of Management and Budget, and the Congress decide the tax laws. The dominant influences are those of big business, which has the resources both to understand and to act.

Then there is foreign policy. The government leads the citizenry to believe it has special expertise which, if it could only be revealed, would support its position against critics. At the same time, it hides the very information which would reveal its position to be indefensible. The mendacity of the government on the Bay of Pigs operation and the withholding of vital information about the Tonkin Gulf events are only two examples of the way the average person becomes a victim of government deception.

In 1990, historian Warren Cohen resigned as adviser to the State Department in its publication of the series *Foreign Relations of the United States,* pointing out that the government was refusing to cover events less than thirty years old. And even what it did publish was not trustworthy. "The United States government is publishing blatantly fraudulent accounts of its activities in Guatemala, Iran, and Southeast Asia in the 1950s" (*World Monitor Magazine,* 1990).

When the United States invaded the tiny island of Grenada in the fall of 1983, no reporters were allowed to observe the invasion, and the American public had little opportunity to get independent verification of the reasons given by the government for the invasion. As a result, President Reagan could glibly tell the nation what even one of his own supporters, journalist George Will, admitted was a lie: that he was invading Grenada to protect the lives of American medical students on the island. He could also claim that documents found on the island indicated plans for a Cuban-Soviet takeover of Grenada; the documents showed no such thing.[10]

Furthermore, the distribution of information to the public is a function of power and wealth. The government itself can color the citizens' understanding of events by its control of news at the source: the presidential press conference, the "leak to the press," the White Papers, the teams of "truth experts" going around the country at the taxpayers' expense. As for private media, the large networks and mass-circulation magazines have the greatest access to the public mind. There is no "equal time" for critics of public policy. . . .

★ 3. Equal Protection

Let us go now from the procedural to the substantive, indeed to the *most* substantive of questions: the right of all people to life itself. Here we find democracy in America tragically inadequate. Not only Locke, one of the leading theorists of the democratic tradition, declared the ultimate right of any person to safeguard his own life when threatened by the government; Hobbes, often looked on as the foe of democratic thought, agreed. Yet, in matters of foreign policy, where the decisions involve life or death for large numbers of Americans, power rests in the hands of the president and a small group of advisers. Despite the constitutional provision that war must be declared by Congress, in reality the President can create situations (as in the Mexican War, as in both world wars) which make inevitable congressional votes for war. And in all post-World War II conflicts (Korea, Vietnam, Iraq) there was no declaration of war by Congress.

It is in connection with this most basic of rights—life itself, the first and most important of those substantive ends which democratic participation is designed to safeguard—that I would assert the need for a global view of democracy. One can at least conceive of a democratic decision for martial sacrifice by those ready to make the sacrifice; a "democratic" war is thus a theoretical possibility. But that presumption of democracy becomes obviously false at the first shot because then *others* are affected who did not decide. . . . Nations making decisions to slaughter their own sons are at least theoretically subject to internal check. The victims on the other side fall without any such chance. For the United States today, this failure of democracy is total; we have the capacity to destroy the world without giving it a chance to murmur a dissent; we did, in fact, destroy a part of southeast Asia on the basis of a unilateral decision made in Washington. There is no more pernicious manifestation of the lack of democracy in America than this single fact.

★ 4. Equality Before the Law

Is there equality before the law? At every stage of the judicial process—facing the policeman, appearing in court, being freed on bond, being sentenced by the judge—the poor person is treated worse than the rich, the black treated worse than the white, the politically or personally odd character is treated worse than the orthodox. A defendant's poverty affects his preliminary hearing, his right to bail, the quality of his counsel. The evidence is plentiful in the daily newspapers, which inform us that an African-American boy fleeing the scene of a two-dollar theft may be shot and killed by a pursuing policeman, while a wealthy man who goes to South America after a million-dollar swindle, even if apprehended, need never fear a scratch. The wealthy price-fixer for General Motors, who costs consumers millions, will get ninety days in jail, the burglar of a liquor store will get five years. An African-American youth, or a bearded white youth poorly dressed, has much more chance of being clubbed by a policeman on the street than a well-dressed white man, given the fact that both respond with equal tartness to a question. . . .

Aside from inequality among citizens, there is inequality between the citizen and his government, when they face one another in a court of law. Take the matter of counsel: the well-trained government prosecutor faces the indigent's court-appointed counsel. Four of my students did a study of the City Court of Boston several years ago. They sat in the court for weeks, taking notes, and found that the average time spent by court-appointed counsel with his client, before arguing the case at the bench, was seven minutes.

★ 5. Distribution of Resources

Democracy is devoid of meaning if it does not include equal access to the available resources of the society. In India, democracy might still mean poverty; in the United States, with a Gross National Product of more than $3 trillion a year, democracy should mean that every American, working a short work-week, has adequate food, clothing, shelter, health care, education for himself and his family—in short, the material resources necessary to enjoy life and freedom. Even if only 20 percent of the American population is desperately poor . . . in a country so rich, that is an inexcusable breach of the democratic principle. Even if there is a large, prosperous middle class, there is something grossly unfair in the fact that in 1995 the richest 1 percent of the population owned over 40 percent of the total wealth, a figure that, throughout our history, has rarely been under 33 percent.

Whether you are poor or rich determines the most fundamental facts about your life: whether you are cold in the winter while trying to sleep, whether you suffocate in the summer; whether you live among vermin or rats; whether the smells around you all day are sweet or foul; whether you have adequate medical care; whether you have good teeth; whether you can send your children to college; whether you can go on vacation or have to take an extra job at night; whether you can afford a divorce, or an abortion, or a wife, or another child. . . .

★ 6. Access to Education

In a highly industrialized society, education is a crucial determinant of wealth, political power, social status, leisure, and the ability to work in one's chosen field. Educational resources in our society are not equitably distributed. Among high-school graduates of the same IQ levels, a far higher percentage of the well-to-do go on to college than the poor.[11] A mediocre student with money can always go to college. A mediocre student without money may not be able to go, even to a state college, because he may have to work to support his family. Furthermore, the educational resources in the schools—equipment, teachers, etc.—are far superior in the wealthy suburbs than in the poor sections of the city, whether white or black.

★ 7. Freedom of Expression

Like money, freedom of expression is available to all in America, but in widely varying quantities. The First Amendment formally guarantees freedom of speech, press, assembly, and petition to all—but certain realities of wealth, power, and status stand in the way of the equal distribution of these rights. Anyone can stand on a street corner and talk to ten or a hundred people. But someone with the resources to buy loudspeaker equipment, go through the necessary red tape, and post a bond with the city may hold a meeting downtown and reach a thousand or five thousand people. A person or a corporation with $100,000 can buy time on television and reach 10 million people. A rich person simply has much more freedom of speech than a poor person. The government has much more freedom of expression than a private individual, because the president can command the airwaves when he wishes, and reach 60 million people in one night.

Freedom of the press also is guaranteed to all. But the student selling an underground newspaper on the street with a nude woman on the cover may be arrested by a policeman, while the airport newsstand selling *Playboy* and ten magazines like it will remain safe. Anyone with $10,000 can put out a newspaper to reach a few thousand people. Anyone with $10 million can buy a few newspapers that will reach a few million people. Anyone who is penniless had better have a loud voice; and then he might be arrested for disturbing the peace.

★ 8. Freedom for Individuality

The right to live one's life, in privacy and freedom, in whatever way one wants, so long as others are not harmed, should be a sacred principle in a democracy. But there are hundreds of laws, varying from state to state, and sometimes joined by federal laws, which regulate the personal lives of people in this country: their marriages, their divorces, their sexual relations. Furthermore, both laws and court decisions protect policemen and the FBI in their use of secret devices which listen in on private conversations, or peer in on private conduct.

★ 9. The Spirit of Cooperation

The maintenance of those substantive elements of democracy which I have just sketched, if dependent on a pervasive network of coercion, would cancel out much of the benefit of that democracy. Democracy needs rather to be sustained by a spirit in society, the tone and the values of the culture. I am speaking of something as elusive as a mood, alongside something as hard as law, both of which would have to substitute cooperation tinged with friendly competition for the fierce combat of our business culture. I am speaking of the underlying drive that keeps people going in the society. So long as that drive is for money and power, with no ceiling on either, so long as ruthlessness is built into the rules of the game, democracy does not have a chance. If there is one crucial cause in the failure of American democracy—not the only one, of course, but a fundamental one—it is the drive for corporate profit, and the overwhelming influence of money in every aspect of our daily lives. That is the uncontrolled libido of our society from which the rape of democratic values necessarily follows.

The manifestations are diverse and endless: the drug industry's drive for profit has led to incredible overpricing of drugs for consumers (700 percent markup, for instance, for tablets to arthritic patients). It was disclosed in 1979 that Johns-Manville, the nation's largest asbestos manufacturer, had deliberately withheld from its workers X-ray results that showed they were developing cancer. In 1984, a company making an intrauterine birth control device—the Dalkon Shield—was found by a Minnesota court to have allowed tens of thousands of women to wear this device despite knowing that it was dangerous to their health (*Minneapolis Star and Tribune,* May 18, 1984). In the mid-1990s, it was revealed that tobacco companies had concealed information showing the narcotic nature of cigarettes. All in the interest of maximizing profit.

If these were isolated cases, reported and then eliminated, they could be dismissed as unfortunate blemishes on an otherwise healthy social body. But the major allocations of resources in our society are made on the basis of money profit rather than social use. . . .

. . . News items buttress what I have said. The oil that polluted California's beautiful beaches in the 1960s . . . was produced by a system in which the oil companies' hunger for profit has far more weight than the ordinary person's need to swim in clean water. This is not to be attributed to Republicanism overriding the concern for the lithe fellow of the Democratic Party. Profit is master whichever party is in power; it was the liberal Secretary of the Interior Stewart Udall who allowed the dangerous drilling to go on. . . .

In 1984, the suit of several thousand veterans against the Dow Chemical Company, claiming that they and their families had suffered terrible illnesses as a result of exposure in Vietnam to the poisonous chemical Agent Orange, was settled. The Dow corporation avoided the disclosures of thousands of documents in open court by agreeing to pay $180 million to the veterans. One thing seemed clear: the company had known that the defoliant used in Vietnam might be dangerous, but it held back the news, and blamed the government for ordering use of the chemical. The government itself, apparently wanting to shift blame to the corporation, declared publicly that Dow Chemical had been motivated in its actions by greed for profit.

★ *10. Opportunity to Protest*

The first two elements in my list for democracy—decision-making and information to help make them are procedural. The next six are substantive, dealing with the consequences of such procedures on life, liberty, and the pursuit of happiness. My ninth point, the one I have just discussed, shows how the money motive of our society corrupts both procedures and their consequences by its existence and suggests we need a different motive as a fundamental requisite of a democratic society. The point I am about to discuss is an ultimate requisite for democracy, a safety feature if nothing else—neither procedures nor consequences nor motivation—works. It is the right of citizens to break through the impasse of a legal and cultural structure, which sustains inequality, greed, and murder, to initiate processes for change. I am speaking of civil disobedience, which is an essential safeguard even in a successful society, and which is an absolute necessity in a society which is not going well.

If the institutional structure itself bars any change but the most picayune and grievances are serious, it is silly to insist that change must be mediated through the processes of that legal structure. In such a situation, dramatic expressions of protest and challenge are necessary to help change ways of thinking, to build up political power for drastic change. A society that calls itself democratic (whether accurately or not) must, as its ultimate safeguard, allow such acts of disobedience. If the government prohibits them (as we must expect from a government committed to the existent) then the members of a society concerned with democracy must not only defend such acts, but encourage them. Somewhere near the root of democratic thought is the theory of popular sovereignty, declaring that government and laws are instruments for certain ends, and are not to be deified with absolute obedience; they must constantly be checked by the citizenry, and challenged, opposed, even overthrown, if they become threats to fundamental rights.

Any abstract assessment of *when* disobedience is justified is pointless. Proper conclusions depend on empirical evidence about how bad things are at the moment, and how adequate are the institutional mechanisms for correcting them. . . .

One of these is the matter of race. The intolerable position of the African-American, in both North and South, has traditionally been handled with a few muttered apologies and tokens of reform. Then the civil disobedience of militants in the South forced our attention on the most dramatic (southern) manifestations of racism in America. The massive African-American urban uprisings of 1967 and 1968 showed that nothing less than civil disobedience (for riots and uprisings go beyond that) could make the nation see that the race problem is an American—not a southern—problem and that it needs bold, revolutionary action.

As for poverty: it seems clear that the normal mechanisms of congressional pretense and presidential rhetoric are not going to change things very much. Acts of civil disobedience by the poor will be required, at the least, to make middle-class America take notice, to bring national decisions that begin to reallocate wealth.

The war in Vietnam showed that we could not depend on the normal processes of "law and order," of the election process, of letters to the *Times,* to stop a series of especially brutal acts against the Vietnamese and against our own sons. It took a nationwide storm of protest, including thousands of acts of civil disobedience (14,000 people were arrested in one day in 1971 in Washington, D.C.), to help bring the war to an end. The role of draft resistance in affecting Lyndon Johnson's 1968 decision not to escalate the war further is told in the Defense Department secret documents of that period. In the 1980s and 1990s civil disobedience continued, with religious pacifists and others risking prison in order to protest the arms race and the plans for nuclear war.

The great danger for American democracy is not from the protesters. That democracy is too poorly realized for us to consider critics—even rebels—as the chief problem. Its fulfillment requires us all, living in an ossified system which sustains too much killing and too much selfishness, to join the protest.

★ *Activist and historian* **Howard Zinn,** *author of* A People's History of the United States, *is Professor Emeritus of History and Political Science at Boston University.*

Endnotes

[1]Robert A. Dahl, *A Preface to Democratic Theory* (Chicago: University of Chicago Press, 1963), p.81.

[2]*Ibid,* p.124.

[3]*Ibid,* p.125.

[4]*Ibid,* p.131.

[5]*Ibid,* pp. 131-32.

[6]*New York Times,* January 25, 27, 1997.

[7]Dahl, *A Preface to Democratic Theory,* p. 146.

[8]Robert Wiebe, "The Confinements of Consensus," *TriQuarterly,* 1966, Copyright by TriQuarterly 1966. All rights reserved.

[9]*New York Times,* September 25, 1984.

[10]The *New York Times* reported, November 5, 1983: "There is nothing in the documents, however, that specifically indicates that Cuba and the Soviet Union were on the verge of taking over Grenada, as Administration officials have suggested."

[11]See the Carnegie Council on Children study, *Small Futures,* by Richard deLore, 1979.

★ ★ ★ ★ ★

Questions

1. To what extent is democracy a function of society as opposed to being an attribute of government?
2. To what extent are the poor at a disadvantage with respect to equal treatment in our courts of justice?
3. To what extent are the poor at a disadvantage with respect to their ability to attain adequate representation for their views and needs?
4. To what extent is American society a democracy for the rich only?
5. To what extent does our society's demand for conformity depreciate the value of our democracy?

☆ ☆ ☆

How Democratic Is America? A Response to Howard Zinn

Sidney Hook

Conservative commentator Sidney Hook attempts to demolish Howard Zinn's critique of American democracy by finding Zinn guilty of violating the principle that philosopher Charles Peirce called the "ethics of words." For Hook, democracy is a political process designed to produce a free society. Hook says that Zinn deliberately confuses democracy with a specific economic condition—the welfare state—designed to produce the good society. Furthermore, Hook insists, Zinn unfairly compares America to an ideal that ignores the natural inequality of human capacities while ignoring the immense progress America has made both with respect to its past and with respect to many other nations in the world.

Charles Peirce, the great American philosopher, once observed that there was such a thing as the "ethics of words." The "ethics of words" are violated whenever ordinary terms are used in an unusual context or arbitrarily identified with another concept for which other terms are in common use. Mr. Zinn is guilty of a systematic violation of the "ethics of words." In consequence, his discussion of "democracy" results in a great many methodological errors as well as inconsistencies. To conserve space, I shall focus on three.

☆ ☆ ☆ ☆ ☆ ☆

★ 1

First of all, he confuses democracy as a political process with democracy as a political *product* or state of welfare; democracy as a "*free* society" with democracy as a "*good* society," where good is defined in terms of equality or justice (or both) or some other constellation of values. One of the reasons for choosing to live under a democratic political system rather than a nondemocratic system is our belief that it makes possible a better society. That is something that must be empirically established, something denied by critics of democracy from Plato to Santayana. The equality which is relevant to democracy as a *political process* is, in the first instance, political equality with respect to the rights of citizenship. Theoretically, a politically democratic community could vote, wisely or unwisely, to abolish, retain, or establish certain economic inequalities. Theoretically, a benevolent despotism could institute certain kinds of social and even juridical equalities. Historically, the Bismarckian political dictatorship introduced social welfare legislation for the masses at a time when such legislation would have been repudiated by the existing British and American political democracies. Some of Mr. Zinn's proposed reforms could be introduced under a dictatorship or benevolent despotism. Therefore, they are not logically or organically related to democracy.

The second error in Mr. Zinn's approach to democracy is "to measure our democracy against an ideal (even if admittedly unachievable) standard . . . even if utopian . . ." without *defining* the standard. His criteria admittedly are neither necessary nor sufficient for determining the presence of democracy since he himself admits that they are applicable to societies that are not democratic. Further, even if we were to take his criteria as severally defining the presence of democracy—as we might take certain physical and mental traits as constituting a definition of health—he gives no operational test for determining whether or not they have been fulfilled. For example, among the criteria he lists for determining whether a society is democratic is this: "Are the members of the society equally protected on matters of life and death—in the most literal sense of that phrase?" A moment's reflection will show that here—as well as in other cases where Zinn speaks of equality—it is impossible for all members to be equally protected on matters of life and death—certainly not in a world in which men do the fighting and women give birth to children, where children need *more* protection than adults, and where some risk-seeking adults require and deserve less protection (since resources are not infinite) than others. As Karl Marx realized, "in the most literal sense of that phrase," there cannot be absolute equality even in a classless society. . . .

The only sensible procedure in determining the absence or presence of equality from a democratic perspective is comparative. We must ask whether a culture is more or less democratic in comparison to the past with respect to some desirable feature of equality (Zinn ignores the fact that not all equalities are desirable). It is better for some people to be more intelligent and more knowledgeable than others than for all to be unintelligent and ignorant. There never is literally equal access to education, to knowledge and training in any society. The question is: Is there more access today for more people than yesterday, and how can we increase the access tomorrow?

Mr. Zinn refuses to take this approach because, he asserts, "it supports complacency." It does nothing of the sort! On the contrary, it shows that progress is possible, and encourages us to exert our efforts in the same direction if we regard the direction as desirable.

It will be instructive to look at the passage in which Mr. Zinn objects to this sensible comparative approach because it reveals the bias in his approach:

"With such a standard," he writes, "Russia in 1910 could point with pride to how much progress they had made toward parliamentary democracy; as Russians in 1985 could point to their post-Stalin progress away from the gulag; as Americans could point in 1939 to how far they had come in solving the problem of economic equality; as Americans in the South could point in 1950 to the progress of the southern African-American."

a. In 1910 the Russians were indeed moving toward greater progress in local parliamentary institutions. Far from making them complacent, they moved towards more inclusive representative institutions which culminated in elections to the Constituent Assembly in 1918, which was bayoneted out of existence by Lenin and the Communist Party, with a minority party dictatorship established.

b. Only Mr. Zinn would regard the slight diminution in terror from the days of Stalin to the regime of Chernenko as progress toward democracy. Those who observe the ethics of words would normally say that the screws of repression had been slightly relaxed. Mr. Zinn seems unaware that as bad as the terror was under Lenin, it was not as pervasive as it is today.1 But no one with any respect for the ethics of words would speak of "the progress of democracy" in the Soviet Union from Lenin to Stalin to Khrushchev to Chernenko. Their regimes were varying degrees of dictatorship and terror.

c. Americans could justifiably say that in 1939 progress had been made in giving workers a greater role, not as Mr. Zinn says in "solving the problem of economic equality" (a meaningless phrase), but in determining the conditions and rewards of work that prevailed in 1929 or previously because the existence of the Wagner Labor Relations Act made collective bargaining the law of the land. They could say this not to rest in complacency, but to use the organized force of their trade unions to influence further the political life of the country. And indeed, it was the organized labor movement in 1984 which in effect chose the candidate of the Democratic Party.

d. Americans in the South in 1950 could rightfully speak of the progress of the southern African-American over the days of unrestricted Jim Crow and lynching bees of the past, not to rest in complacency, but to agitate for further progress through the Supreme Court decision of *Brown v. Board of Education* in Topeka and through the Civil Rights Act of Congress. This has not made them complacent, but more resolved to press further to eliminate remaining practices of invidious discrimination.

Even Mr. Zinn should admit that with respect to some of his other criteria this is the only sensible approach. Otherwise we get unhistorical answers, the hallmark of the doctrinaire. He asks criterion[1]—"To what extent can various people in the society participate in those decisions which affect their lives?" and—criterion 7—"Is there freedom of expression on all matters, and equally for all, to communicate with other members of the society?" Why doesn't Mr. Zinn adopt this sensible comparative approach? Because it would lead him to inquire into the extent to which people are free to participate in decisions that affect their lives *today,* free to express themselves, free to organize, free to protest and dissent today, *in comparison with the past.* It would lead him to the judgment *which he wishes to avoid at all costs,* to wit, that despite the grave problems, gaps, and tasks before us, the United States is *more* democratic today than it was a hundred years ago, fifty years ago, twenty years ago, five years ago with respect to every one of the criteria he has listed. To recognize this is *not* an invitation to complacency. On the contrary, it indicates the possibility of broadening, deepening, and using the democratic political process to improve the quality of human life, to modify and redirect social institutions in order to realize on a wider scale the moral commitment of democracy to an equality of concern for all its citizens to achieve their fullest growth as persons. This commitment to a process, not to a transcendent goal or a fixed, ideal standard.

In a halting, imperfect manner, set back by periods of violence, vigilantism, and xenophobia, the political democratic process in the United States has been used to modify the operation of the economic system. The improvements and reforms won from time to time make the still-existing problems and evils more acute in that people become more aware of them. The more the democratic process extends human freedoms, and the more it introduces justice in social relations and the distribution of wealth, the greater grows the desire for more freedom and justice. Historically and psychologically, it is false to assume that reforms breed a spirit of complacency. . . .

The third and perhaps most serious weakness in Mr. Zinn's view is his conception of the nature of the formal political democratic process. It suffers from several related defects. First, it overlooks the central importance of majority rule in the democratic process. Second, it denies in effect that majority rule is possible by defining democracy in such a way that it becomes impossible. . . .

"Representation by its very nature," claims Mr. Zinn, "is undemocratic." This is Rousseauistic nonsense. For it would mean that no democracy—including all socictics that Mr. Zinn ever claimed at any time to be democratic—could possibly exist, not even the direct democracies or assemblies of Athens or the New England town meetings. For all such assemblies must elect officials to carry out their will. If no representative (and an official is a representative, too) can adequately represent another's needs, there is no assurance that in the actual details of governance, the selectmen, road commissioners, or other town or assembly officials will, in fact, carry out their directives. No assembly or meeting can sit in continuous session or collectively carry out the common decision. In the nature of the case, officials, like representatives, constitute an elite and their actions may reflect their interests more than the interests of the governed. This makes crucial the questions whether and how an elite can be removed, whether the consent on which the rule of the officials or representatives rests is free or coerced, whether a minority can peacefully use these mechanisms, by which freely given consent is registered, to win over or become a majority. The existence of representative assemblies makes democracy difficult, not impossible.

Since Mr. Zinn believes that a majority never has any authority to bind a minority as well as itself by decisions taken after free discussion and debate, he is logically committed to anarchy. Failing to see this, he confuses two fundamentally different things—the meaning or definition of democracy, and its justification.

1. A democratic government is one in which the general direction of policy rests directly or indirectly upon the freely given consent of a majority of the adults governed. Ambiguities and niceties aside, that is what democracy means. It is not anarchy. The absence of a unanimous consensus does not entail the absence of democracy.

2. One may reject on moral or religious or personal grounds a democratic society. Plato, as well as modern totalitarians, contends that a majority of mankind is either too stupid or vicious to be entrusted with self-government, or to be given the power to accept or reject their ruling elites, and that the only viable alternative to democracy is the self-selecting and self-perpetuating elite of "the wise," or "the efficient," or "the holy," or "the strong," depending upon the particular ideology of the totalitarian apologist. The only thing they have in common with democrats is their rejection of anarchy.
3. No intelligent and moral person can make an *absolute* of democracy in the sense that he believes it is always, everywhere, under any conditions, and no matter what its consequences, ethically legitimate. Democracy is obviously not desirable in a headhunting or cannibalistic society or in an institution of the feeble-minded. But wherever and whenever a principled democrat accepts the political system of democracy, he must accept the binding authority of legislative decisions, reached after the free give-and-take of debate and discussion, as binding upon him whether he is a member of the majority or minority. Otherwise the consequence is incipient or overt anarchy or civil war, the usual preface to despotism or tyranny. Accepting the decision of the majority as binding does not mean that it is final or irreversible. The processes of freely given consent must make it possible for a minority to urge amendment or repeal of any decision of the majority. Under carefully guarded provisions, a democrat may resort to civil disobedience of a properly enacted law in order to bear witness to the depths of his commitment in an effort to *reeducate* his fellow citizens. But in that case he must voluntarily accept punishment for his civil disobedience, and so long as he remains a democrat, voluntarily abandon his violation or noncompliance with law at the point where its consequences threaten to destroy the democratic process and open the floodgates either to the violent disorders of anarchy or to the dictatorship of a despot or a minority political party.
4. That Mr. Zinn is not a democrat but an anarchist in his views is apparent in his contention that not only must a democracy allow or tolerate civil disobedience within limits, but that "members of a society concerned with democracy must not only defend such acts, but encourage them." On this view, if southern segregationists resort to civil disobedience to negate the long-delayed but eminently just measures adopted by the government to implement the amendments that outlaw slavery, they should be encouraged to do

so. On this view, any group that defies any law that violates its conscience—with respect to marriage, taxation, vaccination, abortion, education—should be encouraged to do so. Mr. Zinn, like most anarchists, refuses to generalize the principles behind his action. He fails to see that if all fanatics of causes deemed by them to be morally just were encouraged to resort to civil disobedience, even our imperfect existing political democracy would dissolve in chaos, and that civil disobedience would soon become quite uncivil. He fails to see that *in a democracy the processes of intelligence, not individual conscience, must be supreme.*

★ *II*

I turn now to some of the issues that Mr. Zinn declares are substantive. Before doing so I wish to make clear my belief that the most substantive issue of all is the procedural one by which the inescapable differences of interests among men, once a certain moral level of civilization has been reached, are to be negotiated. The belief in the validity of democratic procedures rests upon the conviction that where adult human beings have freedom of access to relevant information, they are, by and large, better judges of their own interests than are those who set themselves up as their betters and rulers, that, to use the homely maxim, those who wear the shoes know best where they pinch and therefore have the right to change their political shoes in the light of their experience. . . .

Looking at the question "How democratic is America?" with respect to the problems of poverty, race, education, etc., we must say "Not democratic enough!" but not for the reasons Mr. Zinn gives. For he seems to believe that the failure to adopt *his* solutions and proposals with respect to foreign policy, slum clearance, pollution, etc., is evidence of the failure of the democratic process itself. He overlooks the crucial difference between the procedural process and the substantive issues. When he writes that democracy is devoid of meaning if it does not include "equal access to the available resources of the society," he is simply abusing language. Assuming such equal access is desirable (which some might question who believe that access to *some* of society's resources—for example, to specialized training or to scarce supplies—should go not equally to all but to the most needful or sometimes to the most qualified), a democracy may or may not legislate such equal access. The crucial question is whether the electorate has the power to make the choice, or to elect those who would carry out the mandate chosen. . . .

When Mr. Zinn goes on to say that "in the United States . . . democracy should mean that every American, working a short work-week, has adequate food, clothing, shelter, health care, . . ." he is not only abusing language, he is revealing the fact that the procedural processes that are essential to the meaning of democracy, in ordinary usage, are not essential to his conception. He is violating the basic ethics of discourse. If democracy "should mean" what Zinn says it should, then were Huey Long or any other dictator to seize power and introduce a "short work-week" and distribute "adequate food, clothing, shelter, health care" to the masses, Mr. Zinn would have to regard his regime as democratic.

After all, when Hitler came to power and abolished free elections in Germany, he at the same time reduced unemployment, increased the real wages of the German worker, and provided more adequate food, clothing, shelter, and health care than was available under the Weimar Republic. On Zinn's view of what democracy "should mean," this made Hitler's rule more democratic than that of Weimar. . . .

Not surprisingly, Mr. Zinn is a very unreliable guide even in his account of the procedural features of the American political system. In one breath he maintains that not enough information is available to voters to make intelligent choices on major political issues like tax laws. (The voter, of course, does not vote on such laws but for representatives who have taken stands on a number of complex issues.) "The dominant influences are those of big business, which has the resources both to understand and to act." In another breath, he complains that the electorate is at the mercy of the propagandist. "The propagandist does not need to lie; he overwhelms the public with so much information as to lead it to believe that it is all too complicated for anyone but the experts."

Mr. Zinn is certainly hard to please! The American political process is not democratic because the electorate hasn't got enough information. It is also undemocratic because it receives too much information. What would Zinn have us do so that the public gets just the right amount of information and propaganda? Have the government control the press? Restrict freedom of propaganda? But these are precisely the devices of totalitarian societies. The evils of the press, even when it is free of government control, are many indeed. The great problem is to keep the press free and responsible. And as defective as the press and other public media are today, surely it is an exaggeration to say that with respect to tax laws "the dominant influences are those of big business." If they were, how can we account for the existence of the income tax laws? If the influence of big business on the press is so dominant and the press is so biased, how can we account for the fact that although 92 percent of the press opposed Truman's candidacy in 1948, he was reelected? How can we account for the profound dissatisfaction of Vice-President Agnew with the press and other mass media?[2] And since Mr. Zinn believes that big business dominates our educational system, especially our universities, how can we account for the fact that the universities are the centers of the strongest dissent in the nation to public and national policy, that the National Association of Manufacturers bitterly complained a few years ago that the economics of the free enterprise system was derided, and often not even taught, in most Departments of Economics in the colleges and universities of the nation?

Mr. Zinn's exaggerations are really caricatures of complex realities. Far from being controlled by the monolithic American corporate economy, American public opinion is today marked by a greater scope and depth of dissent than at any time in its history, except for the days preceding the Civil War. The voice and the votes of Main Street still count for more in a democratic polity than those of Wall Street. Congress has limited, and can still further limit, the influence of money on the electoral process by federal subsidy and regulations. There are always abuses needing reforms. By failing to take a comparative approach and instead focusing on some absolute utopian standard of perfection, Mr. Zinn gives an exaggerated, tendentious, and fundamentally false picture of the United States. There is hardly a sentence in his essay that is free of some serious flaw in perspective, accuracy, or emphasis. Sometimes they have a comic effect, as when Mr. Zinn talks about the lack of "equal distribution of the right of freedom of expression." What kind of "equal distribution" is he talking about? Of course, a person with more money can talk to more people than one with less, although this does not mean that more persons will listen to him, agree with him, or be influenced by him. But a person with a more eloquent voice or a better brain can reach more people than you or I. What shall we do to insure equal distribution of the right of freedom of expression? Insist on equality of voice volume or pattern, and equality of brain power? More money gives not only greater opportunity to talk to people than less money but the ability to do thousands of things barred to those who have less money. Shall we then decree that all people have the same amount of money all the time and forbid anyone from depriving anyone else of any of his money even by fair means? "The government," writes Mr. Zinn, "has much more freedom of expression than a private individual because the president can command the airwaves when he wishes, and reach 60 million people in one night."

Alas! Mr. Zinn is not joking. Either he wants to bar the president or any public official from using the airwaves or he wants all of us to take turns. One wonders what country Mr. Zinn is living in. Nixon spoke to 60 million people several times, and so did Jimmy Carter. What was the result? More significant than the fact that 60 million people hear the president is that 60 million or more can hear his critics, sometimes right after he speaks, and that no one is compelled to listen.

Mr. Zinn does not understand the basic meaning of equality in a free, open democratic society. Its philosophy does not presuppose that all citizens are physically or intellectually equal or that all are equally gifted in every or any respect. It holds that all enjoy a moral equality, and that therefore, as far as is practicable, given finite resources, the institutions of a democratic society should seek to provide an equal opportunity to all its citizens to develop themselves to their full desirable potential.

Of course, we cannot ever provide complete equal opportunity. More and more is enough. For one thing, so long as children have different parents and home environments, they cannot enjoy the same or equal opportunities. Nonetheless, the family has compensating advantages for all that. Let us hope that Mr. Zinn does not wish to wipe out the family to avoid differences in opportunity. Plato believed that the family, as we know it, should be abolished because it did not provide equality of opportunity, and that all children should be brought up by the state.

Belief in the moral equality of men and women does not require that all individuals be treated identically or that equal treatment must be measured or determined by equality of outcome or result. Every citizen should have an equal right to an education, but that does not mean that, regardless of capacity and interest, he or she should have the same amount of schooling beyond the adolescent years, and at the same schools, and take the same course of study. With the increase in national wealth, a good case can be made for an equal right of all citizens to health care or medical treatment. But only a quack or ideological fanatic would insist that therefore all individuals should have the same medical regimen no matter what ails them. This would truly be putting all human beings in the bed of Procrustes.

This conception of moral equality as distinct from Mr. Zinn's notions of equality is perfectly compatible with intelligent recognition of human inequalities and relevant ways of treating their inequalities to further both the individual and common good. Intelligent and loving parents are equally concerned with the welfare of all their children. But precisely because they are, they may provide different specific strategies in health care, education, psychological motivation, and intellectual stimulation to develop the best in all of them. The logic of Mr. Zinn's position—although he seems blissfully unaware of it—leads to the most degrading kind of egalitarian socialism, the kind which Marx and Engels in their early years denounced as "barracks socialism."

It is demonstrable that democracy is healthier and more effective where human beings do not suffer from poverty, unemployment, and disease. It is also demonstrable that to the extent that property gives power, private property in the means of social production gives power over the lives of those who must live by its use, and, therefore, that such property, whether public or private, should be responsible to those who are affected by its operation. Consequently one can argue that political democracy depends not only on the extension of the franchise to all adults, not only on its active exercise, but on programs of social welfare that provide for collective bargaining by free trade unions of workers and employees, unemployment insurance, minimum wages, guaranteed health care, and other social services that are integral to the welfare state. It is demonstrable that although the existing American welfare state provides far more welfare than was ever provided in the past—my own lifetime furnishes graphic evidence of the vast changes—it is still very far from being a genuine welfare state. Political democracy can exist without a welfare state, but it is stronger and better with it.

The basic issue that divides Mr. Zinn from others no less concerned about human welfare, but less fanatical than he, is how a genuine welfare state is to be brought about. My contention is that this can be achieved by the vigorous exercise of the existing democratic process, and that by the same coalition politics through which great gains have been achieved in the past, even greater gains can be won in the future.

For purposes of economy, I focus on the problem of poverty, or since this is a relative term, hunger. If the presence of hunger entails the absence of the democratic political process, then democracy has never existed in the past—which would be an arbitrary use of words. Nonetheless, the existence of hunger is always a *threat* to the continued existence of the democratic process because of the standing temptation of those who hunger to exchange freedom for the promise of bread. This, of course, is an additional ground to the even weightier moral reasons for gratifying basic human needs.

That fewer people go hungry today in the United States than ever before may show that our democracy is better than it used to be but not that it is as good as it can be. Even the existence of one hungry person is one too many. How then can hunger or the extremes of poverty be abolished? Certainly not by the method Mr. Zinn advises: "Acts of civil disobedience by the poor will be required, at the least, to make middle-class America take notice, to bring national decisions that begin to reallocate wealth."

This is not only a piece of foolish advice, it is dangerously foolish advice. Many national decisions to reallocate wealth have been made through the political process—what else is the system of taxation if not a method of reallocating wealth?—without resort to civil disobedience. Indeed, resort to civil disobedience on this issue is very likely to produce a backlash among those active and influential political groups in the community who are aware that normal political means are available for social and economic reform. The refusal to engage in such normal political processes could easily be exploited by demagogues to portray the movement towards the abolition of hunger and extreme poverty as a movement towards the confiscation and equalization of all wealth.

The simplest and most effective way of abolishing hunger is to act on the truly revolutionary principle, enunciated by the federal government, that it is responsible for maintaining a standard of relief as a minimum beneath which a family will not be permitted to sink. . . .

For reasons that need no elaboration here, the greatest of the problems faced by American democracy today is the race problem. Although tied to the problems of poverty and urban reconstruction, it has independent aspects exacerbated by the legacy of the Civil War and the Reconstruction period.

Next to the American Indians, African-Americans have suffered most from the failure of the democratic political process to extend the rights and privileges of citizenship to those whose labor and suffering have contributed so much to the conquest of the continent. The remarkable gains that have been made by African-Americans in the last twenty years have been made primarily through the political process. If the same rate of improvement continues, the year 2000 may see a rough equality established. The growth of African-American suffrage, especially in the South, the increasing sense of responsibility by the white community, despite periodic setbacks resulting from outbursts of violence, opens up a perspective of continuous and cumulative reform. The man and the organization he headed chiefly responsible for the great gains made by African-Americans, Roy Wilkins and the NAACP, were convinced that the democratic political process can be more effectively used to further the integration of African-Americans into our national life than by reliance on any other method. . . .

The only statement in Mr. Zinn's essay that I can wholeheartedly endorse is his assertion that the great danger to American democracy does not come from the phenomena of protest as such. Dissent and protest are integral to the democratic process. The danger comes from certain modes of dissent, from the substitution of violence and threats of violence for the mechanisms of the political process, from the escalation of that violence as the best hope of those who still have grievances against our imperfect American democracy, and from views such as those expressed by Mr. Zinn which downgrade the possibility of peaceful social reform and encourage rebellion. It is safe to predict that large-scale violence by impatient minorities will fail. It is almost as certain that attempts at violence will backfire, that they will create a climate of repression that may reverse the course of social progress and expanded civil liberties of the last generation. . . .

It is when Mr. Zinn is discussing racial problems that his writing ceases to be comic and silly and becomes irresponsible and mischievous. He writes:

> The massive African-American urban uprisings of 1967 and 1968 showed that nothing less than civil disobedience (for riots and uprisings go beyond that) could make the nation see that the race problem is an American—not a southern—problem and that it needs bold, revolutionary action.

First of all, every literate person knows that the race problem is an American problem, not exclusively a southern one. It needs no civil disobedience or "black uprisings" to remind us of that. Second, the massive uprisings of 1967 and 1968 were violent and uncivil, and resulted in needless loss of life and suffering. The Civil Rights Acts, according to Roy Wilkins, then head of the NAACP, were imperiled by them. They were adopted despite, not because, of them. Third, what kind of "revolutionary" action is Mr. Zinn calling for? And by whom? He seems to lack the courage of his confusions. Massive civil disobedience when sustained becomes a form of civil war.

Despite Mr. Zinn and others, violence is more likely to produce reaction than reform. In 1827 a resolution to manumit slaves by purchase (later, Lincoln's preferred solution) was defeated by three votes in the House of Burgesses of the State of Virginia. It was slated to be reintroduced in a subsequent session with excellent prospects of being adopted. Had Virginia adopted it, North Carolina would shortly have followed suit. But before it could be reintroduced, Nat Turner's rebellion broke out. Its violent excesses frightened the South into a complete rejection of a possibility that might have prevented the American Civil War—the fiercest and bloodiest war in human history up to that time, from whose consequences American society is still suffering. Mr. Zinn's intentions are as innocent as those of a child playing with matches.

★ *III*

One final word about "the global" dimension of democracy of which Mr. Zinn speaks. Here, too, he speaks sympathetically of actions that would undermine the willingness and capacity of a free society to resist totalitarian aggression.

The principles that should guide a free democratic society in a world where dictatorial regimes seek to impose their rule on other nations were formulated by John Stuart Mill, the great defender of liberty and representative government, more than a century ago:

> To go to war for an idea, if the war is aggressive not defensive, is as criminal as to go to war for territory or revenue, for it is as little

justifiable to force our ideas on other people, as to compel them to submit to our will in any other aspect. . . . *The doctrine of non-intervention, to be a legitimate principle of morality, must be accepted by all governments.* The despots must consent to be bound by it as well as the free states. Unless they do, the profession of it by free countries comes but to this miserable issue, that the wrong side may help the wrong side but the right may not help the right side. Intervention to enforce non-intervention is always right, always moral *if not always prudent.* Though it may be a mistake to give freedom (or independence—S.H.) to a people who do not value the boon, it cannot be right to insist that if they do value it, they shall not be hindered from the pursuit of it by foreign coercion (*Fraser's Magazine,* 1859, emphasis mine).

Unfortunately, these principles were disregarded by the United States in 1936 when Hitler and Mussolini sent troops to Spain to help Franco overthrow the legally elected democratic Loyalist regime. The U.S. Congress, at the behest of the administration, adopted a Neutrality Resolution which prevented the democratic government of Spain from purchasing arms here. This compelled the Spanish government to make a deal with Stalin, who not only demanded its entire gold supply but the acceptance of the dread Soviet secret police, the NKVD, to supervise the operations. The main operation of the NKVD in Spain was to engage in a murderous purge of the democratic ranks of anti-Communists which led to the victory of Franco. The story is told in George Orwell's *Homage to Catalonia.* He was on the scene.

The prudence of American intervention in Vietnam may be debatable but there is little doubt that [UN ambassador] Adlai Stevenson, sometimes referred to as the liberal conscience of the nation, correctly stated the American motivation when he said at the UN on the very day of his death: "My hope in Vietnam is that resistance there may establish the fact that changes in Asia are not to be precipitated by outside force. This was the point of the Korean War. This is the point of the conflict in Vietnam."

. . . Mr. Zinn's remarks about Grenada show he is opposed to the liberal principles expressed by J. S. Mill in the passage cited above. His report of the facts about Grenada is as distorted as his account of present-day American democracy. On tiny Grenada, whose government was seized by Communist terrorists, were representatives of every Communist regime in the Kremlin's orbit, Cuban troops, and a Soviet general. I have read the documents captured by the American troops. They conclusively establish that the Communists were preparing the island as part of the Communist strategy of expansion.[3]

It is sad but significant that Mr. Zinn, whose heart bleeds for the poor Asians who suffered in the struggle to prevent the Communist takeover in

Southeast Asia, has not a word of protest, not a tear of compassion for the hundreds of thousands of tortured, imprisoned, and drowned in flight after the victory of the North Vietnamese "liberators," not to mention the even greater number of victims of the Cambodian and Cuban Communists.

One summary question may be asked whose answer bears on the issue of how democratic America is. Suppose all the iron and bamboo and passport curtains of the world were lifted today, in what direction would freedom loving and democratic people move? Anyone is free to leave the United States today, except someone fleeing from the law, but in [some of] the countries arrayed against the United States people are penned in like animals and cannot cross a boundary without risking death. Has this no significance for the "global" aspect of our question?

★ *Political and social philosopher* **Sidney Hook** *was a senior research fellow at the Hoover Institution from 1973 to 1989, the year of his death.*

Endnotes

[1]These words and subsequent references to the Soviet Union preceded the reforms initiated under Mikhail Gorbachev and continued with greater intensity under Boris Yeltsin—Editors.

[2]Spiro Agnew, former governor of Maryland and vice president before being forced from office during the first term of Richard Nixon (1968-1972), was a frequent and vociferous critic of the "liberal" press—Editors.

[3]*The Grenada Papers: The Inside Story of the Grenadian Revolution—and the Making of a Totalitarian State as Told in Captured Documents* (San Francisco: Institute of Contemporary Studies, 1984).

★ ★ ★ ★ ★

Questions

1. To what extent is democracy a political process as opposed to a condition of society?

2. To what extent has America made progress in bring political and legal equality to the poor and disadvantaged?

3. To what extent are America's legal procedures inherently discriminatory?

4. To what extent do the poor lack representation because they choose to not participate?
5. To what extent is economic equality necessary to sustain political democracy?

★ ★ ★

The Social Contract

Thomas Hobbes

In the 1640s British philosopher Thomas Hobbes witnessed the horror of the English civil war, characterizing life at the time as "solitary, poore, nasty, brutish, and short." In response to the violence, Hobbes wrote a new philosophy for constructing a civil society. Rejecting the medieval idea that government was established by God, Hobbes suggested that people create a new government by writing a social contract, a set of guidelines for how society shall be ruled (now called a constitution). Since Hobbes viewed people as violent by nature, he proposed an agreement wherein the people would give all of their rights over to a strong individual or group of individuals, which he called a Leviathan. In return, the Leviathan would protect them so that they could live normal lives. Although later democratic societies provide individuals many more rights than Hobbes thought advisable, Hobbes is widely recognized as writing the first systematic modern social contract theory.

The *right of nature*, which writers commonly call *jus naturale*, is the liberty each man has to use his own power as he will himself, for the preservation of his own nature, that is to say, of his own life, and consequently of doing anything which in his own judgement and reason, he shall conceive to be the aptest means thereunto.

By *liberty* is understood, according to the proper signification of the word, the absence of external impediments, which impediments may oft take away part of a man's power to do what he would, but cannot hinder him from using the power left him, according as his judgment and reason shall dictate to him.

★ ★ ★ ★ ★ ★

From Thomas Hobbes, *Leviathan* (1651). Spelling and punctuation have been modernized for this selection.

A law of nature, *lex naturalis*, is a precept or general rule, found out by reason, by which a man is forbidden to do that which is destructive of his life or takes away the means of preserving the same, and to omit that by which he thinks it may be best preserved. For though they that speak of this subject use to confound *jus* and *lex*, *right* and *law*, yet they ought to be distinguished, because right consists in liberty to do or to forbear, whereas law determines and binds to one of them, so that law and right differ as much as obligation and liberty, which in one and the same matter are inconsistent.

And because the condition of man, as hath been declared in the precedent chapter, is a condition of war of every one against every one, in which case every one is governed by his own reason, and there is nothing he can make use of that may not be a help unto him in preserving his life against his enemies; it follows that in such a condition every man has a right to every thing, even to one another's body. And therefore, as long as this natural right of every man to every thing endures, there can be no security to any man, how strong or wise soever he be, of living out the time which nature ordinarily allows men to live. And consequently it is a precept, or general rule of reason, *that every man ought to endeavour peace as far as he has hope of obtaining it, and when he cannot obtain it, that he may seek, and use, all helps and advantages of war.* The first branch of which rule contains the first and fundamental, law of nature: which is, *to seek peace and follow it.* The second, the sum of the right of nature: which is, *by all means we can to defend ourselves.*

From this fundamental law of nature, by which men are commanded to endeavour peace, is derived this second law: *that a man be willing, when others are so too, as far-forth as for peace and defense of himself he shall think it necessary, to lay down this right to all things, and be contented with so much liberty against other men as he would allow other men against himself.* For as long as every man holds this right of doing anything he likes; so long are all men in the condition of war. But if other men will not lay down their right, as well as he, then there is no reason for anyone to divest himself of his, for that were to expose himself to prey, which no man is bound to, rather than to dispose himself to peace. This is that law of the Gospel: *whatsoever you require that others should do to you, that do ye to them.* And that law of all men, *quod tibi fierinon vis, alteri ne feceris.*

To *lay down* a man's right to any thing is to *divest* himself of the *liberty* of hindering another of the benefit of his own right to the same. For he that renounces or passes away his right, gives not to any other man a right which he had not before, because there is nothing to which every man had not right by nature, but only stands out of his way that he may enjoy his own original right without hindrance from him, not without hindrance from another. So that the effect which redounds to one man by another man's defect of right, is but so much diminution of impediments to the use of his own right original. Right is laid aside either by simply renouncing it or by transferring it to another. By *simply* renouncing: when he cares not to whom the benefit thereof redounds. By transferring: when he intends the benefit thereof to some certain person or persons. And when a man hath in either manner abandoned or granted away his right, then is he said to be obliged, or bound, not to hinder those to whom such right is granted, or abandoned from the benefit of it, and that he *ought*, and it is his duty, not to make void that voluntary act of his own, and that such hindrance is injustice and injury, as being *sine jure*, the right being before being renounced or transferred. So that *injury*, or *injustice*, in the controversies of the world is somewhat like to that which in the disputations of scholars is called *absurdity*. For as it is there called an absurdity to contradict what one maintained in the beginning, so in the world it is called injustice and injury voluntarily to undo that which from the beginning he had voluntarily done. The way by which a man either simply renounces or transfers his right, is a declaration, or signification, by some voluntary and sufficient sign, or signs, that he does so renounce or transfer, or has so renounced or transferred the same to him that accepts it. And these signs are either words only, or actions only, or—as it happens most often—both words and actions. And the same are the bonds by which men are bound and obliged: bonds that have their strength, not from their own nature, for nothing is more easily broken than a man's word, but from fear of some evil consequence upon the rupture.

Whensoever a man transfers his right or renounces it, it is either in consideration of some right reciprocally transferred to himself, or for some other good he hopes for thereby. For it is a voluntary act: and of the voluntary acts of every man the object is some *good to himself*. And therefore there be some rights which no man can be understood by any words, or other signs, to have abandoned or transferred. As first a man cannot lay down the right of resisting them that assault him by force to take away his life, because he cannot be understood to aim thereby at any good to himself. The same may be said of wounds, and chains, and imprisonment: both because there is no benefit consequent to such patience, as there is to the patience of suffering another to be wounded or imprisoned, as also because a man cannot tell when he sees men proceed against him by violence, whether they intend his death or not. And lastly the motive and end for which this renouncing and transferring of right is introduced, is nothing else but the security of a man's person in his life and in the means of so preserving life as not to be weary of it. And therefore if a man by words, or other signs, seem to despoil himself of the end for which those signs were intended, he is not to be understood as if he meant it or that it was his will, but that he was ignorant of how such words and actions were to be interpreted. The mutual transferring of right is that which men call *contract*.

. . .

There is difference between transferring of right to the thing, the thing, and transferring or tradition, that is, delivery of the thing itself. For the thing may be delivered together with the translation of the right, as in buying and selling with ready money, or exchange of goods or lands, and it may be delivered some time after. Again, one of the contractors may deliver the thing contracted for on his part, and leave the other to perform his part at some determinate time after, and in the meantime be trusted; and then the contract on his part is called pact, or covenant: or both parts may contract now to perform hereafter, in which cases he that is to perform in time to come, being trusted, his performance is called keeping of promise, or faith, and the failing of performance, if it be voluntary, violation of faith.

When the transferring of right is not mutual, but one of the parties transfers in hope to gain thereby friendship or service from another, or from his friends; or in hope to gain the reputation of charity, or magnanimity; or to deliver his mind from the pain of compassion; or in hope of reward in heaven; this is not contract, but gift, free gift, grace: which words signify one and the same thing.

Signs of contract are either express or by inference. Express are words spoken with understanding of what they signify: and such words are either of the time present or past; as, I give, I grant, I have given, I have granted, I will that this be yours: or of the future; as, I will give, I will grant, which words of the future are called promise.

Signs by inference are sometimes the consequence of words; sometimes the consequence of silence; sometimes the consequence of actions; sometimes the consequence of forbearing an action: and generally a sign by inference, of any contract, is whatsoever sufficiently argues the will of the contractor.

Words alone, if they be of the time to come, and contain a bare promise, are an insufficient sign of a free gift and therefore not obligatory. For if they be of the time to come, as, tomorrow I will give, they are a sign I have not given yet, and consequently that my right is not transferred, but remains till I transfer it by some other act. But if the words be of the time present, or past, as, I have given, or do give to be delivered tomorrow, then is my tomorrow's right given away today; and that by the virtue of the words, thought here were no other argument of my will. And there is a great difference in the signification of these words, *volo hoc tuum essecras*, and *cras dabo*; that is, between I will that this be your tomorrow, and, I will give it to you tomorrow: for the word I will, in the former manner of speech, signifies an act of the will present; but in the latter, it signifies a promise of an act of the will to come: and therefore the former words, being of the present, transfer a future right; the latter, that be of the future, transfer nothing. But if there be other signs of the will to transfer a right besides words; then, though the gift be free, yet may the right be understood to pass by words of the future: as if a man propound a prize to him that comes first to the end of a race, the gift is free; and though the words be of the future, yet the right passes: for if he would not have his words so be understood, he should not have let them run.

In contracts the right passes, not only where the words are of the time present or past, but also where they are of the future, because all contract is mutual translation, or change of right; and therefore he that promises only, because he hath already received the benefit for which he promises, is to be understood as if he intended the right should pass: for unless he had been content to have his words so understood, the other would not have performed his part first. And for that cause, in buying, and selling, and other acts of contract, a promise is equivalent to a covenant, and therefore obligatory.

He that performs first in the case of a contract is said to merit that which he is to receive by the performance of the other, and he hath it as due. Also when a prize is propounded to many, which is to be given to him only that wins, or money is thrown amongst many to be enjoyed by them that catch it; though this be a free gift, yet so to win, or so to catch, is to merit, and to have it as due. For the right is transferred in the propounding of the prize, and in throwing down the money, though it be not determined to whom, but by the event of the contention. But there is between these two sorts of merit this difference, that in contract I merit by virtue of my own power and the contractor's need, but in this case of free gift I am enabled to merit only by the benignity of the giver: in contract I merit at the contractor's hand that he should depart with his right; in this case of gift, I merit not that the giver should part with his right, but that when he has parted with it, it should be mine rather than another's. And this I think to be the meaning of that distinction of the schools between *meritum congrui* and *meritum condigni*. For God Almighty, having promised paradise to those men, hoodwinked with carnal desires, that can walk through this world according to the precepts and limits prescribed by him, they say he that shall so walk shall merit paradise *ex congruo*. But because no man can demand a right to it by his own righteousness, or any other power in himself, but by the free grace of God only, they say no man can merit paradise *ex condigno*. This, I say, I think is the meaning of that distinction; but because disputers do not agree upon the signification of their own terms of art longer than it serves their turn, I will not affirm anything of their meaning: only this I say; when a gift is given indefinitely, as a prize to be contended for, he that wins merits, and may claim the prize as due.

If a covenant be made wherein neither of the parties perform presently, but trust one another, in the condition of mere nature (which is a condition of war of every man against every man) upon any reasonable suspicion, it is void: but if there be a common power set over them both, with right and force sufficient to compel performance, it is not void. For he that performs first has no assurance the other will perform after, because the bonds of words are too weak to bridle men's ambition, avarice, anger, and other passions, without the fear of some coercive power; which in the condition of mere nature, where all men are equal, and judges of the justness of their own fears, cannot possibly be supposed. And therefore he which performs first does but betray himself to his enemy, contrary to the right he can never abandon of defending his life and means of living.

But in a civil estate, where there a power set up to constrain those that would otherwise violate their faith, that fear is no more reasonable; and for that cause, he which by the covenant is to perform first is obliged so to do.

The cause of fear, which makes such a covenant invalid, must be always something arising after the covenant made, as some new factor other sign of the will not to perform, else it cannot make the covenant void. For that which could not hinder a man from promising ought not to be admitted as a hindrance of performing. He that transfers any right transfers the means of enjoying it, as far as lies in his power. As he that sells land is understood to transfer the herbage and whatsoever grows upon it; nor can he that sells a mill turn away the stream that drives it. And they that give to a man the right of government in sovereignty are understood to give him the right of levying money to maintain soldiers, and of appointing magistrates for the administration of justice.

To make covenants with brute beasts is impossible, because not understanding our speech, they understand not, nor accept of any translation of right, nor can translate any right to another: and without mutual acceptation, there is no covenant.

To make covenant with God is impossible but by mediation of such as God speaks to, either by revelation supernatural or by His lieutenants that govern under Him and in His name: for otherwise we know not whether our covenants be accepted or not. And therefore they that vow anything contrary to any law of nature, vow in vain, as being a thing unjust to pay such vow. And if it be a thing commanded by the law of nature, it is not the vow, but the law that binds them.

The matter or subject of a covenant is always something that falls under deliberation, for to covenant is an act of the will; that is to say, an act, and the last act, of deliberation; and is therefore always understood to be something to come, and which judged possible for him that covenants to perform.

And therefore, to promise that which is known to be impossible is no covenant. But if that prove impossible afterwards, which before was thought possible, the covenant is valid and binds, though not to the thing itself, yet to the value; or, if that also be impossible, to the unfeigned endeavour of performing as much as is possible, for to more no man can be obliged.

Men are freed of their covenants two ways; by performing, or by being forgiven. For performance is the natural end of obligation, and forgiveness the restitution of liberty, as being are transferring of that right in which the obligation consisted.

Covenants entered into by fear, in the condition of mere nature, are obligatory. For example, if I covenant to pay a ransom, or service for my life, to an enemy, I am bound by it. For it is a contract, wherein one receives the benefit of life; the other is to receive money, or service for it, and consequently, where no other law (as in the condition of mere nature) forbids the performance, the covenant is valid. Therefore prisoners of war, if trusted with the payment of their ransom, are obliged to pay it: and if a weaker prince make a disadvantageous peace with a stranger, for fear, he is bound to keep it; unless (as hath been said before) there arises some new and just cause of fear to renew the war. And even in Commonwealths, if I be forced to redeem myself from a thief by promising him money, I am bound to pay it, till the civil law discharge me. For whatsoever I may lawfully do without obligation, the same I may lawfully covenant to do through fear: and what I lawfully covenant, I cannot lawfully break. A former covenant makes void a later. For a man that hath passed away his right to one man today hath it not to pass tomorrow to another: and therefore the later promise passed no right, but is null.

A covenant not to defend myself from force, by force, is always void. For, as I have shown before, no man can transfer, or lay down his right to save himself from death, wounds, and imprisonment, the avoiding whereof is the only end of laying down any right: and therefore the promise of not resisting force in no covenant transfers any right, nor is obliging. For though a man may covenant thus, unless I do so, or so, kill me, he cannot covenant thus, unless I do so, or so I will not resist you when you come to kill me. For man by nature chooses the lesser evil, which is danger of death in resisting, rather than the greater, which is certain and present death in not resisting. And this is granted to be true by all men, in that they lead criminals to execution, and prison, with armed men, notwithstanding that such criminals have consented to the law by which they are condemned.

A covenant to accuse oneself, without assurance of pardon, is likewise invalid. For in the condition of nature where every man is judge, there is no place for accusation: and in the civil state the accusation is followed with punishment, which, being force, a man is not obliged not to resist. The same is also true of the accusation of those by whose condemnation a man falls into misery; as of a father, wife, or benefactor. For the testimony of such an accuser, if it be not willingly given, is presumed to be corrupted by nature, and therefore not to be received: and where a man's testimony is not to be credited, he is not bound to give it. Also accusations upon torture are not to be reputed as testimonies. For torture is to be used but as means of conjecture, and light, in the further examination and search of truth: and what is in that case confessed tends to the ease of him that is tortured, not to the informing of the torturers, and therefore ought not to have the credit of a sufficient testimony: for whether he deliver himself by true or false accusation, he does it by the right of preserving his own life.

The force of words being (as I have formerly noted) too weak to hold men to the performance of their covenants, there are in man's nature but two imaginable helps to strengthen it. And those are either a fear of the consequence of breaking their word, or a glory or pride in appearing not to need to break it. This latter is a generosity too rarely found to be presumed on, especially in the pursuers of wealth, command, or sensual pleasure, which are the greatest part of mankind. The passion to be reckoned upon is fear; whereof there be two very general objects: one, the power of spirits invisible; the other, the power of those men they shall therein offend. Of these two, though the former be the greater power, yet the fear of the latter is commonly the greater fear. The fear of the former is in every man his own religion, which hath place in the nature of man before civil society. The latter hath not so; at least not place enough to keep men to their promises, because in the condition of mere nature, the inequality of power is not discerned, but by the event of battle. So that before the time of civil society, or in the interruption thereof by war, there is nothing can strengthen a covenant of peace agreed on against the temptations of avarice, ambition, lust, or other strong desire, but the fear of that invisible power which they everyone worship as God, and fear as a revenger of their perfidy. All therefore that can be done between two men not subject to civil power is to put one another to swear by the God he fears: which swearing, or oath, is a form of speech, added to a promise, by which he that promises signifies that unless he perform he renounces the mercy of his God, or calls to him for vengeance on himself. Such was the heathen form, Let Jupiter kill me else, as I kill this beast. So is our form, I shall do thus, and thus, so help me God. And this, with the rites and ceremonies which every one uses in his own religion, that the fear of breaking faith might be the greater.

By this it appears that an oath taken according to any other form, or rite, than his that swears is in vain and no oath, and that there is no swearing by anything which the swearer thinks not God. For though men have sometimes used to swear by their kings, for fear, or flattery; yet they would have it thereby understood they attributed to them divine honour. And that swearing unnecessarily by God is but profaning of his name: and swearing by other things, as men do in common discourse, is not swearing, but an impious custom, gotten by too much vehemence of talking.

It appears also that the oath adds nothing to the obligation. For a covenant, if lawful, binds in the sight of God, without the oath, as much as with it; if unlawful, binds not at all, though it be confirmed with an oath.

★ **Thomas Hobbes** *(1588-1679) was an English political theorist and philosopher.*

★ ★ ★ ★ ★

Questions

1. What aspects of Hobbes' thought are incorporated into the Constitution of the United States?
2. Is a constitution truly a social contract if the people who live under it, like today's Americans, never had a chance to vote for or against it?
3. Considering the violence of the 20th century, was Hobbes right about human nature?

★ ★ ★

State of Nature. State of War (1690)

John Locke

Thomas Jefferson's belief that people have the right to "life, liberty, and the pursuit of happiness," was based on the ideas of British philosopher John Locke (1632-1704). Following Thomas Hobbes' (1588-1679) suggestion that government should be based upon a social contract—an agreement among the members of society about the basic structure of government—Locke wrote a political philosophy. He proposed that, in their natural condition (a state of nature), people desire to accumulate property and associate freely, but that some occasionally take advantage of others. He suggested that people construct a social contract guaranteeing the freedom of the individual to manufacture and trade freely. This could be done by establishing a government with limited powers to represent the political aspirations of the people. Because Locke believed that governments could be altered and dissolved if they were not serving the people's needs, Jefferson and his compatriots adopted his philosophy to legitimize their revolution.

★ The State of Nature

To understand political power aright, and derive it from its original, we must consider, what state all men are naturally in, and that is, a state of perfect freedom to order their actions, and dispose of their possessions and persons, as they think fit, within the bounds of the law of nature, without asking leave, or depending upon the will of any other man.

★ ★ ★ ★ ★ ★

From John Locke, *Two Treatises of Government* (1690).

A state also of equality, wherein all the power and jurisdiction is reciprocal, no one having more than another; there being nothing more evident, than that creatures of the same species and rank, promiscuously born to all the same advantages of nature, and the use of the same faculties, should also be equal one amongst another without subordination or subjection, unless the lord and master of them all should, by any manifest declaration of his will, set one above another, and confer on him, by an evident and clear appointment, an undoubted right to dominion and sovereignty.

This equality of men by nature, the judicious Hooker looks upon as so evident in itself, and beyond all question, that he makes it the foundation of that obligation to mutual love amongst men, on which he builds the duties they owe one another, and from whence he derives the great maxims of justice and charity. His words are:

> The like natural inducement hath brought men to know that it is no less their duty, to love others than themselves; for seeing those things which are equal, must needs all have one measure; if I cannot but wish to receive good, even as much at every man's hands, as any man can wish unto his own soul, how should I look to have any part of my desire herein satisfied, unless myself be careful to satisfy the like desire, which is undoubtedly in other men. We all being of one and the same nature to have any thing offered them repugnant to this desire, must needs in all respects grieve them as much as me; so that if I do harm, I must look to suffer, there being no reason that others should shew greater measure of love to me, than they have by me shewed unto them, my desire therefore to be loved of my equals in nature as much as possible may be, imposeth upon me a natural duty of bearing to themward fully the like affection; from which relation of equality between ourselves and them that are as ourselves, what several rules and canons natural reason hath drawn, for direction of life, no man is ignorant.
>
> —*Eccl. Pol.* lib.i.

But though this be a state of liberty, yet it is not a state of license: though man in that state have an uncontroulable liberty to dispose of his person or possessions, yet he has not liberty to destroy himself, or so much as any creature in his possession, but where some nobler use than its bare preservation calls for it. The state of nature has a law of nature to govern it, which obliges every one, and reason, which is that law, teaches all mankind, who will but consult it, that being all equal and independent, no one ought to harm another in his life, health, liberty, or possessions: for men being all the workmanship of one omnipotent, and infinitely wise maker; all the servants of one sovereign master, sent into the world by his order, and about his business; they are his property, whose workmanship they are, made to last during his, not one another's pleasure: and being furnished with like faculties, sharing all in one community of nature, there cannot be supposed any such subordination among us, that may authorize us to destroy one another, as if we were made for one another's uses, as the inferior ranks of creatures are for ours. Every one, as he is bound to preserve himself, and not to quit his station willfully, so by the like reason, when his own preservation comes not in competition, ought he as much as he can to preserve the rest of mankind, and not unless it be to do justice on an offender, take away, or impair the life, or what tends to the preservation of the life, the liberty, health, limb, or goods of another.

And that all men may be restrained from invading others rights, and from doing hurt to one another, and the law of nature be observed, which willeth the peace and preservation of all mankind, the execution of the law of nature is, in that state, put into every man's hands, whereby every one has a right to punish the transgressors of that law to such a degree, as may hinder its violation. For the law of nature would, as all other laws that concern men in this world, be in vain, if there were nobody that in the state of nature had a power to execute that law, and thereby preserve the innocent and restrain offenders. And if any one in the state of nature may punish another for any evil he has done, every one may do so: for in that state of perfect equality where naturally there is no superiority or jurisdiction of one over another, what any may do in prosecution of that law, every one must needs have a right to do.

And thus, in the state of nature, one man comes by a power over another; but yet no absolute or arbitrary power, to use a criminal, when he has got him in his hands, according to the passionate heats, or boundless extravagancy of his own will; but only to retribute to him, so far as calm reason and conscience dictate, what is proportionate to his transgression, which is so much as may serve for reparation and restraint: for these two are the only reasons why one man may lawfully do harm to another, which is that we call punishment. In transgressing the law of nature, the offender declares himself to live by another rule than that of reason and common equity, which is that measure God has set to the actions of men for their mutual security, and so he becomes dangerous to mankind, the tie, which is to secure them from injury and violence, being slighted and broken by him. Which being a trespass against the whole species, and the peace and safety of it, provided for by the law of nature, every man upon this score, by the right he hath to preserve mankind in general, may restrain, or where it is necessary, destroy things noxious to them, and so may bring such evil on any one, who hath transgressed that law, as may make him repent the doing of it, and thereby deter him, and, by his example others, from doing the like mischief. And in this case, and upon this ground, every man hath a right to punish the offender, and be executioner of the law of nature.

I doubt not but this will seem a very strange doctrine to some men; but before they condemn it, I desire them to resolve me, by what right any prince or state can put to death, or punish an alien, for any crime he commits in their country. 'Tis certain their laws, by virtue of any sanction they receive from the promulgated will of the legislative, reach not a stranger: they speak not to him, nor, if they did, is he bound to hearken to them. The legislative authority, by which they are in force over the subjects of that commonwealth, hath no power over him. Those who have the supreme power of making laws in England, France or Holland, are to an Indian, but like the rest of the world, men without authority: and therefore, if by the law of nature every man hath not a power to punish offenses against it, as he soberly judges the case to require, I see not how the magistrates of any community can punish an alien of another country; since, in reference to him, they can have no more power than what every man naturally may have over another.

Besides the crime which consists in violating the law, and varying from the right rule of reason, whereby a man so far becomes degenerate, and declares himself to quit the principles of human nature and to be a noxious creature, there is commonly injury done and some person or other, some other man receives damage by his transgression; in which case he who hath received any damage, has, besides the right of punishment common to him with other men, a particular right to seek reparation from him that has done it: and any other person, who finds it just, may also join with him that is injured, and assist him in recovering from the offender so much as may make satisfaction for the harm he has suffered.

From these two distinct rights, the one of punishing the crime for restraint, and preventing the like offense, which right of punishing is in every body; the other of taking reparation, which belongs only to the injured party, comes it to pass that the magistrate, who by being magistrate hath the common right of punishing put into his hands, can often, where the public good demands not the execution of the law, remit the punishment of criminal offenses by his own authority, but yet cannot remit the satisfaction due to any private man for the damage he has received. That, he who has suffered the damage has a right to demand in his own name, and he alone can remit: the damnified person has this power of appropriating to himself the goods or service of the offender, by right of self-preservation, as every man has a power to punish the crime, to prevent its being committed again, by the right he has of preserving all mankind, and doing all reasonable things he can in order to that end: and thus it is, that every man, in the state of nature, has a power to kill a murderer, both to deter others from doing the like injury, which no reparation can compensate, by the example of the punishment that attends it from every body, and also to secure men from the attempts of a criminal, who having renounced reason, the common rule and measure God hath given to mankind, hath, by the unjust violence and slaughter he hath committed upon one, declared war against all mankind, and therefore may be destroyed as a lion or a tyger, one of those wild savage beasts, with whom men can have no society nor security: and upon this is grounded that great law of nature, *Whoso sheddeth man's blood, by man shall his blood be shed.* And Cain was so fully convinced, that every one had a right to destroy such a criminal, that after the murder of his brother, he cries out, *Every one that findeth me, shall slay me*; so plain was it writ in the hearts of all mankind.

By the same reason may a man in the state of nature punish the lesser breaches of that law. It will perhaps be demanded, with death? I answer, each transgression may be punished to that degree, and with so much severity, as will suffice to make it an ill bargain to the offender, give him cause to repent, and terrify others from doing the like. Every offense, that can be committed in the state of nature, may in the state of nature be also punished equally, and as far forth as it may, in a commonwealth: for though it would be besides my present purpose, to enter here into the particulars of the law of nature, or its measures of punishment; yet, it is certain there is such a law, and that too as intelligible and plain to a rational creature, and a studier of that law, as the positive laws of commonwealths: nay, possibly plainer; as much as reason is easier to be understood, than the fancies and intricate contrivances of men, following contrary and hidden interests put into words; for so truly are a great part of the municipal laws of countries, which are only so far right, as they are founded on the law of nature, by which they are to be regulated and interpreted.

To this strange doctrine, *viz.*, that in the state of nature every one has the executive power of the law of nature, I doubt not but it will be objected, that it is unreasonable for men to be judges in their own cases, that self-love will make men partial to themselves and their friends: and on the other side, that ill-nature, passion and revenge will carry them too far in punishing others; and hence nothing but confusion and disorder will follow; and that therefore God hath certainly appointed government to restrain the partiality and violence of men. I easily grant that civil government is the proper remedy for the inconveniencies of the state of nature, which must certainly be great where men may be judges in their own case, since 'tis easy to be imagined, that he who was so unjust as to do his brother an injury, will scarce be so just as to condemn himself for it; but I shall desire those who make this objection, to remember, that absolute monarchs are but men; and if government is to be the remedy of those evils, which necessarily follow from men's being judges in their own cases, and the state of nature is therefore not to be endured, I desire to know what kind of government that is, and how much better it is than the state of nature, where one man commanding a multitude, has the liberty to be judge in his own case, and may do to all his subjects whatever he pleases, without the least question or controul those who execute his pleasure? and in whatsoever he doth, whether led by reason, mistake or passion, must be submitted to? which men in the state of nature are not bound to do one to another. And if he that judges, judges amiss in his own, or any other case, he is answerable for it to the rest of mankind.

'Tis often asked as a mighty objection, where are, or ever were there any men in such a state of nature? To which it may suffice as an answer at present, that since all princes and rulers of *independent* governments all through the world, are in a state of nature, 'tis plain the world never was, nor never will be, without numbers of men in that state. I have named all governors of *independent* communities, whether they are, or are not, in league with others: for 'tis not every compact that puts an end to the state of nature between men, but only this one of agreeing together mutually to enter into one community, and make one body politic; other promises, and compacts, men may make one with another, and yet still be in the state of nature. The promises and bargains for truck, etc. between the two men in the desert island, mentioned by Garcilasso de la Vega, in his history of Peru; or between a Swiss and an Indian, in the woods of America, are binding to them, though they are perfectly in a state of nature, in reference to one another: for truth and keeping of faith belongs to men, as men and not as members of society.

To those that say, there were never any men in the state of nature, I will not only oppose the authority of the judicious Hooker, *Eccl. Pol.* lib. i. sect. 10, where he says,

> the laws which have been hitherto mentioned, *i.e.* the laws of nature, do bind men absolutely, even as they are men, although they have never any settled fellowship, never any solemn agreement amongst themselves what to do, or not to do: but forasmuch as we are not by ourselves sufficient to furnish ourselves with competent store of things, needful for such a life as our nature doth desire, a life fit for the dignity of man; therefore to supply those defects and imperfections which are in us, as living singly and solely by ourselves, we are naturally induced to seek communion and fellowship with others: this was the cause of men uniting themselves at first in politic societies.

But I moreover affirm, that all men are naturally in that state, and remain so, till by their own consents they make themselves members of some politic society; and I doubt not in the sequel of this discourse, to make it very clear.

★ *The State of War*

The state of war is a state of enmity and destruction; and therefore declaring by word or action, not a passionate and hasty, but a sedate, settled design upon another man's life, puts him in a state of war with him against whom he has declared such an intention, and so has exposed his life to the other's power to be taken away by him, or any one that joins with him in his defense, and espouses his quarrel, it being reasonable and just I should have a right to destroy that which threatens me with destruction; for by the fundamental law of nature, man being to be preserved, as much as possible, when all cannot be preserved, the safety of the innocent is to be preferred; and one may destroy a man who makes war upon him, or has discovered an enmity to his being, for the same reason that he may kill a wolf or a lion, because such men are not under the ties of the commonlaw of reason, have no other rule, but that of force and violence, and so may be treated as beasts of prey, those dangerous and noxious creatures that will be sure to destroy him whenever he falls into their power.

And hence it is that he who attempts to get another man into his absolute power does thereby put himself into a state of war with him; it being to be understood as a declaration of a design upon his life. For I have reason to conclude that he who would get me into his power without my consent would use me as he pleased when he had got me there, and destroy me too when he had a fancy to it, for nobody can desire to have me in his absolute power, unless it be to compel me by force to that which is against the right of my freedom—*i.e.,* make me a slave. To be free from such force is the only security of my preservation and reason bids me look on him as an enemy to my preservation, who would take away that freedom which is the fence to it; so that he who makes an attempt to enslave me thereby puts himself into a state of war with me. He that in the state of nature would take away the freedom that belongs to any one in that state must necessarily be supposed to have a design to take away everything else, that freedom being the foundation of all the rest; as he that, in the state of society, would take away the freedom belonging to those of that society or commonwealth must be supposed to design to take away from them everything else, and so be looked on as in a state of war.

This makes it lawful for a man to kill a thief who has not in the least hurt him, nor declared any design upon his life, any farther than, by the use of force, so to get him in his power as to take away his money, or what he pleases, from him; because using force, where he has no right to get me into his power, let his pretense be what it will, I have no reason to suppose that he who would take away my liberty would not, when he had me in his power, take away everything else. And therefore it is lawful for me to treat him as one who has put himself into a state of war with me—*i.e.*, kill him if I can; for to that hazard does he justly expose himself whoever introduces a state of war, and is aggressor in it.

And here we have the plain difference between the state of nature and the state of war, which however some men have confounded, are as far distant as a state of peace, goodwill, mutual assistance, and preservation; and a state of enmity, malice, violence and mutual destruction are one from another. Men living together according to reason without a common superior on earth, with authority to judge between them, are properly in the state of nature. But force, or a declared design of force upon the person of another, where there is no common superior on earth to appeal to for relief, is the state of war; and 'tis the want of such an appeal gives a man the right of war even against an aggressor, though he be in society and a fellow-subject. Thus, a thief whom I cannot harm, but by appeal to the law, for having stolen all that I am worth, I may kill when he sets on me to rob me but of my horse or coat, because the law, which was made for my preservation, where it cannot interpose to secure my life from present force, which if lost is capable of no reparation, permits me my own defense and the right of war, a liberty to kill the aggressor, because the aggressor allows not time to appeal to our common judge, nor the decision of the law, for remedy in a case where the mischief may be irreparable. Want of a common judge with authority puts all men in a state of nature; force without right upon a man's person makes a state of war both where there is, and is not, a common judge.

But when the actual force is over, the state of war ceases between those that are in society and are equally on both sides subjected to the fair determination of the law; because then there lies open the remedy of appeal for the past injury, and to prevent future harm; but where no such appeal is, as in the state of nature, for want of positive laws, and judges with authority to appeal to, the state of war, once begun, continues with a right to the innocent party to destroy the other whenever he can, until the aggressor offers peace, and desires reconciliation on such terms as may repair any wrongs he has already done, and secure the innocent for the future; nay, where an appeal to the law, and constituted judges, lies open, but the remedy is denied by a manifest perverting of justice, and a barefaced wresting of the laws to protect or indemnify the violence or injuries of some men or party of men, there it is hard to imagine any thing but a state of war: for wherever violence is used, and injury done, though by hands appointed to administer justice, it is still violence and injury, however colored with the name, pretenses, or forms of law, the end whereof being to protect and redress the innocent, by an unbiassed application of it, to all who are under it; wherever that is not *bona fide* done, war is made upon the sufferers, who having no appeal on earth to right them, they are left to the only remedy in such cases, an appeal to heaven.

To avoid this state of war (wherein there is no appeal but to heaven, and wherein every the least difference is apt to end, where there is no authority to decide between the contenders) is one great reason of men's putting themselves into society and quitting the state of nature. For where there is an authority, a power on earth, from which relief can be had by appeal, there the continuance of the state of war is excluded, and the controversy is decided by that power.

. . .

★ **John Locke** *(1632-1704) was an English philosopher whose two major works were* Two Treatises of Government *and* The Essay Concerning Human Understanding.

★ ★ ★ ★ ★

Questions

1. What ideas of John Locke are reflected in the Constitution of the United States?
2. John Locke asserted a right to revolution. To what extent does this right exist in the United States today?
3. In what respects are Locke's views of human nature accurate? In what ways are they inaccurate?

☆ ☆ ☆

Of The Social Contract

Jean-Jacques Rousseau

Among the questions that have divided political thinkers for centuries is the matter of the "nature of man," the essential qualities that determine human behavior. This topic arises whenever people look for a way to treat the causes of such social problems as poverty, crime, and injustice, instead of merely treat the symptoms. While some, like English philosopher Thomas Hobbes and Austrian physician Sigmund Freud, have argued that people are inherently prone to violence, Rousseau contended that people are naturally good, born free from destructive tendencies, but become aggressive when confronted by unhealthy social customs and oppressive institutions. When Rousseau asserts that "Man is born free, and everywhere he is in chains," he places the blame for the ills of society squarely on the shoulders of centuries of governments, churches, and economic systems constructed for the benefit of some to the detriment of others.

☆ Book 1

I wish to inquire whether, in the civil order, it is possible to have some legitimate and sure rule of administration, taking men as they are and the laws as they can be. In this inquiry, I shall always try to unite what right permits with what interest prescribes so that justice and utility are in no way divided.

I embark upon the task without proving the importance of my subject. Someone will ask me if I am a prince or a legislator in order to write on Politics. I answer no, and that is why I am writing on Politics. If I were a prince or a legislator, I would not waste my time saying what is necessary to do; I would do it or keep silent.

☆ ☆ ☆ ☆ ☆ ☆

"Of the Social Contract," by Jean-Jacques Rousseau, reprinted from *Of the Social Contract,* 1762.

Born a citizen of a free State and a member of the sovereign, whatever feeble influence my voice could have in public affairs, the right to vote suffices to impose upon me the duty to instruct myself in them. Happy am I whenever I meditate on Governments, always to find in my inquiries new reasons to love that of my country!

★ *Chapter I*

The Subject of the First Book

Man was born free, but everywhere he is in chains. Whoever thinks himself the master of others is nevertheless more a slave than they. How did this change come about? I do not know. What can render it legitimate? I think I can resolve this question.

If I were to consider only force and the effect derived from it, I would say: as long as a People is constrained to obey and obeys, it does well; as soon as it can shake off the yoke and succeeds, it does even better; because, recovering its liberty by the same right that stole it away, either a people is justified in taking freedom back or there was no justification to deprive a people of it. But the social order is a sacred right which serves as a basis of all the others. However, this right does not come from nature; it is therefore founded on conventions. The problem is to know what are these conventions. Before going on to that, I must establish what I have just asserted.

★ *Chapter II*

Of the First Societies

The most ancient of all societies and the only natural one is the family. Yet children remain tied to the father only as long as they need him for their preservation. As soon as this need ceases, the natural tie is dissolved. Children, released from the obedience that they owe the father, and he released from the cares and owed the children, they all return equally to independence. If they continue to stay united, it is no longer naturally, it is voluntarily; and the family itself is maintained only by convention.

This common freedom is a consequence of the nature of man. His first law is to watch over his own preservation; his first cares are those that he owes to himself; and as soon as he reaches the age of reason, he alone being judge of the proper means to preserve himself, becomes thereby his own master.

The family therefore may be called the first model of political societies: the ruler is the image of the father, the people is the image of the children; and all, being born equal and free, alienate their freedom only for their utility. The only difference is that in the family the love of the father for his children compensates him for the cares that he renders them; while in the State the pleasure of commanding takes the place of this love which the ruler does not have for his people.

Grotius denies that all human power is established for the benefit of those who are governed; he cites slavery as an example. His most characteristic way of reasoning is to establish right by fact.[1] One could use a more consistent method, but not one more favorable to Tyrants.

It is then doubtful, according to Grotius, whether mankind belongs to a hundred men or whether this hundred men belong to mankind; and he appears, throughout his book, to learn to the first of these opinions; this is also the sentiment of Hobbes. Thus we see the human species divided into herds of cattle, each with its ruler, who protects it in order to devour it.

As a shepherd has a superior nature to that of his herd, so the shepherds of men, their rulers, also have a superior nature to that of their people. The emperor Caligula reasoning from this analogy readily concluded, according to the report of Philo, that kings were Gods, or that peoples were beasts.

The reasoning of this Caligula coincides with that of Hobbes and Grotius. Aristotle, before them all, had also said that men are not naturally equal, but that some are born for slavery and others for domination.

Aristotle was correct; but he took the effect for the cause. Any man born in slavery is born for slavery; nothing is more certain. Slaves lose everything in their chains, even the desire to escape from them. They love their servitude as the companions of Ulysses loved their brutish condition.[2] If then there are slaves by nature, it is because there have been slaves against nature. Force made the first slaves; their cowardice has perpetuated their slavery.

I have said nothing of the king Adam, nor of the emperor Noah, father of three great Monarchs who divided the universe among themselves, as did the children of Saturn, whom some have thought to recognize in them. I hope some may be grateful to me for this moderation; for, having descended directly from one of these Princes and perhaps from the oldest branch, how do I know but what on the verification of titles I might find myself the legitimate king of mankind? In any case, one cannot deny that Adam was Sovereign of the world, as was Robinson of his island, as long as he was the only inhabitant, and what was convenient in this empire was that the monarch, secure on his throne, had to fear neither rebellion, nor wars, nor conspirators.

★ Chapter III

Of the Right of the Strongest

The strongest is never strong enough always to be the master, unless he transforms his force into right, and obedience into duty. Hence, the right of the strongest; right apparently mean ironically, but actually established as principle. But will we never have an explanation of this word? Force is a physical power; I do not see what morality can result from its effects. To yield to force is an act of necessity, not of will. At most it is an act of prudence. In what sense can it be a duty?

Let us suppose for a moment that this so-called right exists. I say that it results only in inexplicable nonsense. For, as soon as it is force that makes right, the effect changes with the cause. Every force that overcomes the first succeeds to its right. As soon as one can disobey with impunity, one does so legitimately; and, since the strongest is always correct, it is only a question of acting in such a way that one may be the strongest. But what kind of right is it that perishes when force ceases? If it is necessary to obey by force, one does not need to obey by duty; and if one is not forced to obey, one is no longer obligated. Therefore this word, right, adds nothing to force; it does not mean anything here.

Obey power. If this means yield to force, the precept is good but superfluous; I answer that it will never be violated. All power comes from God, I avow; but so does all disease. Is that to say that it is forbidden to call a doctor? A brigand surprises me in a recess of a forest: not only is it necessary by force to give my purse, but, even if I could withhold it, am I obligated in conscience to give it? After all, the pistol he holds is also a power.

Let us agree then that force does not make right, and that one is only obligated to obey legitimate powers. Thus my first question always returns.

★ Chapter IV

Of Slavery

Since no man has a natural authority over his fellow, and since force produces no right, what remains are convention as the basis of all legitimate authority among men.

If an individual, says Grotius, can alienate his freedom and make himself the slave of a master, why could not a whole people alienate its freedom and make itself subject to a king? There are many equivocal words here that would need explanation; but let us confine ourselves to the word *alienate.* To alienate is to give or sell. Now, a man who makes himself the slave of another does not give himself; he sells himself, at the very least for his subsistence. But a people, for what does it sell itself? Far from furnishing his subjects their subsistence, a king gets his own only from them; and, according to Rabelais, a king does not live on little. Do subjects then give their persons on the condition that their goods also be taken? I do not see what is left them to preserve.

It will be said that the despot assures his subjects civil tranquility. Very well, but what do they gain, if the wars that his ambition brings upon them, if his insatiable avidity, if the harassments of his ministers desolate them more than would their own dissensions? What do they gain, if this tranquility itself is one of their miseries? One also lives tranquility in dungeons; is that enough to be well off there? The Greeks imprisoned in the cave of the Cyclops lived there tranquility, awaiting their turn to be devoured.

To say that a man gives himself gratuitously is to say a thing absurd and inconceivable; such an act is illegitimate and null, if only because he who does it is not in his right mind. To say the same thing of a whole people is to suppose a people of madmen; madness does not make right.

Even if each man could alienate himself, he could not alienate his children. They are born men and free. Their freedom belongs to them, and no one but themselves has a right to dispose of it. Before they are of the age of reason, the father can lay down the conditions for their preservation, for their well being. But he cannot give them away irrevocably and without condition, because such a gift is contrary to the ends of nature and exceeds the rights of paternity. So, for an arbitrary government to be legitimate, it would be necessary that each generation of people be able to accept or reject the master, but then this government would no longer be arbitrary.

To renounce one's freedom is to renounce what makes one a man, to renounce the rights of humanity as well as its duties. There is no possible compensation for someone who renounces everything. Such a renunciation is incompatible with the nature of man, and to remove all freedom from his will is to remove all morality from his actions. Finally, it is an empty and contradictory convention that lays down on one side an absolute authority and on the other an obedience without limit. Is it not clear that one is not obligated at all to someone from whom one has the right to exact everything? And does not this condition alone, without equivalent, without exchange, nullify the act? For what right can my slave have against me, since all that he has belongs to me? And if his right is mine, to speak of this right of mine against myself is senseless.

Grotius and the others derive from war another origin of the so-called right of slavery. The victor having, according to them, the right to kill the vanquished, the latter can buy back his life at the price of his freedom, a convention all the more legitimate in that it profits both parties.

But it is clear that this so called right to kill the vanquished does not result in any manner from the state of war. Men, living in their primitive independence, have not among themselves constant enough relation to constitute either the state of peace or the state of war. From this alone, they are not at all naturally enemies. It is the relation of things and not of men that constitutes war; and the state of war cannot be born from simple and personal relations but only from property relations. Private war or war between one man and another cannot exist either in the state of nature, where there is no fixed property, or in the social state, where everything is under the authority of the laws.

Individual combats, duels, and encounters are acts which do not constitute a state. And as for private wars, authorized by the Establishments of Louis IX, king of France, and suspended by the peace of God, these are abuses of feudal government, an absurd system, if ever there was one, and contrary to the principles of natural right and to any good polity.

War then is not a relation between man and man but a relation between State and State, in which individuals are enemies only accidentally, not as men, nor even as citizens,[3] but as soldiers; not as members of the fatherland, but as its defenders. Finally each State can have for enemies only other States, not men, because between things of different natures there can be no true relation.

This principle also conforms to the established maxims of all times and to the constant practice of all civilized peoples. Declarations of war are not so much announcements to powers as to their subjects. The foreigner, whether king, individual, or people, who steals, kills or detains the subjects without declaring war on a prince is not an enemy; he is a brigand. Even in open war, a just prince in an enemy land properly seizes all that belongs to the public, but he respects the person and the goods of individuals. He respects the rights upon which his own are founded. The end of war being the destruction of the enemy State, one has a right to kill its defenders as long as they bear arms. But as soon as they lay them down and surrender, ceasing to be enemies or instruments of the enemy, they again become simply men, and one no longer has any right to their life. Sometimes it is possible to kill the State without killing a single one of its members, but war gives no right that is not necessary to its end. These principles are not those of Grotius. They are not based on the authority of poets, but they derive from the nature of things and are based on reason.

In regard to the right of conquest, it has no other basis than the law of the strongest. If war does not give the victor the right to massacre the vanquished peoples, this right which he does not have cannot serve as a basis of that to enslave them. One has the right to kill the enemy only when one cannot enslave him. The right to enslave him does not come from the right to kill him. It is therefore an iniquitous exchange to make him buy with his freedom his life over which one has no right. In establishing the right of life and death upon the right of slavery, and the right of slavery upon the right of life and death, is it not clear that one falls into a vicious circle?

Even assuming this terrible right to kill everyone, I say that a slave made in war or a conquered people is not bound in any way to its master except to obey him as long as forced to do so. In taking an equivalent for the lives of the enslaved or conquered, the victor has not done them a favor; instead of killing them without profit, he has killed them usefully. Far from his acquiring any further authority over them in addition to force, the state of war subsists between them as before; their very relation is the effect of it; and the practice of the right of war does not suppose a peace treaty. They have made a convention; granted, but this convention, far from destroying the state of war, supposes its continuation.

Thus, in whatever way one looks at things, the right of slavery is null, not only because it is illegitimate but because it is absurd and signifies nothing. These words, *slavery* and *right,* are contradictory; they are mutually exclusive. Between a man and another man or between a man and a people, this statement is equally senseless. *I make a convention with you, one wholly at your expense and wholly to my profit, one that I will observe as long as it pleases me and one that you will observe as long as it pleases me.*

★ Chapter V

That It Is Always Necessary to Go Back to a First Convention

Even if I granted all that I have hitherto refuted, the champions of despotism would be no better off. There will always be a great difference between subduing a multitude and ruling a society. If dispersed men, however numerous they might be, were successively enslaved by one man, I only see there a master and some slaves. I do not see a people and its ruler. Perhaps, if one wishes, this is an aggregation but not an association. There is here neither public good nor body politic. This man, if he had enslaved half the world, is still only an individual. His interest, separated from that of the others, is always only a private interest. If this same man were to perish, his empire after him remains dispersed and without connection, as an oak dissolves and falls into a heap of ashes after fire has consumed it.

A people, says Grotius, can give itself to a king. According to Grotius, a people is therefore a people before giving itself to a king. This gift itself is a civil act; it assumes public deliberation. Therefore, before examining the act by which a people elects a king, it would be good to examine the act by which a people is a people. For this act necessarily being prior to the other is the true foundation of the society.

Indeed, if there were no prior convention, where, unless the election were unanimous, would be the obligation upon the minority to submit to the choice of the majority? And whence do the hundred who want a master get the right for the ten who do not so wish? The law of plurality voting is itself an establishment of convention and assumes unanimity at least on one occasion.

★ Chapter VI

Of the Social Compact

I assume that men have reached a point where the obstacles injurious to their preservation in the state of nature, overwhelm the forces that each individual can employ to maintain himself in this state. Then this primitive state can no longer subsist, and mankind would perish if it did not change its way of life.

Now, since men cannot engender new forces, but only unite and direct those that exist, they no longer have any other means to preserve themselves than to form, by aggregation, a sum of forces that can prevail over those obstacles, to bring these forces into play by a single motive power and to make them act in concert.

This sum of forces can arise only from the coming together of several men. But the force and the freedom of each man being the original instruments of his preservation, how will he commit them without injuring himself and without neglecting the cares that he owes himself? This difficulty, leading back to my subject, may be expressed in these terms.

"To find a form of association which defends and protects the person and goods of each associate with all the common force; and in which, each uniting with all nevertheless obeys only himself and remains as free as before." Such is the fundamental problem to which the social contract gives the solution.

The clauses of this contract are so determined by the nature of the act that the least modification would render them null and void. They are such that, even though they may perhaps never have been formally expressed, they are everywhere the same, everywhere tacitly admitted and recognized. But when the social compact is violated, each associate resumes his original rights and retakes his natural freedom, while losing the conventional freedom for which he renounced natural freedom.

These clauses properly understood all reduce to one, namely, the total alienation of each associate with all his rights to the whole community. Because in the first place, each giving himself completely, the situation is the same for all. And the situation being the same for all, it is in no one's interest to make it onerous for others.

Moreover, the alienation being done without reservation, the union is as perfect as it can be and no associate any longer has anything to demand back. For if some rights were left to individuals where there were no common superior to decide between them and the public, each individual being his own judge in some cases would soon claim to be it for all. The state of nature would subsist and the association would necessarily become tyrannical or useless.

Finally, each giving himself to all gives himself to no one. And since there is no associate over whom he does not acquire the same right that he yields over himself, he gains the equivalent of all that he loses and more force to preserve that which he has.

If then one removes from the social compact that which is not its essence, one will find that it is reduced to the following terms. *Each of us places in common his person and all his power, under the supreme direction of the general will; and we as a body receive each member as an indivisible part of the whole.*

At once, in place of the particular person of each contractor, this act of association produces a moral and collective body, composed of as many members as there are voices in the assembly. And by this same act, the body receives its unity, its common *I,* its life and its will. In other times, this public person so formed by the union of all others took the name *City*[4] and now takes that of *Republic* or *body politic* which is called by its members *State* when it is passive, *Sovereign* when it is active, *Power* in comparison to others like itself. In regard to the associates, they take collectively the name *people* and call themselves individually *Citizens* as participants in the sovereign authority and *subjects* as being under the laws of the State. But these terms are often confused and are taken one for another. It suffices to know how to distinguish them when they are used in all their precision.

★ Chapter VII

Of the Sovereign

This formula shows that the act of association contains a reciprocal commitment between the public and the individuals, and that each individual, contracting, as it were, with himself is doubly committed: as a member of the Sovereign to individuals and as a member of the State to the Sovereign. But the maxim of civil right that no one is bound by commitments made with himself cannot be applied here, for there is a great difference between making an obligation with oneself and with the whole of which one is part.

It is necessary to note further that public deliberation which, due to the two different relations under which each of the subjects is seen, can obligate all to the Sovereign, cannot, by the opposite reason, obligate the Sovereign to itself. And consequently, it is against the nature of the body politic for the Sovereign to impose a law on itself which it could not break. Only being able to consider itself as under one and the same relation, the Sovereign is then a case of an individual contracting with himself. From this it appears that there neither is nor can be any kind of fundamental law obligatory upon the body of people, not even the social contract. This does not mean that this body could not very well commit itself with others in matters that do not derogate from this contract, for in regard to the foreigner, it becomes a simple being, an individual.

But the body politic or the Sovereign, drawing its existence only from the sanctity of the contract, can never, even toward others, obligate itself to anything that derogates from the original act, such as alienating some portion of itself or submitting to another Sovereign. To violate the act by which it exists, would be to annihilate itself; and that which is nothing can produce nothing.

As soon as this multitude is thus united in one body, one of the members cannot be injured without attacking the body, much less the body be injured without the members feeling it. Thus duty and interest equally obligate the two contracting parties mutually to aid each other, and the same men should seek to bring together under this dual relationship all the advantages that depend on it.

Now, the Sovereign, being formed only of the individuals who compose it, neither has nor can have any interest contrary to theirs. Consequently, the Sovereign power has no need to give guarantees to its subjects, because it is impossible that the body should want to harm all its members, and we shall presently see that it can do no harm to anyone in particular. The Sovereign, solely because of what it is, is always all that it should be.

But it is not so with the subjects' relation to the Sovereign. Despite the common interest, nothing would vouch for their commitment if the Sovereign did not find means of assuring their fidelity.

In fact, each individual may, as a man, have a particular will contrary or dissimilar to the general will which he has as a Citizen. His particular interest may speak to him quite differently than the common interest. His existence, absolutely and naturally independent, may make him regard what he owes to the common cause as a gratuitous contribution, the loss of which will be less harmful to others than the payment is onerous to himself. And considering the moral person who constitutes the State as an imaginary being because it is not a man, he would enjoy the rights of the citizen without wishing to fulfill the duties of the subject. The progress of this injustice would cause the ruin of the body politic.

In order then that the social compact not be an empty formula, it tacitly contains this commitment which alone can give force to the others: that whoever shall refuse to obey the general will shall be constrained to do so by the whole body. This means nothing other than that he will be forced to be free, because this is the condition which, giving each Citizen to the Fatherland, guarantees him from all personal dependence, the condition which designs and activates the political machine and which alone renders civil commitments legitimate—without it, they would be absurd, tyrannical, and subject to the most enormous abuses.

✯ Chapter VIII

Of the Civil State

This passage from the state of nature to the civil state produces in man a very remarkable change, by substituting justice for instinct in his conduct and giving morality to his actions which they previous lacked. It is only then that, the voice of duty taking the place of physical impulse and right the place of appetite, man, who until then had only thought of himself, finds himself forced to act on other principles and to consult his reason before listening to his inclinations. Although in this state he is deprived of several advantages that he gets from nature, he gains in it others so great, his faculties are exercised and developed, his ideas are extended, his sentiments are ennobled, his entire soul is raised to such a peak, that even if the abuses of this new condition were often to degrade him below that which he left, he ought to bless ceaselessly the happy moment that tore him from it forever, and which, from a stupid and limited animal made an intelligent being and a man.

Let us reduce this balance to terms easily compared. What man loses by the social contract is his natural freedom and an unlimited right to all that tempts him and that he can attain. What he gains is civil freedom and property in all that he possesses. In order not to be mistaken concerning these compensations, it is necessary carefully to distinguish natural freedom which is bounded only by the forces of the individual from civil freedom which is limited by the general will; and possession which is only the effect of force or the right of the first occupant, from property which can only be founded upon a positive title.

One might add to the preceding that moral freedom is also acquired in the civil state, and it alone truly makes a man master of himself. For the impulse of mere appetite is slavery, and to obey law which one has prescribed for oneself is freedom. But I have already said too much on this matter, and the philosophical sense of the word *freedom* is no part of my subject here.

★ Chapter IX

Of Real Property

At the moment that the community is founded, each member gives himself to it just as he is, he and all his forces which include the goods that he possesses. It is not that, by this act, possession changes its nature by changing hands and becomes property in the hands of the Sovereign. But as the forces of the City are incomparably greater than those of an individual, public possession is also in fact stronger and more irrevocable, without being more legitimate, at least for foreigners. For the State in respect to its members is master of all their goods by the social contract, which serves as the basis of all rights of the State. But from the perspective of other Powers, it is only the right of the first occupant, which the State obtains from individuals.

The right of the first occupant, though more real than that of the stronger, becomes a true right only after the establishment of the right of property. Every man naturally has the right to everything that is necessary to him, but the positive act which makes him proprietor of some good excludes him from all the rest. His part being settled, he ought to limit himself to it, and no longer has any claim on the community. This is why the right of the first occupant, so weak in the state of nature, is respected by every civil man. By this right, one respects less what belongs to others than what does not belong to oneself.

In general, to authorize the right of the first occupant over any piece of land, the following conditions are necessary: first, that this piece of land not yet be inhabited by anyone; second, that one only occupy as much as one needs for subsistence; and in the third place, that one take possession of it, not by an empty ceremony but by work and cultivation, the sole sign of property which, in the absence of juridical title, should be respected by others.

In resting the right of the first occupant upon need and work, is that not in fact extending it as far as it can go? Can some limits not be given to this right? Will it be enough to set foot on a piece of common land to allege that at that moment one becomes master of it? Will it be enough to have the momentary force to separate other men from it in order to deprive them of the right of ever returning? How can a man or a people seize an immense territory and deprive mankind of it except by a punishable usurpation, since the rest of men are thereby deprived of a place of residence and sustenance which nature gives men in common? When Nuñez Balboa, standing on the shore, took possession of the south sea and all south American in the name of the crown of Castille, was this enough to dispossess all the inhabitants and to exclude all the Princes of the world from it? On this basis, such ceremonies would proliferate endlessly, and the Catholic King from his chamber might have taken possession of the whole universe, afterwards only cutting from this empire what other Princes already possessed.

One can see how the united and contiguous lands of individuals become the public territory, and how the right of sovereignty, extending from the subjects to the terrain that they occupy, becomes both real and personal, for it places the possessors in the greatest dependence and makes of their very forces the guarantees of their fidelity. This advantage does not appear to have been grasped by the ancient monarchs who called themselves Kings of the Persians, of the Scythians, of the Macedonians, seeming to regard themselves as the rulers of men rather than as masters of the country. Those of today more cleverly call themselves Kings of France, of Spain, of England, etc. In thus holding the land, they are very sure of holding its inhabitants.

What is singular in this alienation is that in accepting the goods of individuals, the community is far from despoiling them of them. It only serves to assure individuals of legitimate possession of their goods, changing usurpation into a true right, and possession into property. Then the possessors being considered as depositories of the public good, their rights being respected by all members of the State and maintained by all its forces against the foreigner, by a cessation advantageous to the public and more so to themselves, they have, so to speak, acquired all that they have given up. This is a paradox easily explained by the distinction between the rights which the sovereign and the proprietor have over the same basic object, as will be seen hereafter.

It may also happen that men begin to unite before possessing anything, and that subsequently seizing a terrain sufficient for all, they enjoy it in common, or they divide it among themselves equally or in the proportions established by the Sovereign. However this acquisition is made, the right that each individual has over his own part is always subordinate to the right of the community over all, without which there would be neither solidity of the social bond nor real force in the exercise of Sovereignty.

I shall end this chapter and this book with a remark which may serve as the basis of the whole social system. The fundamental compact, instead of destroying natural equality, substitutes a moral and legitimate equality for that physical inequality which nature had set up among men, and men however unequal in force and genius, all became equal by convention and right.[5]

End of the First Book

★ *One of the most important theorists of the eighteenth century, French philosopher* **Jean-Jacques Rousseau** *lived a life of controversy and wrote works that challenged traditional notions of human character and social convention.*

Endnotes

[1]"Learned inquiries into public right are often only the history of ancient abuses, and one becomes improperly stubborn when one troubles oneself to study them too hard." (*Treatise on the Interests of France with Her Neighbors.* M. L. M. d'A.) This is precisely what Grotius did.

[2]See a little treatise by Plutarch titled, *That Animals Use Reason.*

[3]The Romans who understood best and respected the right of war more than any nation on earth, carried their scruples in this regard so far that a citizen was not permitted to serve as volunteer without engaging himself expressly against the enemy and against a specifically named enemy. A legion having been reformed in which Cato the younger saw his first service under Popillus, Cato the elder wrote Popillus that if he wished his son to continue to serve under him, he must administer a new military oath to him, because the first having been annulled, he could no longer bear arms against the enemy. And the same Cato wrote his son to take care not to go into combat until he had taken the new oath. I know the examples of the Siege of Clusium and other particular facts may be used against me; but I cite the laws, the practices. The Romans are those who least often transgressed their laws; and they are alone in having such noble laws.

[4]The true sense of this word has been almost entirely obliterated among the moderns. Most take a town for a City and a bourgeois for a Citizen. They do not know that houses make a town but that Citizens make a City. In another time, this same mistake cost the Carthaginians dearly. I have not read of the title, *Cives,* ever having been given to the subjects of any Prince, not in antiquity to the Macedonians, nor in our day to the English, despite their being closer to freedom than all the others. Only the French with great familiarity take on the name of *Citizens,* because they have no true idea of it, as one can see in their Dictionaries. Otherwise, in usurping it, they would fall into the crime of *Lèse-Majesté.* Among them, this name expresses a virtue and not a right. When Bodin wanted to speak of our Citizens and Bourgeois, he made the gross blunder of taking the one for the other. M. d'Alembert did not make the same mistake, and in his article on *Geneva* has properly distinguished the four orders of men (or five, counting ordinary foreigners) who are in our town, and of which only two compose the Republic. No other French author, that I know, has understood the true sense of the word *Citizen.*

[5]Under bad governments, this equality is only apparent and illusory; it serves only to maintain the poor in their misery and the rich in their usurpation. In fact, the laws are always useful to those who possess and harmful to those who have nothing; from which it follows that the social state is advantageous to men only when they all have something and no one has too much.

★ ★ ★ ★ ★

Questions

1. When Rousseau asserts that "Man is born free, and everywhere he is in chains," what does he mean?
2. Are people essentially good or essentially evil?
3. To what extent does a "general will" exist in American politics?
4. If social problems are caused primarily by human nature, what is the best approach to find solutions?
5. If social problems are caused primarily by political, economic and social institutions, what is the best approach to change them?

☆ ☆ ☆

Public Policymaking: An Introduction

James E. Anderson, Texas A&M University

☆ The Study of Public Policy

In the course of their daily lives people are affected, directly and indirectly, obviously and subtly, by an extensive array of public policies. Take, for example, automobile owners. If an automobile was purchased on time, the Truth in Lending Act required provision of accurate information by the lender on the cost of credit. The vehicle features safety equipment, such as a padded dash and seat belts, required by the National Highway Traffic Safety Administration and a catalytic converter to reduce tailpipe emissions necessitated by Environmental Protection Agency rules. Out on the highway, financed jointly by the state and national governments, our driver needs to be aware of state and local traffic regulations, or risk direct contact with law enforcement officials. State policy requires that the automobile be insured and that both it and the driver be licensed. The price of the gasoline it consumes is indirectly affected by national energy policies and directly increased by national and state excise taxes. The vehicle's gas mileage must meet the national corporate average fuel economy (CAFÉ) standard.

Public policies in a modern, complex society are indeed ubiquitous. They confer advantages and disadvantages, cause pleasure, irritation, and pain, and collectively have important consequences for our well-being and happiness. They constitute a significant portion of our environment. This being so, we should know something about public policies, including how they are formed,

☆ ☆ ☆ ☆ ☆ ☆

Reprinted from *Public Policymaking*, (2003), by permission of Houghton Mifflin.

budgeted, implemented, and evaluated. There are also scientific, professional, and political reasons for studying public policies and policymaking.

Scientifically the systematic and rigorous study of the origins, development, and implementation of public policies will enhance our knowledge of political behavior and governance, as well as of public policy per se. How is policymaking affected by federalism and the separation of powers? Were pressure groups or public opinion or the media influential in the adoption of a policy? Why did government cease to be concerned with a problem? Concern with questions of this sort are designated as *policy study*.

Professionally, a person may pursue a career as a policy analyst or evaluator. Practitioners of *policy analysis*, which draws heavily upon economic theory and statistical and mathematical analytical techniques, have been growing in number in recent decades.[1] Policy analysis has an applied orientation and seeks to identify the most efficient alternative (i.e., the one that will yield the largest net social benefit) for dealing with a current problem, such as the control of air pollution or the disposal of household garbage. A variant of policy analysis is evaluation research, which assesses how well policies attain their goals and the other societal effects that they may have.

Politically, many people want to engage in *policy advocacy*, using knowledge of public policy to formulate and promote "good" public policies that will have the "right" goals, that is, goals which serve their purposes. They may think of themselves as liberals, conservatives, libertarians, communitarians, or socialists and disagree greatly in their notions of what is good or just. The research efforts of policy advocates are frequently skewed by their wish to generate data and analysis in line with their preferences. In contrast, policy study is motivated by the intent to be impartial.

This book draws on the scientific policy studies approach to develop a basic understanding of the policymaking process, which is here viewed as an inherently political process involving conflict and struggle among people (public officials and private citizens) with conflicting interests, values, and desires on policy issues. In describing and analyzing the policymaking process, the scientific policy studies approach has three basic aims.[2] First, its primary goal is to explain the adoption of a policy rather than to identify or prescribe "good" or proper policy. Analysis, rather than advocacy, is its style. Second, it rigorously searches for the causes and consequences of public policies by applying social-scientific methodology, which is not restricted to the use of quantitative data and methodology. At a minimum, it does require that one should strive to be rational, empirical, and objective. Third, this approach aims to develop reliable theories and explanations about public policies and their politics. Thus policy studies can be both theoretical and somewhat relevant to the more practical aspects of policymaking. It has been said that nothing is as practical as a good theory.

What Is Public Policy?

In general usage, the term *policy* designates the behavior of some actor or set of actors, such as an official, a governmental agency, or a legislature, in an area of activity such as public transportation or consumer protection. Public policy also may be viewed as whatever governments choose to do or not to do. Such definitions may be adequate for ordinary discourse, but because we set out in this book to do a systematic analysis of public policy, a more precise definition or concept is needed to structure our thinking and to facilitate effective communication with one another.

In this book a *policy* is defined as a *relatively stable, purposive course of action followed by an actor or set of actors in dealing with a problem or matter of concern.* This definition focuses on what is actually done instead of what is only proposed or intended; differentiates a policy from a decision, which is essentially a specific choice among alternatives; and views policy as something that unfolds over time.

Public policies are those developed by governmental bodies and officials. (Nongovernmental actors and factors may of course influence public-policy development.) The special characteristics of public policies stem from their being formulated by what political scientist David Easton has called the "authorities" in a political system, namely, "elders, paramount chiefs, executives, legislators, judges, administrators, councilors, monarchs, and the like." These are, he says, the persons who "engage in the daily affairs of a political system," are "recognized by most members of the system as having responsibility for these matters," and take actions that are "accepted as binding most of the time by most of the members so long as they act within the limits of their roles."[3] In short, public policies are those produced by government officials and agencies. They also usually affect substantial numbers of people.

There are several implications of this concept of public policy as a relatively stable, purposive course of action followed by government in dealing with some problem or matter of concern. First, the definition links policy to purposive or goal-oriented action rather than to random behavior or chance occurrences. Public policies in modern political systems do not, by and large, just happen. They are instead designed to accomplish specified goals or produce definite results, although these are not always achieved. Proposed policies may be usefully thought of as hypotheses suggesting that specific actions be taken to achieve particular goals. Thus, to increase farm income, the national government utilizes income subsidies and production controls. These programs have indeed enhanced the incomes of many farmers, but by no means all.

The goals of a policy may be somewhat loosely stated and cloudy in content, thus providing general direction rather than precise targets for its implementation. Those who want action on a problem may differ both as to what should be done and how it should be done. Ambiguity in language then can become a means for reducing conflict, at least for the moment. Compromise to secure agreement and build support may consequently yield general phrasing and lack of clarity in the statement of policy goals.

Second, policies consist of courses or patterns of action taken over time by governmental officials rather than their separate, discrete decisions. It is difficult to think of such actions as a presidential decision to honor a movie actor or a Social Security Administration decision to award disability benefits to Joe Doaks as public policies. A policy includes not only the decision to adopt a law or make a rule on some topic but also the subsequent decisions that are intended to enforce or implement the law or rule. Industrial health and safety policy, for example, is shaped not only by the Occupational Safety and Health Act of 1970 but also by a stream of administrative rules and judicial decisions interpreting, elaborating, and applying (or not applying) the act to particular situations.

Third, public policies emerge in response to *policy demands*, or those claims for action or inaction on some public issue made by other actors—private citizens, group representatives, or legislators and other public officials—upon government officials and agencies. Such demands may range from general insistence that a municipal government "do something" about traffic congestion to a specific call for the national government to prohibit theft of pet dogs and cats for sale to medical and scientific research organizations. In short, some demands simply call for action; others also specify the action desired.

In response to policy demands, public officials make decisions that give content and direction to public policy. These decisions may enact statutes, issue executive orders or edicts, promulgate administrative rules, or make judicial interpretations of laws. Thus the decision by Congress to enact the Sherman Antitrust Act in 1890 was a policy decision; another was the 1911 Supreme Court ruling that the act prohibited only unreasonable restraints of trade rather than all restraints of trade. Each was of major importance in shaping that course of action called *antitrust policy*. (The Sherman Act also prohibits monopolization and attempts to monopolize.) Such decisions may be contrasted with the innumerable relatively routine decisions that officials make in the day-to-day application of public policy. The Department of Veterans Affairs, for example, makes hundreds of thousands of decisions every year on veterans' benefits; most, however, fall within the bounds of settled policy and can be categorized as routine decisions.

Policy statements in turn usually are formal expressions or articulations of public policy. Among these are legislative statutes, executive orders and decrees, administrative rules and regulations, and court opinions, as well as statements and speeches by public officials indicating the government's intentions and goals and what will be done to realize them. Policy statements are sometimes notably ambiguous. Witness the conflicts that arise over the meaning of statutory provisions or judicial holdings, or the time and effort expended analyzing and trying to divine the meaning of policy statements by national political leaders, such as the president of the United States or the chair of the Federal Reserve Board. Different levels, branches, or units of government may also issue conflicting policy statements, as on such matters as environmental pollution or liability for consumer products.

Fourth, policy involves what governments actually do, not just what they intend to do or what officials say they are going to do. If a legislature enacts a law requiring employers to pay no less than a stated minimum wage but nothing is done to enforce the law, and subsequently little change occurs in economic behavior, it seems reasonable to contend that public policy actually takes the form of nonregulation of wages.

Relevant here is the concept of *policy output*, or the action actually taken in pursuance of policy decisions and statements. This concept focuses our attention on such matters as amounts of taxes collected, miles of highway built, welfare benefits paid, restraints of trade eliminated, traffic fines collected, and foreign-aid projects undertaken. These can usually be enumerated with little difficulty. Examining policy outputs, we may find that a policy differs somewhat or even greatly from what policy statements indicate it should be. Policy outputs should be distinguished from *policy outcomes*, which focus on a policy's societal consequences. For example, do longer prison terms reduce crime rates? Do air pollution control programs improve public health? Outputs can be counted; outcomes are often difficult or impossible to measure.

Fifth, a public policy may be either positive or negative. Some form of overt governmental action may deal with a problem on which action is demanded (positive), or governmental officials may decide to do nothing on some matter on which government involvement was sought (negative). In other words, governments can follow a policy of laissez faire, or hands off, either generally or on some aspects of economic activity. Such inaction may have major consequences for a society or some groups, as in the late 1970s, when the national government decided to cease regulating commercial airline rates and routes.

Inaction becomes a public policy when officials decline to act on a problem—that is, when they decide an issue negatively. This choice differs from nonaction on a matter that has not become a public issue, has not been brought to official attention, and has not been considered or debated. A slightly ludicrous example is the lack of governmental action on the taking of earthworms—the activity has no seasons and no bag limits. Is this a public policy? The answer is no, because it is not an issue and no decisions have been made.

Finally, public policy, at least in its positive form, is based on law and is authoritative. Members of a society usually accept as legitimate the facts that taxes must be paid, import controls must be obeyed, and highway speed limits must be complied with, unless one wants to run the risk of fines, jail sentences, or other legally imposed sanctions or disabilities. Thus public policy has an authoritative, legally coercive quality that the policies of private organizations do not have. Indeed, a major characteristic distinguishing government from private organizations is its monopoly over the legitimate use of coercion. Governments can legally incarcerate people; private organizations cannot.

Some public policies may be widely violated even though they are authoritative, such as national prohibition in the 1920s and many highway speed limits. Moreover, enforcement may be limited, piecemeal, or sporadic. Are these still public policies? The answer is yes, because they were on the statute books and enforcement was provided for. Whether such policies are effective or wise is another matter. Authoritativeness is a necessary but not a sufficient condition for effective public policy.

Categories of Public Policies

Governments at all levels in the United States—national, state, and local—have been increasingly active in developing public policies. Every year a large volume of laws and ordinances flows from the nation's national, state, and local legislative bodies. That volume of laws in turn is greatly exceeded by the quantity of rules and regulations produced by administrative agencies acting on the basis of legislative authorizations. This proliferation of public policies has occurred in such traditional areas of governmental action as foreign policy, transportation, education, welfare, law enforcement, business and labor regulation, and international trade. Much activity has also come in areas that received little attention until the last two or three decades: economic stability, environmental protection, equality of opportunity, medical care, nuclear energy, and consumer protection.

During a typical two-year term of Congress 300 to 400 public laws will be enacted. Though the legislative process was disrupted by bitter partisan conflict over the possible impeachment of President Bill Clinton, Congress still managed in 1998 to adopt several important pieces of legislation. These dealt with such matters as an overhaul of public housing, higher education, vocational education, charter schools, Head Start, Internal Revenue Service reform, surface transportation, veterans' benefits, chemical weapons, and

International Monetary Fund financing. Involving mostly changes or additions to current policies, all of the laws incorporate biases that benefit some groups and disadvantage other groups, which is indeed an intrinsic feature of public policies. Rarely does a public policy make everyone better off.

Given the large number and complexity of public policies in the United States, the task of trying to make sense of them is enormous. This section will summarize a number of general typologies that political scientists and others have developed for categorizing public policies. These typologies will prove much more useful in distinguishing among and generalizing about policies than some of the more traditional and widely used categorization schemes, such as by issue area (labor, welfare, civil rights, and foreign affairs), institution (legislative policies, judicial policies, and departmental policies), and time (New Deal era, post-World War II, and late nineteenth century). Although these categories are convenient for designating various sets of policies and organizing discussions about them, they are not helpful in developing generalizations, because they do not reflect the basic characteristics and content of policies. The discussion of typologies will also provide the reader with a notion of the scope, diversity, and different purposes of public policies.

Substantive and Procedural Policies

First, policies may be classified as either *substantive* or *procedural. Substantive policies* involve what government is going to do, such as constructing highways, paying welfare benefits, acquiring bombers, or prohibiting the retail sale of liquor. Substantive policies directly allocate advantages and disadvantages, benefits and costs, to people. *Procedural policies*, in contrast, pertain to how something is going to be done or who is going to take action. So defined, procedural policies include laws providing for the creation of administrative agencies, determining the matters over which they have jurisdiction, specifying the processes and techniques that they can use in carrying out their programs, and providing for presidential, judicial, and other controls over their operations.

A procedural policy of great importance is the federal Administrative Procedure Act (APA) of 1946. This statute, a response to the growth of administrative agency discretion in the twentieth century, prescribes procedures to be used by agencies in notice and comment or informal rule-making. For example, APA requires notice of the proposed rule-making, opportunity for interested persons to participate in the proceeding through oral or written submissions, publication of a proposed rule at least thirty days before it becomes effective, and opportunity for interested persons to petition for issuance, amendment, or repeal of a rule. The act's requirements for adjudication are much more detailed, but in both instances it is intended to ensure openness and fairness in agency decision-making. Another example of a procedural policy is the requirement that an environmental impact statement be prepared by agencies proposing major actions affecting the environment by the National Environmental Policy Act (NEPA). Its purpose is to cause agencies to give consideration to environmental effects before making their decisions. In itself NEPA adds nothing to the substance of policy; it neither prohibits nor requires particular agency actions toward the environment.

Procedural policies may have important substantive consequences. That is, how something is done or who takes the action may help determine what is actually done. Frequently, efforts are made to use procedural issues to delay or prevent adoption of substantive decisions and policies. An agency's action may be challenged on the ground that improper procedures were followed, as under APA, when it is really the substance of the action that is being resisted. Some Washington lawyers have become highly skilled in manipulating procedural rules to delay agency action. Thus, because of procedural delays and complications (most of them produced by the maneuverings of the defendant company), it took the Federal Trade Commission thirteen years to complete a case compelling the manufacturer to remove the word "liver" from a product named "Carter's Little Liver Pills." (The product has no effect on one's liver.)

Distributive, Regulatory, Self-Regulatory, and Redistributive Policies

This typology differentiates policies by their effect on society and the relationships among those involved in policy formation.[4]

Distributive policies involve allocation of services or benefits to particular segments of the population—individuals, groups, corporations, and communities. Some distributive policies may provide benefits to one or a few beneficiaries, as in the Chrysler loan guarantee of the late 1970s, which kept the company from bankruptcy, and the subsidies for the operation of American merchant ships. Others may provide benefits for vast numbers of persons, as is true for agricultural income-support programs, tax deductions for home mortgage interest payments, free public school education, and job-training programs.

Distributive policies typically involve using public funds to assist particular groups, communities, or industries. Those who seek benefits usually do not compete directly with one another, although in some instances they do, as in the selection of the site for the Superconducting Super Collider, where there could be only one winner. The SSC was a costly scientific venture, later cancelled, which was supposed to help determine the nature of matter. Nor do their benefits represent a direct cost to any specific group; rather, the costs are assessed to the public treasury, which is to say all taxpayers. Thus, distributive policies appear to create only winners and no specific losers, although obviously someone does pay their financial cost.

The standard example of distributive policy has been rivers and harbors improvement and flood control legislation (water projects), carried out by the Army Corps of Engineers. In recent years it has been surpassed as an example of pork-barrel legislation (or simply, "pork") by transportation legislation. The 1998 surface transportation law, entitled the Transportation Equity Act for the 21st Century, provides for $218 billion in spending over a six-year period. In addition to its general provisions the act contains authorization for many hundreds of special highway, mass transit, and bus projects requested by members of Congress from both parties. The cost of these pork projects was estimated to be more than $20 billion. Most states and congressional districts shared in the bacon.

These projects are scattered all around the country and have little connection with one another, which supports Professor Theodore J. Lowi's contention that distributive policies "are virtually not policies at all but are highly individualized decisions that only by accumulation can be called a policy."[5] Each locality and its supporters seek authorization and funding for their own project without challenging the right of others to do likewise. Most projects consequently have some friends and no enemies in Congress, and presidents usually leave them alone. President Jimmy Carter upset the apple cart in 1977, when he successfully eliminated some water projects on the grounds that they were wasteful and unnecessary. Many members of Congress were antagonized by this action, either because they favored the targeted projects or resented presidential intervention in an area long under congressional domination. A few of the projects later were restored.

Regulatory policies impose restrictions or limitations on the behavior of individuals and groups. That is, they reduce the freedom or discretion to act of those regulated, whether bankers, utility companies, meat-packers, or saloonkeepers. In this sense they clearly differ from distributive policies, which increase the freedom or discretion of the persons or groups affected.

When we think of regulatory policies we usually focus on business regulatory policies, such as those pertaining to control of pollution or regulation of transportation industries. Among others, these sorts of policies were the focus of the movement for deregulation. The most extensive variety of regulatory policies, however, is that which deals with criminal behavior against persons and property. What are called social regulatory policies deal with such topics as affirmative action, school prayer, gun control, pornography, and abortion, and involve the regulation of personal behavior.[6]

The formation of regulatory policy usually features conflict between two groups or coalitions of groups, with one side seeking to impose some sort of control on the other side, which customarily resists, arguing either that control is unnecessary or that the wrong kind of control is being proposed. Amid this opposition, regulatory decisions involve clear winners and losers, although the winners usually get less than they initially sought. (When the winners are public interest groups, they may not gain direct material benefits from policies which, like the Clean Air Act, provide broad social benefits.) It is often difficult, however, to identify all the purposes and consequences of regulatory policies. Regulatory policies take several forms.

Some regulatory policies set forth general rules of behavior, directing that actions be taken or commanding that others not be taken. The Sherman Act in effect tells businesses, "Thou shalt not monopolize or attempt to monopolize or act to restrain trade." These prohibitions are enforced by actions brought in the federal courts against violators. In contrast, public-utility regulation by state governments involved detailed control of entry into the business, standards of service, financial practices, and rates charged by electric, telephone, and other utility companies. Comparatively, antitrust regulation entails much less restriction of business discretion than does public-utility regulation.

Consumer-protection policies illustrate other variations in regulatory policies. Some statutes, such as the Pure Food and Drug Act of 1906 and the Drug Amendments of 1962, set standards for quality that drug manufacturers must comply with. Thus, before new drugs can be put on the market, they must be shown to meet the standards for safety in use and efficacy for the purposes intended. Other consumer legislation, such as the Consumer Credit Protection Act, requires creditors to provide borrowers with accurate information on interest and other financing costs for credit purchases. The first sort of policy is intended to prevent products that do not meet designated standards from entering the marketplace; the second type is meant to provide consumers with enough information to make informed decisions.

Some regulatory policies, such as those which restrict entry into a business such as television broadcasting or electric power distribution, are implemented by decisions that confer benefits on some and deny them to others. Of the several applicants for a television broadcast license for a city that may be before the Federal Communications Commission, only one can be propitiated. These can be called *competitive regulatory policies* because they limit the number of providers of specific goods and services. They also may regulate the quality of services that can be provided to consumers.[7]

Self-regulatory policies are similar to competitive regulatory policies in that they involve restricting or controlling some matter or group. Unlike competitive regulatory policies, however, self-regulatory policies are usually more controlled by the regulated group as a means of protecting or promoting the interests of its members. Several hundred professions and occupations, ranging from tree surgeons and auctioneers to lawyers and physicians, are licensed in one or more states; about sixty are licensed in a majority of states. Commonly licensed health professionals include chiropractors, dentists, dental hygienists, emergency medical technicians, optometrists, pharmacists, physicians, podiatrists, practical and registered nurses, psychologists, sanitarians, and social workers.[8]

The usual policymaking pattern here is for a professional or occupational group acting on its own to seek licensing legislation from the state legislature. Outside the ranks of the interested group, interest in the matter usually is slight. The result is enactment of a licensing law, whose implementation is delegated to a board dominated by members from the licensed group. In time, entry into the licensed occupation or profession may be restricted and the prices charged for its specialized services may increase. It is unclear to what extent licensing improves the quality of services available to the public.[9]

Supervised self-regulation may also occur. Under the Agricultural Marketing Agreement Act of 1937, the producers and handlers of fruits, vegetables, and specialty crops such as almonds sold on the fresh market collectively act to obtain marketing orders from the Agricultural Marketing Service (AMS). Put into effect with the approval of two-thirds of the producers of a commodity, these orders are binding on all producers and may authorize research and promotional programs, set standards for quality, and control movement of such products as oranges and grapefruit to market so as to ensure "orderly marketing." Marketing orders, which are managed by producer-dominated administrative committees and are subject to AMS supervision, are intended to improve the economic situation of producers.[10]

Redistributive policies involve deliberate efforts by the government to shift the allocation of wealth, income, property, or rights among broad classes or groups of the population, such as haves and have-nots, proletariat and bourgeoisie. "The aim involved is not use of property but property itself, not equal treatment but equal possession, not behavior but being."[11] In American society redistributive policies ultimately involve disagreements between liberals (pro) and conservatives (con) and tend to be highly productive of conflict.

The usual pattern in redistributive policy shifts resources from haves to have-nots. It is possible, however, for the flow to reverse. Farm subsidy payments under the agricultural income-support programs go mostly to large commercial farmers; small-scale farmers derive few benefits, yet everyone who pays taxes contributes to financing of the programs. Typically, however, such instances are not debated as redistributive,[12] perhaps because of reluctance to acknowledge that sometimes the haves benefit at the expense of the have-nots.

Redistributive policies are difficult to enact because they involve the reallocation of money, rights, or power. Those who possess money or power rarely yield them willingly, regardless of how strenuously some may discourse upon the "burdens" and heavy responsibility attending their possession. Because money and power are good coinage in the political realm, those who possess them have ample means to resist their diminution.

Policies that have (or have had) some redistributive influence include the graduated income tax, Medicare and Medicaid, the War on Poverty, the Voting Rights Act, and legislative reapportionment. The Johnson administration's War on Poverty represented an effort to shift wealth and other resources to blacks and poor people. Encountering much resistance from conservatives and lacking strong presidential support, it was gradually dispersed and dismantled. Although most of the individual antipoverty programs (such as Head Start and the community action or service programs) still function, they have lost much of their redistributive quality. The Voting Rights Act, which on the whole has been enforced with considerable strength by the Justice Department, has helped to produce a substantial increase in black voter registration, voting, and state and local officeholding in the South.

The graduated income tax, which is based on the principle of ability to pay (those who have more income can fairly be expected to pay at progressively higher rates) has now lost much of its redistributive potential. The top marginal rate once was as high as 91 percent. In the early 1980s the rates ranged from 14 to 50 percent over a dozen income brackets, which still held out the possibility of considerable redistribution. The Tax Reform Act of 1986, enacted by Congress with strong support from President Reagan, who believed that high marginal tax rates both infringed on individual liberty and discouraged economic growth, provided for only two tax brackets at 15 and 28 percent.[13] Brackets of 31, 36, and 39.6 percent were added in the 1990s, however. These marginal tax rates will be reduced over the next several years by tax reduction legislation enacted in 2001 at the urging of the George W. Bush administration.

Redistributive policies are not only difficult to obtain, they are also hard to retain, as the discussion of the income tax indicates. Equality of result or condition (that is, equality in income or standard of living) is not overly appealing to most Americans, whatever they think about equality of opportunity.

Material and Symbolic Policies

Public policies may also be described as either material or symbolic, depending upon the kind of benefits they allocate.[14] Material policies actually either provide tangible resources or substantive power to their beneficiaries, or impose real disadvantages on those who are adversely affected. Legislation requiring employers to pay a prescribed minimum wage, appropriating money for a public-housing program, or providing income-support payments to farmers is material in content and effect.

Symbolic policies, in contrast, have little real material impact on people. They do not deliver what they appear to deliver; they allocate no tangible advantages and disadvantages. Rather, they appeal to people's cherished values, such as peace, patriotism, and social justice. A prime example of a symbolic policy is the Kellogg-Briand Pact of 1928, by which the United States and fourteen other countries agreed to outlaw war. Comment on its impact seems unnecessary.

Burning of the United States flag as a symbolic form of political protest has agitated members of Congress for several years. In 1989 the Flag Protection Act provided criminal penalties for any person who "knowingly mutilates, defaces, physically defiles, burns, maintains on the floor or ground, or tramples upon any flag of the United States." Quickly challenged, the act was declared unconstitutional by the U.S. Supreme Court as an infringement on the freedom of expression protected by the first amendment. The Court's ruling touched off a public and political furor. An effort in the early 1990s to amend the Constitution to prohibit desecration of the flag failed. However, in 1995, the House, stimulated by the new Republican majority, approved (312 to 120) an amendment authorizing the national and state governments to ban "physical desecration of the flag of the United States."[15] It failed to win approval in the Senate. There is much symbolism at stake in this struggle.

Occasionally a policy that appears to be mostly symbolic may turn out to have important consequences. The Endangered Species Act of 1973, which is intended to help ensure the survival of rare animals and plants, initially appeared to be a statement of good intentions with few costs. Little opposition attended its enactment. As implemented, however, the act has had important effects, sometimes being used to block construction projects, timber cutting, and other activities that would threaten or destroy the habitats of endangered species, such as spotted owls, California gnatcatchers, and the red-cockaded woodpecker.[16]

Most policies are neither entirely symbolic nor wholly material. The symbolic and material categories should instead be viewed as the poles of a continuum, with most policies being ranged along the continuum depending upon how symbolic or material they are in practice. The Sherman Act, as an instrument for "trust busting," for breaking up large monopolistic companies, has long been symbolic. With the exception of AT&T, no trusts have been broken up since the Progressive Era. On the other hand, beginning with the Carter administration and continuing on into the Clinton administration, the Sherman Act has been applied with some vigor against collusive behavior such as price fixing, bid rigging, and market allocation. Here it has had substantial material impact.

Policies that are ostensibly material as labeled by legislative language may be rendered essentially symbolic by administrative action or by the legislature's failure to provide adequate funds for their implementation. The public-housing goals of the Housing Act of 1949 and later laws were made substantially symbolic by the subsequent failure of Congress to provide the authorized level of funding for housing construction.[17] On the other hand, policies may move from the more symbolic to the more material category. Professor Bruce I. Oppenheimer argues that policy for controlling oil pollution was largely symbolic during the years 1947 to 1966.[18] Legislation was on the books but little was done to enforce it. After 1966, the control of oil pollution became much more effective as a consequence of growing public concern about pollution, increased enforcement activity, and additional congressional legislation, such as the 1986 Oil Pollution Act.

The material-symbolic typology is especially useful to keep in mind when analyzing effects of policy because it directs attention beyond formal policy statements. It also alerts us to the important role of symbols in political behavior.

Policies Involving Collective Goods or Private Goods

Public policies may also involve the provision of either collective (indivisible) goods or private (divisible) goods.[19] The nature of collective goods is such that if they are provided for one person, they must be provided for all. Moreover, one person's consumption of a collective good does not deny it to others. A standard example is national defense: there is no effective way to provide it for some citizens and exclude others from its benefit, enjoyment, or other consequences, nor to calculate that some citizens benefit more from it than others. Thus an economically rational person would never voluntarily pay for national defense, choosing rather to be a free rider and let others stand the costs. Hence defense must be provided, if we want it, by government and financed by taxation. Other examples of collective goods are clean air, public safety, traffic control, and mosquito abatement.

Private goods, in contrast, may be broken into units and purchased or charged by the individual user or beneficiary, and are available in the marketplace. Others may be excluded from their use. Various social goods provided by government (garbage collection, postal service, medical care, museums, public housing, and national parks) have some characteristics of private goods. Charges and fees are sometimes, but not always, levied on users. Whether such goods, which conceivably could be provided by the market economy, will be provided by the government is a function of political decisions influenced by tradition (parks), notions of the proper functions of government (the post office), the desire of users or beneficiaries to shift some of their costs to others (federal crop insurance), and the like.

Some argue that only collective goods should be the subject of public policy. The tendency, however, has been more and more to convert private goods into social goods by government action. Many consider ill health, unemployment, environmental pollution, industrial accidents and disease, and misrepresentation in the marketplace to be collective rather than individual problems—matters affecting the entire population, hence involving public goods for which the entire society should pay. Generally, the more something is thought to have the qualities of a public good, the more likely people are to accept its provision by government. If it seems clear that some benefit more directly than others, there may also be a desire to levy charges, fees, or taxes on the direct beneficiaries to cover part of the cost. Thus we encounter user fees at national parks, tuition at public colleges, rent in public-housing projects, and tolls for some bridges and highways.

The privatization movement, encouraged in the 1980s by the Reagan administration, represented a counterforce to the long-run tendency to expand the scope of social goods. Based on free-market economic theory, privatization supports transferring many government assets or programs to the private sector and contracting with private companies to handle many public services, whether the collection of garbage or the operation of prisons. "The private sector, it is argued, will perform these functions more efficiently and economically than the public sector."[20]

The results of the privatization movement at the national level are mixed. A successful example is the sale of Conrail, which operated several railroads in the Northeast and Midwest, to a private corporation. Nothing, however, came out of proposals by the Reagan administration and others to sell public lands in the western states to private buyers.[21] Even western ranchers and other supporters of the "sagebrush rebellion," which promoted transferring ownership of public lands to state and local governments, lost interest in privatization. Their access to public grazing lands with low lease rates would have been jeopardized by privatization. Congress was also quite skeptical about the sale of public lands.

Approaches to Policy Study

Political and social scientists have developed many models, theories, approaches, concepts, and schemes for analyzing policymaking and its related component, decision-making. Indeed, political scientists have often displayed more facility and zeal for theorizing about public policymaking than for actually studying policy and the policymaking process. Nonetheless, theories and concepts are needed to guide the study of public policy, to facilitate communication, and to suggest possible explanations for policy actions. Those who aspire to systematically study the policymaking process need some guidelines and criteria of relevance to focus their effort and to prevent aimless meandering through the fields of political data. What we find when we engage in research depends partly upon what we are looking for; policy concepts, models, and theories give direction and structure to our inquiry.

This section will survey several theoretical approaches to the study of public policy. But first we must distinguish between policymaking and decision-making, a distinction students of public policy do not always make with clarity, if at all. Decision-making involves making a discrete choice from among two or more alternatives, such as whether or not to read further in this book. Theories of decision-making deal with the criteria and processes used in making such choices. A *policy*, as defined earlier, is "a relatively stable, purposive course of action followed by an actor or set of actors in dealing with a problem or matter of concern." Policymaking thus typically encompasses a flow and pattern of action that extends over time and includes many decisions, some routine and some not so routine. Rarely will a policy be synonymous with a single decision. Here is a mundane illustration: it would not be accurate for a person to state that it was his policy to bathe on Saturday nights, if in fact he did so infrequently, however elegant and thoughtful the decision-making process that led to his doing so on a rare Saturday. It is the course of action, the pattern or regularity, that defines policy, not an isolated event. In the example, the policy is best thought of as going dirty.

The theoretical approaches discussed here include political systems theory, group theory, elite theory, institutionalism, and rational-choice theory. Although most of these approaches were not developed specifically for analyzing policy formation, they can readily be bent to that purpose. They are useful to the extent that they direct our attention to important political phenomena, help clarify and organize our thinking, and suggest explanations for political activity or, in our case, public policies. Limitations and criticisms are mentioned as the discussion proceeds.

Political Systems Theory

Public policy may be viewed as a political system's response to demands arising from its environment. The political system, as Easton defines it, comprises those identifiable and interrelated institutions and activities (what we usually think of as governmental institutions and political processes) in a society that make authoritative allocations of values (decisions) that are binding on society. The environment consists of all phenomena—the social system, the economic system, the biological setting—that are external to the boundaries of the political system. Thus at least analytically one can separate the political system from all the other components of a society.[22]

Inputs into the political system from the environment consist of demands and supports. Demands are the claims for action that individuals and groups make to satisfy their interests and values. Support is rendered when groups and individuals abide by election results, pay taxes, obey laws, and otherwise accept the decisions and actions undertaken by the political system in response to demands. The amount of support for a political system indicates the extent to which it is regarded as legitimate, or as authoritative and binding on its citizens.

Outputs of the political system include laws, rules, judicial decisions, and the like. Regarded as the authoritative allocations of values, they constitute public policy. The concept of feedback indicates that public policies (or outputs) made at a given time may subsequently alter the environment and the demands arising therefrom, as well as the character of the political system itself. Policy outputs may produce new demands, which lead to further outputs, and so on in a never-ending flow of public policy (see Figure 1.1).

The usefulness of systems theory in studying public policy is limited by its highly general and abstract nature. It does not, moreover, say much about the procedures and processes by which decisions are made and policy is developed within the "black box" called the political system. Indeed, systems theory depicts government as simply responding to demands made upon it, and its results are sometimes characterized as "input-output studies." (For an illustration, see the discussion in the section headed Socioeconomic Conditions.) Nonetheless, this approach can be helpful in organizing inquiry into policy formation. It also alerts us to some important facets of the political process, such as these: How do inputs from the environment affect the content of public policy and the operation of the political system? How in turn does public policy affect the environment and subsequent demands for policy action? How well is the political system able to convert demands into public policy and preserve itself over time?

Group Theory

According to the group theory of politics, public policy is the product of the group struggle. One writer states, "What may be called public policy is the equilibrium reached in this [group] struggle at any given moment, and it represents a balance which the contending factions or groups constantly strive to weight in their favor."[23] Many public policies do reflect the activities of groups. Examples include the AFL-CIO and minimum-wage legislation, farm groups and agricultural subsidies, the National Rifle Association and gun-

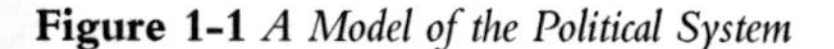

Figure 1-1 *A Model of the Political System*

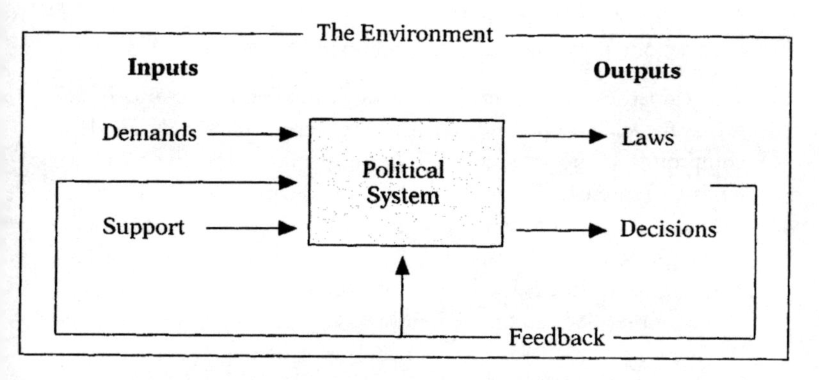

control policies, and the National Education Association and federal aid to public schools.

Group theory rests on the contention that interaction and struggle among groups are the central facts of political life. A group is a collection of individuals that may, on the basis of shared attitudes or interests, make claims upon other groups in society. It becomes a political interest group "when it makes a claim through or upon any of the institutions of government."[24] And many groups do just that. The individual is significant in politics only as a participant in or a representative of groups. It is through groups that individuals seek to secure their political preferences.

A central concept in group theory is that of access. To have influence and to be able to help shape governmental decisions, a group must have access, or the opportunity to express its viewpoints to decision-makers.[25] Obviously, if a group is unable to communicate with decision-makers, if no one in government will listen, its chances of affecting policymaking are slim. Access may result from the group's being organized, from its having status, good leadership, or resources such as money for campaign contributions. Social lobbying—the wining, dining, and entertaining of legislators and other public officials—can be understood as an effort to create access by engendering a feeling of obligation to the groups involved. Then, when a group wishes to discuss policy matters with an official, it will have an opportunity to present its case or have its telephone calls returned. Contributions to legislators by political action committees (PACs) are also often justified as a way of acquiring or maintaining access.

In the nature of things, some groups will have more access than others. Public policy at any given time will reflect the interests of those who are dominant. As groups gain and lose power and influence, public policy will be altered in favor of the interests of those gaining influence against the interests of those losing it.

The role of government ("official groups") in policy formation is described by one proponent of group theory:

> The legislature referees the group struggle, ratifies the victories of the successful coalitions, and records the terms of the surrenders, compromises, and conquests in the form of statutes. Every statute tends to represent compromises because the process of accommodating conflicts of group interests is one of deliberation and consent. The legislative vote on any issue tends to represent the composition of strength, i.e., the balance of power, among the contending groups at the moment of voting....Administrative agencies of the regulatory kind are established to carry out the terms of the treaties that the legislators have negotiated and ratified....The judiciary, like the civilian bureaucracy, is one of the instrumentalities for the administration of the agreed rules.[26]

Group theory focuses on one of the major dynamic elements in policy formation, especially in pluralist societies such as the United States, but it seems both to overstate the importance of groups and to understate the independent and creative role that public officials can play in the policy process. Indeed, many groups have been generated by public policies. The American Farm Bureau Federation, which developed around the agricultural extension program, is a notable example, as is the National Welfare Rights Organization. Public officials also may acquire a stake in particular programs and act as an interest group supporting their continuance. In the United States some welfare-agency employees, including social workers, prefer current programs, with their emphasis on supervision and services (as well as benefits), to a guaranteed annual income, which would probably eliminate some of their jobs.

Another shortcoming of group theory is that in actuality many people (e.g., the poor and disadvantaged) and interests (such diffuse interests as natural beauty and social justice) are either not represented or only poorly represented in the group struggle. As Professor E. E. Schattschneider remarks about the underorganization of the poor, "The flaw in the pluralist heaven is that the heavenly chorus sings with a strong upper-class accent."[27] Those who are not represented will have little voice in policymaking and thus their interests are likely to be slighted therein.

Finally, from a methodological perspective, it is misleading and inefficient to try to explain politics and policymaking solely in terms of interests and the group struggle. This bias leads to neglect of many other factors, such as ideas and institutions, which abound and which independently affect the development of policy. The reductionism or unicausal explanation that results when all political phenomena are crammed into the group concept should therefore be avoided.[28]

Elite Theory

Approached from the perspective of elite theory, public policy can be regarded as reflecting the values and preferences of a governing elite. The essential argument of elite theory is that public policy is not determined by the demands and actions of the people or the "masses" but rather by a ruling elite whose preferences are carried into effect by public officials and agencies.

Professors Thomas Dye and Harmon Zeigler provide a summary of elite theory:

1. Society is divided into the few who have power and the many who do not. [Only a small number of persons allocate values for society; the masses do not decide public policy.]
2. The few who govern are not typical of the masses who are governed. Elites are drawn disproportionately from the upper socioeconomic strata of society.
3. The movement of non-elites to elite positions must be slow and continuous to maintain stability and avoid revolution. Only non-elites who have accepted the basic elite consensus can be admitted to governing circles.
4. Elites share a consensus on the basic values of the social system and the preservation of the system. [In the United States, the elite consensus includes private enterprise, private property, limited government, and individual liberty.]
5. Public policy does not reflect demands of the masses but rather the prevailing values of the elite. Changes in public policy will be incremental rather than revolutionary. [Incremental changes permit responses to events that threaten a social system with a minimum of alteration or dislocation of the system.]
6. Elites may act out of narrow self-serving motives and risk undermining mass support, or they may initiate reforms, curb abuse, and undertake public-regarding programs to preserve the system and their place in it.
7. Active elites are subject to relatively little direct influence from apathetic masses. Elites influence masses more than masses influence elites.[29]

So stated, elite theory is a challenging theory of policy formation. Policy is the product of elites, reflecting their values and serving their ends, one of which may be a desire to provide in some way for the welfare of the masses. Dye argues that development of civil-rights policies in the United States during the 1960s can be suitably explained by elite theory. These policies were "a response of a national elite to conditions affecting a small minority of Americans rather than a response of national leaders to majority sentiments." Thus, for example, the "elimination of legal discrimination and the guarantee of equality of opportunity in the Civil Rights Act of 1964 was achieved largely through the dramatic appeals of middle-class black leaders to the conscience of white elites."[30]

This interpretation presents a narrow perspective on both who is affected by or interested in civil-rights policies and the explanation for adoption of the Civil Rights Act of 1964. Certainly leadership in Congress and the executive branch was very important, but so too were civil-rights protests and marches, public opinion, and support from an array of nonblack organizations. The civil-rights movement of the 1960s was far more than an effort by black leaders to appeal to the conscience of white elites.

Elite theory focuses our attention on the role of leadership in policy formation and on the reality that, in any political system, a few govern the many. Whether elites rule and determine policy, with little influence from the masses, is a difficult proposition to handle. It cannot be proved merely by assertions that the "establishment runs things," which has been a familiar plaint in recent years. Political scientist Robert Dahl argues that to defend the proposition successfully one must identify "a controlling group, less than a majority in size, that is not a pure artifact of democratic rules ... a minority of individuals whose preferences regularly prevail in cases of differences of preferences on key political issues."[31] It may be that elite theory has more utility for analysis and explanation of policy formation in some political systems, such as developing or Eastern European countries, than in others, such as the pluralist democracies of the United States and Canada. Sociologist William Domhoff has long argued, however, that there is an American upper class, based on the ownership and control of large corporations, which is in fact a governing class.[32]

Institutionalism

The study of government institutions (or organizations) is one of the oldest concerns of political science. This is not surprising, since political life generally revolves around governmental institutions such as legislatures, executives, courts, and political parties; public policy, moreover, is authoritatively determined and implemented by these institutions.

Traditionally, the institutional approach concentrated on describing the more formal and legal aspects of governmental institutions: their formal structure, legal powers, procedural rules, and functions or activities. Formal relationships with other institutions might also be considered, such as legislative-executive relations. Usually little was done to explain how institutions actually operated as opposed to how they were supposed to operate, to analyze public policies produced by the institutions, or to discover the relationships between institutional structure and public policies.

Subsequently, political scientists turned their attention in teaching and research to the political processes within governmental or political institutions; concentrating on the behavior of participants in the process and on political realities rather than formalism. In the study of the legislatures, interest shifted from simply describing the legislature as an institution to analyzing and explaining its operation over time, from its static to its dynamic aspects. Thus in the academic curriculum the course on the legislature often came to be about the legislative process.

Institutionalism, with its emphasis on the formal or structural aspects of institutions, can nonetheless be usefully employed in policy analysis. An institution is, in part, a set of regularized patterns of human behavior that persist over time and perform some significant social function or activity. It is their differing patterns of behavior that really distinguish courts from legislatures, from administrative agencies, and so on. These regularized patterns of behavior, which we often call rules or structures, can affect decision-making and the content of public policy. Rules and structural arrangements are usually not neutral in their effects; rather, they tend to favor some interests in society over others and some policy results over others. It is contended that some of the Senate rules (and traditions, which often have the effect of rules), such as those relating to unlimited debate and action by unanimous consent, favor the interests of legislative minorities over majorities. Many actions in the Senate, such as bringing bills up for consideration and closing off debate on them, are done by unanimous consent. Thus one senator, so inclined, can block action by the Senate.

In the American federal system, which allocates governmental power among the national and state governments, several arenas of action are created. Some groups may have more influence if policy is made at the national level, whereas others may benefit more from state policymaking. Civil-rights groups, for example, have received a better response in Washington, D.C., than in the capitals of the southern states. Groups advocating adoption of English as the nation's official language, however, have fared better at the state level. Between 1983 and 1997, twenty states adopted such laws, but the Congress has been unsympathetic. Indeed, the Voting Rights Act provides that in some states ballots must be printed in foreign languages as well as English.

In summary, institutional structures, arrangements, and procedures often have important consequences for the adoption and content of public policies. They provide part of the context for policymaking, which must be considered along with the more dynamic aspects of politics, such as political parties, groups, and public opinion, in policy study. By itself, however, institutional theory can provide only partial explanations of policy. It has little to say about what drives the policy process.

Rational-Choice Theory

The rational-choice theory, which is sometimes called *social choice, public-choice,* or *formal theory*, originated with economists and involves applying the principles of microeconomic theory to the analysis and explanation of political behavior (or nonmarket decision-making). It has now gained many adherents among political scientists.

Perhaps the earliest use of rational-choice theory to study the political process is Anthony Downs's *Economic Theory of Democracy*.[33] In this influential book, Downs assumes that voters and political parties act as rational decision-makers who seek to maximize attainment of their preferences. Parties formulated whatever policies would win them most votes, and voters sought to maximize the portion of their preferences that could be realized through government action. In attempting to win elections, political parties moved toward the center of the ideological spectrum to appeal to the greatest number of voters and maximize their voting support. Thus, rather than providing voters with "meaningful alternatives," parties will become as much alike as possible, thereby providing an "echo rather than a choice."

Let us now look more closely at the major components of rational-choice theory. One of its basic axioms is that political actors, like economic actors, act rationally in pursuing their own self-interest. Thus economist James Buchanan, a leading proponent of rational-choice theory, contends that politicians are guided by their self-interest rather than an altruistic commitment to such goals as statesmanship or the national interest. "This should be no surprise," says Buchanan, "because governments are made up of individuals, and individuals operate from self-interest when they are engaged in a system of exchange, whether this is in the market economy or in politics."[34] Individuals who are engaged in decision-making exchanges or transactions, such as voting, also have preferences that vary from person to person. Being rational, individuals are able to comprehend and rank their preferences from most to least desired. In making decisions (whether economic or political), they are guided by these preferences and will seek to maximize the benefits they gain. In short, people are self-interested utility maximizers, not the uninformed, confused, or irrational choice-makers often depicted in analyses of political behavior.

A second basic axiom of rational-choice theory involves methodological individualism. The individual decision-maker is the primary unit of analysis and theory. The individual's preferences or values are assumed to be more important than other values—collective, organizational, or social. Conversely, rational-choice theorists argue that the actions of organizations and groups can be satisfactorily explained in terms of the behavior of a model individual. Nothing substantial will be lost by so doing in explaining the behavior of all persons.

For example, a rational-choice explanation of why Congress delegates discretionary power to administrative agencies begins with the assumption that the preference of members of Congress is to get reelected.[35] To this end, legislators delegate power to agencies, knowing that in exercising that power the agencies will create problems for their constituents. Legislators will then be called on by their constituents to assist them with their bureaucratic problems and, in return for assistance, the grateful constituents will vote to reelect the legislators. The pursuit of self-interest by the members of Congress thus explains the delegation of power and the growth of bureaucracy.

Some rational-choice theorists have explored the effects of incomplete or imperfect information and uncertainty on policymaking.[36] Political decision-makers are said to be possessed of differing amounts of information (a condition called *information asymmetry*) and are uncertain about the outcomes or consequences of laws and policies when they are implemented. In Congress, legislative committee members, as policy specialists and the basic developers of legislation, are best informed about the relationship between a proposed policy and its likely consequences. In comparison, the rank-and-file members of Congress, who make the final decisions on the enactment of legislation, have only limited knowledge of the policy-consequences relationships. Conceivably this information asymmetry would permit committee members to act strategically and secure the enactment of policies of benefit primarily to themselves (and their constituents).

Various rules and practices in Congress, however, help ensure that legislators will have incentives both to specialize in analyzing public problems and crafting policies and to make information generally available to the members of Congress. The problem is to identify the institutional arrangements that help reduce uncertainty. This "information-theories" variant of rational choice continues to assume that legislators are utility maximizers with differing interests. Their utility, however, is determined by policy outcomes rather than by policies per se. About outcomes, as we have seen, there is uncertainty.

Rational-choice studies of political behavior are often characterized by rigid and narrow assumptions, mathematical equations, abstractions, and remoteness from reality. Even William C. Mitchell, an early enlistee in the rational-choice movement, remarks that as it appears in textbooks, rational-choice theory "hardly involves government, politicians, bureaucrats, and interest groups. Little of the exposition ... has anything to do with the fiscal or regulatory lives of the community or state."[37] A more positive view holds that "in its pure form it is one, but only one, useful, partial explanation of politics."[38]

Rational-choice theory both alerts us to the importance of self-interest as a motivating force in politics and policymaking, and provides a better understanding of decision-making processes. Many contend, however, that politics is not nearly as devoid of altruism and concern for the public interest as the rational-choice theorists assume. The adoption of "good public policy," for example, is frequently a goal of members of Congress.[39] And public-interest groups, such as the National Wildlife Federation, are motivated by more than immediate self-interest.[40]

Commentary

Because individual political scientists often manifest strong preference for one or another of these theoretical approaches (or others, such as incrementalism, which is presented as a decision-making theory in the chapter titled "Policy Adoption"), there is no consensus on which is the "best" or the most satisfactory. Each approach focuses attention on different aspects of policymaking and politics, and thus seems more useful for understanding some situations or events than others.

Group theory and elite theory are mutually exclusive explanations of how the policy process operates and, most important, of who controls or dominates and benefits from it. Or, succinctly: Who rules? Sharp intellectual struggles have been waged between group (or pluralist) theorists and elite theorists about who controls decision-making on public policy in American communities. Much heat if not light was generated by this controversy, which has quieted down without the issue having been fully resolved.[41]

Systems theory and institutionalism both focus on the process of policymaking, albeit in different ways, and are not incompatible. Institutionalism can be used to help explain what goes on within the "black box" (the political system), which is neglected by systems theory. Because neither theory directly confronts the question of who rules, either group or elite theory could be combined with them to some degree. Rational-choice theory, because of its narrow focus, must stand pretty much by itself. Institutions appear as the individual writ large; little attention is given to the policy environment, how issues are brought to the attention of government, or how policy preferences are developed. Like institutionalism, however, rational-choice theory does show much interest in how rules and structures help determine the outcomes of decision-making. Rational-choice scholars often occupy themselves with demonstrating how the manipulation of rules could produce preferred decisions.

On the question of who rules, rational-choice theory asserts that democratically elected officials will promote their own interest rather than the people's. This conviction frequently leads to the normative (and conservative) conclusion that less government is better government. Group theorists feel that the interests of dominant groups (however determined) prevail, and for elite theorists the few (a ruling class) govern in their own interest, perhaps with some concern for the condition of the masses.

The various theories thus raise some controversial questions about politics and the policymaking process. They also tend to skew research findings. Not surprisingly, pluralists find groups in control, elite theorists detect dominance by an elite, and rational-choice theorists find that self-interest dominates. These theories are therefore not merely neutral alternatives for guiding analysis. What one finds in policy research depends in important part on what one is looking for, just as those who go about town "looking for trouble" are more apt to find it than are more peaceful citizens.

The differing concerns of these theoretical approaches can be further clarified by briefly observing how their proponents might look at political campaign finance reform. A major goal of reformers has been to ban "soft money"—funds that can be raised in unlimited amounts from corporations, labor unions, and wealthy persons and spent for party-building activities, such as voter registration and get out the vote campaigns. Soft money can also be expended on generic or issue advertising to promote generally a political party or to influence the election prospects of particular candidates, so long as this is done without specifically endorsing their defeat or election. The Democratic and Republican parties together raised more than half a billion dollars in soft money during the 1999–2000 election cycle.

A group theorist would view the struggle to enact a campaign finance reform law as a contest for advantage among various business, labor, and public-interest groups and their supporters, as well as the political parties. Lobbying and other group tactics would be scrutinized. An institutionalist, in comparison, would focus on the problems presented by congressional structure and procedure in securing the enactment of legislation. These could include getting the bill to the House floor for debate, overcoming filibusters in the Senate, resolving differences in House and Senate versions of the bill, and avoiding a presidential veto. Much attention would be given to how a bill becomes law.

A rational-choice proponent would see members of Congress calculating how the content of reform legislation would affect the ability to raise campaign money and to get reelected. Another of his concerns would be strategic behavior, as when opponents propose amendments which, if adopted, would make the bill unacceptable to some of its supporters (a "poison pill"), or when reformers craft amendments to help gain or retain supporters. Self-interest would be seen as informing legislative behavior.

An elite theorist would see the legislative struggle here as one of interest primarily to top-level legislative and political leaders. Both proponents and opponents of reform would contend that what they were trying to do was best for the public. The elitist would hold that the mass public was neither interested or informed, especially on the details of legislation.

Finally, a systems theorist would likely rivet on how government action was influenced by inputs (demands, pressures, information) from its political, social, and economic environment. Limited attention at best would be devoted to the details of how a bill becomes law. In time the systems theorist would be attentive to how the government's decisions on campaign finance reform affected its operation and future demands on it.

To conclude, a person should avoid becoming too dogmatically or rigidly bound to one model or approach. As a rule it is desirable to be eclectic and flexible, using those theories and concepts that seem most useful for the satisfactory and fair-minded description and explanation of political inquiry. The goal should be the objective explanation of political behavior rather than the validation of a preferred theoretical approach. Each of the theories that have been discussed, if drawn upon skillfully and selectively, can contribute to a fuller understanding of policymaking.

Methodological Difficulties in Studying Public Policy

Methodological problems afflict all research, although social scientists appear both more self-conscious about their methodology and more intellectually inclined to batter themselves for methodological infirmities than do natural and physical scientists. Policy research, especially given the complexity of its subject matter, has its full share of methodological problems. Such problems may impede or limit policy research, and may make it more than a little frustrating at times, but they neither prevent it nor negate the need for it. An awareness of some of these problems, however, may help prevent wasted efforts, needless errors, unsound conclusions, and insomnia.

Solid, conclusive evidence, facts, or data, as one prefers, on the motives, values, and behavior of policy-makers, the nature and scope of public problems, the impact of policies, and other facets of the policy process are often difficult to acquire or simply not available. The urge to convert assumptions or speculations about what happened into facts is something to be resisted, along with the uncritical acceptance of the often self-serving statements or incomplete explanations emanating from public officials and other participants in the policy process. Sometimes numerical measures of political phenomena such as policy impacts are used without sufficient care in determining their validity. Is the number of infant deaths (in their first year) per 1,000 live births a good indicator of the general level of health care in a society that has much income inequality? Do salary levels and similar data really measure the professionalism of civil servants? The acquisition of hard facts about who did what, why, and with what effect should be the goal of research. We need to be able to say with some certainty why members of Congress respond to constituency interests on some issues and not others, or what role the media play in setting agendas.

In explaining behavior in the policy process, one needs empirical data that will permit the demonstration or sound inference of cause-and-effect relationships. Once a person gets involved in quantitative data-based analysis, it is important to resist the notion that collecting empirical data is of prime importance and that the more data one has, the more one can explain. One can drown in a sea of data as well as thirst for lack thereof. To account for or explain behavior, theory is needed that will guide analysis in potentially fruitful directions, as well as good judgment in the selection of policy measures. As much as possible, hypotheses about cause-and-effect relationships need to be developed and tested on the basis of the best available evidence.

The notion that policy analysis is worthwhile only when it involves the analysis of quantitative data with statistical techniques—the higher powered the better—should also be resisted. There is no reason to assume that if something cannot be counted, it does not count. Some policy areas and problems have not been very amenable to rigorous quantitative measurement and analysis, although this may not always continue to be the case. Many aspects of social welfare and economic regulatory policies currently fit into this category. How does one measure the comparative influence of pressure groups, agency values, and economic analysis on rulemaking by EPA or OSHA? The prosecution of insider traders by the Securities and Exchange Commission? The total benefits of a public-housing program? And how does one appraise the power of ideas, as distinct from interests, in developing programs for the handicapped? Such questions present real puzzles.

Yet it should be stressed that explicit theory, quantitative data, and careful, rigorous analysis have not been as frequently utilized in studying policy as would be possible or desirable. Thus political scientist Marver H. Bernstein's hoary contention that regulatory agencies pass through a four-stage life cycle (gestation and birth, youth, maturity, and old age), frequently culminating in their "capture" (which is not well-specified) by the regulated groups, is often cited as though it were a clearly supported phenomenon.[42] Bernstein provides impressionistic support but by no means strong proof for his life-cycle theory. (He does not follow a single commission through all of the stages of the cycle.) It still lacks systematic empirical support. Conventional wisdom of this sort frequently rests on a rather frail intellectual foundation. Another example, also in the regulatory area, is economist George Stigler's theory of economic regulation. It holds that, as a rule, regulation is sought by the affected industry and operated for its benefit.[43] This theory will not do much to explain a raft of consumer protection, industrial health and safety, and environmental programs, or the deregulation legislation of the late 1970s and early 1980s.

Many perceptive and informative studies of policy formation employ little or no statistical analysis. Examples are Charles O. Jones's *Clean Air*; Alan Stone's *Economic Regulation and the Public Interest*; Barbara J. Nelson's *Making an Issue of Child Abuse*; and I. M. Destler's *American Trade Politics*.[44] The quality of intellectual analysis and careful use of sound data (or information) are more important than whether and to what extent quantitative analysis is employed when it comes to determining the worth of a study. To be rigorous, analysis does not have to be quantitative, and not all quantitative analysis is rigorous. Those who use quantitative techniques have been known to quarrel with enthusiasm and even some rancor over the reliability or appropriateness of their techniques and the validity of their findings. Also, to be fair-minded, one should avoid developing a phobia for quantitative or statistical analysis, as some did in reaction to the behavioral movement in political science. Much can be learned through quantitative analysis.

Data gained by interviews and questionnaires administered to public officials and other players in the policy process are often invaluable and may not otherwise be available to researchers. Care is required, however, in using both such techniques and the data acquired. Questions must be properly framed to elicit the needed information. Questions which are "loaded" and therefore bias responses, or which are so general as to create strong doubt about their intent, need to be avoided. Officials and others may not always respond fully or candidly to questions, their memories may be hazy, and they may overstate their own role in events. Data gained from these sources obviously should not be viewed as gospel. Rather, they should be checked against other sources, used with care, and regarded as representing particular viewpoints on some event. Good judgment is called for.

Many studies of policymaking take the form of case studies; that is, they focus on particular programs, statutes, or areas of public policy. Case studies have been the butt of much criticism because, being narrowly based, they do not permit sound generalization. "What is a case study a case of?" is a common gibe. Preferred studies are those dealing with all the cases in a universe, such as all regulatory commissions or sunset laws, or a meaningful sample thereof, such as Supreme Court decisions on the rights of the accused or the benefit decisions made by a welfare agency. These afford a better basis for generalizations. Case studies, however, do have a variety of uses.[45] They can be used to test theories, to develop new theories, to provide detailed, contextual analysis of events, to analyze deviant cases that contradict our generalizations, and to help provide an "intuitive feel" for the subtleties and nuances of the policy process and the practice of politics. There is plenty of room in the study of policy for both case studies and more general and comparative studies. To draw on a Republican analogy, policy study should be viewed as a "big tent."

The Plan of This Book

The central concern of this book is the policy process, which is a shorthand way of designating the various a processes and practices by which public policies are formed. There is not, however, a single process by which policies are made. They do not come off of an assembly line as do automobiles or television sets. Rather, variations in the subjects of policies will produce variations in the style and techniques of policymaking. Foreign policy, taxation, railroad regulation, health-care financing, professional licensing, and reform of local government each are characterized by a distinguishable policy process—different participants, procedures, techniques, decision rules, and the like. Policymaking may also vary depending upon whether its primary organizational location is the legislature, the executive, the judiciary, or administrative agencies. Policymaking within administrative agencies is more likely to be characterized by hierarchy, secrecy (or low visibility), and the involvement of experts or professionals than is legislative policymaking.[46] And certainly one will discover differences in the formation of tax policy in the United States, Great Britain, and Mexico.

This variability does not mean, however, that there are no common functions or elements, and that it is impossible to formulate generalizations on policy formation. Given the diversity and complexity in policymaking processes, the development of some sort of "general theory" that has broad explanatory power is an unrealistic aspiration.[47] But we can achieve a useful start toward what political scientists call "theory building" by striving to develop sound generalizations about such topics as who is involved in policy formation, on what sorts of issues, under what conditions, in what ways, and to what effect. Nor should we neglect to ask about how policy problems develop or obtain a place on governmental agendas. Such questions are not as simple as they may first appear.

To provide a conceptual framework to guide the examination of the policy process in the ensuing chapters, I view it as a sequential pattern of activities or functions that can readily be distinguished analytically although they may be empirically more difficult to pull apart. The following categories or stages are employed (see their portrayal in Table 1.1). Some illustrative questions are included.

1. *Problem identification and agenda setting.* The focus here is on how the problems that may become the targets of public policies are identified and specified. Why only some problems, out of all that exist, receive consideration by policy-makers requires an examination of agenda setting; that is, how governmental bodies decide what problems to address. What is a public problem? Why does some condition or matter become a public problem? How does a problem get on a governmental agenda? Why do some problems not achieve agenda status?
2. *Formulation.* This encompasses the creation, identification, or borrowing of proposed courses of action, often called alternatives or options, for resolving or ameliorating public problems. Who participates in policy formulation? How are alternatives for dealing with a problem developed? Are there difficulties and biases in formulating policy proposals?
3. *Adoption.* This involves deciding which proposed alternative, including taking no action, will be used to handle a problem. In American legislatures this function is performed by majorities. How is a policy alternative adopted or enacted? What requirements must be met? Who are the adopters? What is the content of the adopted policy?
4. *Implementation.* (A synonym is administration.) Here attention is on what is done to carry into effect or apply adopted policies. Often further development or elaboration of policies will occur in the course of their administration. Who is involved? What, if anything, is done to enforce or apply a policy? How does implementation help shape or determine the content of policy?
5. *Evaluation.* This entails activities intended to determine what a policy is accomplishing, whether it is achieving its goals, and whether it has other consequences. Who is involved? Who is advantaged and disadvantaged by a policy? What are the consequences of policy evaluation? Are there demands for changes in or repeal of the policy? Are new problems identified? Is the policy process restarted because of evaluation?

Within this simplified framework, the formation and implementation of policies are seen as political in that they involve conflict and struggle among individuals and groups, officials and agencies, with conflicting ideas, interests, values, and information on public-policy issues. Policymaking is "political"; it involves "politics." That is, its features include conflict, negotiation, the exercise of power, bargaining, and compromise—and sometimes such nefarious practices as deception and bribery. There is no good reason to resist or disparage this conclusion, or to imitate those who derogate policies that they do not like with such statements as, "It's nothing but politics." Although it is sometimes implied or even asserted that if enough analysis were done, if enough facts and data were gathered, all "right-thinking" people would agree on the appropriate course of action to handle a problem, this is not the way the world works. Quite reasonable people can disagree on policy issues because they have differing interests, values, and affiliations. Politics is the way a democratic society resolves such differences.

The policy-process (sometimes it is called the *policy cycle*) approach to policy study has several advantages. First, and most important, the policy-process approach centers attention on the officials and institutions who make policy decisions and the factors that influence and condition their actions. We need to be concerned about more than the complexity of public problems, the goals of the polity, the general forms policy responses can take, and similar matters. Knowledge of these is clearly of value; but we also want to know who makes policy decisions and how they do it. Consequently, answers are needed for such questions as: What is the legislature's role in policymaking? How does its structure affect decision-making? What sorts of factors or considerations influence the legislator's decisions? The policy-process approach not only helps us learn about policymaking and policy, it also causes us to take a more holistic view of how government works.

Second, policymaking usually incorporates the stages or categories of activity that I have described. Its sequential nature thus helps one capture and comprehend the flow of action in the actual policy process. However, in actuality the formulation and adoption stages may blend together, as when proposed legislation on welfare reform is modified during consideration in committees and on the House and Senate floors in order to win votes needed for its enactment. Administrative agencies issue rules elaborating policy, as in the case of public-lands policy, while implementing it. The adoption of a policy, such as restrictions on abortion, solves a problem for some people while it creates a problem for others, who then restart the policy process in an effort to modify or repeal the disliked policy. Even in such instances, the policy-process approach can be used to analytically distinguish the various activities involved.

TABLE 1-1 *The Policy Process*

Policy Terminology	Stage 1: Policy Agenda	Stage 2: Policy Formulation	Stage 3: Policy Adoption	Stage 4: Policy Implementation	Stage 5: Policy Evaluation
Definition	Those problems, among many, that receive the serious attention of public officials	Development of pertinent and acceptable proposed courses of action for dealing with a public problem	Development of support for a specific proposal so that a policy can be legitimized or authorized	Application of the policy by the government's administrative machinery	Efforts by the government to determine whether the policy was effective and why or why not
Common sense	Getting the government to consider action on the problem	What is proposed to be done about the problem	Getting the government to accept a particular solution to the problem	Applying the government's policy to the problem	Did the policy work?

Source: Adapted from James E. Anderson, David W. Brady, and Charles Bullock III, *Public Policy and Politics in the United States*, 2d ed. (Monterey, Calif: Brooks/Cole, 1984).

Third, the policy-process approach is flexible and open to change and, refinement.[48] Additional stages can be introduced if experience indicates that they would strengthen description and analysis. Perhaps budgeting should be recognized as a separate stage of the process. Various forms of data collection and analysis, whether quantitative (statistical), historical, legal, or normative (value-oriented), are compatible with it. It can be used to study a single policy (e.g., the Americans with Disabilities Act) or to compare the enactment and implementation of several civil-rights laws. Group, institutional, and other approaches to policy study can be fitted into it. The group approach may help explain policy adoption; institutionalism can cast light on its implementation. Systems theory may help alert us to some of its societal consequences.

Fourth, the policy-process approach helps present a dynamic and developmental, rather than static and cross-sectional, view of the policy process. It is concerned with the evolution of policy and requires that one think about what moves action on policy from one stage of the process to another. Moreover, it helps emphasize relationships, or interactions, among the participants in policymaking. Political parties, interest groups, legislative procedures, presidential commitments, public opinion, and other matters can be tied together as they drive and help explain the formation of a policy. Further, one can seek to discover how action at one stage of the process affects action at later stages. For example, how does the design and content of legislation ease or complicate its implementation? How does implementation affect its impact?

Fifth, the policy-process approach is not "culture bound." It can readily be used to study policymaking in foreign political systems. It also lends itself to manageable comparisons, such as how problems reach governmental agendas, or how policies are adopted in various countries. A few such comparisons are included in this book.[49]

The structure of the remainder of the book looks like this: the chapter titled "The Policy-Makers and Their Environment" surveys the environment or context of policymaking and the official and unofficial participants in the policy process. "Policy Formation: Problems, Agendas, and Formulation" examines the nature of policy problems and agendas, agenda-setting processes, and the formulation of policy proposals. The chapter "Policy Adoption" is concerned with decision-making and the adoption of public policies. The "Budgeting and Public Policy" chapter takes up the budgetary process because of its important effects on the implementation of public policies. The struggle to balance the budget is also considered. "Policy Implementation" discusses several aspects of policy implementation and explores why people comply with politics. The chapter titled "Policy Impact, Evaluation, and Change" deals with policy impacts, the evaluation of policies, and policy termination, which occasionally may follow evaluation. A case study on airline regulation and deregulation examines the rise, elaboration, and termination of an important public policy over several decades. In "Concluding Comments," some conclusions and comments on the American policy process are presented.

★ ★ ★ ★ ★

For Further Exploration

- ***http://www.movingideas.org***

  The Policy Action Network site provides numerous links to liberal think tanks and foundations devoted to a variety of public policy issues such as economic, health, education, and media policies.

- ***http://www.policy.com/***

  This site provides information related to public policy issues at the federal, state and local levels. Included in this web site are daily policy briefings, as well as a policy "issue of the week."

- ***http://www.ncpa.org***

  Although it is conservative in nature, the homepage of The National Center for Policy Analysis (NCPA) provides a wealth of descriptive material on specific domestic and foreign policy issues.

- ***http://www.pbs.org/newshour/***

  The Online NewsHour provides a site titled "Forum," where several current policy issues are debated each month. This site also contains transcripts of the various policy discussions and roundtable issues that were broadcast on *The NewsHour with Jim Lehrer.*

★ ★ ★ ★ ★

Suggested Readings

Kenneth Bickers and John T. Williams, *Public Policy Analysis* (Boston: Houghton Mifflin, 2001). This readable examination of the policy process introduces the reader to rational choice theory.

Frank R. Baumgartner and Beth L. Leech, *Basic Interests: The Importance of Groups in Politics and Political Science* (Princeton: Princeton University Press, 1998). No one interested in groups and politics should ignore this outstanding analysis of group theory and the literature on groups.

Charles L. Cochran and Eloise F. Malone, *Public Policy: Perspectives & Choices*, 2nd ed. (New York: McGraw-Hill, 1999). This book, which draws broadly on the social sciences, combines a general treatment of policy-making with a discussion of several substantive policy areas.

Thomas R. Dye, *Top Down Policymaking* (New York: Chatham House, 2001). This controversial examination of the policymaking process in the United States argues that it is dominated by a national elite.

Carl E. Van Horn, Donald C. Baumer, and William T. Gormley, Jr., *Politics and Public Policy*, 2nd ed. (Washington, D.C.: CQ Press, 1992). Six policy domains—boardroom, bureaucratic, cloakroom, chief executive, court-room, and livingroom politics—are utilized in a wide-ranging examination of the policy process.

Paul A. Sabatier, ed., *Theories of the Policy Process* (Boulder, Colo.: Westview Press, 2001). The challenging essays in this anthology present a variety of theoretical lenses for studying the policy process.

Notes

[1]On policy analysis see Robert D. Behn, "Policy Analysis and Politics," *Policy Analysis*, VII (Spring 1981), pp. 199-226; and Peter J. May, "Politics and Policy Analysis," *Political Science Quarterly*, Vol. 101 (Spring 1986), pp. 109-125.

[2]Thomas R. Dye, *Understanding Public Policy*, 7th ed. (Englewood Cliffs, N.J.: Prentice-Hall, 1992), p. 7.

[3]David Easton, *A Systems Analysis of Political Life* (New York: Wiley, 1965), p. 212.

[4]The basic typology is from Theodore J. Lowi, "American Business, Public Policy Case Studies, and Political Theory," *World Politics*, XVI (July 1964), pp. 677-715. The self-regulatory category is from Robert Salisbury, "The Analysis of Public Policy" in Austin Ranney, ed. *Political Science and Public Policy* (Chicago: Markham, 1968), pp. 151-175.

[5]Lowi, op. cit., p. 690.

[6]Raymond Tatalovich and Byron W. Daynes, eds., *Moral Controversies in American Politics: Cases in Social Regulatory Politics* (Armonk, N.Y.: M. E. Sharpe, 1998).

[7]Randall B. Ripley and Grace A. Franklin, *Congress, the Bureaucracy, and Public Policy* (Pacific Grove, Calif.: Brooks/Cole, 1991), pp. 20-21.

[8]Kenneth J. Meier and E. Thomas Garman, *Regulation and Consumer Protection*, 3rd ed. (Houston: Dome Publications, 1998), pp. 41-42.

[9]For a discussion of licensing, see *ibid*., chap. 3.

[10]James E. Anderson, "Agricultural Marketing Orders and the Process and Politics of Self-Regulation," *Policy Studies Review*, II (August 1982), pp. 97-111.

[11]Lowi, op. cit., p. 691. On redistributive policies, see Ripley and Franklin, *Congress, the Bureaucracy, and Public Policy*, op. cit., chap. 6.

[12]Randall B. Ripley, *Policy Analysis in Political Science* (Chicago: Nelson Hall, 1985), pp. 68-69.

[13]Paul E. Peterson and Mark Rom, "Lower Taxes, More Spending, and Budget Deficits," in Charles O. Jones, ed., *The Reagan Legacy: Promise and Performance* (Chatham, N.J.: Chatham House, 1988), pp. 218-221.

[14]On the symbolic aspects of policies, see Murray Edelmann, *The Symbolic Uses of Politics* (Urbana: University of Illinois Press, 1964), chap. 2; and Charles D. Elder and Roger W. Cobb, *The Political Uses of Symbols* (New York: Longman, 1983).

[15]*Congressional Quarterly Weekly Report*, Vol. 53 (July 1, 1995), p. 1933.

[16]Brian Czech and Paul R. Krausman, *The Endangered Species Act* (Baltimore: Johns Hopkins University Press, 2001).

[17]Richard O. Davis, *Housing Reform During the Truman Administration* (Columbia: University of Missouri Press, 1966), chap. 10.

[18]Bruce I. Oppenheimer, *Oil and the Congressional Process* (Lexington, Mass.: Heath, 1974), pp. 130-145.

[19]Cf. L. L. Wade and R. L. Curry, Jr., *A Logic of Public Policy* (Belmont, Calif.: Wadsworth, 1970), chap. 5; and Charles L. Cochran and Eloise F. Malone, *Public Policy* (New York: McGraw-Hill, 1995), pp. 17-19.

[20]Ronald C. Moe, "Exploring the Limits of Privatization," *Public Administration Review*, XLVII (November-December 1987), p. 453.

[21]R. McGregor Cawley, *Federal Land, Western Anger* (Lawrence: University Press of Kansas, 1993).

[22]David Easton, "An Approach to the Analysis of Political Systems," *World Politics*, IX (April 1957), pp. 383-400; and Easton, *A Systems Analysis of Political Life* (New York: Wiley, 1965).

[23]Earl Latham, *The Group Basis of Politics* (New York: Octagon Books, 1965), p. 36.

[24]David Truman, *The Governmental Process* (New York: Knopf, 1951), p. 37.

[25]Alan C. Isaak, *Scope and Methods of Political Science* (Chicago: Dorsey Press, 1988), pp. 269-270.

[26]Latham, op. cit., pp. 35-36, 38-39.

[27]E. E. Schattschneider, *The Semisovereign People* (New York: Holt, Rinehart and Winston, 1960), p. 35.

[28]See generally, Frank R. Baumgartner and Beth L. Leech, *Basic Interest: The Importance of Groups in Politics and Political Science* (Princeton, N.J.: Princeton University Press, 1998).

[29]Thomas R. Dye and L. Harmon Zeigler, *The Irony of Democracy*, 10th ed. (Belmont, Calif.: Wadsworth, 1996), pp. 4-5. See also Thomas R. Dye, *Top Down Policymaking* (New York: Chatham House, 2001).

[30]Dye, op. cit., pp. 59-63.

[31]Robert A. Dahl, "A Critique of the Ruling Elite Model," *American Political Science Review*, LII (June 1958), p. 464.

[32]G. William Domhoff, *Who Rules America?* (Englewood Cliffs, N.J.: PrenticeHall, 1967); G. William Domhoff, *The Power Elite and the State: How Policy Is Made in America* (New York: Walter deGruyter, 1990).

[33]Anthony Downs, *An Economic Theory of Democracy* (New York: Harper & Row, 1957).

[34]Roger Lewin, "Self-Interest in Politics Earns a Nobel Prize," *Science*, CCXXXIV (November 21, 1986), p. 941.

[35]Morris P. Fiorina, *Congress: Keystone of the Washington Establishment*, 2nd ed. (New Haven: Yale University Press, 1989).

[36]This discussion leans heavily upon Keith Krehbiel, *Information and Legislative Organization* (Ann Arbor: University of Michigan Press, 1992); and Thomas W. Gilligan and Keith Krehbiel, "Asymmetric Information and Legislative Rules with a Heterogeneous Committee," *American Journal of Political Science*, XXXIII (May 1989), pp. 459-490.

[37]William C. Mitchell, "Textbook Public Choice: A Review Essay," *Public Choice*, XXVIII (1982), p. 99.

[38]Louis F. Weschler, "Methodological Individualism in Politics," *Public Administration Review*, XLIII (May-June 1982), p. 294.

[39]See Richard J. Fenno, Jr., *Congressmen in Committees* (Boston: Little, Brown, 1973). Fenno indicates that members of Congress are variously influenced by the desires to be reelected, to help enact good public policy, and to acquire influence in the House.

[40]Those wishing to explore rational choice theory further can begin with Kenneth A. Shepsle and Mark S. Bonchek, *Analyzing Politics: Rationality, Behavior, and Institutions* (New York: Norton, 1997). For a critique see Donald P. Green and Ian Shapiro, *Pathologies of Rational Choice Theory* (New Haven: Yale University Press, 1994).

[41]See Philip J. Trounstine and Terry Christensen, *Movers and Shakers: The Study of Community Power* (New York: St. Martin's, 1982).

[42]Marver H. Bernstein, *Regulating Business by Independent Commission* (Princeton: Princeton University Press, 1955), pp. 74-95.

[43]George Stigler, "The Theory of Economic Regulation," *Bell Journal of Economic and Management Science* (Spring 1971), pp. 3-21.

[44]Charles O. Jones, *Clean Air* (Pittsburgh, Pa.: University of Pittsburgh Press, 1975); Alan Stone, *Economic Regulation and the Public Interest* (Ithaca, N.Y.: Cornell

University Press, 1977); Barbara J. Nelson, *Making an Issue of Child Abuse* (Chicago: University of Chicago Press, 1984); and I. M. Destler, *American Trade Politics*, 2nd ed. (Washington, D.C.: Institute of International Economics, 1992). All are political scientists.

[45]See Harry Eckstein, "Case Study and Theory in Political Science," in Fred I. Greenstein and Nelson W. Polsby, eds., *The Handbook of Political Science*, Vol. 7, *Strategies of Inquiry* (Reading, Mass.: Addison-Wesley, 1975), pp. 79-137.

[46]Francis E. Rourke, *Bureaucracy, Politics, and Public Policy*, 3rd ed. (Boston: Little, Brown, 1984), pp. 145-158.

[47]See David Easton, *The Political System* (New York: Knopf, 1953), chap. 2.

[48]See, generally, Richard Rose, "Concepts for Comparison," *Policy Studies Journal*, I (Spring 1973), pp. 122-127.

[49]For criticisms of the sequential process approach, see Charles E. Lindblom and Edward J. Woodhouse, *The Policy Making Process*, 3rd ed. (Englewood Cliffs, N.J.: Prentice Hall, 1993), pp. 10-12; and *Policy Change and Learning: An Advocacy Coalition Approach*, Paul A. Sabatier and Hank Jenkins-Smith, eds. (Boulder, Colo.: Westview, 1993), chap. 1.

★ ★ ★

Politics and Public Policy

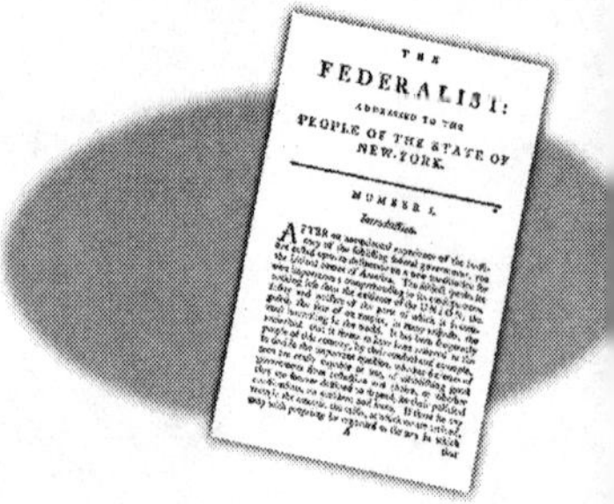

James Q. Wilson

Complain, complain, complain. Listen in on any discussion of politics today, and almost all you hear is complaint. According to political scientist James Q. Wilson, most of these complaints concern two things. The first is politicians, who are seen as untrustworthy servants of special interests. The second is public policy on virtually any subject you choose. Surprise! At this point readers might well expect Wilson to come to the defense of the system, or at least to tell us that it's not so bad after all. Wrong. Instead, Wilson insists that the complaints are valid, but that we are blaming the wrong people. The real culprits are our Founding Fathers, because it is the system—defined by our Constitution—that is at fault. According to Wilson, "The Constitution was written not to make governing easy but to make it hard; not to facilitate choices, but to impede them; not to empower leaders, but to frustrate them."

Talk to almost any citizen about American government and you will get a long list of complaints that generally fall into two groups. The first are gripes about politics: "Politicians are self-serving captives of special-interest groups, interested only in their own reelection. Judges are too liberal (or too conservative). The media are too interested in trivial scandals (or not interested enough in important scandals). The president and Congress are in gridlock, unable or unwilling to take decisive action." The second group are grievances about policies: "It's outrageous that for so long we had a budget deficit; why can't we manage to live within our means? Why can't the government do something about (take your pick) crime, drug

★ ★ ★ ★ ★ ★

abuse, racism, poor schools, air pollution, welfare dependency, or international competition?"

A lot of people think that there is a connection between our political problems and our policy failures. In their opinion, we don't solve the problems of the deficit, or crime, or racism, or international competition because our politicians are self-serving, the press doesn't do its job right, the courts are filled with wrong-headed judges, and special-interest groups are too powerful. Many people who think that way decided to support Ross Perot when the Texas businessman announced that he would run for president as an independent in 1992. They apparently were saying that we could solve our problems if only we had strong, dedicated leaders. This view of how to fix the system, or even whether the system needs fixing at all, has some truth to it, but for the most part it is too simple. Having read this book so far, you should understand that the way our system works is not mainly the result of the people in charge of it, but mainly (though not entirely) the result of the Constitution *that shapes it*. The Constitution was written not to make governing easy but to make it hard; not to facilitate choices, but to impede them; not to empower leaders, but to frustrate them. The written and unwritten constitutions of European democracies are very different: they were designed to allow the government to govern, subject only to the periodic checks of a popular election. Here, popular participation is encouraged; there, it is discouraged. Here, the courts can overturn presidential and congressional actions; there, they cannot. Here, many officials have the power to say "no" and none has the power to say "yes" and make it stick; there, a prime minister can say "yes" and make it stick.

★ How the American System Affects Policy Making

This system for making policy creates quite predictable results, and among them are the very aspects of politics that so many Americans find distasteful. Consider the effects of four constitutional provisions on how we make policy:

1. *The separation of powers* This has at least two important results. First, the president and Congress are rivals, even when they are from the same political party. The White House and Congress compete for power over the policies and personnel of the government. Stalemates are the rule, not the exception, and they are overcome only by a national crisis, a powerful tide of public opinion, or tough political bargaining. For example, if the president wants to cut the

deficit by reducing spending and Congress wants to cut it by increasing taxes, a political standoff will occur, as during much of the Reagan and Bush administrations. Second, members of Congress first and foremost represent their districts and states. Virtually no bill becomes a law unless it is first adjusted to reflect the differing demands of local constituencies. A president may complain that members of Congress work to get "unnecessary" benefits—roads, bridges, parks, and airports—for their districts, but he forgets that this is exactly what the voters want from their members. Calling it "pork-barrel politics" doesn't change that fundamental political reality.

2. *Federalism:* The states have an independent political position. As a result, it is very hard to have a truly "national" policy on anything. And even when we do have a national policy, the states play a big role in implementing it. For example, the states have had a large say in setting and administering welfare benefits, enforcing pollution-control programs, and building major highways, even though most of the money has come from Washington. And they play the dominant role in schooling, law enforcement, and land-use controls and pay most of those bills.
3. *Judicial review:* The federal courts can declare an act of the president or Congress unconstitutional and can decide suits brought by people arguing either that a federal agency has exceeded its legal authority or that it has not done all that the law requires. The courts have obviously played a decisive role in racial integration and civil-liberties cases, but they also play an important, though less visible, role in implementing laws affecting the environment, occupational safety and health, and highway construction.
4. *Freedom of speech and assembly:* The First Amendment guarantees the right of individuals to speak their minds and lobby their senators and representatives. This right cannot be preserved for individuals and denied to groups; after all, groups are just collections of like-minded individuals. As a result, placing any meaningful restrictions on the activities of lobbyists is next to impossible (except, of course, to ensure that they do not engage in corruption, such as bribery).

When you add together the effects of these four features of our Constitution, you get a uniquely American system of government policy making. Though it has many distinctive features, the best word to describe our system of government is *adversarial*—that is, a system that encourages participation by people who have an incentive to fight rather than cooperate. Freedom of speech protects a person's right to participate; the separation of powers and federalism means that any participant can usually find a political ally; the decentralized organization of Congress (which is one effect of federalism and the separation of powers) gives each member an incentive to call attention to himself or herself by making speeches, taking positions, and (above all) attacking adversaries; and the courts provide a convenient (though expensive) arena in which to wage endless struggles.

One can see our adversarial system at work in many policy arenas. Business and government fight over what environmental protection rules to enforce. (You may be surprised to learn that in much of Europe, they cooperate rather than fight in deciding the rules.) Environmental groups attack business, portraying it in the worst possible light; antiabortion groups attack proabortion groups (and vice versa). When a government agency issues an unpopular order, we don't usually respond by obeying but by claiming that our rights have been violated and threatening to sue or hold a protest march. Not all these situations occur as the inevitable result of our Constitution; the next chapter discusses the historical forces that have intensified these problems in recent decades. But however much events have aggravated these tendencies, the tendencies themselves arise directly from the kind of government that we have chosen.

Adversarial politics puts a premium on the ability to dramatize issues, gain publicity, mount demonstrations, and attack opponents. It downplays the ability to conduct quiet negotiations, make commitments, or accept personal responsibility.

In making policy in a participatory, adversarial system, politicians have no incentive to say that the government shouldn't tackle a problem or doesn't know how to solve it and every incentive to claim that government must "do something" and they know just what to do. The more such things are done, the more interest groups will have an incentive to organize lobbying efforts and open offices in Washington. The more such offices are opened, the greater the pressure to draft more bills and the smaller the chances that any given bill will make much sense.

Adversarial politics also colors our judgment as to the actual level of corruption and misconduct in our government. The checks and balances of our constitutional system and the individualistic style of political campaigning give everybody an incentive to dig up dirt and blow the whistle on a rival. By contrast, in parliamentary regimes such as those in Europe, these checks and balances and individualistic rivalries are much less common, and therefore the incentive to expose a rival also diminishes. As a result, lying and corruption seem more prevalent here than abroad when in fact we may have less; it is just that here more gets exposed—or invented.

Given these features of our system, what is surprising is that anything gets done at all. But it does. Preoccupied as we are with all the government's failings, we sometimes forget its accomplishments. Since the end of World War II, our government has built an interstate highway system, passed a set of civil-rights laws, created the Medicare program for the elderly, adopted a series of increasingly tough environmental laws, explored outer space, deregulated the airlines, waged and won a forty-five-year Cold War against the former Soviet Union, and sustained a level of economic growth and freedom sufficient to make millions of people from all parts of the world want to immigrate to this country. It paid a price, of course, for all of this: higher taxes, more regulations, and new groups to assimilate, but the taxes and the deficit are lower here than in most other large industrial nations.

★ *How Things Get Done*

Since our complex political system makes it easy for all kinds of people and groups to wield at least some power, we should not expect policies to get made in only one way. If we had a less participatory, less adversarial system, it would be much easier to explain policy making. In Japan, for example, appointed officials-bureaucrats have much more power than their American counterparts, and so much Japanese policy making is the result of government agencies making proposals that are only modestly changed, if changed at all, by the legislature. (One result is the sad state of the Japanese banking system.) In Great Britain, the prime minister enjoys a great deal of power for as long as his or her party has a majority in the House of Commons, and so discussing British policy making involves explaining why the prime minister favors one policy over another.

In the United States everybody gets into the act. Some policies are proposed by the president and enacted (after many changes) by Congress; others are proposed by members of Congress and enacted despite presidential objections. (The Congress may override the president's veto or sufficiently modify the proposal to get him to withhold his veto.) When a congressional majority forms around a proposal, it is not always the result of one party (say, the Democrats) outvoting the other (the Republicans); rather, the majority often consists of a coalition of Democrats and Republicans winning out over a smaller coalition of other Democrats and Republicans.

Figure 1 *A Way of Classifying and Explaining the Politics of Different Policy Issues*

	Perceived Costs: Distributed	Perceived Costs: Concentrated	Perceived Benefits
	Majoritarian Politics	Entrepreneurial Politics	Distributed
	Client Politics	Interest-group Politics	Concentrated

★ Four Kinds of Political Coalitions

The key to understanding policy making in the United States is understanding how these coalitions form. There are various theories of coalition formation. Many will be familiar to you even though you may not have thought of them as "theories" or given them these labels (see Figure l).

Client Politics

In this view, a small group that would benefit from the policy rounds up the necessary votes. The group may be dairy farmers who want federal subsidies for the milk they produce, labor unions that want to ensure that only union members can get jobs working on federal projects, sugar-beet growers who want to restrict imports of cheaper sugar produced abroad, or a town that wants a new airport. These groups are called "clients" because they will be beneficiaries of the policy if it is adopted. Many people have this in mind when they talk about "special-interest" or "pork-barrel" politics.

The reason such groups can win is that nobody else stands to lose enough to make it worthwhile to organize and fight against the policy. Subsidies to dairy farmers or restrictions on importing foreign-made sugar will raise the price of milk and sugar for the consumer, but usually not by enough for consumers to worry about it. And even if the price increase is large, most consumers will not be aware of it. (Dairy subsidies may cost people about twenty cents per gallon of milk, but hardly anyone knows that and those who know don't care that much.) And even if consumers know and care, it would be very hard for them to organize any opposition to these policies. Imagine trying to persuade your friends to protest against the dairy lobby just to get the price of milk reduced—maybe!—by twenty cents a gallon. Most people would say it wasn't worth the time and trouble. The same is true of policies that require that workers be paid the "prevailing" wage (which is usually the union wage) for building a new federal courthouse. Hardly anybody cares enough about the amount by which this policy increases the cost of the building to do anything about it. And most people don't care whether Jonesville gets a new airport or Smithtown gets a new bridge; all they care about is getting these things for their towns, too. It is easy to see why Congress votes for these proposals. Somebody who stands to gain a lot supports each proposal, often with campaign contributions, personal lobbying, and threats of voter reprisals if the group gets turned down. Hardly anyone opposes it, and those who do rarely represent any well-organized or highly motivated group. Voting for these things is, in political jargon, a no-brainer: any idiot would do it.

Because there is a clear beneficiary and no real opponent, client politics usually does not involve the political parties. Both Democrats and Republicans favor these proposals, albeit not unanimously (there are always a few in each party who want to defend the unorganized interests that may be adversely affected).

Some people think that all politics is client politics. They talk about how the "fat cats" and the "big interests" always get their way in Congress. But all politics is not client politics. For example, just about every organized interest in Washington opposed the 1986 tax reform act because they feared they would lose some cherished tax loopholes. But they lost anyway. The auto industry opposed the Auto Safety Act of 1966, but they lost. Most of the airlines opposed the airline deregulation bill of 1978, but they lost. To see why, we have to look at other ways by which political coalitions form and congressional votes are rounded up.

Entrepreneurial Politics

This theory explains why client groups sometimes lose. In this case a very unusual kind of coalition is formed consisting of people who claim, rightly or wrongly, to speak on behalf of the large number of people who would benefit from a policy that imposes heavy costs on some small group. As we saw above, client groups often win because the average citizen has too small a stake in the outcome to take the trouble to fight. But sometimes a leader or a few activists will have the ability or good luck to be regarded as the spokespersons for the unorganized majority. To the extent they are successful in being perceived this way, they can often defeat client groups, either by repealing some *policy* the client group already enjoys or by imposing some new tax, regulation, or restriction on it.

The people who can do this are called policy entrepreneurs. Ralph Nader is a familiar example. For decades he has successfully portrayed himself as the champion of the consumer. He has taken on automobile companies (by arguing for safety regulations) and even Congress itself (by fighting its efforts to vote itself a pay increase). But there are many other examples, not all of them from the liberal side of the political spectrum. The late Howard Jarvis mobilized voters in California to vote for a ballot measure (called Proposition 13) that sharply restricted the ability of local governments to levy property taxes or increase tax assessments.

Becoming a successful policy entrepreneur is not easy. Washington is filled with people who want to lead various causes; they spend countless hours wandering from one congressional office to the next looking for allies, usually finding none. Though some of their causes are nutty, some are worthwhile, but winning allies takes more than just having a good cause.

The key requirement is the ability to dramatize the issue. This usually means making it front-page news. Ralph Nader is a master at this, beginning with his revelation that General Motors had attempted to spy on him when he was leading a campaign for an auto-safety law. Instantly the issue was transformed from auto safety (in which few Americans were interested) into "ruthless big business" (in which many were interested). Events can create policy entrepreneurs. The 1968 oil spill on the beaches of Santa Barbara, California, made it easier for the organizers of the first Earth Day to dramatize environmental problems. Since then the environmental movement has highlighted (not always accurately) other events to further its gains, such as the story about toxic waste supposedly harming the residents of Love Canal or apples treated with the chemical Alar allegedly harming people who ate them.

Dramatizing an issue is easier if you can portray the opponent of your policy as not just wrong but evil, if your opponent has made a newsworthy blunder, if friendly reporters and editors willingly print or broadcast the story, if the story can be cast in terms with which the public readily sympathizes, and if like-minded congressional staffers are willing to persuade a member of Congress to hold a well-publicized hearing to investigate the issue. Understanding entrepreneurial politics, therefore, involves understanding the kinds of symbols and appeals to which attentive members of the public, journalists, and congressional staffers respond. These change from generation to generation. Once "Americanism" and "anticommunism" were powerful motivators; today it's "cancer" and "the environment." The proponents of hand-gun control labored for years to find a compelling symbol that would produce votes for their proposal and almost found it when James Brady, President Reagan's former press secretary, was shot in the head during a failed attempt to assassinate the president. Bills restricting access to handguns soon became known as "Brady bills," and Brady himself testified in support of them. But for many Americans, the "right to bear arms" is an even more powerful symbol than the sight of a seriously wounded public official, and so only modest restrictions have been enacted.

Interest-Group Politics

This theory says that policies are made as a result of the pulling and pushing of rival, organized interests. Some political scientists call it the pluralist theory of politics. In this view the winning coalition consists of whichever side has amassed the most votes. There is generally no way to predict which side that will be; everything depends on the relative size, strength, and energy of rival interest groups. But in any particular case, you may be able to predict the winner by measuring size, strength, and energy. You might ask, for example, which side has the most members, makes the biggest campaign contributions through political action committees (PACs), or has the best access to the mass media. For example, when the North American Free Trade Agreement (NAFTA) came up for congressional vote in 1993, unions that feared they would lose jobs to Mexican workers fought against it, while businesses that saw a chance to increase sales to Mexico argued for it. The struggle was furious; the proponents narrowly won.

Interest-group politics occurs whenever some specific group, town, occupation, or industry stands to gain significantly from the proposal and some other specific group, town, occupation, or industry stands to lose a lot. Each side will have enough at stake to make it worthwhile to organize, spend money, buy advertisements, mail letters, and buttonhole legislators. That occurs, for example, when labor unions want a law restricting a business from closing a plant and businesses oppose such a law, or when American auto-makers and unionized autoworkers want a law reducing the importation of Japanese-built cars and people who sell Japanese cars want no such reductions. For interest-group politics to occur, the stakes do not have to involve money. People may feel so strongly about some issue that they will fight tooth and nail even though they stand to gain nothing of monetary value. This is obviously the case with the struggle between proabortion and antiabortion groups. Many of the participants in these battles will not personally be affected by the outcome, but they have strong convictions nonetheless.

Members of Congress don't like an intense, evenly matched interest-group battle because it forces them to take sides. This is especially true of members who have in their districts large numbers of people on both sides of the issue. As citizens we are often irritated by the tendency of politicians to be mealy mouthed, talking about important issues in ways that avoid taking a clear position. We should realize that this tendency does not reveal a flaw in their character, however. If we were in their shoes, we would probably do exactly the same thing unless, of course, we didn't care about getting reelected. And if winning office wasn't important, you wouldn't be in politics in the first place.

Political parties usually don't play a very big role in settling interest-group conflicts for the same reason individual members wish that they didn't have to take sides. Most such conflicts split the parties right down the middle. Because both the Democrats and the Republicans would like to win the support of autoworkers, union members, or business leaders, party leaders are careful to not go too far in backing one side or another. Some interest-group issues, however, happen to coincide with party labels. Abortion is one of these: though most Americans tend to take a middle position (tolerating abortion, but only under certain limited circumstances), those who strongly favor free choice are usually concentrated in the Democratic party while those who strongly oppose it are overwhelmingly Republican.

Interest-group politics doesn't end when Congress decides the issue. Each side will lobby hard to influence the kinds of people who get appointed to carry out the law. In many cases the losing side will take its case to the courts, trying to block or modify enforcement of the law, and in all cases the struggle will continue before whatever administrative agency is charged with implementing it. Since there are so many places in American government where interest groups can plead their case—the president, the White House staff, the bureaucratic agency, the media, various congressional committees—the struggle is never over.

Some writers like to describe American politics as involving nothing but interest-group competition, or pluralism. But as we have seen with client politics, this isn't always the case. And it also isn't the case with the fourth kind of politics.

Majoritarian Politics

In this kind of political coalition the great majority of the people stand to benefit in some significant way and the great majority must pay the cost. This is what many people have in mind when they say, "the people ought to rule." Here they do. The only question is whether the benefits people expect to get will or will not exceed the costs they expect to pay. If the perceived benefits exceed the perceived costs, the proposal will have a lot of support.

That was the case when the Social Security Act was passed in 1935 and when Medicare was enacted thirty years later. These were popular measures because they held out to people the prospect of getting a lot—a retirement check, free medical care when they were old—in exchange for paying what started out as a rather small payroll tax. When people thought the United States was being pushed around by foreign countries—at one time, the Soviet Union; later, Iraq—they supported higher defense spending. When they thought these threats had lessened, they called for cuts in defense spending.

Obviously public opinion is the key factor in determining the outcome of majoritarian politics. Interest groups may reinforce what the public believes, but the group effort is usually not the decisive factor. For example, the American Association of Retired Persons (AARP) opposes cuts in Social Security benefits, but this popular program is unlikely to experience any serious cuts even if the AARP did not exist. Political parties don't play much of a role either, because popular programs get support from both sides of the aisle. The only exception to this occurs when a new policy is first debated and no one is certain how popular it will be. Then one party may favor it and the other oppose it. This happened when the Democrats backed Social Security and the Republicans were initially critical of it; it also occurred more recently when the Republicans backed military action against Iraq (Operation Desert Storm) and most congressional Democrats opposed it. But both parties quickly jump onto the same bandwagon when public opinion about the policy is clear (as the Republicans did with Social Security in the 1950s and the Democrats did with the Persian Gulf War in the 1990s).

Majorities in Congress can be produced by any one of these four types of politics. As a result, no single explanation of policy making is correct, and the careful student should avoid using slogans that imply that there is a single explanation. Some people complain that the rich rule (but that statement isn't consistent with their tax rate, which is higher than that of the nonrich), some say that big business dominates (but that doesn't square with the passage of so many environmental policies opposed by business), some argue that organized labor calls the shots (but that theory can't explain why free-trade policies opposed by labor generally win out), and still others claim that party bosses or congressional leaders have all the clout (but this argument doesn't account for the small role that the party leaders play in client or majoritarian politics and the difficulty they have keeping their party members in Congress toeing the line). On any given issue, one or another group may be very powerful, but no group is powerful across all or even most issues.

★ Some Cautionary Remarks

Having described these four types of politics, I want to caution the reader against certain common mistakes in applying this schema. First, not every issue fits neatly into one or another of these categories. Many don't fit at all and some fit into two simultaneously; this is especially true for foreign policy. Second, how people perceive the effects of a policy will change, in turn changing the political coalitions around that policy. For example, making less-polluting cars seemed like a good idea to everybody until some of the newer cars turned out to be less powerful and more expensive than the previous models. At that point, some autoworkers began worrying that they would lose their jobs because foreign manufacturers were doing a better job of complying with the new rules than were American carmakers. Similarly, Social Security looked like a great idea until the taxes to pay for it got very high, making it harder to increase benefits. At one time, federal subsidies for tobacco farmers seemed like a harmless case of client politics; people who bought cigarettes didn't care that they cost a few pennies more because of the subsidies. But when the adverse health consequences of smoking became better known, many members of Congress began to question the wisdom of such subsidies.

The words *client, entrepreneurial,* or *majoritarian* are intended only to explain the policy process, not to label the policies as good or bad. Client politics can be good (as when some very deserving group, such as disabled children, is the object of tax-supported research) or dubious (as when somebody receives subsidies to produce something that they ought to be able to produce without the subsidy). Entrepreneurial politics can lead to good outcomes (as when big cities reduce their smog levels) or questionable outcomes (as when useful drugs are kept off the market for years because of the fear that a few cases will yield adverse side effects). Majoritarian politics is certainly consistent with popular rule, but the public doesn't always see its own interests clearly. People may love the idea of having their medical bills paid in part by Medicare without understanding that as currently designed, it will bankrupt the country in another decade or two. They may like the idea of cleaner air but not see that one good way to achieve this is to tax gasoline so that people drive less.

Finally, bear in mind that the confusion and deadlocks of American politics, since they are caused largely by our constitutional system, cannot easily be corrected without changing that system fundamentally. Very few quick fixes or clever new leaders can make much of a difference. Moreover, the system that produces these problems also provides some very great advantages. The Constitution may encourage an adversarial system, but such a system is less likely to trample on our personal liberties than one that is less adversarial, less participatory, and more orderly. We all want our leaders to have the guts to make the tough decisions, but sometimes what we have in mind by way of a "tough decision" is something that gores the other fellow's ox. Strong leaders can gore your ox, too.

★ *Summary*

American politics is a confusing, sometimes dispiriting spectacle because so many people have a chance to get into the act and the system encourages adopting an adversarial tone. Many people think they have little influence in government; that is sometimes true, but only because so many people try to have influence. This participatory, adversarial system arises directly out of our constitutional arrangements, especially the separation of powers, federalism, political freedom, and judicial review. That system also makes it very difficult for any one group to dominate the policy-making process. There are four different ways in which winning coalitions are pulled together to enact a policy: client politics, entrepreneurial politics, interest-group politics, and majoritarian politics.

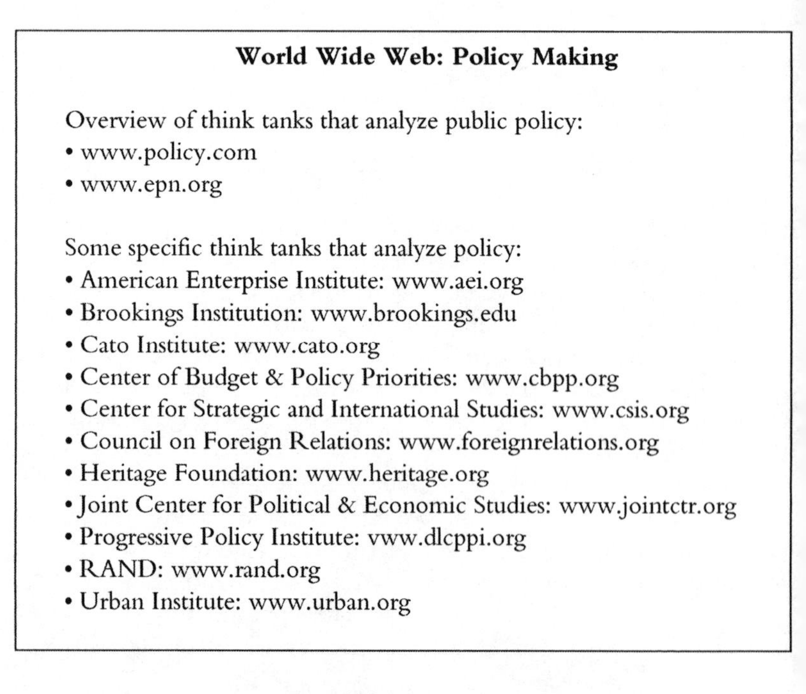

World Wide Web: Policy Making

Overview of think tanks that analyze public policy:
- www.policy.com
- www.epn.org

Some specific think tanks that analyze policy:
- American Enterprise Institute: www.aei.org
- Brookings Institution: www.brookings.edu
- Cato Institute: www.cato.org
- Center of Budget & Policy Priorities: www.cbpp.org
- Center for Strategic and International Studies: www.csis.org
- Council on Foreign Relations: www.foreignrelations.org
- Heritage Foundation: www.heritage.org
- Joint Center for Political & Economic Studies: www.jointctr.org
- Progressive Policy Institute: vww.dlcppi.org
- RAND: www.rand.org
- Urban Institute: www.urban.org

Suggested Readings

Derthick, Maria, and Paul J. Quirk. *The Politics of Deregulation.* Washington, D.C.: Brookings Institution, 1985. A brilliant analysis of how three industries—airlines, trucking and telecommunications—were deregulated despite industry opposition.

Kingdon, John W. *Agendas, Alternatives, and Public Policies.* Boston: Little, Brown, 1984. Insightful account of how issues, especially those involving health and transportation, get on (or drop off) the federal political agenda.

Polsby, Nelson W. *Political Innovation in America.* New Haven, Conn.: Yale University Press, 1984. Explains how the federal government adopted eight policy innovations.

Wilson, James Q., ed. *The Politics of Regulation.* New York: Basic Books, 1980. Analyzes regulatory politics in nine agencies using the four types of politics described in this chapter.

★ *Since beginning his career as a professor of government at Harvard University in the 1960's, James Q. Wilson has earned a reputation as a criminologist, economist and political analyst.*

★ ★ ★ ★ ★

Questions

1. To what extent does the separation of powers inherent in our national government create paralysis on important issues?
2. To what extent does federalism hinder our ability to develop a national agenda on any topic?
3. To what extent does judicial review thwart the will of the majority?
4. To what extent do lobbyists and their political action committees reserve to themselves the power to make many of the most important government decisions?
5. Is it time to replace our Constitution with one that is more effective and democratic?

★ ★ ★

How to Read "The Federalist"

George W. Carey

In his introduction to the Federalist Papers, conservative George W. Carey critiques commonly held views of the essays that, after the Declaration of Independence and Constitution, are often held to be the most important documents in American history. Carey dismisses charges that the Papers are a hodge-podge, mere journalism, and propaganda. He insists that although the Constitution may be interpreted in various ways, Publius (Hamilton, Madison, and Jay) provides an accurate depiction of the Constitution as the Founding Fathers meant it to be understood. Carey concludes that the Federalist Papers "remains, above all, the book to which conservatives must go in order to learn how to wrest from the hands of Liberals their most elective weapon, namely, the charge that our traditional political system is 'undemocratic.'"

The book you are about to read is, by common consent among scholars and publicists, the third in point of time of the four "basic documents" of the American political tradition: the Declaration of Independence, the Constitution itself, *The Federalist,* the Bill of Rights. No one putting forward a "list" of the documents that deserve that status would be likely to omit it, and so far as we know no one has ever seriously contended that similar status should be accorded to any fifth or sixth document. Put otherwise: *The Federalist* is a "must" for anyone who seeks an "intellectual" understanding of our tradition and of the political system under which we have governed ourselves, happily and well some of us would say, for nigh onto two hundred years. The first thing we want to say, then, in the Introduction to this new printing of the book is this: We cannot too strongly urge upon the reader, who for

★ ★ ★ ★ ★ ★

reasons we shall be speaking of in a moment is not unlikely to be reading it (actually reading *it,* as opposed to this or that one of its "papers" that turns up in an anthology) for the first time, his obligation—yes obligation—to linger over its every paragraph, turn over and over in his mind its every idea, steep himself in it, master it, and make it his own. And this equally whether he is a defender of the political system produced by the four "basic documents" or a critic of the system, determined to "reform" it along "more democratic" lines, and so bring it abreast of the prevailing political ideas of our time: political equality, majority rule, and individual rights. In either role, he will speak and act out of ignorance insofar as *The Federalist* is not part of his intellectual baggage.

But why, the reader may well ask, save as a matter of just knowing American history, should that be true? Were my college or university teachers not correct in telling me that *The Federalist* is not "serious" political philosophy? That it is not really a "book" at all, but a hodge-podge of articles, hastily written at that and by three different authors, all busy with other matters and not in very close touch with one another, for newspapers? That, far from being serious political philosophy, it is first and foremost a venture in what we today call "political propaganda," whose overriding purpose was, quite simply, to persuade the reluctant peoples of the thirteen states to accept and ratify the Constitution written at Philadelphia, and so form a Union? That insofar as it is anything more than mere political propaganda, it is a mere "schoolteacherish" expounding of the several articles of the Constitution, which goes on and on for several hundred pages, saying nothing much that one cannot, on one's own, dig out of the text of the Constitution itself? That, in any case, ours is a "changing Constitution," a "growing Constitution," which constantly adapts itself to "new" problems, "new" situations, "new" needs, "new" ideas that have won acceptance by the American people—so that no brief for or commentary on the Constitution written so long ago could have the contemporary relevance and importance that you attribute to *The Federalist?* Does the "book" you ask us to "steep" ourselves in really belong in that list of "basic documents," save in the sense that the Constitution probably wouldn't have been ratified but for the skillful propaganda job it accomplished? Has it not been included in the list (by what you call the "common consent of scholars and publicists") by, so to speak, courtesy, because of the influence it exerted at a crucial moment in our history, but only for that reason? Well, these are good questions and, given the intellectual climate at our universities, which unavoidably trickles down into the high schools and out into the forum of public discussion, natural questions for the reader to ask as he weighs our statement of *The Federalist*'s claim to his attention. So we shall take them up, one at a time (though not in that order), and, as we hope, dispose of them to the reader's satisfaction.

Is The Federalist *a hodge-podge of "hastily"-written ventures in "mere" journalism?*

On two points, no argument: (a) most of the pieces of which it is composed (not all of them) were indeed first published in newspapers, and (b) the pieces were indeed composed in a remarkably brief period of time. But to concede these two points is by no means to concede that they are "mere" journalism, and so beneath our notice as political philosophy. To write quickly is by no means the same thing as to write "hastily" (think of the Gettysburg Address!): that depends, in any given instance, on, first, the amount and quality of the thinking, about the topic in hand, that the writer who writes quickly has done, and, second, his just plain ability to write well under pressure of time. Now: nothing can be more certain than that the authors (but see below about "authors") of *The Federalist* had thought long and hard about the major problems (again see below) to which the book, as opposed to the individual pieces, addresses itself; that all three had been deeply involved in the most important affairs of the emergent Republic over many, many years—came, therefore, to this venture in "quick" writing with a kind of preparation that must have made it impossible for them to write about those affairs in a way properly describable as "hasty"; and that each of them brought to the task in hand very considerable intellectual and literary abilities. The query which we are answering is, in other words, question-begging, and the problem as to the status of *The Federalist* as political philosophy is *not* to be decided in terms of its having been published first in newspapers (newspapers were the *only* medium through which the authors could have got across their teaching in the time available), or in terms of the book's having been executed in less time than, say, Locke's *Second Treatise on Civil Government* (in which, let us say in passing, it is easier to discover flaws of the kind we associate with "haste" than ever it would be in *The Federalist*). Let the reader, at the very least, dismiss these two irrelevancies from his mind before he tackles the book—if only because, as we can assure him out of a considerable knowledge of the relevant literature, those who have dismissed *The Federalist* as "journalistic" and "hasty" tend to be quite stingy with citations of chapter and verse to support their thesis. So, too, with the charge that *The Federalist* is a hodge-podge: true though it be that it originally appeared as articles in newspapers, and that it was written in a few months, it is a *book,* executed with loving care and based (as, for example, Locke's *Second Treatise,* at least on the face of it, certainly is *not*) on a well-thought-out plan.

Is The Federalist *primarily a venture in "propaganda," with the over-riding intention of getting the Constitution ratified?*

Here, again, we can make some concessions to the objector whom we are answering and still, we believe, dispose of the main point he seeks to make. *The Federalist* is, certainly, on one level, *"polemical"* in character—that is, it is the affirmative "side" of a "debate" (with the opponents and critics of the proposed new Constitution), addressed to the "judges" in the debate, the people of America, in the hope of rallying doubters to the support of the "Federalist" cause. Its polemical hand, moreover, is not always gentle: at numerous junctures, for example, it calls into question the good faith of the "negative" in the debate, as also its knowledgeability and good sense, frequently, it "hits hard," in a fashion more likely to knock the opponent out than to show him up as a poor boxer. It is, if you like, a book manifestly intended, *inter alia,* to "influence" "events," by people's hearts and minds in a desired direction; and if all books written with that purpose in view, if, in other words, that is what you mean by "propaganda," then *The Federalist,* along with many of the masterpieces of political philosophy, is indeed "propaganda." So much by way of concessions. But again our reply is, the query is itself, question-begging, because it presupposes that the authors, and their allies, wrote out of a genuine fear that the new Constitution would be rejected. That, however, is a highly questionable assumption, and those who have given currency to the idea that adoption of the Constitution was a "near thing," so that swift and perhaps even desperate *démarches* by its supporters were called for, have, to date offered us extremely little documentation of their thesis; beside which, as far as *The Federalist* is concerned, their chronology is all wrong. By the time any significant number of the pieces that make up *The Federalist* had appeared, ratification of the Constitution was legally and constitutionally speaking, already "in the bag": ratification, by the number of states required by the Constitution in order for it to go into effect, was already assured, though two "indispensable" states, both to be sure states in which there was more, and more vocal opposition to the Constitution than elsewhere, Virginia and New York, had not yet acted. The authors of *The Federalist* may well then, have been hoping to influence the outcome in those two states though to concede that is by no means to concede that they believed that either might actually fail to ratify. (Another possibility: though already sure of a majority in both, they wished to increase the *size* of the relevant majorities.) And, in any event, it is certainly not to concede that the "overriding" purpose of their book was "propagandistic" even to this limited extent. Though nominally addressed to the People of New York, the authors, as the reader will quickly see if he keeps his weather eye peeled, are writing for and to the people of *all* states, that is, to the American people *as a whole*—who as we have noted had, in effect, already ratified, and for large numbers of whom, therefore, ratification was no longer an issue. Why? We offer it as our opinion, based upon long study of the text and long meditation, that their primary purpose on the level here in question, was to make sure that the peoples of the several states, in ratifying, fully understood what exactly they were committing themselves to, what exactly they were doing. And as our further opinion that the correct adjective to apply to a book with such a purpose is "educational," not "propagandistic," pedagogical, *not,* in the pejorative sense of the term, primarily polemical at all. Indeed, one of the most valuable themes that weaves in and out of the book's argument is provided by the numerous passages that, taken together, lay down what amounts to a set of rules, an *ethos,* as to how public discussion, worthy of gentlemen, should be conducted by a sober, intelligent, and intellectually honest self-governing people. The opponents of the Constitution, *The Federalist* insists, constantly violate these rules and should, for that reason alone were other reasons lacking, be disregarded. One might say that the rules in question were the rules that had been observed in the deliberations of the Constitutional Convention itself. One might say, also, that what we mean by "propaganda" today is precisely public utterance that violates the ethos those rules embody. And if that is what we mean by it, *The Federalist,* taken as a whole, is oceans apart from propaganda.

Does the fact that The Federalist *had three different authors, not in very close touch with one another, detract from the book's claim to our attention?*

The Federalist is indeed the product of three different pens: That of Alexander Hamilton, who initiated the project and, in general, masterminded the pro-Constitution forces through the period between Philadelphia and the ratification by his home state of New York. That of James Madison, a Virginian, who wrote the two most famous of the single papers (Federalist 10, Federalist 51). That of John Jay, who wrote the key pieces on the "advantages" of union in the remarkable first section of the book (see below), but early withdrew from active participation because of illness. The reader will wish to know at least this much about these men. Only one of them, Madison, had played a conspicuous role in the actual writing of the Constitution the book defends and explicates. (Hamilton, though a delegate, was a minority voice in the delegation from his state, had, therefore, strictly speaking, no vote, and frequently absented himself from the proceedings; Jay was not a delegate at all.) All three were graduates of distinguished institutions of higher learning: Hamilton and Jay of King's College (Columbia), Madison of Princeton. Hamilton, a man of great talent and energy, had by the age of 30 made himself an outstanding figure in the New York bar; during the Revolutionary War, still in his early twenties, had held critically important posts, both staff and line, under Washington's command; was destined to be the Secretary of the Treasury in the first Cabinet under the new Constitution, and the great issue-drawer of the Washington administration; had, as a lad of 17, before the Revolution, already been writing lengthy and sophisticated tracts in defense of the colonies. Jay, the oldest and perhaps, at the time *The Federalist* was written, the best-known of the three, was also a prominent New

York lawyer; had played a leading role in the governmental affairs of his state just before and during the war, especially in connection with the administration of the loyalty oath; had been Secretary of Foreign Affairs for a time under the Articles of Confederation, so that the Treaty of Peace with Britain (1783) had been the product of negotiations he had conducted; was destined to be the first Justice of the Supreme Court. Madison, a man of remarkably broad "scholarly" interests, had served conspicuously in the Continental Congress; had perhaps given more, and deeper, thought to the form a future "Union" constitution ought to take than any other delegate to the Convention at the time it assembled, so that while it is perhaps an exaggeration to speak of him as the "Father of the Constitution," it is not too much to say that he has a better claim to that title than any single rival claimant; he was destined to be an influential member of the First Congress, where he wrote and "floor-managed" the Bill of Rights (of which he was the "Father" in the strictest sense of the term, and perhaps also the "Mother").

All of that the reader should be told before reading the book, lest he accuse the writers of this Introduction of having withheld information to which (as he can prove by pointing to the Introductions of countless editions of *The Federalist*) he is entitled. All of that, we say, he should be told, in order to take notice of it, and then, if we dare say so, promptly forget. *The Federalist* is written in the first person singular, and signed "Publius"—which is to say, it is not only put forward as the product of a single pen, but in a very special sense, the critical sense, *is* the work of a single pen. That pen, to be sure, we now know to have passed from hand to hand among three able writers, but three able writers each of whom, by entering into the project, at least tacitly agreed, for purposes of the project, to contribute not in his individual, personal capacity, but in a *role*—that is, as "Publius." Though it is now fashionable, in the successive editions of *The Federalist,* to "assign" the respective papers to one or another of the three "authors," the reader will enjoy the book more, and profit more from it, if he ignores these designations and substitutes for them, in his mind, the original signature "Publius." This for several reasons: (1) He will improve his chances of understanding the book as the people to whom it was addressed understood it, and as the authors intended it to be understood. For the fact that "Publius" was a man with three heads—thus, also the identity of those heads—was not known to the first generation that read him (not until 1802 was it revealed in America—ten years later, curiously, than in France—that "Publius" was Hamilton plus Madison plus Jay). (2) He will improve his chances of understanding the book, period. For one thing, he will be able to approach each individual paper, as the original readers could, without his opinions concerning the author getting "between" him and the argument. (One of the three "authors," Hamilton, has, of course, had a "bad press" over the decades, even amongst conservatives, many of whom do not lightly forgive him for his views on governmental "interference" with the economy; and his name, at the head of a paper, is not unlikely to get the reader's back up—in a way that "Publius" would not.) For another thing, to think of each of the individual papers as the handiwork of the particular writer we now know (to our misfortune, the present writers would say) to have written it is, quite simply, to misunderstand the character of "Publius'" enterprise, and thus to misunderstand the book. Let us put it this way: Precisely the point about *The Federalist,* precisely the point which, once grasped, opens it up to our understanding, is that it is a re-enactment, in miniature, of the *miracle* of the Philadelphia convention itself—the miracle that produced a document which (a) reflected accurately the deepest convictions of nobody present as to the shape it should have taken, and to which, nevertheless, (b) nearly everybody present (we must never forget Mason) was prepared to give his all-out support. The Constitution was made possible, one might say, first and foremost because in the course of its proceedings the individual delegates became increasingly willing to "write off" their own pet ideas, to subordinate their personal preferences, to the overriding necessity of arriving at a *consensus*. Put otherwise, and we consciously paraphrase a famous passage from perhaps the most famous of modern ventures in political philosophy: The Constitution became possible because, increasingly, the delegates were willing to ask themselves not "What do *I,* personally, think the Constitution ought to be?" but rather "How *much* of what I think can I insist on with any hope of getting others to go along with me?" and "How *much* of what we can all get together on is there any hope of getting accepted by the American people?" (Not, as that famous book puts it, "What do I will?", but "What is the general will?") *The Federalist* we are saying, re-enacts that political miracle—as, we would add, with the exception of the tragic years that produced the Civil War, American political life has re-enacted it over and over again ever since—and eventuates in a public act that became possible only because the authors were prepared to submerge their individual personalities, their individual political philosophies, in the common enterprise. Hamilton precisely does not write as Hamilton, but as "Publius," that is, as a collaborator of Madison and Jay, in writing the book that is needed to continue the work of the Convention by helping to get the Constitution ratified, to make sure (as we have put it above) that the American people, in ratifying it, understand what they are doing, and, lastly, to accomplish still another purpose to which we shall allude below. Thus the question—a great favorite among writers of Introductions to *The Federalist*—"Was Hamilton 'sincere' in his contributions to the book?"—is of all silly questions perhaps the silliest. The man Hamilton, the man Madison, the man Jay—each of them, as he writes assuming the mantle of Publius, is, in the very nature of the case, in no position to shoot the works with his pet notions about politics. He must, as he writes this or that piece that is to go into the book, ask himself: "Will my two collaborators go along with this?" The "contradictions" between what "Hamilton" wrote in *The Federalist* and what he wrote elsewhere are, therefore, neither here nor there; and it is sad that so much American "scholarship," which might have been employed for better purposes, should have gone into exposing such contradictions. *The Federalist* must be read as the common ground on which Hamilton, Madison, and Jay could meet in defense of the proposed Constitution—as the consensus, between Hamilton, Madison, and Jay, as to what did need to be said at the moment in order to assure the destiny of the United States of America. The whole business as to the authorship of the individual papers, which has been the topic of a major controversy in American letters is, then, a red herring, which the reader had best dismiss as a red herring before he begins to read the book.

Is The Federalist, *if not mere propaganda, a mere "schoolteacherish" explication of the Philadelphia Constitution?*

Of all the questions we are raising in this Introduction, this is the easiest to answer, and to answer with a flat "No, indeed!" The Philadelphia Constitution, the Constitution submitted by the Convention for ratification by the American people, is, to put the matter in its simplest terms, not one but many constitutions—a crossroads, from which, once having situated itself there, the people of America might have moved in any of several directions, might have moved (as, to our sorrow, we rediscover every now and then) to this or that one of many alternative political systems under which we might have governed ourselves. The point is not, as the present writers well know, an easy one to grasp—which is why we implore the reader, *inter alia,* to re-read, and re-read carefully, the Philadelphia Constitution, *the Constitution without the Bill of Rights,* before he plunges into the book he is about to read. Not easy to grasp, we say, and for two reasons: First, because it is now difficult for even the most knowledgeable reader to read the Philadelphia Constitution with an "innocent eye"; he is in the habit of thinking of the Constitution as the Constitution *plus* the Bill of Rights, and is likely, therefore, as he reads *The Federalist,* to forget from page to page that the Constitution it purports to explicate is precisely a Constitution that has no Bill of Rights. (More: as the reader will discover, perhaps to his horror, *The Federalist* is *opposed* to a Bill of Rights, to the whole idea of a Bill of Rights—as, by unanimous vote, the Philadelphia Convention declared itself to be opposed to one.) Second, because of the influence of *The Federalist* itself, which expounds a single one of the numerous alternative "readings" of the Constitution, but precisely that one which we, for good reason (the question of a Bill of Rights apart), are in the habit of "seeing" in it. The Philadelphia Constitution, for example—read it with a deliberately cultivated innocent eye and you will see that for yourself—does *not* provide for a government of three "equal and coordinate" branches, though it also does not exclude the possibility of one. The Philadelphia Constitution does *not* provide "judicial review" of statutes enacted by the Congress and signed by the President, but also does not exclude the possibility of it. The Philadelphia Constitution appears, on the face of it, to be an invitation to a political system in which Congress shall be hardly less "powerful" than the Parliament of Great Britain: nothing in the text, for example, forbids Congress to use the impeachment power, or the power of the "purse," to force the President and the Supreme Court to subordinate themselves to *its* will, but it does not demand that the invitation be accepted. The Philadelphia Constitution does *not* provide for, but also does not forbid, a "plebiscitary" political system—that is, one in which the great decisions about legislation and public policy shall be made by the electorate, choosing between alternative "programs" at the polls and thus giving a "mandate" to its new Congress and its new President. The choice amongst such possibilities as these the Constitution leaves up to the good (or bad) sense of the American people, whom it thus leaves "free" to give itself, and give itself *constitutionally,* any one of a wide variety of political systems. Now: "Publius" has, first, his own "special" way of reading the Constitution, and, second, a great wish to persuade the American people not only to choose *his* reading over all alternative readings, but to convince itself that no other reading is so much as possible. But let us postpone further development of this point until we raise, and attempt to answer, our next question. Suffice it to say, for the moment, that you will not understand *The Federalist* unless you bear in mind that, on one side at least, it is an attempt, oceans apart from mere "school-teacherish" explication of the Constitution, to impose upon that constitution a particular meaning that is present in it *only* potentially.

Is The Federalist *a "basic document" of the American political tradition?*

We have already answered this question by implication, but let us now spell the answer out. "Publius'" attempt to impose a particular reading upon the Philadelphia Constitution has been so successful that one is tempted to say: The Constitution expounded in *The Federalist*—because it has, in its crucial dimensions, only one not several meanings and points forward to only one not several possible political systems—is not really the Philadelphia Constitution at all. One is tempted, indeed, to say that we should in strict propriety distinguish between the Philadelphia Constitution and what we might fairly call "*The Federalist* Constitution," and, further, that it is under the latter, the Philadelphia Constitution as refined by "Publius," and refined so daringly as to make of *The Federalist* a further and drastic step in constitution-building, that we have lived and governed ourselves since 1789. The Philadelphia Constitution, as we have already noted, leaves the door wide open to "legislative supremacy," and places in the hands of Congress "weapons" that make of it a "coordinate" but *not* equal, a coordinate but *superior* branch of the Federal government, in position, whenever it sees fit to do so, to bring the other two branches to their knees. In "Publius'" Constitution, by contrast, so little is said about those weapons as, in effect, to spirit them away; and we have yet to witness the spectacle of Congress' impeaching a President because it dislikes, *e.g.* his foreign policy, or of Congress' "packing" the Supreme Court in order to force the reversal of a Supreme Court decision it finds abhorrent. The Philadelphia Constitution contents itself with saying that the judicial power shall be vested in a Supreme Court—which, as our good friend Brent Bozell has conclusively demonstrated in a book soon to be published, certainly did not mean to the men who wrote those words that the Supreme Court can and shall refuse to enforce, or declare null and void, legislative acts that it deems "unconstitutional." "Publius'" Constitution, by contrast, reads those words in the Philadelphia Constitution as meaning precisely that; and it is "Publius'" meaning, not the Philadelphia meaning, that Americans, through long habituation, now see in them—so that our political system is often described as one not of "legislative supremacy" but of "*judicial* supremacy." The Philadelphia Constitution says—the point is similar to but not identical with that which we have made about legislative supremacy—nothing about "separation of powers." "Publius," by contrast, makes of "separation of powers," of the notion, to put it briefly, that it is "unconstitutional" for any one of the three branches to "encroach" upon the powers and prerogatives of the other two, *the* basic doctrine of the Constitution; and, lo and behold, we teach our children, from an early moment in their education, that "separation of powers" lies at the very heart of our constitutional theory. The Philadelphia Constitution, with certain minor exceptions, leaves a bare majority of the two houses of Congress free to attribute to itself the full powers of Congress, and work its will without regard to the views of the minority. "Publius," though he perhaps never goes so far as to suggest that a bare majority of the two houses of Congress can *not,* under the Constitution, arrogate to itself the plenitude of congressional power, teaches throughout *The Federalist* the doctrine that legislation under the Constitution should reflect the "deliberate sense" not of the majority of the American people but of the American people as a whole, and it is "Publius'" teaching, not the plain language of the Philadelphia Constitution, that we have, in general, taken to heart and lived by: the congressional majority in the United States does not, and does not think itself entitled to, ram legislation through without consulting the views and wishes of the congressional minority (so that the normal legislative act is in America, and always has been, a "deal" hammered out, in the course of lengthy deliberation and negotiation, between majority and minority, and by no means the act that the majority, had it consulted only its own views and wishes, would have put on the statute book). The Philadelphia Constitution is, as we have suggested above, potentially an "invitation" to the American people to govern itself by plebiscitary *mandates*—that is, to insist, in the conduct of its elections, that these be fought over sharply drawn "policy" issues, so that the real policy decisions get themselves made by the electorate (Congress and the President being reduced, so to speak, to the ministerial role of carrying out popular mandates). "Publius" teaches us that the American people should elect to Congress the "best" and "wisest" men, not the men whose policies they happen to approve of; even if he does not come out and say so, he clearly contemplates elections that are *not* plebiscitary in character, elections that precisely do not ventilate, and so submit for decision by the people themselves, the great choices among policy alternatives; and, as the reader hardly needs to be told, nothing is so rare in America as an election, whether of a new Congress or a new President or both, that produces a clear-cut popular decision about public policy, and the word "mandate," in its British sense, is not, even today, part of our political vocabulary. (Though there are those amongst us who would like, by "reforming" our political system in a plebiscitary, that is allegedly "more democratic" direction, to make it that.) The Philadelphia Constitution leaves the American people and their representatives free to make what use they like of Article V, that is, of the amending process, and might well have made of our politics a sort of permanent constitution convention. "Publius," by contrast, convinced as he is of the need for a *stable* constitution and fighting shy (as we have already seen him do) of "great debates" calculated to produce decisions by the people, teaches the unwisdom of frequent use of the amending power; and no one would, we think (so infrequently have we resorted to the amending process), deny that "Publius'" teaching is to all intents and purposes a part of our "real" Constitution. (The latter reads, in effect: the power to amend the Constitution shall be used sparingly.) Finally—again a point similar to but not identical with one we have already made—the Philadelphia Constitution in no wise discourages, save perhaps by its provision for staggered elections, overnight action by Congress on great controversial issues, on, for example, proposals for drastic social or economic "change" that might, if enacted, require for their enforcement large-scale coercion. "Publius," given the lengths to which he "pushes" his characteristic doctrines of "separation of powers" and "judicial review," teaches by implication that the proponents of drastic change in America, even if they have a majority out in the country, must (as one of the present writers has put it in a recent essay) cool their heels in the ante-room of our politics until they can achieve a consensus among the three branches and so, since the branches represent different constituencies out among the people, a popular consensus as well; and, as the essay just mentioned argues (rightly, we think), we have no experience in America, apart from the Civil War, of governmentally imposed social or economic change that has called for large-scale enforcement by bayonets. "Publius'" Constitution, that is to say, has a built-in "conservative" bias that is not readily discernible in the Philadelphia Constitution.

We conclude: to omit *The Federalist* from the list of "basic documents" of the American political system would be to leave unaccounted for, on the documentary level, many of the major features of that system. Or, to put the point a little differently: much of the teaching of *The Federalist,* through tacit ratification by the American people, has assumed a status that it would be foolish to call other than "constitutional."

Is The Federalist *nevertheless "dated"—that is, no longer so "relevant" as to warrant the claim we have made for it at the beginning of this Introduction?*

Again the question is one to which we have already, at least by clear implication, given an answer, but one which, especially in an Introduction to an edition of *The Federalist* to be distributed by the Conservative Book Club, wants spelling out and driving home. Increasingly, over the past sixty-odd years, the American political system has been under attack from Liberal quarters, is under attack today in college classrooms presided over by the typical American political scientist, on the grounds that it is fundamentally "undemocratic." More: the Liberals have a carefully worked-out program for "reforming" that system. We must, the Liberals insist, provide ourselves with a new kind of political party, capable of presenting to the electorate at election time a clear choice between competing "ideologies" and competing policy alternatives, and so turn our elections into plebiscites that will lay bare the genuine "will of the people." We must see to it that every President goes into office with a mandate to carry out certain policies, and with a congressional majority pledged to give him unquestioning support in doing so. We must get rid of those features of our political system—staggered elections, the "seniority principle" in our congressional committees, the filibuster, etc.—that prevent the immediate translation of the will of the majority into legislation. We must infuse into the system, by whatever means necessary, the principle of "one man, one equal vote"—must, especially, "reapportion" our legislative assemblies alike on the federal level and that of the states, in a fashion consonant with that principle. We must free the Supreme Court from the outmoded notion that it is somehow bound by the plain language of the Constitution, and learn to think of it as, literally, the "conscience" of the nation, bound by nothing save the requirements of lofty moral principle. We must increase the powers of the President. We must above all, impose upon the system a clearly understood new purpose, namely, that of making our citizens increasingly "equal." Now: the reader of this Introduction will hardly need to be told that the Liberal attack in question is an attack not so much on the Philadelphia Constitution as, to recur to the distinction we have drawn above, on "Publius'" Constitution; and *The Federalist,* though it will not, as Mr. Russell Kirk has lately accused one of the present writers of believing, "solve all our problems," remains *the* book to which conservatives must go to learn the "case" for, the "philosophy" that underlies those features of the American political system that the Liberals dislike and wish to abolish. It remains, above all, the book to which conservatives must go in order to learn how to wrest from the hands of the Liberals their most elective weapon, namely, the charge that our traditional political system is "undemocratic." Precisely the claims that "Publius" makes, and substantiates, for the system—let us emphasize the point, on the off-chance that the reader may begin to read *The Federalist* under the impression that "Publius" is against democracy—are, first, that it is a *democratic* republic, because it provides for self-government (or, in Lincoln's phrase, government by the people) with justice, and, second, that any democratic republic constructed along other lines will prove unworkable because it will lead, automatically, to "tryanny" (which "Publius" understood to be the very negation of self-government and thus of true democracy). We must learn, we conservatives, that the issue is *not* whether the American system is or is not "democratic," but which of two competing definitions of "democracy"—that which equates it with government by the "deliberate sense" of the people, acting through their elected representatives, and that which equates it with direct majority rule and equality—should prevail, and, in doing so, learn to expose the falseness of the Liberal's claim that the reforms he proposes can properly be defended in the name of democracy. Here again, *The Federalist* remains the book to go to for instruction, as, also, for reinforcement of our will to realize the destiny which "Publius" holds up to the American people as their destiny, namely: to demonstrate to all mankind that self-government—self-government with justice, of course—is *possible.* That, again, of course, is precisely the destiny that the Liberals, by equating justice with equality and thus rendering it meaningless, are calling upon us to reject; let *them* have their head, and we shall speedily have the "tyranny" that *The Federalist* teaches us how to avoid. Let the conservative, then (we will not urge the point again on the Liberal, who will not read the book anyway), accept "his obligation—yes, obligation"—to linger over "Publius'" every paragraph, turn over and over in his mind "Publius'" every idea, steep himself in "Publius'" book, master it, and make it his own.

★ *A professor of government at Georgetown University,* **George W. Carey** *is an associate editor of* Modern Age *and editor of* The Political Science Reviewer.

★ ★ ★ ★ ★

Questions

1. In view of the last 200 years of history, to what extent do the Federalist Papers include a cohesive and comprehensive treatment of the strengths and weaknesses of the Constitution?
2. In view of the last 200 years of history, to what extent was Publius correct in his reservations about direct democracy?
3. To what extent is a democratic republic not a democracy?
4. In view of the many changes the Constitution has undergone in the last 200 years (especially the expansion of rights to women and minorities), do the anti-democratic elements of the original Constitution seem justified?
5. What revisions to the Constitution are still warranted to make it more democratic?

★ ★ ★

American Exceptionalism

Seymour Martin Lipset

When French aristocrat Alexis de Tocqueville wrote his extraordinarily insightful commentary Democracy in America *on a visit here in the 1830s, he characterized America as* exceptional, *that is, distinctly different from other countries. Thus, according to political scientist Seymour Martin Lipset, began an enduring historical and journalistic fashion that Lipset calls American exceptionalism. In Lipset's definition,* exceptional *is neither better nor worse, merely different. As he sets out to discover in what ways America is actually exceptional, Lipset identifies a peculiarly American set of attitudes—an American ideology that sometimes leads to misunderstanding and yet is an enduring source of vitality.*

Americans once proudly emphasized their uniqueness, their differences from the rest of the world, the vitality of their democracy, the growth potential of their economy. Some now worry that our best years as a nation are behind us. Americans distrust their leaders and institutions. The public opinion indicators of confidence in institutions are the lowest since polling on the subject began in the early sixties. These concerns suggest the need to look again at the country in comparative perspective, at the ways it differs from other economically developed nations. As I have frequently argued, it is impossible to understand a country without seeing how it varies from others. Those who know only one country know no country.

The idea of American exceptionalism has interested many outside the United States. One of the most important bodies of writing dealing with this country is referred to as the "foreign traveler" literature. These are articles

★ ★ ★ ★ ★ ★

and books written by visitors, largely European, dealing with this way in which America works as compared with their home country or area. Perhaps the best known and still most influential is Alexis de Tocqueville's *Democracy in America*. The French aristocrat came here in the 1830s to find out why the efforts at establishing democracy in his native country, starting with the French Revolution, had failed while the American Revolution had produced a stable democratic republic. The comparison, of course, was broader than just with France; no other European country with the partial exception of Great Britain was then a democracy. In his great book, Tocqueville is the first to refer to the United States as exceptional—that is, qualitatively different from all other countries. He is, therefore, the initiator of the writings on American exceptionalism. . . .

When Tocqueville or other "foreign traveler" writers or social scientists have used the term "exceptional" to describe the United States, they have not meant, as some critics of the concept assume, that America is better than other countries or has a superior culture. Rather, they have simply been suggesting that it is qualitatively different, that it is an outlier. Exceptionalism is a double-edged concept. As I shall elaborate, we are the worst as well as the best, depending on which quality is being addressed.

The United States is exceptional in starting from a revolutionary event, in being "the first new nation," the first colony, other than Iceland, to become independent. It has defined its raison d'etre ideologically. As historian Richard Hofstadter has noted, "It has been our fate as a nation not to have ideologies, but to be one." In saying this, Hofstadter reiterated Ralph Waldo Emerson's and Abraham Lincoln's emphases on the country's "political religion," alluding in effect to the former's statement that becoming American was a religious, that is, ideological act. The ex-Soviet Union apart, other countries define themselves by a common history as birthright communities, not by ideology.

The American Creed can be described in five terms: liberty, egalitarianism, individualism, populism, and laissez-hire. Egalitarianism, in its American meaning, as Tocqueville emphasized, involves equality of opportunity and respect, not of result or condition. These values reflect the absence of feudal structures, monarchies, and aristocracies. As a new society, the country lacked the emphasis on social hierarchy and status differences. . . .

The belief that the traditional values which underlie American exceptionalism will continue to determine American behavior at the end of the twentieth century has been challenged by those who call for a fundamental change in our national values to stop a moral decline. These critics do not see that what they find fault with is the dark side of American exceptionalism;

developments which, like many of the positive features, derive from the country's organizing principles. These include rising crime rates, increased drug use, the dissolution of the traditional family, sexual promiscuity, and excessive litigiousness.

Public opinion data over the past thirty years reveal a consistently pessimistic outlook regarding the ethical stock of America. The Gallup organization has measured this sentiment in polls over three decades. Even in 1963, only 34 percent responded affirmatively to the question whether they were "satisfied with the honesty and standards of behavior of people in the country today?" while 59 percent were dissatisfied. In 1973, 22 percent were satisfied and 72 percent were not; by 1992, the gap widened to 20 percent and 78 percent. Americans have always yearned for the "good old days." Yet, as the statistics show, the trend over the past few decades is toward great pessimism about the country. People are more negative with regard to moral prospects than before. In mid-1994, three-quarters of Americans told pollsters that the country is in moral and spiritual decline. Over two-thirds believe it is seriously off track.

Though some of these social trends are recent and disturbing, adhere have surprisingly long-standing roots in American society The critics have exaggerated many of the problems in the quest to demonstrate decay. There is, however, no denying that the impression of a change in basic values exists, and to dismiss public perception as somehow wrong or misinformed is to deny the reality of individual experience. The most forceful and well-intentioned attempts to address these perceptions have sought to hold the emphasis on individualism and competitiveness as being responsible for the rending of the nation's social and political fabric, and the corresponding decline in adherence to traditional norms. And to be sure . . . these values are significant forces in American culture, with widespread impact on Americans' views of their social obligations.

American values are quite complex, particularly because of paradoxes within our culture that permit pernicious and beneficial social phenomena to arise simultaneously from the same basic beliefs. The American Creed is something of a double-edged sword: it fosters a high sense of personal responsibility, independent initiative, and voluntarism even as it also encourages self-serving behavior, atomism, and a disregard for communal good. More specifically, its emphasis on individualism threatens traditional forms of community morality, and thus has historically promoted a particularly virulent strain of greedy behavior At the same time, it represents a tremendous asset, encouraging the self-reflection necessary for responsible judgment, for fostering the strength of voluntary communal and civic bonds, for principled opposition to wars, and for patriotism. . . .

The moral content of Americanism is only meaningful insofar as it is expressed within a social context, and that context is civil society. Commentaries, derived from Tocqueville, on the importance of civil associations permeate classically liberal (i.e., libertarian) treatments of democratic life, which argue that an idealized individualism is more attractive and more readily attainable than any idealized collectivism.

Central to this American conception of individualism is the importance of civil society and voluntary associations. Zbigniew Rau comments: "Civil society is an association of rational agents who decide for themselves whether to join it and how to act in it. . . . Therefore, the creation of and participation in civil society is caused by and further promotes the reassertion of its members as fully rational and moral agents." These associations—including churches, civic organizations, school boards, and philanthropic volunteer groups—are lifelong training grounds of citizenship and leadership, and create communication networks, conclusions Tocqueville drew from American practice. They strengthen moral bonds and facilitate the understanding of democracy.

But taking part in civil society does not simply mean belonging to collective entities and thereby embedding oneself within a social identity. Rather, it is a dynamic and sometimes problematic process of engagement between the individual and associations linked to interests and ideas. . . .

Although civil society, association life, is, as Tocqueville also noted, stronger here than elsewhere, the American data, much of which has been assembled by Robert Putnam, indicate that "civic engagement," to use his term, and political commitment have declined in the past three decades. He notes that "participation in many types of civic associations from religious groups to labor unions, from women's clubs to fraternal clubs from neighborhood gatherings to bowling leagues has fallen off."

Most, but not all, of the available evidence bears out these generalizations. A Roper survey taken in August 1993 indicates that the percentage of people who have "attended a public meeting on town or school affairs" has dropped by more than a third, from 23 percent in 1973 to 16 percent in 1993. NORC data indicate that the proportion who attended a political rally or speech, who served on a committee, or who were officers of a club or organization also fell off over this twenty-year period. All told, those reporting involvement in at least one of six civic activities declined from 50 to 43 percent.

One of the most critical forms of community participation in the United States has been in parent-teacher associations (PTA), reflecting Americans' high commitment to education. Putnam reports a very significant drop-off in membership in the PTA from the 1960s to the present, from 12 million in

1964 to 5 million in 1982, though there is some indication that membership may have rebounded somewhat to 7 million in recent years. Survey data gathered by NORC from 1974 to 1993 indicate that fraternal organizations have experienced a steady decline.

There are some contradictory trends. As noted above, Gallup Polls find that the proportion of people indicating that they have volunteered for charitable, "social service," or "non-profit" organizations has doubled between 1977 and the 1990s. Ethnic organizations have increased their total membership in percentage terms. And Putnam reports a type of civic organization that has grown in membership in recent years, groups like the National Organization of Women, the Sierra Club, and the American Association of Retired People (AARP). The latter increased from 400,000 dues-paying members in 1960 to 33 million in 1993. But these Putnam sees as essentially checkbook organizations, which do not promote civic engagement. Their members pay dues, but rarely attend any meetings and seldom, if ever, knowingly encounter other members. They are not mechanisms for communication or the learning of politically relevant skills. In any case, looking at the international data, Putnam reaffirms the conclusion that Americans are "more trusting and civically engaged than most other people in the world."

Putnam discusses various possible causes for the falloff in activity, including the movement of women into the labor force, the decline in the size and stability of the family, and high rates of geographic mobility, and finds good reason to reject these hypotheses. He notes the importance of television in helping to individualize the use of leisure time and points to various time-budget studies documenting the steady increase in time devoted to television, which has "dwarfed all of the changes in the way Americans spend their days and nights." NORC finds that the percentage of the population who watch television for only an hour a day or less decreased from 37 in 1964, to 27 in 1978, to 22 in 1989, and then went up to 25 in 1993. Those looking at the tube for four hours or more a day climbed from 19 percent in 1964 to 28 percent in 1993. Conversely, the proportion reading newspapers every day fell from 73 percent in 1967 to 46 percent in 1993. Other technological developments have had similar effects. For example, the growth in the technology for listening to music—the cassette tape, compact disc, and the Walkman—has helped privatize Americans and reduced their interpersonal contacts outside work. . . .

Popular involvement in civil society apart, the evidence has been growing that all is not well with the American polity. Over the past three decades, opinion polls show that the citizenry is increasingly distrustful of its political leaders and institutions. When asked about their "confidence" in government, large majorities, here as in almost every country, report that they have "none," "little," or "a fair amount" of trust in the president and the legislative bodies. Those who are strongly positive are minorities, usually small ones.

The United States provides a striking example of this breakdown of respect for authority. Confidence in all United States institutions inquired about in the opinion surveys declined precipitously and steadily from the mid-1960s, though the greatest part of the fall occurred early in that decade. The Louis Harris Poll, which has investigated the subject since 1966, reported in 1994 the lowest level of confidence in government institutions ever. Those expressing a "great deal" of confidence in the executive branch of government constituted only 12 percent of a national sample in 1994, as compared to 24 percent in 1981, and 41 percent in 1966. Trust in Congress was even lower—8 percent in 1994, contrasted with 16 percent in 1981, and 42 percent in 1966. Daniel Yankelovich reports a drastic shift for the worse in response to the question, "How much of the time can you trust the government to do what's right?" In 1964, 76 percent said "always" or "most of the time." The proportion so answering fell to 44 percent in 1984, and then to an all-time low of 19 percent in 1994, a finding reported in the latest Luntz Poll for the Hudson Institute as well. . . .

Given the anger about politics in the United States, what accounts for the continued stability of the American system? Why do we not witness grievous forms of mass unrest? Why is the major protest movement, led by Ross Perot, basically centrist, even conservative with respect to economic and social policy? Part of the answer to the conundrum is that most Americans are not unhappy about their personal lives or prospects; if anything, the opposite is true. They still view the United States as a country that rewards personal integrity and hard work, as one that, government and politics apart, still works. The American Dream is still alive, even if the government and other institutions are seen as corrupt and inefficient. A 1994 survey-based study of "The American Dream" conducted for the Hudson Institute finds that over four-fifths, 81 percent, agree with the statement, "I am optimistic about my personal future," while about two-thirds, 64 percent are "optimistic about America's future." Three-quarters, 74 percent, agreed that "In America, if you work hard, you can be anything you want to be." And almost 72 percent felt that "As Americans, we can always find a way to solve our problems and get what we want." And not surprisingly, when asked to choose between "having the opportunity to succeed and having security from failing," over three-quarters, 76 percent, opt for the former; only a fifth, 20 percent, prefer the security option.

Gallup polling for Times-Mirror in 1994 presents similar results. Over two-thirds, 67 percent, expect their financial situation to improve a lot or some; only 14 percent say it will get worse. Large majorities reject the statement that "Success in life is pretty much determined by forces outside our control." Most affirm the traditional American laissez-faire ideology, with its emphasis on individualism, with 88 percent agreeing with the statement, "I admire people who get rich by working hard," and 85 percent agreeing that "Poor people have become too dependent on government assistance programs." More significantly, perhaps, 78 percent endorse the view: "The strength of this country today is mostly based on the success of American business."

The American political system, though distrusted and ineffective in dealing with major social issues, is clearly not in danger. Most Americans remain highly patriotic and religious, believe they are living in the best society in the world, and think that their country and economy, in spite of problems, still offer them opportunity and economic security.

★ *A senior fellow at the Hoover Institution,* **Seymour Martin Lipset** *is the Hazel Professor of Public Policy at George Mason University.*

★ ★ ★ ★ ★

Questions

1. What values do most Americans hold in common?
2. To what extent is this common set of values uniquely American?
3. In what ways is American history uniquely different from the histories of other countries?
4. To what extent does American individualism threaten or weaken our sense of responsibility to our communities?
5. To what extent does American exceptionalism produce arrogance?

☆ ☆ ☆

The Struggle for American Culture

James A. Morone, Brown University

Is there an American political culture? Do Americans share a set of attitudes and assumptions powerful enough to shape their politics?[1] A generation ago, most social scientists thought so. Important books bore titles like *The American Mind* (Henry Steel Commager 1950), *The American Political Tradition* (Richard Hofstadter 1948), or *The Americans: The National Experience* (Daniel Boorstin 1965). Critics occasionally damned the cultural consensus for its suffocating homogeneity (Hingham 1959), but few questioned its existence.

Today, agreement over a shared American culture has vanished. Some observers insist that it is still going strong. Americans, they argue, remain deeply committed to their core beliefs—things like individualism, equal opportunity, political rights, and government bashing (Greenstone 1986, 1993; Huntington 1981). Others fear that centrifugal cultural forces bode serious trouble. America increasingly "belittles *unum* and glorifies *pluribus*," writes Arthur Schlesinger Jr. Ethnic militancy "nourishes prejudices, magnifies differences, and stirs antagonisms...Will the Center hold? or will the melting pot give way to the Tower of Babel" (1993 17-18)? And still others cheer precisely the diversity that Schlesinger laments. American political culture, they argue, was more the hegemony of the powerful than any real harmony among the people. From this perspective, that "Babel" is the welcome sound of overlooked voices (Thelen and Hoxie 1994; Fox and Lears 1993; Foner 1990).

Did the Americans really share a political culture? If they had it, did they lose it? If they lost it, should they feel distressed or liberated?[2]

The United States had—and has—a dominant political culture. But in contrast to the common picture of culture as a static concept, American culture is almost constantly contested and continuously evolving. Each gener-

☆ ☆ ☆ ☆ ☆ ☆

Reprinted from *Political Science and Politics 29*, (September 1996), by permission of Cambridge University Press.

ation of immigrants brings new perspectives; so do marginal groups struggling for legitimacy. There is nothing inevitable about the ideas and groups which win and become part of the cultural mainstream, and those that lose and are pushed to the margins.

In one sense, Patrick Buchanan got it exactly right at the 1992 Republican Party convention: "We are...in a culture war...for the soul of America" (1992). He failed to add that the war has waxed and waned in America for more than three hundred years (Morone 1996).

★ *Liberalism*

Begin with the classic vision of American political culture, the one they all agreed on forty years ago. The foundation was set by Alexis de Tocqueville. "It seems to me that I can see the entire destiny of America contained in the first Puritan who stepped ashore" (Tocqueville 1981, vol 1, 382; Tocqueville 1969, 279).[3] In Tocqueville's "storybook truth" about America's origin, those early settlers arrived in a vast unpopulated land. They did not face feudal and clerical oppressions, they were "born equal instead of becoming so" (Tocqueville 1981, vol II, 130; Tocqueville 1969, 509; Hartz 1955, 3).

In contrast to the people stirring in early modern Europe, these American settlers did not need class movements or state power to clear paths of upward mobility. In the new world there was no *ancien regime*; no revolutionary tradition to attack it; no reactionary conservatism to counterattack. The result would be a profound faith in individualism. Americans came to believe in personal social mobility, and (eventually) in competitive economic markets. In short, they became unshakable liberals (Hartz 1955; Greenstone 1986).

At the heart of liberalism lies a sharp demarcation between private and public spheres (Rosenblum 1989). The private sphere is protected from political meddling. Individuals all begin with essential rights. Beyond that, they define and pursue their own self-interest. In the private realm, government interference is deplored, success in economic markets honored, failure scorned. (Those first Puritans, after all, took economic success and failure as divine hints about salvation and perdition.) As for the public sphere, Americans would hone their notorious dread of government. Their political institutions would develop by fits and starts and checks and balances into the incoherent, contemporary apparatus (Morone 1990).

Recent analysis stresses the range of possibility within liberalism. At one extreme, of course, lie free economic markets. However, if the competition is to be fair, if individuals are to enjoy equal opportunity at success, then perhaps government should guarantee certain prerequisites: good education, basic nutrition, decent housing, access to health care (Katznelson 1996). In this more expansive sense, liberalism can be stretched almost to the edge of democratic socialism. (This division within American liberalism, incidentally, can be traced back to the differences between the Yankee-Whigs and Jacksonians) (Greenstone 1993).

The liberal grip on American culture seems to explain why social reforms (from either left or right) are so terribly hard to secure. At the same time, the heritage of a more expansive liberalism offers the faint prospect of significant political reform—the theory can be made to fit with an occasional reforming success.

In many hands, liberalism goes further. This is not just the way Americans are, it is what they aspire to be. The roots of the normative strain lie back in the sermon delivered on the first flagship of the Puritans' Great Migration (1630): "Wee are entered into a Covenant with God for this worke...Wee must Consider that wee shall be a citty on a hill, the eies of all people are uppon us" (Winthrop 1931, 294-295). Future generations would repeatedly return to the heady image of a special national mission, a divinely sanctioned experiment unfolding in the new world with the rest of the world—all eyes—waiting for results. Three hundred fifty years later, Sacvan Bercovitch would write of his "astonishment, as a Canadian immigrant, at learning about the prophetic history of America." Here was "a population that, despite its bewildering mixture of race and creed, could believe in something called the American mission, and could invest that patent fiction with all the emotional, spiritual, and intellectual appeal of a religious quest" (Bercovitch 1978, 11).

The mission, in Winthrop's sense, meant constructing a society so well ordered that the world (well, England) would find it an irresistible model. As modern American liberalism inherited the mission, it offered the world a model of economic opportunity and a distinctive political creed: equality, liberty, rights, and consent of the governed. Sure, there has been xenophobia, nativism, racism; but across American time, these are all matched and trumped by the principles embedded in the American creed. From this perspective, American political history reads like the inexorable (although bumpy) march of liberal democracy. Americans secured basic political rights with their Constitution; political rights expanded in the Jacksonian period (to the "common man"), after the civil war (to "the freemen"), during the progressive years (to women), during the 1960s (based on race and gender, again). Throughout, immigrants were assimilated and marginal groups empowered (Huntington 1981; Fuchs 1990).

In short, here is an ideology that constrains power and shrinks the realm of political action. But on this narrowed field, it restlessly integrates, protects, liberates, and empowers. Sophisticated descriptions picture liberalism as a "boundary condition," a pervasive influence interacting with other American forces (Greenstone 1986). In more enthusiastic hands, the liberal culture becomes the most potent force in American political development.

★ The Limits of Liberalism

Almost every aspect of the liberal tradition has been criticized: it ignores alternative voices, oversimplifies cultural history and overlooks an unhappy heritage of profound illiberality. An alternative perspective begins with an entirely different foundation than the one Tocqueville and Hartz read into the early American experience. After all, for every Puritan who sailed from old world intolerance, two hundred Africans were driven to the new world in chains. While Puritans made their covenant with God, the slaves endured what Jon Butler calls an "African spiritual holocaust." Authorities in the new world extirpated the rich African religious traditions. The slaves, concludes Butler, "were robbed of more than their lives; they were robbed, as well, of traditional collective means of comprehending life and loss" (1990, 162; see Raboteau, 1978; Wills 1990).

Eventually, the slaves in the United States turned to Christianity and applied it to their own condition. Like the Puritans, they saw themselves as the chosen people of Israel. In their version, God's people had not been delivered into the New Jerusalem (a city on a hill) but languished in Egyptian bondage. This American narrative emphasized consolation, mutual assistance and hope—for God tempered those whom He would exalt. The teleology in this American story turned on escape from bondage and freedom in the promised land (Du Bois 1969, chapter 10).

The slave's vision would develop across American time. It passed into wide political currency in the tumult of antebellum America (most famously in the rhetoric of Abraham Lincoln) and, again, in the sermons and speeches of the southern civil rights movement of the 1950s and 1960s.

Incorporating these early Americans (rather than setting them aside as exceptional) yields a very different reading of the culture. It is not so easy to waive away feudal oppressions, revolutionary upheaval, counterrevolutionary conservatism, or the state as guarantor of social mobility. Very different—but still recognizable—strands of American thought come into focus: community becomes more important, individualism less so; more populism and mutual assistance and less fear of government and market competition. It is not that all these themes derive from the experience of the bondsmen and women (after all, most can be found in Tocqueville). Rather, starting the story in a different place emphasizes different aspects of the American cultural heritage.

Looking at different voices also rewrites the American historical trajectory embedded in celebratory liberalism. "The dynamic of American development," writes Rogers Smith, "cannot simply be seen as a rising tide of liberalizing forces submerging contrary beliefs" (1993 558-9; see Smith, 1996). Bigotry fights back. Sometimes, it wins. Triumphs of the American creed are followed by nativist relapses. There is nothing linear or inevitable about the progress of liberal progress.

Take a closer look, for example, at the first great expansion of liberal rights during the Jacksonian period. (In fact, many of the reforms occurred on the state level prior to the Jackson Administration itself.) Immigrants and, more generally, men without property did win political participation—despite the violent opposition of American nativists. Although there is a murky line between the progress of an American creed and the raw partisan politics of early parties seeking votes, the expansion of political participation is undeniable (Morone 1990, chapter 2).

However, the same Jacksonian coalition that promoted voting rights conducted an extraordinarily violent campaign to remove native Americans from the East. Even Tocqueville demurred.

> One cannot imagine the frightful afflictions that accompanied these forced migrations. When the Indians leave their ancestral fields they are already exhausted and worn down...Behind them there is famine, before them war, everywhere misery...With my own eyes I have witnessed miseries [and] afflictions beyond my power to portray...The sight will never leave my memory (Tocqueville 1981, vol I, 435-6; Tocqueville 1961, 323-324).

If the Irish won broad political rights in the 1830s, native Americans decisively lost basic human rights. This was not a policy on the margins of the administration. In his Farewell Address, "Indian removal" is the first issue that Jackson turns to and he does not mince his words: "The states which had so long been retarded in their improvement by the Indian tribes residing in the midst of them are at length relieved from this evil ..." (Jackson 1897, 1513).

Scoring the results of the national creed requires observers to draw boundaries—to make judgments about who and what counts. Reading the Irish experience might yield an interpretation of Jacksonian America grounded in American liberal values. Shifting the focus to native Americans makes that perspective difficult to sustain. Nor in the case of native Americans, would there be future efforts to redeem the Jacksonian era wrongs.

The analysis can be repeated for each flourish of American liberal progress. The civil war, for example, offers another deeply ambiguous political moment. Slaves were liberated, then resubjugated through a long process that culminated early in the next ostensibly liberalizing moment, the Progressive era. The progressive fully participated in illiberal Darwinian racial theories. The Progressive era can be read as a step in the march of democracy only by blinking away racial repression.

Ultimately, the critique against the liberal consensus turns on a simple point: celebrating a single, homogenous, American political culture means listening to only some of the voices—to a large extent, the powerful ones.

The most dramatic omission lies in the African American experience. Social scientists simply did not take it seriously. Frederick Jackson Turner, for example, waived away the entire slavery experience, a mere "incident" (Turner 1896, 24). Morrison, Commager, Hartz—the estimable social scientists who explored the liberal tradition—all overlooked, brushed aside or patronized. Somehow, "the absence of feudal and clerical oppressions" stood for everyone (a mistake, incidentally, that Tocqueville did not make). W. E. B. Du Bois wrote furiously against the tide: "In propaganda against the negro since emancipation in this land, we face one of the most stupendous efforts...to discredit human beings, an effort involving universities, history, science, social life and religion" (Du Bois 1992, 727).

Critics of the liberal consensus argue that race is just the first omission on a long list. Images of consensus flourished only because social scientists overlooked multiple competing traditions and voices (Rogers Smith 1993, 1996). Perhaps the most popular exhibition in the case against the old school is the fear expressed in the 1962 presidential address of the American Historical Association. Carl Bridenbaugh of Brown University warned his colleagues of the gathering academic storm. Once upon a time, argued Bridenbaugh, scholars were men who shared a common culture. No more. The coming generation of historians, "are products of lower middle-class or foreign origins, and their emotions not infrequently get in the way of historical reconstructions. They find themselves in a very real sense outsiders on our past..." (Bridenbaugh 1963, 322-3). Bridenbaugh's fear was well founded. Outsiders no longer, the new generation insisted on their share of "our past." But where does this leave American political culture?

It is not that liberalism is wrong. On the contrary, it offers powerful insights into the unarticulated assumptions that lie under a great deal of American politics. But it is incomplete. Anti-government individualism is balanced by populist reform movements; the sacralization of the marketplace is matched by potent religious revivals; the ethos of democratic inclusion contrasts with inegalitarian "cultural, religious, ethnic,...racial, and gender hierarchies" (Smith 1993, 549-550).

Rather than a single consistent culture, argues Michael Kammen, the American experience yields a series of paradoxes (1972, chap 4). And no wonder. This is a relatively young nation which celebrates social and economic mobility while it remakes itself through successive generations of newcomers. All this makes American political culture a protean commodity, always subject to revision. Each generation wrestles over the norms and values of the polity. Of course, they never start *tabula rasa*—each generation stands in a long American cultural tradition. But at the same time, the outcomes—the contours of American culture—are not fixed in either liberal or illiberal ways. The political culture is shaped by struggle.

★ The Struggle for American Culture

Culture conflicts tend to follow a pattern. Immigrants arrive with their differences. Politically marginal groups claim new rights or seek to shift power relations between races, classes, groups or genders. Older, well-established Americans resist. In the conflict, two criticisms of the threatening "other" recur with particular intensity. First, the newcomers undermine American values they do not understand or appreciate. Second, the upstarts are morally corrupt—and their corruption portends national declension.

Benjamin Franklin articulated the standards of the decline jeremiad two decades before the revolution:

> This will in a few years be a German colony. Instead of their learning our language, we must learn theirs, or live as in a foreign county. Already the English begin to quit particular Neighborhoods, surrounded by Dutch, being made uneasy by the Disagreeableness of Dissonant Manners; and in Time, Numbers will probably quit the Province...Besides, the Dutch under-live, and are thereby enabled to under-work and under-sell the English; who are thereby extremely incommoded, and consequently disgusted, so there can be no cordial Affection or Unity...between the two Nations (Franklin 1752, 43).

Here is an early version of the underclass. Franklin's pessimism (he later recanted) touches points that remain tender today: apprehension over "our language," anxiety about cultural inundation, the uneasy sense of racial difference, allegations of laziness and social division articulated as middle class flight. Underlying the specific complaints lurks the question about shared culture: can we be a single people? With *them*?

Future critics would be more explicit about the "dissonant manners" that so disgusted the English neighbors. Some newcomers, for instance, were not Protestant. The United States and Protestantism both sprang from revolts against centralized authority. Citizenship and faith reinforced one another. In contrast, Catholicism stood alongside European monarchies as a bulwark of the *ancien regime*. Catholics were ruled by a foreign Pope, they deferred to their clergy, they were incapable of independent (much less republican) thought. Their priests kept convents full of unmarried woman which true American mobs occasionally burned to the ground (Billington 1938; Norton 1986).

The litany went on, across time, race and ethnicity: The Chinese were "cruel, cunning and savage," as social reformer Jacob Riis put it; they posed "a constant and terrible menace to society" (1890, 97, 102). Jews were "moral cripples with dwarfed souls." Italians were "gross little aliens" who lacked the power to take rational care of themselves (Ross 1913, 154, 101, 113). Beyond the immigrants lay all the other American others. Differences arose—arise—from race, class, gender, region, urban life and even diseases (of which AIDS is only the latest). Each has been read as a culture-threatening menace.

Ironically, the registries of moral flaws provoke such alarm precisely because of the partial truth embedded in the liberal argument. A relatively open, immigrant society casts a skeptical eye on potential new members. Moreover, the success of the mythic American mission rests on the exemplary nature of the domestic order—such stakes ratchet up anxiety about the borders of the community and the allocation of social privileges within it.

The cultural debate heats up when the structure of American society appears to be flux: moments of large-scale immigration (like the present), broad economic change (like the present) and shifting social relations (particularly when they involve changing racial or gender relations—again, like the present). Not surprisingly, contemporary politics reverberate with culture conflicts. The conflicts set off ancient anxieties.

First, these new outsiders cannot appreciate "our" culture. They resist assimilation, demand to be educated in foreign languages and cling to their alien ways. In part, the alarm comes from poor historical memory (perhaps abetted by the last generation's overly enthusiastic reading of a shared culture). As Benjamin Franklin testified, new Americans have long spoken their dissonant languages and clung to alien habits. Even the contemporary debate over bi-lingual education has precedents; Wisconsin's Bennet Law, for example, set off a national uproar in 1889 by requiring schools to teach in English—in effect, shutting down the German-speaking Catholic schools (Kelley 1993).

Mike Royko put it well in his description of Chicago in the ostensibly homogeneous 1950s:

> North of the loop was Germany. To the Northwest Poland. To the west were Italy and Israel...Southwest were Bohemia and Lithuania. And to the South was Ireland...You could always tell what state you were in...by the odors of the food, the sound of the...language, and by whether a stranger hit you in the head with a rock; (Royko 1971, 30-1).

Second, the new culture wars return Americans to old conflicts over moral order. This might seem odd, from a liberal perspective; liberalism is generally read as removing such matters from public discourse. But Americans are only occasional liberals. Every group noted in this essay—native Americans, Irishmen, Puritans, Germans, Yankee-Whigs, African captives—has provoked sustained, often deeply illiberal, moral tumult (Morone 1996).

Today, the moral tumult is not hard to hear. Christian activists ardently campaign over abortion, the state of marriage, the suppression of homosexuality, the role of women, the restoration of Christian morals, an end to affirmative action. On the other side, gay activists run for office in both major parties, the Olympic torch bypasses Cobb County (Georgia) for its anti-gay ordinances, the gender gap becomes a major staple of political analysis as women tilt toward Democrats, and, by some estimates, Islam is poised to become one of the ten largest American religious groups.

Is there an American culture? Certainly. But it is a perpetual work in progress. Americans are fighting over it now. They have fought over it since the first Puritan stepped ashore. At least in that sense Tocqueville was right to read the "entire destiny of America" in that landing.

Notes

[1]For definitions of political culture, see Almond (1956); Pye (1968); Geertz (1973, especially chaps 4, 8); Levine (1992); and Kelley (1993).

[2]There is another great, unanswered, question: to what extent does political culture explain political outcomes? What is its explanatory power relative to, say, structural or institutional factors? See Greenstone (1986) and Skocpol (1992, 15-20) for useful discussions.

[3]My translation. I give two citations for Tocqueville quotations—the first is the French edition, the second a standard translation.

References

★Almond, Gabriel A. 1956 "Comparative Political Systems." *Journal of Politics* 18(3):391-409.

★Bercovitch, Sacvan. 1978. *The American Jeremiad.* Madison, WI: University of Wisconsin Press.

★Boorstin, Daniel. 1965. *The Americans: The National Experience.* New York: Random House.

★Bridenbaugh, Carl. 1963. "The Great Mutation." *American Historical Review.* 69 (January):322-3.

★Buchanan, Pat. 1992. "The Election Is About Who We Are: Taking Back the Country." Delivered at the Republican National Convention. Houston, Texas. August 17.

*Butler, Jon. 1990. *Awash in a Sea of Faith: Christianizing the American People.* Cambridge, MA: Harvard University Press.

*Commager, Henry Steel. 1950. *The American Mind.* New Haven: Yale University Press.

*Du Bois, W. E. B. 1969. [Original, 1903] *The Souls of Black Folk.* New York: New American Library.

*——. 1992. [Original, 1935] *Reconstruction.* New York: Atheneum.

*Foner, Eric. 1990. ed. *The New American History.* Philadelphia: Temple University Press.

*Fox, Richard Wrightman and T. Jackson Lears. 1993. eds. *The Power of Culture.* Chicago: The University of Chicago.

*Franklin, Benjamin. 1752. Letter to James Parker. In The Importance of Gaining and Preserving the Friendship of the Indians to the British Interest Considered, ed. Archibald Kennedy. London: E. Cave.

*Fuchs, Lawrence, H. 1990. *The American Kaleidoscope: Race, Ethnicity and the Civic Culture.* Hanover, NH: University Press of New England.

*Geertz, Clifford, 1973. *The Interpretation of Cultures.* New York: Basic Books.

*Greenstone, J. David. 1993. *The Lincoln Persuasion: Remaking American Liberalism.* Princeton, NJ: Princeton University Press.

*——. 1986. "Political Culture and American Political Development: Liberty, Union, and the Liberal Bipolarity." *Studies in American Political Development* Vol. 1:1-49.

*Hingham, John. 1959. "The Cult of American Consensus: Homogenizing Our History." *Commentary* (February):93-100

*Hofstadter, Richard. 1948. *The American Political Tradition and The Men Who Made It.* New York: Knopf.

*Huntington, Samuel, P. 1981. *American Politics: The Promise of Disharmony.* Cambridge, MA: Harvard University Press.

*Jackson, Andrew. 1897. [original, 4 March, 1837]. "Farewell Address." In *Messages and Papers of the Presidents.* James Richardson, ed. Washington: Bureau of National Literature Vol II:1511-27.

*Kammen, Michael. 1972. *People of Paradox.* New York: Random House.

*Katznelson, Ira. 1996. *Liberalism's Crooked Circle.* Princeton, NJ: Princeton University Press.

*Kelley, Robert. 1992. "Political Culture." In *Encyclopedia of American Social History.* Mary Kupiec Cayton, Elliot J. Gorn, Peter W. Williams, eds. New York: Charles Scribner's Sons. Vol III: 2269-N81.

*Levine, Lawrence W. *1993 The Unpredictable Past: Explorations in American Cultural History.* New York: Oxford University Press.

*Morone, James A. 1990. *The Democratic Wish: Popular Participation and the Limits of American Government.* New York: Basic Books.

★——. 1996. Sin: The Moral Dimension of American Politics. Work in Progress.

★Norton, Anne. 1986. *Alternative Americas: A Reading of Antebellum Political Culture.* Chicago: University of Chicago Press.

★Pye, Lucian. 1968. "Political Culture." In *International Encyclopedia of the Social Sciences.* David Sills, ed. New York: Macmillan Company and the Free Press. Vol 12:218–25.

★Raboteau, Albert J. 1978. *Slave Religion.* New York: Oxford University Press.

★Riis, Jacob. 1890. *How the Other Half Lives.* New York: Scribners.

★Ross, E. A. 1913. *The Old World In the New.* New York: Century Co.

★Rosenblum, Nancy L. 1989. *Liberalism and the Moral Life.* Cambridge, MA: Harvard University Press.

★Royko, Mike. 1971. *Boss.* New York: Plume.

★Skocpol, Theda. 1992. *Protecting Soldiers and Mothers.* Cambridge, MA: Harvard University Press.

★Smith, Rogers M. 1993. "Beyond Tocqueville, Myrdal and Hartz: The Multiple Traditions in America." *American Political Science Review,* 87(3):549–66.

★——. 1996. *Civic Ideals: Conflicting Visions of Citizenship in American Public Law.* New Haven: Yale University Press.

★Schlesinger, Arthur M. Jr. 1991. *The Disuniting of America: Reflections on a Multicultural Society,* New York: Norton.

★Thelen, David and Frederick E. Hoxie. 1994. eds. *Discovering America.* Chicago: University of Illinois Press.

★Tocqueville, Alexis de. 1981. *de la Democratie en Amerique.* Paris: GF-Flammarion.

★Tocqueville, Alexis de. 1969. George Lawrence. trans. *Democracy in America.* Garden City, NY: Doubleday.

★Winthrop, John. 1931. [originally, 1630] "A Modell of Christian Charity," *The Winthrop Papers.* Boston: Massachusetts Historical Society. Volume II:282–95.

★Wills, Gary. 1990. *Under God: Religion and American Politics.* New York: Simon and Schuster.

★ ★ ★ ★ ★

★ ***James Morone*** *is Professor of Political Science at Brown University. His* The Democratic Wish: Popular Participation and the Limits of American Government *won the American Political Science Association's 1991 Gladys M. Kammerer Award. He can be reached via email at* james-morone@brown.edu

☆ ☆ ☆

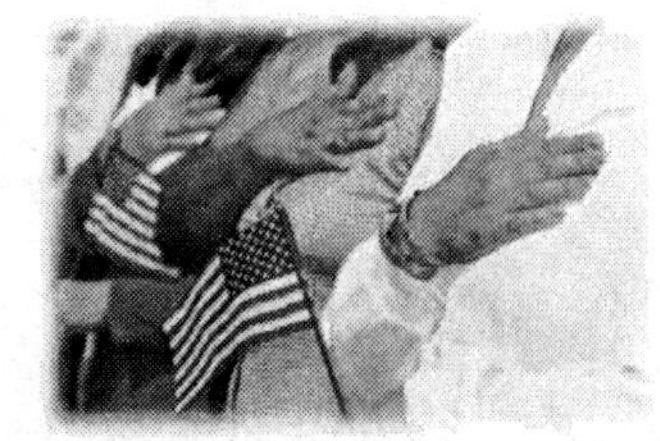

Understanding Political Theory

**Department of Social Sciences,
U.S. Military Academy**

Although "political theory" is a label that is applied to a variety of writings on politics, this article helps students who are new to political science to understand that within the discipline this phrase commonly carries two disparate definitions. The first, called normative or traditional, includes discourses on such issues as what constitutes a good society, what is the best form of government, how is a cohesive political community achieved, and how should we define justice, create equality, or actualize freedom. The second definition is called behavioral or scientific. It eschews "value judgments" in favor of establishing guidelines for observing, describing and analyzing objective information about political behavior. This article provides an easily understandable introduction to the varieties of approaches utilized under both definitions.

☆ Two Approaches to Political Theory

The term theory in American political science suffers from a condition Aristotle calls homonymy, which means nothing more than that the term theory means different things in different contexts. Advocates of the scientific study of politics construe theory as part of the scientific method. Political philosophers construe theory as part of the philosophic enterprise. Most political philosophers, who are in the business of studying and teaching Plato,

☆ ☆ ☆ ☆ ☆ ☆

Machiavelli, Locke, or contemporary topics such as human rights and democracy, have no trouble using the terms philosophy and theory interchangeably. For instance, we might study Aristotle's theory (or philosophy) of politics or John Rawls's theory (or philosophy) of liberal democracy.

Students of political philosophy routinely engage normative questions, i.e., questions whose answers assume the form of, "This *ought* to be done because it is right or *just*" or "That *ought not* to be done because it is wrong or *unjust.*" Many people characterize philosophic efforts as mere opinions; however, one must realize that some opinions, by virtue of their craftsmanship, logical consistency, or vision, are better than others. Just as we presumptively value a general's opinion on how to conduct an attack more than the man in the street's opinion on the same matter, so should we give the political philosopher some benefit, however cautiously and temporarily, that what he has to say about normative issues should be of some interest to those who care about democracy, justice, and the dignity of the human person.

Moreover, philosophic theories need not be solely normative; they may also comprise descriptive analyses of complex issues that are simply not susceptible to routine scientific treatment. An example of this sort of problem is the origin of ethical norms in a society. We know for a fact that ethical norms exist; the difficult task is to explain how they came to exist. One philosopher who has tackled this problem is Aristotle, whose writing on this issue is principally descriptive, not normative. Now regardless of whether the philosopher produces a normative or descriptive analysis, his work will be unable to shake the one stubborn characteristic of political philosophy: his work will inspire argument. Consensus is hard to come by in political theory, and this is not likely to change despite the cogency of reasons offered in support of one or another theory.

Today political philosophy (with its brand of theory) is one sub-field within the larger discipline of political science (in which a different brand of theory prevails). In this context, political philosophy assumes a place alongside the scientific analysis of American politics, international relations, and comparative politics. This situation is uncomfortable, because what the political philosopher thinks knowledge is differs from what [e.g.] the American politics student thinks it is; consequently, scholars of each discipline will arrive at different notions of theory and its purpose.

New students in American politics, international relations, or comparative politics soon discover that our experimental or empirical knowledge (in contradistinction to our normative knowledge) of political phenomena arises from the application of a scientific procedure. One can see this procedure at play in the vast majority of political-science journals. Scientific scholars routinely (1) posit a research question (e.g., What is the relationship between the

Senate, the Supreme Court, and Pressure Groups?); (2) offer a theory that speculates on the relationship between specific variables (e.g., Pressure groups shape senators' preferences by providing information on how judicial nominees will likely vote once on the bench and by informing senators about how strongly his constituents feel about a particular nominee); and (3) develop specific hypotheses or predictions based on the theory (e.g., pressure groups' lobbying has a significant effect on senators' votes for or against approval of judicial nominees). Today's political "scientists" consider the fruits of the foregoing method to be reliable political knowledge or fact, which is in no way to be confused with the philosophical musings or wisdom found in philosophical dialogues and treatises.

When confronted with the question of what constitutes genuine political knowledge, men and women of the twenty-first century, for a variety of reasons, reflexively side with the empirical political scientists and look askance at the normative political philosophers. Today's students celebrate the concrete discoveries emanating from a "scientific" approach to politics and greet the "opinions" of the philosophers with, "That's what you think! Prove it!" But the philosophical enterprise has merit. Contemporary political science prides itself on being wise about a whole host of things: how people vote, how they make their party affiliation, the role of congressional committees, and the power of the president. But assume for a moment that final, scientific knowledge on the topics of political behavior and institutions was settled once and for all (say, in the same way as we have settled that the earth revolves around the sun). Would we be any wiser about the most important and fundamental political questions?

Put otherwise, is it within the jurisdiction of the scientific method to settle once and for all what constitutes *morally justifiable* reasons for going to war? Or the thresh-hold human-rights violations must cross before sufficient justification for intervening in the internal affairs of a sovereign state might be in order? Or the causes, both spiritual and psychological, of the Holocaust and terrorism, both of which are undeniably political phenomena yet not readily susceptible to scientific analysis? Or the relation between a nation-state's ethical climate and its democratic hygiene? A satisfactory "scientific" study of these questions has not appeared, and it is likely not forthcoming. The reason is that political knowledge or wisdom far exceeds what can be known through a scientific method. This fact is plain even on the most commonsense level with reference to wisdom in general (as opposed to, say, political wisdom). When someone asks you for advice and you honestly intend to help, the sort of wisdom you will offer up to your friend will likely not result from your having stated a research question, posited a theory, and speculated on hypothesis. At the very least, what you consider to be a sound criterion for knowledge in moral and ethical matters will not be appropriate to your study of whether pressure groups affect senators' decisions (and vice versa).

It is all too easy to set the two brands of theory against each other. For our purposes, it is best to consider the normative task of the philosophers and the scientific task of the scientists as cooperative ventures, and it is in such a spirit that our study of politics will proceed. There are two guiding questions we should keep in mind: (1) Who governs? and (2) How democratic is America? The first question requires a thoroughly descriptive or empirical answer. This question is shorthand for Harold Lasswell's famous definition of politics, "the study of who gets what, when, and how." When we set our sights on answering this question, we neither require nor desire opinions about right and wrong—we simply want to know who governs and how resources get allocated. This enterprise is purely empirical and descriptive.

The second question—"How Democratic is America?"—is a bit more complex since to answer this question we must first settle on a definition of democracy. We know that defining democracy, as Howard Zinn's and Sidney Hook's polemic reveals, is a passionate enterprise full of passionate *oughts* and *counter-oughts*. No "scientific" method can distill the *true* meaning of democracy. Nonetheless, without a body of persons applying their intellectual rigor to the normative enterprise of defining democracy, we would have neither the ability to know how democratic we can become, how democratic we have become, or even whether we should be democratic at all (as opposed to, say, theocratic or oligarchic).

An exhaustive study of politics requires the political philosopher's normativity and wisdom as well as political scientist's empiricism and facts. An *introductory* course in politics, however, is properly empirical and factual. A beginning student of politics requires facts before anything else; e.g., he should know the answer to such basic questions as "What is a legislature?" "What is a bureaucracy?" and "What are elections?" Until students master these fundamentals, political science ought to compel a measure of reticence. After all, before one opines, one ought to know *something.*

As a valedictory to this brief sketch on the role of theory in politics, I offer a final caveat: Good empirical science has a normative foundation, and good political philosophy is empirical. The question of "Who governs?" makes sense primarily in a democracy. Prior to our asking this question, we have—perhaps unconsciously—revealed a normative preference for democracy. We could just as well have chosen to study the shapes of clouds or snowflake patterns. By asking "Who governs?" we establish our empirical, scientific investigations on a normative basis, i.e., our *preference* for democracy. Similarly, if the theoretical musings of our political philosophers are to have any bearing on concrete human persons and their societies, such musings had best devote attention to real, concrete problems and have a solid appreciation of human nature. That is, political philosophy should be empirical.

In any event, a new student of politics must gain facts, and our method of doing so will follow the scientific method. We thus put aside *for now* the approach of Hobbes, Locke, Montesquieu, and Rousseau (much less Plato and Aquinas) and attempt to learn the theoretical approach of the empirical political scientist.[1]

★ A Scientific Approach to Political Analysis

How do we come to know about our world? At a basic level, individuals learn about reality through experience. Stories of interest-group activities may lead us to believe that some politicians are "captured" by the special interests. Or a personal encounter with a government agency (e.g., the Department of Motor Vehicles) may confirm a suspicion that the bureaucrats really rule the world. These experiences do contribute to personal knowledge, but do they support a clear picture of reality? Can we really be confident in our view of the political world if we base this knowledge on random media reporting and anecdotal evidence alone? It seems as though such knowledge is far too dependent on chance encounters and personal experience.

A scientific approach to political questions assumes that knowledge is possible by investigating patterns of behavior, regularities of action, and recurring responses in political behavior.[2] Scientists use theories and hypotheses to structure their studies of these patterns. In this context, a theory is an intellectual tool that provides us with a way to organize the complex reality that surrounds us in order to make sense of the world.[3] Every scientific theory has three purposes: 1) it serves as an aid to understanding a complex subject, 2) it serves as a tool for explaining past or current events, and 3) it serves as a tool for making predictions about future events. The political scientist uses theory in much the same way as the physical scientist; the objects under investigation are all that differ.

Scientific theory consists of a set of related statements that, in combination, offer testable propositions about reality. These statements must be testable in order to be of scientific value. Unchallengeable statements that attempt to explain everything really explain nothing. For example, the theory that individuals will always act in their own self-interest is useless if one is free to define "self-interest" in any way. Such an approach could explain Mother Theresa's actions by arguing that altruism is merely another personal goal. One must gather data to support or falsify a truly testable statement, and this is a critical feature of a scientific proposition about reality.

Scientists call these testable statements *hypotheses*. A hypothesis specifies the relationship among the phenomena being explained. It consists of a dependent variable and one or more independent variables, and it states how they are connected or related.[4] The dependent variable is the effect or result that we are trying to explain. For example, the scientist might be interested in voter turnout in America. Scientists choose to study independent variables that might logically influence the dependent variable. In the case of voting, we might wish to study how education level influences the level of participation. If we suspect that the two variables vary directly, the hypothesis in this case would take the form: "If education levels increase, then the percentage of persons who vote also increases." This is a testable statement, since we can gather data on voter education levels and compare this to the non-voting population to support or falsify the hypothesis. Note that the hypothesis employs an "If . . . then" structure. This technique of hypothesis construction ensures the inclusion of both independent and dependent variables. The independent variable(s) follow "If," while the dependent variable follows "then." Political scientists develop and refine these interconnected hypotheses into overarching theories to answer questions about the political world.

An important part of hypothesis testing is *operationalization*. This term refers to the conversion or redefinition of relatively abstract notions into concrete terms that will allow us to measure results. It involves moving from the conceptual level (thinking about a question) to the operational level (deciding how to study it).[5] The first step in operationalization is to create an operational hypothesis or proposition. Second, one must propose several research questions to guide the research effort.

A proposition contains more specifically defined variables, and it places the hypothesis into a specific context. In the above example, we question how education levels affect voting behavior. We begin to operationalize this question when we define the variables, "education level" and "voting." A common definition of education level relies on the amount of formal schooling one has undergone. One must also confine the study to a specific period of time and a specific region. In this case, the study might look at voting behavior during the 1996 election in New York. Armed with this definition, the social scientist is able to define consistently the independent variable for voting precincts in a specific sample area. We must also operationalize the dependent variable so we can be sure to measure properly its variation. In this case, the scientist might rely upon polling data that asks New Yorkers whether or not they voted in the 1996 federal elections. The operational hypothesis or "proposition" takes the form: "If citizen levels of formal schooling rise in New York, then polling data is likely to indicate greater participation in federal elections."

The real point of operationalization is to help the scientist determine what kind of evidence is useful to a particular study. This method involves creating research questions that one must answer in order to test the relationship specified in a proposition. The above proposition suggests several important questions to the researcher. How did levels of formal education vary in different New York voting precincts in 1996? What does polling data indicate about voter turnout given a certain level of education? Did more highly educated voters report greater participation? These questions guide the scientist in his research effort. In this case, the researcher should look for published reports on average education levels in a sample of voting districts. Specific polling data is important to gauging variance in the dependent variable. The researcher may also have to conduct interviews or administer surveys to find out how voter turnout varied in these districts. This step of offering precise definitions of the variables in each hypothesis and a series of specific research questions is absolutely critical to scientific inquiry.

Operationalization is a task that is full of potential pitfalls. Every definition of variables has implications for the validity of the research process. The definition of education used above neglects certain measures of "education" like unstructured reading or job experience. It also assumes that the "education" at any given grade level is constant and uniform throughout New York. Respondents who must self-report their own voting behavior might be inclined to lie in order to appear to be good citizens.[6] Voters in New York State may not be representative of voters nationwide. The problematic nature of operationalization tends to limit the number of valid conclusions to be drawn from any attempt at scientific inquiry. However, this effort is the only way to achieve any level of validity. Without explicit operationalization, a study becomes an ad-hoc and futile exercise with no application to the real world.

Political science is not unlike any science that attempts to model reality in a controlled and systematic fashion. A meteorologist finds uniformities in weather patterns to predict the probability of sunshine or to explain why we sometimes get snow in April. "When we do political science, we set out to discover uniformities in the political world."[7] Like the meteorologist, the political scientist is not always right. But, while a scientific approach is not the only way to understand reality, it is the most efficient and reliable method.

★ An Approach to the Question: "Who Governs?"

One of the most important uniformities that we can identify in the political world involves the use of power and suggests answers to the question "Who governs?" Answers to this question help us to understand why our society allocates values as it does. It goes beyond a description of who gets what to the more important question of who determines the distribution of benefits. This knowledge has implications for how we participate. If the political parties govern, then our choice of party label and our voting decisions become critical. If interest groups truly hold power, then we should pursue our policy goals by joining the appropriate faction. If power is concentrated in the private sector, then public elections may have no real impact on who governs. In this case, it makes little sense to vote. The answer to "Who governs?" has implications for how we evaluate the health of our democracy. Does our system allow for meaningful participation, and how well does it protect democratic values? Could our system be better? The answer to who governs will inform our normative evaluations of our government and politics.

When we explain who governs, we explain politics. Politics describes the process by which our society decides the "authoritative allocation of values." More simply, it is the process that determines, "who gets what, when, and how."[8] When media critics and politicians deride the fight over a particular piece of legislation as mere "politics," they do not do justice to the term. There is nothing more important to a political system than its politics, because this process determines who will win and who will lose in the fight for scarce resources and the associated allocation of values. We should not be misled into thinking that politics and values are separate spheres, or that we should not try to "legislate morality." Whenever government issues a policy decision, whether it is an increase in welfare expenditure, or a prohibition against the partial-birth abortion method, or the creation of a budget, some value or set of values are elevated at the expense of another set. In some cases, accommodation and cooperation may characterize the path to a particular policy result. At other times, interested groups may battle relentlessly with all means at their disposal to influence the outcome. But, whether contested or congenial, bipartisan or fiercely divided, the process that leads to policy is still politics.

Any theory of governance (i.e. politics) must include several hypotheses. Interesting variables that contribute to an understanding of the questions of "Who governs?" and "How democratic is America?" include:

1. *Key Actors,* defined as those individuals or groups who have the most influence in politics and policymaking.
2. *Power,* defined as the ability to influence the allocation of values.
3. *Participation,* defined as the level of citizen involvement in political decisions.
4. *Institutions,* defined as the public and/or private structures that facilitate the use of power.
5. *Policymaking,* defined as the authoritative decisions of government.

Each of these variables gives rise to interesting research questions. What factors (independent variables) contribute to a political actor's political power, and what is the resultant distribution of power? What kinds of individual activities allow for substantial citizen participation? What factors determine the role of institutions in society, and how do all of these activities affect policymaking? An understanding of these phenomena and the independent variables that affect them can give us a clearer picture of who governs and the state of democracy in America.

Various theories of American politics approach these dependent variables in different ways, and they emphasize different independent variables. Pluralism emphasizes the role of groups in policy formation, while elite theory focuses on institutional positions of concentrated power. State-centered theory emphasizes the role of governmental institutions and personalities. In each case, however, the basic analytic task is to specify and test hypotheses in the following way:[9]

1. Determine which observation or policy result one wishes to explain.
2. Offer some tentative hypotheses. In other words, specify how certain independent variables may affect important dependent variables.
3. Operationalize the hypotheses, and gather evidence relevant to testing the specified connection.
4. Analyze the hypotheses in light of the available evidence and draw conclusions about the validity of the relationship.

Evidence may support or refute the specified relationship. Do not "test" a hypothesis in order to support a preconceived notion about a relationship. For example, a study that refutes an expected relationship between education level and voting is just as valuable as one that supports such a relationship. Negative findings are important. These individual hypothesis tests also allow us to refine our theories about who governs. As we gain confidence in several related hypotheses, we tend to bolster the general theory that unifies them. Because a theory cannot model reality perfectly, we never *prove* our propositions. But, such theories do gain validity, and we can rely increasingly upon the connections that they specify.

A final evaluative step is to judge the result. Here we ask the question, "How democratic is America?" The answer to this question includes an evaluation of the process that characterizes who governs and the product of that governance. Political institutions that allow for fair and open citizen participation would typify the wide distribution of power normally associated with a democratic process. Policies that support the democratic values of freedom, social and economic equality, tolerance, and diversity might lead to confidence in the health of "democratic" outcomes in our society. Note that a democratic process does not necessarily lead to "democratic" outcomes. The democratic process in America once tolerated slavery, for example. Thus, we must judge the process and the product separately. This final evaluative step is crucial to a full understanding of who governs.

Endnotes

[1]For worthwhile treatments of the relationship between science and political philosophy, consult Leo Strauss's *Natural Right and History* and *What is Political Philosophy?* Additionally, Eric Voegelin's *The New Science of Politics* is instructive.

[2]Bruce Russett and Harvey Starr, "A Scientific Study of World Politics," in *Understanding International Relations, 2d edition,* eds. Daniel Kaufman, Joseph Collins, and Thomas Schneider (New York: McGraw Hill, 1994), 138.

[3]Russett and Starr, 139.

[4]Alan S. Zuckerman, *Doing Political Science* (Boulder, CO: Westview Press, 1991), 7.

[5]Jarol B. Manheim and Richard C. Rich, *Empirical Political Analysis* (White Plains, N.Y.: Longman Press, 1995), 9.

[6]Zuckerman, 9.

[7]Zuckerman, 1.

[8]Thomas A. Spragens, Jr., *Understanding Political Theory* (New York: St. Martin's Press, 1976), 2.

[9]Russett and Starr, 143.

★ ★ ★ ★ ★

Questions

1. What are the essential characteristics of and approaches to normative political theory?
2. What are the strengths and weaknesses of normative political theory?
3. What are the essential characteristics of and approaches to scientific political theory?
4. What are the strengths and weaknesses of scientific political theory?
5. Which type of political theory promises the greatest benefits to the future of society?

★ ★ ★

Pluralism: The Nature and Objectives of Political Science

**U.S. Military Academy,
Department of Social Sciences**

Prepared by the Department of Social Sciences of the U.S. Military Academy, this introduction to political science in general and pluralism in particular provides a perspective of the discipline which values both normative and behavioral schools. The article introduces students to the basic questions of political theory and then proceeds to examine the assumptions and characteristics of pluralism. The authors discuss the key actors, institutions, distribution of power, and policy-making procedures of American pluralism and then address pluralism's critics.

★ The Nature and Objectives of Political Science

The term "science" comes from the ancient Greek term episteme, or knowledge. In the past, that body of knowledge of which people were confident

★ ★ ★ ★ ★ ★

was science. With the great advances in physics and the other natural sciences, the term science came to describe that body of material that was capable of being "proved" through some variation of the scientific method. Consequently, use of the senses in experimentation, quantitative analysis, and some method of verifying results composed the study of modern science. With this development came the rise of the fact-value distinction, in which that knowledge susceptible to the scientific method was labeled as fact and the product of true science, whereas values, not capable of being "proved," came to be seen as the result of mere subjective thinking. Thus, if one asserts a truth such as, "Capital punishment is morally illicit (or licit)," one can always respond with, "That's what you think! Prove it!"

Now, American political science does have some persons who succumb to the fact-value distinction and believe that quantitative analysis alone constitutes good political science. In some cases, this attitude accompanies a belief that no progress is possible in the study of ethics (which ever since Aristotle has been a part of the study of politics). Nonetheless, there is in many quarters an appreciation for the fact that the study of politics requires rigorous analyses of both facts and values. The political philosopher Eric Voegelin once observed that Aristotle, in working through the many problems related to ethics and politics, set the foundation for the full range of subjects in political science. These problems have yet to lose their relevance. Political science includes the study of:

(a) ethics, the origins of ethical norms, and the standard bearers of ethical norms

(b) historical and political knowledge and how it changes over time, particularly as it relates to the self-understanding of a people

(c) the rise and fall of political regimes

(d) social tensions (rich vs. poor, immature vs. mature, etc.)

(e) the variety of political forms (or constitutions), lawmaking, and the limits of lawmaking

(f) community substance, or the "glue" that holds a politically organized people together

In the foregoing subjects you will notice that three of them appear especially suitable topics for modern scientific or descriptive study (history, rise and fall of political units, and constitutions and lawmaking). The remaining three lend themselves especially (but not solely) to analyses of values or norms (ethics, social tensions, and community substance). A responsible way to look at problems within political science is to do what Aristotle did: If he made recommendations about what we might today call values, he did so based on empirical knowledge; that is, he did not simply pull things out of thin air, but he thought hard about political problems and ensured that his suggestions had a firm basis in real-world phenomena.

It is this approach to political science that we take in this course. Our study in SS202 revolves around two central questions: "Who governs?" and "How democratic is America?" The first question requires that you become knowledgeable of a wide range of materials (the Constitution and its sources; the institutional and behavioral aspects of American politics, e.g., federalism and voting, respectively; and policymaking). But you will also be asked, based on the factual knowledge you gain from a scientific analysis of politics, to offer some craftsmanlike thoughts on a "value" question, i.e., "How democratic is America?" Thus, you will have to come up with a plausible understanding of democracy as well as assess the extent to which the facts of American politics meets your criteria for democracy. Here we touch upon issues inherent in the Zinn and Hook debate, which should serve as a starting point from which to begin your normative evaluation of the American political system.

★ A Thumbnail Sketch of Political Theory

America is a relatively young country. The Constitutional framers had the benefit of thousands of years of recorded political thought and experience upon which to base a new scheme of government. In this course, you have already read a few key excerpts from some of these foundational thinkers, including Hobbes, Locke, Montesquieu, and Rousseau. Other thinkers, such as Plato, St. Augustine, and David Hume influenced the framers as well. However, as one reads the Publius's account of the extend republic to mitigate factions in Federalist 10 and his account of the separation of powers to mitigate tyranny (or the accumulation of the three functions of government under one entity) in Federalist 51 (as you will in this course), the contributions of Locke and Montesquieu on American political thought are particularly evident. It is arguable that these two Federalist papers, and the embodiment of the papers' ideas in the U.S. Constitution are the two most significant pieces of American political thought in terms of their impact upon the resulting American political culture.

In the 1920s and 1930s, the first generation of American "political scientists" formulated what we will refer to as "elite theory." Academics such as Charles Merrian, Harold Laswell and the columnist Walter Lippman concluded that "[e]lites inevitably dominate the masses through the manipulation of symbols."[1] They also concluded that given the level of public ignorance, this elite domination was both good and proper. Elite theory will be covered in more depth later in the course.

Publius's Federalist 10 served as an inspiration for the *pluralist* theory, though Publius's account was not itself strictly pluralist. Building on the earlier work of John Dewey and Harold Laski, David Truman set the theory forth in his seminal work, *The Governmental Process* (1950). Pluralist theory, and later offshoots of this theory, dominated the study of American politics for the decades of the 1950s, 1960s, and 1970s. Claiming that American politics could be best described as a competition among interested (or "pressuring") groups for relatively scarce governmental policy benefits, Truman argued at best that America is governed by the people, through the groups in which they choose to participate. This theory held sway for the next few decades, and it shaped much of the resulting empirical and normative analysis that came after.

Viewing the American political universe in the late 1950s, E. E. Schattschneider and others—including William H. Riker and his students—grew to believe that Truman's pluralist theory of interest groups was only partially correct, if correct at all. Schattschneider set forth his view, in *The Semisovereign People* (1960), of an American political world in which political parties, dominated by the upper middle classes, were the most significant political actors and served as a coherent means of administering government in a system of shared and fragmented powers. Related to this concept is the idea that all government institutions (and quasi-governmental ones, like political parties) have a place in answering the question, "who governs in America?" It is this idea of "state-centered" analysis where the "State" is the key actor that we will discuss as our third theory later in this course.

★ *Pluralism*

Pluralism, just like each theoretical attempt to answer the question "Who governs?" provides a description of the process behind American politics. Pluralism is based upon group theory and maintains that the best way to understand American politics is through the analysis of group interaction. The unit of analysis is the group which is defined as a collection of individuals with some common values, purposes, and demands who join together to advance those purposes and demands. Pluralists are not interested in individual consciousness or the collective interests of society—at least not for purposes of analysis. Group theorists trace their theoretical origins back to James Madison in Federalist 10. However, unlike Madison, modern pluralists have a fundamentally positive view of group interaction in society.

Assumptions

Pluralist theorists make some basic assumptions that need to be clarified. First, they, like Publius, assume that people are rational, individualistic, and self-interested. Therefore, a situation of mutual animosities tends to exist in society. If so motivated, ordinary individuals, through group activity, can have a substantial impact on other groups in society and upon governmental decision-making.

Second, political resources include not only money and position, but also such assets as prestige, expertise, knowledge, organizational skills, large membership, intensity of activity, and media access. Any combination of these assets may provide an advantage to groups in competition. The distribution of these resources is constantly changing and, therefore, a relatively perfect competition between groups is possible. Groups are not equal; some groups may have more access than others to both particular resources and governmental institutions. As Robert Dahl points out in *Who Governs?*, control over decisions is unevenly distributed; neither individuals or groups are political equals.[2]

Elements

This course has two central questions: Who governs? and How democratic is America? To help answer these questions we will use five elements to help frame each of the theories. They are:

- Key Actors
- Role of the People (Participation)
- Power/Resources
- Role of Institutions, and
- Policymaking

In addition, we will examine and contrast each theory's definition of the foundations of American governance:

- Politics—Who governs? and
- Democracy—How democratic is America?

By applying this framework, we will gain a broad understanding of each of the theories. Armed with this understanding, we can develop hypotheses and test the utility of the theories in explaining politics in America. We will begin by discussing key political actors.

Who are the key political actors according to pluralism?

The key political actors according to pluralism are interest groups. These groups are formed by individuals who have common interests in an issue. They use the strength of their membership as well as consolidated resources of their members to attempt to influence government officials to support them. It is only through groups that individuals can have influence over policy.

What is the role of the people?

Pluralists assert that the role of individuals in politics is as members of groups. They contend that groups are the best and most effective way to allow for participation in a democratic society. There are many reasons why there are so many groups in the United States and why this form of participation is so effective.

- First, Americans have a "propensity to join" groups. We are a nation of "joiners."
- Second, the Constitution and its interpretation have produced few implicit and no explicit barriers to group membership and group formation.
- Third, people supplement the power of their vote by supporting groups that lobby and pressure government on their behalf. Similarly, an individual can express his/her interests in the political process by joining and supporting groups.
- Fourth, the complexity of modern society lends itself to the formation of many different types of groups. Thus, there is a "universality of groups" in every sector of society with competing and conflicting interests. This notion is similar to Madison's discussion of an "extended republic." Madison foresaw that the "mischief of factions" would be held in check through a representative system of government in a large republic. Allowing groups to multiply and flourish diverts their drive to undermine liberty into conflict with other groups.

What about the seeming apathy and ignorance of the American public about politics and political institutions? How do pluralists account for non-participation? Pluralists explain the dynamics of non-participation by citizens in the political system by stating that non-participation may reflect the health of the society and may not be a problem. Citizens might not be participating through the normal channels in the political system due to their satisfaction with the existing conditions of society. They have yet to be moved to join groups or participate in other ways to redress their grievances. Furthermore, full participation by all members of society on every issue of public policy might be deleterious to the political process. On occasion, groups may be able to resolve issues with each other, without resorting to the government. If the institutions of government considered all policy issues, and all the citizens of a polity participated in decision making on all issues, the political system could not sustain all that activity. As the quantity of participation increases, the quality of that participation may suffer. However, a pluralist would argue that it is important that no one deny individual citizens either the ability to mobilize into groups or the right of access into the policy process to achieve their goals.

What resources do groups leverage to exert pressure on public officials?

Pluralists understand political power to be the ability of one political actor to influence the behavior of another actor. In other words, political power is understood behaviorally as the ability of one group to win in the competition with other groups and to influence the other groups or political institutions to do as it wishes.

A couple of other factors should be noted concerning this definition of power. First, when one says that we understand power "behaviorally," that means that we can observe the wielding of political power. We can see someone or some group exercising political power when they influence others to do as they wish. Second, this notion of political power is not based upon any one particular resource. Groups can generate political power from a number of different resources including effective strategy, organizational skills, and pressure upon government. Poor groups are therefore able to generate political power by compensating for their lack of financial resources by effective group mobilization, strategy, leadership, organization, and the application of other non-monetary resources.

What is the role of institutions?

The role of political institutions, such as Congress and the presidency is to provide access for groups and serve as a neutral arena for carrying out the competition between groups. Governmental institutions do not "rule" a polity as much as they represent the various views that exist within the polity. Governmental institutions should also protect the right of groups to organize. The cornerstones of our institutional framework, the separation of powers and federalism, guarantee that groups will find adequate access to government at many different points. After the competition between groups is completed, the institutions of government act as ratifying agents by passing legislation and making executive decisions that codify the agreements and compromises reached between the groups. The important point to note here is that in the pluralist model, political institutions have little independent role in governing other than representing various views that exist in society and acting as the referee in the competition between groups.

How is policy made?

According to pluralism, policy making is a function of the competition, conflict, and compromise between groups. Since the distribution of resources is fairly fluid, no one group can dominate the entire political spectrum or process. One group may "win" on one particular issue, but lose on the next. As V. O. Key notes in his discussion of political power, political elites do not control enough resources to dominate the political process. Pluralists see government as being a network of activities rather than merely being a set of formal institutions.

A political system that operates in this manner tends toward equilibrium as bargaining replaces conflict and violence. The compromises that result from this process ensure moderate policy and political stability. *The first mechanism is overlapping membership.* If a person is a member of two groups that are in conflict over an issue, she will likely advocate a middle-of-the-road compromise solution to avoid alienating fellow members of both groups. For example, the business owner whose store is in competition over spaces in his town's new parking lot with his local church will likely pursue a moderate solution to avoid alienating potential customers. According to pluralists, since Americans tend to join many groups, there is a great likelihood that this mechanism often comes into play in the political process.

The second equilibrating mechanism is acceptance of an underlying political consensus or "rules of the game." Pluralists contend that stability in American politics is facilitated by the presence of this consensus that is derived from our political culture. This consensus is generally held by almost everyone, but especially by governmental and interest group leaders. These "rules" are settled precepts of the political system that are never at issue "in principle" in any political conflict. These "rules" insure that groups conduct political debate within certain boundaries and include: (1) the prevailing political culture; (2) the rule of law; (3) the Bill of Rights; (4) the provision of effective means for political participation through groups; and (5) the provision of equal access to governmental institutions. In other words, pluralists see the government, to include the court system, as the legitimate arena for resolving disputes. The acceptance of this consensus allows for political debate and long term change and helps to insure long term stability.

The third equilibrating mechanism is potential groups. Pluralists contend that even the interests of unorganized groups are protected in this political system because of their latent potential to mobilize. Governmental decision makers, as well as interest group leaders, will not advocate solutions that radically violate the interests of unorganized groups for fear that those groups will mobilize and become significant actors in the process.

How does pluralism describe politics?

Politics according to pluralism is the competition between groups for access to government and influence over policy and the policy benefits that government can provide. Again, to understand politics, it is first necessary to understand the interaction of groups. The actions of and interactions between governmental institutions or elected officials are of secondary importance.

What then does pluralism say about democracy in America?

According to the pluralist theory, democracy is an unfettered market allowing each group to seek comparative advantage in competing for political power. In other words, similar to the theory of capitalism in the study of economics, democracy is a political free market. Democracy is found in the process of competition between groups and it is the process itself that is fundamental to democracy. The rules that govern the competition are most important. Pluralists feel that democracy is served as long as free competition is allowed even if the outcome of that competition seems somewhat inequitable.

Why is this system preferable to other forms of government?

Pluralists contend that if a political system works these ways it has many advantageous qualities. This system provides access for the average citizen as he can participate in politics through groups with little investment of scarce resources, such as money and time. This system also contributes to democracy as it accommodates the preferences of those who are most intensely concerned as opposed to a simple majority. This is so because those citizens who are the most concerned about a particular issue are the ones who bother to mobilize into groups and it is they who should have a say in the outcome of political matters.

Some pluralists argue that it is through group activity that individuals may acquire interest in the larger political system. Without feeling the sense of belonging, individuals may feel isolated and alienated from the larger society. Involvement in group activity may increase one's sense of political efficacy and provide the link between the individual and the rest of society.

Most importantly, this group system promotes outcomes that approximate the public interest through a "self-corrective" mechanism resulting in an "automatic society." In other words, the interactions and compromise of competing groups will automatically result in policies that are in the general public interest insofar as such an interest exists. Finally, pluralists contend that this type of political participation limits the coercive power of government. The existence of many competing groups in the extended republic insures that these groups will take advantage of the many points of access to government presented by the separation of powers and federalism. As they take advantage of these various points of access, the ability of government to violate the rights of its citizens is reduced.

The Criticism of Pluralism

As we have noted, pluralism is only one of several theories of politics and merely the first of three we will review in SS202. The pluralist model has its critics. While outlining the development of pluralism as a theory, G. David Garson, in "American Political Science and the Interest Group Concept of Politics," from *Power and Politics in the United States,* also examines some of the flaws of this perspective. He posits the following questions for consideration:

1. Is the pluralist definition of power complete?

2. Is participation in groups and the mobilization of groups as easy as the pluralists assume?
3. Are the reasons pluralists give for non-participation compelling? What other reasons might exist for non-participation in the political system?
4. Are political resources evenly divided throughout society? Is the distribution of those resources constantly changing?
5. Do all groups have equal access to government?
6. Is government truly a passive referee in the conflict between groups?
7. Does the pluralist model render government illegitimate as a source of power and control in government?

Consider these questions as we discuss Elite Theory in the next lesson.

Endnotes

[1]John G. Gunnell, *The Descent of Political Theory* (Chicago, University of Chicago, 1993), 124.

[2]Robert A. Dahl. *Who Governs?* (New Haven, CT: Yale University Press, 1961), 145.

★ ★ ★ ★ ★

Questions

1. To what extent does pluralism ensure democracy?

2. The world pluralism implies that many people participate in government. To what extent do elites actually dominate American politics?

3. What groups of Americans have taken the greatest advantage of the opportunities pluralism presents?

4. To what extent is it necessary to join a group to be effective in American politics?

5. To what extent did the Founding Fathers anticipate a pluralist society?

★ ★ ★

Elite Theory

**Department of Social Sciences,
U.S. Military Academy**

While pluralism asserts that the many interest groups in society participate in making public policy, thereby ensuring that a large proportion of the population is represented in the process, elite theorists claim that in reality a relatively few rich and influential people actually make most of the decisions. This article introduces students to the basic propositions of elite theory, especially as explained by political scientists Thomas Dye and Harmon Ziegler, and then examines the theory's assumptions and characteristics. The article's authors focus on the dynamics of elitism and the tension between elitism and democracy.

Elite theorists contend that the mass of American society plays virtually no substantive role in either the decision-making process or governing. The means to participate are limited, if not meaningless. Dye and Ziegler put an interesting twist on this argument by claiming that this is a desirable phenomenon (see Christopher Lasch's *The Revolt of the Elites and the Betrayal of Democracy* for a dissenting view). They claim that the average American has little political awareness. Moreover, the great mass of Americans has little commitment to the values that make democracy possible. The true irony of democracy is that democracy survives in the face of a large, undemocratic—yet apathetic and uninvolved—mob.

★ The Assumptions of Elite Theory

Elite theorists make some basic assumptions about human nature that need to be clarified. In almost Hobbesian proportions, elite theorists believe that

★ ★ ★ ★ ★ ★

while citizens might be individualistic, rational, self-centered maximizers of utility, they are for the most part incapable of governing. The state of nature for the vast majority of us is the state of war; life for the masses is indeed nasty, brutish, and short.

Unlike pluralism, where the focus is on the tendency of people to form groups, elite theorists assume that Man has the tendency to form hierarchical relationships in society. By definition, elites (sovereigns) are needed to impose order on the anarchy of the masses. In something of a twist, however, this system is the best for all concerned. Indeed, democracy would be impossible without it.

The first chapter in Dye and Zeigler (D&Z) is intended to introduce this new theoretical perspective with which we can examine American politics. D&Z offer us an explanation that is different from our discussion of pluralism as a theory. Often, both of these theories (and "state-centered" theory as well) describe the same features in American government but emphasize different factors or give different explanations of those features. Similar to our discussion last time, we will frame our discussion of elite theory in terms of the five political elements and the theory's definition of politics and democracy. We will look at how elite theorists answer the following basic questions:

- Who are the key actors?
- What is political power and where does it reside in our society?
- How do individuals participate in a democracy?
- What are the roles of institutions?
- How does policy-making take place and what does this process tell us about who governs?

In addition, we will determine how elite theorists describe politics and how this theory explains the democratic process and product of American politics.

Who are the Key Actors?

Elites are those people in leadership positions of various governmental and nongovernmental institutions. The elite classes come from the upper socioeconomic strata of American society. They are primarily white, male, Anglo-Saxon, Protestant citizens of established families. They are highly educated at prestigious private universities. Perhaps a good mnemonic is to think of elites as the top *5%* of commerce, government, finance, the legal profession, academia, etc. They move easily from public to private institutions, thus giving rise to "the revolving door" principle. Under this idea, the leadership of the nation's institutions move from position to position; however, they maintain their authority as they move.

D&Z openly admit that the existence of elite and mass does not exclude movement between the divisions. In fact, in their model, upward mobility is not only possible, it is a necessary (but perhaps not sufficient) condition for stability. The possibility of improving one's lot tends to pacify both elite and mass, thereby allowing the system to perpetuate itself, even flourish.

The Elite Consensus

D&Z use the term consensus to describe a core of values and beliefs that all elites hold to be prerequisites for our system of government. These values spring very much from the concepts of natural law as espoused by such political thinkers as John Locke and Montesquieu. Private property, individual liberty, and limited government are the basis of the elite consensus that exists in the United States. This core of beliefs allows the system to perpetuate even given the movement of individuals through "the revolving door." All elites are on "the same sheet of music" if you will, and that fact alone allows the system to survive, if not succeed. D&Z note that this elite consensus is not the product of some conspiracy.

Elites are more committed to democratic values than are the masses; however, that fact does not eliminate elite threats to democracy. Elite threats arise during periods of crisis, when fear of mass activism leads to elite repression. Elite threats to democracy are always present. They are nonetheless more likely under conditions of crisis.

Elite-model Political Participation

Participation is an interesting concept in D&Z. Much of their argument is a critique of the pluralist view. According to elite theory, elections are merely a symbolic exercise and a tool to indoctrinate the masses into thinking they have an impact in the political system. They are an effort by elites to maintain control. Political parties fail to provide any meaningful choices in elections. Candidates stand on image and not substance. In D&Z, the masses are easily fooled by media campaigns with little substance. There is always a danger that counter-elites will mobilize the masses in protest movements. However, over time most movements are integrated into the prevailing culture and become increasingly conservative and hierarchical, relying on elite leadership for success.

D&Z recognize the existence and importance of interest groups but they assert that groups themselves are hierarchical and merely represent the interests of both the institutional elites and the elite leadership and core activities of a particular interest group. The leadership of these groups tend to come from other established governmental and non-governmental institutions in this country. The rank and file membership's interests are seldom sought out much less met by the leadership of any given organized interest.

Elite Political Power

Political power under the elite view is the purview of the rich and famous. Power is a function of institutional position, be it either in governmental or non-governmental institutions. It is the ability to maintain control over the functions of society.

The power resulting from the control of resources and functions of society manifests itself in two ways. The first manifestation is that elites have the power to make decisions that affect the rest of society. This concept hopefully requires no further elaboration. The second—and I feel much more interesting manifestation—is the power of non-decisions. By this term, D&Z imply an agenda-setting power that elites possess that effectively stifles political discourse. Elites possess the power to keep potentially threatening issues from entering the public arena. D&Z imply that this agenda-setting power is central to perpetuating elite rule, because it ensures that divisive issues—those truly relevant to the "masses" and which might threaten elite power—will never come to the fore.

Elite-model Political Institutions

Closely tied to D&Z's discussion of power is their discussion of political institutions. D&Z claim that power in America is organized into the major societal institutions. Unlike the other two theories we have studied, their definition of institution includes both *private* and *public* structures. These structures are the repositories of power within society. Implicitly, then, institutions become instruments of control. They must be structured so as to lend stability to the political system. Institutions are critical to maintaining elite control of society. It is important to understand however that the more a particular political institution tries to represent the masses, the more undemocratic its efforts are. Political elites must conform to the elite consensus or be ostracized (e.g. Pat Buchanan). Political institutions reflect elite consensus. Political debate is not an ideological or partisan affair but as a part of the slow shift the elite consensus.

Public Policymaking

On the whole, elites, in an on-going effort to maintain control, have established cumbersome controls over the policy making process to avoid radical changes to the status quo. Seemingly large changes in public policy take time to effect as it takes time to change the elite consensus. Most public policy making is incremental in nature.

Policy making over time has shifted from Congress, the president, and the courts to the bureaucracy as society has grown larger and more complex. Bureaucracy has increasingly undertaken a larger role in rule making and regulatory policy as well as adjudicating violators of their regulations. Most policy making is a function of so-called "iron triangles": alliances of special interests, executive agencies or departments, and congressional committees.

The Nature of Elite Politics

If we believe the underlying assumptions surrounding elite theory, then politics (and policymaking for that matter) is nothing more than the give and take between elites who essentially agree on the fundamental values of society. Politics exists within the narrow sphere of disagreement that exists within the elite universe. Like pluralism, politics is competition; however, elite theorists contend that the field of competition is narrow.

Democracy, "Elite-style"

Much of D&Z attempts to discredit pluralism. The authors constantly compare their understanding of pluralism with classical democracy. D&Z's main effort is to undermine pluralism by pointing where pluralism fails to conform with classical democracy.

Interestingly enough, D&Z does not specifically argue what democracy within the elite universe is. By default, we must assume that it isn't. Perhaps more accurately, democracy within the larger society is at most symbolic. D&Z do not disqualify those phenomena we traditionally associate with democracy: political participation, representation, voting, et al. Within the elitist heaven, though, these activities serve a symbolic function by allowing the people to "choose" between two more or less identical agendas.

People who subscribe to the accuracy of pluralism would view democracy as a process ("an unfettered market allowing each group to seek comparative advantage in competing for political power"). Elite theorists, however, would say that elites view democracy as a product. In other words, elites feel that democracy is not dependent on who made the decisions, but instead on how the decisions affect the people. Elites seek to preserve for the masses: individual dignity, limited government, equality of opportunity, private property, freedom of speech and press, religious tolerance, and due process of law. In this way, an undemocratic process results in a "democratic" product.

★ ★ ★ ★ ★

Questions

1. To what extent does elitism preclude democracy?
2. Given the fact that America hosts more than 80,000 separate governmental units, to what extent do elites actually dominate American politics?
3. Are America's elites still primarily white-male-Anglo-Saxon-Protestants?
4. To what extent is it necessary to join the right group to be effective in American politics?
5. To what extent did the Founding Fathers intentionally create an elitist society?

★ ★ ★

The Irony of Democracy

Thomas R. Dye and Harmon Zeigler

Abraham Lincoln may have been a great man, but he was certainly wrong: America has never and will never enjoy a government of, by, or for the people. This is the indictment of American democracy set forth by political scientists Thomas Dye and Harmon Ziegler in this excerpt from their introductory text. "Elites—not masses—govern the United States." The irony of democracy is precisely this: "elites must govern wisely if 'government by the people' is to survive." For Dye and Ziegler, elitism is not a theory or a goal but simply a fact of life. If democracy demands that most people must participate in governing, all hope for democracy is lost. If it means, however, that the interests of the people somehow find voice in the actions of elites, hope for democracy remains.

Government is always government by the few, whether in the name of the few, the one, or the many.

Harold Lasswell

Elites—not masses—govern the United States. Life in a democracy, as in all societies, is shaped by a handful of people. Major political, economic, and social decisions are made by tiny minorities, not the masses of people.

Elites are the few who have power; the *masses* are the many who do not. Power is deciding who gets what, when, and how; it is participation in the decisions that shape our lives; the masses are the many whom lives are shaped by institutions, events, and leaders over which they have little direct control.

★ ★ ★ ★ ★ ★

"The Irony of Democracy," by Thomas R. Dye and Harmon Zeigler, reprinted from *The Irony of Democracy: An Uncommon Introducation to American Politics,* Thompson Learning, 2000.

Political scientist Harold Lasswell writes, "The division of society into elite and mass is universal," and even in a democracy "a few exercise a relatively great weight of power, and the many exercise comparatively little."[1]

Democracy is government "by the people," but the survival of democracy rests on the shoulders of elites. This is the irony of democracy: elites must govern wisely if government "by the people" is to survive. The masses do not lead; they follow. They respond to the attitudes, proposals, and behavior of elites.

This book, *The Irony of Democracy,* explains American political life using elite theory. It presents the evidence of U.S. political history and contemporary political science to describe and explain how elites function in a modern democratic society. But before we examine American politics we must understand more about *elitism, democracy,* and *pluralism.*

★ *The Meaning of Elitism*

The central idea of elitism is that all societies are divided into two classes: the few who govern and the many who are governed. The Italian political scientist Gaetano Mosca expressed this basic concept as follows:

> In all societies—from societies that are very underdeveloped and have largely attained the dawnings of civilization, down to the most advanced and powerful societies—two classes of people appear—a class that rules and a class that is ruled. The first class, always the less numerous, performs all of the political functions, monopolizes power, and enjoys the advantages that power brings, whereas the second, the more numerous class, is directed and controlled by the first, in a manner that is now more or less legal, now more or less arbitrary and violent.[2]

Elites, not masses, govern *all* societies. Elites are not a product of capitalism or socialism or industrialization or technological development. All societies—socialist and capitalist, agricultural and industrial, traditional and advanced—are governed by elites. All societies require leaders, and leaders acquire a stake in preserving the organization and their position in it. This motive gives leaders a perspective different from that of the organization's members. An elite, then, is inevitable in any social organization. As French political scientist Roberto Michels put it nearly a century ago, "He who says organization, says oligarchy."[3] The same is true for societies as a whole. According to the distinguished American political scientist Harold Lasswell, "The discovery that in all large-scale societies the decisions at any given time are typically in the hands of a small number of people" confirms a basic fact:

"Government is always government by the few, whether in the name of the few, the one, or the many."[4]

Elitism also asserts that the few who govern are not typical of the masses who are governed. Elites control resources: power, wealth, education, prestige, status, skills of leadership, information, knowledge of political processes, ability to communicate, and organization. Elites in the United States are drawn disproportionately from wealthy, educated, prestigiously employed, socially prominent, white, Anglo-Saxon, and Protestant groups in society. They come from society's upper classes; those who own or control a disproportionate share of the societal institutions: industry, commerce, finance, education, the military, communications, civic organizations, and law.

Elitism, however, does not necessarily bar individuals of the lower classes from rising to the top. In fact, a certain amount of "circulation of elites" (upward mobility) is essential for the stability of the elite system. Openness in the system siphons off potentially revolutionary leadership from the lower classes; moreover, an elite system is strengthened when talented and ambitious individuals from the masses enter governing circles. However, social stability requires that movement from non-elite to elite positions be a slow, continuous assimilation rather than a rapid or revolutionary change. Only those non-elites who have demonstrated their commitment to the elite system itself and to the system's political and economic values can be admitted to the ruling class.

Elites share a general consensus about the fundamental norms of the social system. They agree on the basic rules of the game, as well as on the importance of preserving the social system. The stability of the system, and even its survival, depends on this consensus. Political scientist David Truman writes, "Being more influential, they [the elites] are privileged; and being privileged, they have, with very few exceptions, a special stake in the continuation of the system in which their privileges rest."[5] However, elite consensus does not prevent elite members from disagreeing or competing with each other for preeminence. But this competition takes place within a very narrow range of issues; elites agree on more matters than they disagree on. Disagreement usually occurs over *means* rather than *ends*.

In the United States, the bases of elite consensus are the sanctity of private property, limited government, and individual liberty. Political historian Richard *Hofstadter* writes about American elite struggles:

> The fierceness of political struggles has often been misleading; for the range of vision embodied by the primary contestants in the major parties has always been bounded by the horizons of property and enterprise. However much at odds on specific issues, the major political traditions have shared a belief in the rights of property, the

> philosophy of economic individualism, the value of competition; they have accepted the economic virtues of capitalist culture as necessary qualities of man.[6]

Elitism implies that public policy does not reflect demands of "the people" so much as it reflects the interests and values of elites. Changes and innovations in public policy come about when elites redefine their own values. However, the general conservatism of elites—that is, their interest in preserving the system—means that changes in public policy will be *incremental* rather than revolutionary. Public policies are often modified but seldom replaced.

Elites may act out of narrow self-serving interests or enlightened, "public-regarding" motives. Occasionally elites abuse their powers and position and undermine mass confidence in their leadership. At other times, elites initiate reforms designed to preserve the system and restore mass support. Elitism does not necessarily mean that the masses are exploited or repressed, although these abuses are not uncommon. Elitism means only that the responsibility for mass welfare rests with elites, not with masses.

Finally, elitism assumes that the masses are largely passive, apathetic, and ill informed. Mass sentiments are manipulated by elites more often than elite values are influenced by the sentiments of the masses. Most communication between elites and masses flows downward. Masses seldom make decisions about governmental policies through elections or through evalution of political parties' policy alternatives. For the most part, these "democratic" institutions—elections and parties—have only symbolic value: they help tie the masses to the political system by giving them a role to play on election day. Elitism contends that the masses have at best only an indirect influence over the decision-making behavior of elites.

In brief, elite theory may be summarized as follows:

- Society is divided into the few who have power and the many who do not.
- The few who govern are not typical of the masses who are governed. Elites are drawn disproportionately from the upper socioeconomic strata of society.
- The movement of nonelites to elite positions must be slow and continuous to maintain stability and avoid revolution. Only nonelites who have accepted the basic elite consensus enter governing circles.
- Elites share a consensus on the basic values of the social system and the preservation of the system. They disagree only on a narrow range of issues.

- Elites may act out of narrow self-serving motives and risk undermining mass support, or they may initiate reforms, curb abuse, and undertake public-regarding programs to preserve the system and their place in it.
- Active elites are subject to relatively little direct influence from the apathetic masses. Elites influence masses more than masses influence elites.

★ The Meaning of Democracy

Ideally, *democracy* means individual participation in the decisions that affect one's life. Traditional democratic theory has valued popular participation as an opportunity for individual self-development: responsibility for governing one's own conduct develops one's character, self-reliance, intelligence, and moral judgment—in short, one's dignity. The classic democrat would reject even a benevolent despot who could govern in the interest of the masses. As the English political philosopher J. S. Mill asked, "What development can either their thinking or active faculties attain under it?" Thus the argument for citizen participation in public affairs depends not on its policy outcomes but on the belief that such involvement is essential to the full development of human capacities. Mill argued that people can know truth only by discovering it for themselves.[7]

Procedurally, in the democratic model, a society achieves popular participation through majority rule and respect for the rights of minorities. Self-development presumes self-government, and self-government comes about only by encouraging each individual to contribute to the development of public policy and by resolving conflicts over public policy through majority rule. Minorities who have had the opportunity to influence policy but whose views have not won majority support accept the decisions of majorities. In return, majorities permit minorities to attempt openly to win majority support for their views. Freedom of speech and press, freedom to dissent, and freedom to form opposition parties and organizations are essential to ensure meaningful individual participation. This freedom of expression is also critical in ascertaining the majority's real views.

The underlying value of democracy is individual dignity. Human beings, by virtue of their existence, are entitled to life, liberty, and property. A "natural law," or moral tenet, guarantees every person liberty and the right to property, and this natural law is morally superior to human law. John Locke, the English political philosopher whose writings most influenced America's founding elites, argued that even in a "state of nature"—that is, a world of no governments—an individual possesses inalienable rights to life, liberty, and property. Locke meant that these rights are independent of government; governments do not give them to individuals, and no government may legitimately take them away.[8]

Locke believed that a government's purpose is to protect individual liberty. People form a "social contract" with one another to establish a government to help protect their rights; they tacitly agree to accept government authority to protect life, liberty, and property. Implicit in the social contract and the democratic notion of freedom is the belief that governmental authority and social control over the individual must be minimal. This belief calls for removing as many external restrictions, controls, and regulations on the individual as possible without violating the freedom of other citizens.

Another vital aspect of classical democracy is a belief in the equality of all people. The Declaration of Independence states that "all men are created equal." Even the Founding Fathers believed in equality for all persons *before the law,* regardless of their personal circumstances. A democratic society cannot judge a person by social position, economic class, creed, or race. Many early democrats also believed in *political equality:* equal opportunity of individuals to influence public policy. Political equality is expressed in the concept of "one person, one vote."

Over time, the notion of equality has also come to include *equality of opportunity* in all aspects of American life: social, educational, and economic, as well as political. Each person should have an equal opportunity to develop his or her capacities to the fullest potential. There should be no artificial barriers to success in life. All persons should have the opportunity to make of themselves what they can, to develop their talents and abilities to their fullest, and to be rewarded for their skills, knowledge, initiative, and hard work. However, the traditional democratic creed has always stressed *equality of opportunity,* not *absolute equality*. Thomas Jefferson recognized a "natural aristocracy" of talent, ambition, and industry, and liberal democrats since Jefferson have always accepted inequalities that arise from individual merit and hard work. Absolute equality, or "leveling," is not part of liberal democratic theory.

In summary, democratic thinking reflects the following ideas:

- Popular participation in the decisions that shape the lives of individuals in a society.
- Government by majority rule, with recognition of the rights of minorities to try to become majorities. These rights include the freedom of speech, press, assembly, and petition and the freedom to dissent, to form opposition parties, and to run for public office.
- A commitment to individual dignity and the preservation of the liberal values of life, liberty, and property.

- A commitment to equal opportunity for all individuals to develop their capacities.

★ Elitism in a Democracy

Democracy requires popular participation in government. (The Greek root, of the word *democracy* means "rule by the many.") But popular participation in government can have different meanings. To our nation's Founders, who were quite ambivalent about the wisdom of democracy, it meant that the people would be given representation in government. The Founders believed that government rests ultimately on the *consent* of the governed. But their notion of republicanism envisioned decision making by *representatives* of the people, rather than direct decision making by the people themselves. The Founders were profoundly skeptical of direct democracy, in which the people initiate and decide policy questions by popular vote. They had read about direct democracy in the ancient Greek city-state of Athens, and they were fearful of the "follies" of democracy—James Madison wrote,

> Such democracies have ever been spectacles of turbulence and contention; have ever been found incompatible with personal security of the Rights of property and have in general been as short in their lives as they have been violent in their deaths.[9]

The Fear of Direct Democracy

The Founders were most fearful that unrestrained majorities would threaten liberty and property and abuse minorities and individuals, "the weaker party and the obnoxious individual." They recognized the potential contradiction in democratic theory—government by majority rule can threaten the life, liberty, and property of minorities and individuals.

Thus, *the U.S. Constitution has no provision for national referenda.* It was not until 100 years after the Constitution was written that political support developed in some states for more direct involvement of citizens in policy making. The beginning of the twentieth century, populists in the farm states of the Midwest and the mining states of the West introduced the initiative and referendum.

Today only voters in the states can express their frustrations with elite governance directly. The initiative is a device whereby a specific number or percent of voters, through the use of a petition, may have a proposed state constitutional amendment or a state law placed on the ballot for adoption or rejection by the electorate of a state. This process bypasses the legislature and allows citizens to propose both laws and constitutional amendments. The referendum is a device by which the electorate must approve decisions of the legislature before them become law or become part of the state constitution, or approve of proposals placed on the ballot by popular initiative.[10]

The Impracticality of Direct Democracy

Yet even if it were desirable, mass government is not really feasible in a large society. Lincoln's rhetorical flourish—"a government of the people, by the people, for the people"—has no real-world meaning. What would "the people" look like if all of the American people were brought together in one place?

> Standing shoulder to shoulder in military formation, they would occupy an area of about sixty-six square miles.
>
> The logistical problem of bringing 250 million bodies together is trivial, however, compared with the task of bringing about a meeting of 250 million minds. Merely to shake hands with that many people would take a century. How much discussion would it take to form a common opinion? A single round of five-minute speeches would require five thousand years. If only one percent of those present spoke, the assembly would be forced to listen to over two million speeches. People could be born, grow old and die while they waited for the assembly to make one decision.
>
> In other words, an all-American town meeting would be the largest, longest, and most boring and frustrating meeting imaginable. What could such a meeting produce? Total paralysis. What could it do? Nothing.[11]

Representative Democracy and the Inevitability of Elites

The solution to the practical problem of popular government is the development of institutions of representation—elections, parties, organized interest groups—as bridges between individuals and their government. *But this solution leads inevitably to elitism, not democracy.*

Individuals in all societies, including democracies, confront the iron law of oligarchy. As organizations and institutions develop in society, power is concentrated in the hands of the leadership. Society becomes "a minority of directors and a majority of directed." Individuals are no match for the power of large institutions.

Power is the ability to influence people and events by granting or withholding valuable resources. To exercise power, one must control valuable resources. Resources are defined broadly to include not only wealth, but also position, status, celebrity, comfort, safety, and power itself. Most of the nation's resources are concentrated in large organizations and institutions—in corporations, banks, and financial institutions; in television networks, newspapers, and publishing empires; in organized interest groups, lobbies, and law firms; in foundations and think tanks; in civic and cultural organizations; and, most important, in government. The government is the most powerful of all these organizations, not only because it has accumulated great economic resources, but because it has a monopoly on physical coercion. Only government can legitimately imprison and execute people.

Elite Competition as the Basis of Democracy

In a democratic society, unlike a totalitarian one, multiple elites exist. A defining characteristic of Western democratic nations is the relative autonomy of various elites—governmental, economic, media, civic, cultural, and so on.[12] In contrast, a defining characteristic of totalitarian societies is the forced imposition of unity on elites. Fascism asserted the unity of the state in Hitler's words: "Ein volk, Ein Reich, Ein Fuhrer" (one people, one state, one leader). Socialism asserts the government's control of economic as well as political resources, and communism extols "the dictatorship of the proletariat" and assigns the Communist party the exclusive right to speak for the proletariat.

But in Western democracies, elites have *multiple institutional bases* of power. Not all power is lodged in government, nor is all power derived from wealth. Democracies legitimize the existence of opposition parties as well as of organized interest groups. The power and independence of a media elite is a distinctive feature of U.S. democracy. Even within U.S. government, relatively autonomous multiple elites have emerged—in the Congress; in the judiciary; in the executive; and even within the executive, in a variety of bureaucratic domains. But it is really the power and autonomy of nongovernmental elites, and their recognized legitimacy, that distinguishes the elite structures of democratic nations from those of totalitarian states.

Mass support for American government

Can you trust government to do what is right?

"How much of the time do you think you can trust the government in Washington to do what is right? Always? Most of the time? None of the time?" Percentage of respondents saying government can be trusted "always" or "most of the time."

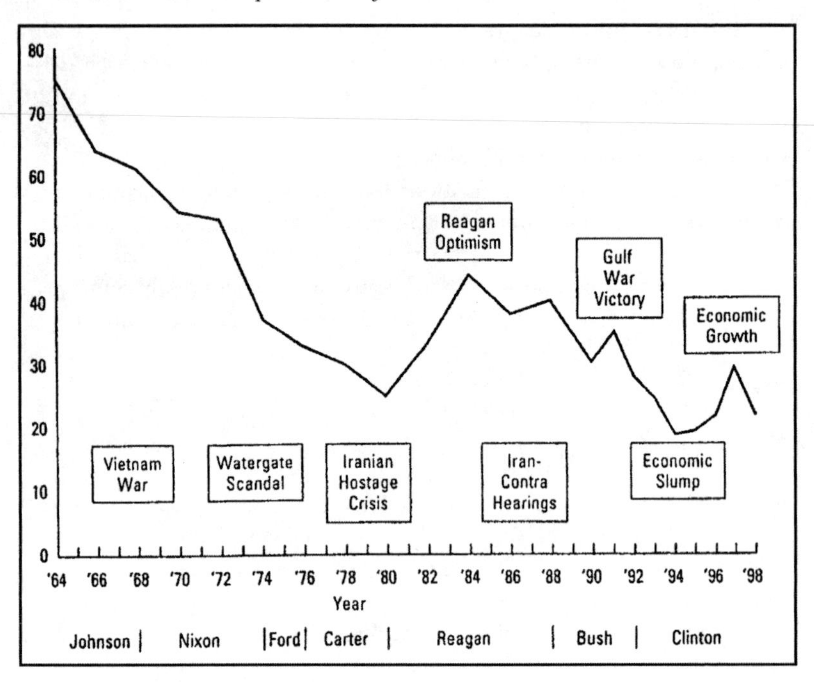

Source: Prepared by the authors from National Election Surveys, University of Michigan, data. 1994 figure from *Time*/CNN poll reported in *Time* (September 26, 1994): 49.

★ The Meaning of Pluralism

No scholar or commentator, however optimistic about life in the United States, would assert that the U.S. political system has fully realized all the goals of democracy. No one contends that citizens participate in all decisions shaping their lives or that majority preferences always prevail. Nor does anyone argue that the system always protects the rights of minorities, always preserves the values of life, liberty, and property, or provides every American with an equal opportunity to influence public policy.

However, *pluralism* seeks to affirm that American society is nevertheless democratic by asserting that:

- Society is divided into numerous groups, all of which make demands upon government and none of which dominates decision making.
- Although citizens do not directly participate in decision making, their many leaders make decisions through a process of bargaining, accommodation, and compromise.
- Competition among leadership groups helps protect individuals' interests. Countervailing centers of power—for example, competition among business leaders, labor leaders, and government leaders—can check one another and keep each interest from abusing its power and oppressing the individual.
- Although individuals do not participate directly in decision making, they can exert influence through participating in organized groups, as well as parties and elections.
- Leadership groups are open; new groups can form and gain access to the political system.
- Although political influence in society is unequally distributed, power is widely dispersed. Access to decision making is often determined by how much interest people have in a particular decision. Because leadership is fluid and mobile, power depends on one's interest in public affairs, skills in leadership, information about issues, knowledge of democratic processes, and skill in organization and public relations.
- Multiple leadership groups operate within society. Those who exercise power in one kind of decision do not necessarily exercise power in others. No single elite dominates decision making in all issues.
- Public policy does not necessarily reflect majority preference but is an equilibrium of interest interaction—that is, competing interest group influences are more or less balanced, and the resulting policy is therefore a reasonable approximation of society's preferences.

Pluralism, then, is the belief that democratic values can be preserved in a system where multiple, competing elites determine public policy through bargaining and compromise, voters exercise meaningful choices in elections, and new elites can gain access to power.

Focus

Mass Distrust of America's Elite

How much trust do the masses have in America's leadership? Is a "crisis of authority" confronting America's elite?

Elites have always been concerned about the possibility of mass disaffection and the opportunities that such disaffection might present for demagogues and revolutionaries. The Constitutional Convention of 1787 was inspired in part by Shays' Rebellion and the concern that the Revolutionary War had unleashed mass hostility toward established authority. John Adams worried about a general crisis in authority following the revolt against the British Crown:

> We have been told that our struggle has loosened the bonds of government everywhere, that children and apprentices were disobedient, that schools and college were grown turbulent, that Indians slighted their guardians, and negroes grew insolent to their masters. . . . [Now we have the] intimation that another tribe [women], more numerous and powerful than all the rest, were grown discontent.[a]

"A major concern of the nation's elite throughout the 1960s and 1970s was the decline of mass trust in national leadership. Public opinion polls showed that fewer and fewer people were willing to trust the government in Washington to do what is right" (see the figure).

Defeat and humiliation in war always and everywhere undermines mass support for a nation's leadership. Perhaps the most important negative influence on mass confidence in America's elite was the experience of the Vietnam War. This tragic war was followed immediately by the Watergate scandal and the first forced resignation of a president. President Carter did little to reverse the decline in mass confidence; America's humiliation by Iranian revolutionaries who took U.S. embassy personnel as hostages produced the nadir of confidence in 1980.

The long-term effect of negative media reporting—of world events and of political, military, and business leadership—is to increase social distrust and political cynicism. Television in particular has lowered general levels of trust and confidence. Because the strongest bias in network news reporting is toward conflict and controversy, scandal and corruption—bad news drives out the good news—it is unlikely in the media age that mass confidence in American institutions and leadership can ever be restored to previous high levels.

Yet clearly mass trust can be increased. No doubt the relative peace and prosperity of the 1980s made improvement possible. But the personality of Ronald Reagan and his calculated efforts to restore optimism, pride, and patriotism had a profound effect on Americans. It is somewhat ironic that Ronald Reagan, a conservative critic of big government, helped to partially restore public confidence in "the government in Washington." But the spurt proved to be transient. Although the Gulf War in early 1991 produced the usual "rally 'round the flag" effect, mass trust in government declined again as economic recession settled over the nation.

Public trust in government has risen slightly in recent years, probably as a result of improved economic conditions. Yet mass trust remains low by historic standards.

What does it matter whether the masses trust their political leaders? It is likely that mass distrust and cynicism toward politics and government contributes to a weakening of political party affiliations, low voter turnouts, opposition to taxation, and the prevalence of anti-Washington themes in political campaigns. But perhaps more importantly, mass disaffection from national leadership underlies much of the political immobility, or "gridlock," confronting the national government—its inability to deal effectively with pressing national issues. When trust in leadership is high, leaders have greater flexibility in dealing with national issues. They enjoy a reserve of mass confidence, enabling them to call upon citizens to make short-term sacrifices in pursuit of long-term national goals. But when trust is low, leaders are pressured to make shortsighted decisions, seeking immediate mass gratification, often at the expense of the nation's future well-being.

[a]Charles Francis Adams, ed., *Letters of John Adams,* vol. I (Boston: Charles C. L. Little and James Brown, 1841), pp. 96-97; cited in Seymour Martin Lipset and William Schneider, *The Confidence Gap* (New York: Free Press, 1988).

★ How Elitism and Pluralism Differ

Elite theory differs from the prevailing pluralist vision of democracy in several key respects. Both theories agree that societal decision making occurs through elite interaction, not mass participation; that the key political actors are the leaders of large organizations and institutions, not individual citizens; and that public policy generally reflects the interests of large organizations and institutions, not majority preferences. Indeed, because of these similarities, some critics of pluralism assert that it is really a disguised form of elitism—that is, elitism hiding in democratic rhetoric.[13] Yet despite these recognized parallels with pluralist theory, elite theory offers a fundamentally different view of power and society.

First of all, elite theory asserts that the most important division in society is between elites and masses, between the few who govern and the many who do not. Elites in all organizations and institutions in society share a common experience—the exercise of power. Occupying positions of power provides elites with a common motive—the preservation of their organization and their position in it. Pluralism overlooks this central division of society into elites and masses and emphasizes the fragmentation of society and competition between leadership groups. Elitism emphasizes the importance to leaders of maintaining their positions of power, while pluralism emphasizes their devotion to their group interests.

Elite theory asserts that the mass membership of organizations, parties, interest groups, and institutions in society rarely exercises any direct control over the elite leadership. Group membership does *not* ensure effective individual participation in decision making. Rarely do corporations, unions, armies, churches, governmental bureaucracies, or professional associations have any internal democratic mechanisms. They are usually run by a small elite of officers and activists. Leaders of corporations, banks, labor unions, interest groups, television networks, churches, universities, think tanks, and civic associations remain in control year after year. Very few people attend meetings, vote in organizational elections, or make their influence felt within their organization. The pluralists offer no evidence that the giant organizations and institutions in American life really represent the views or interests of their individual members.

Elite theory suggests that accommodation and compromise among leadership groups is the prevailing style of decision making, not competition and conflict. Pluralism contends that competition among leadership groups protects the individual. But why should we assume that leadership groups compete with each other? More likely, each elite group allows other elite groups to govern in their own spheres of influence without interference. According to elite theory, accommodation rather than competition is the prevailing style of elite interaction: "You scratch my back and I'll scratch yours." Where interests occasionally overlap, elite differences are compromised in order to maintain stability. It is true that multiple, relatively autonomous elites exist in a democratic society; but this multiplicity does not guarantee competition or a balance among centers of power.

Elite theory takes account of *all* power holders in society, private as well as public. Pluralism focuses on governmental leaders and those who interact directly with them. Because governmental leaders are chosen in elections, pluralism asserts that leaders can be held accountable to the people. But even if governmental elites can be held accountable through elections, how can corporation executives, media elites, union leaders, and other persons in positions of private leadership be held accountable? Pluralism usually dodges this important question by focusing primary attention on *public,* government-elite decision and largely ignoring private, nongovernment-elite decision making.

Elitism emphasizes the shared characteristics of leaders, not only their common interest in preserving the social system and their place in it, but also their many shared experiences, values, and goals. Pluralism emphasizes diversity among leaders—differences in backgrounds, ideologies, and viewpoints. Even when elitists show that a disproportionate share of America's leadership is composed of wealthy, educated, prestigiously employed, white, upper- and upper-middle-class males, pluralists respond by asserting that these background characteristics are poor predictors of the decision-making behavior of

Table 1 How elitism and pluralism differ in their views of power and society

	Elite Theory	*Pluralist Theory*
Most Important Political Division(s) in Society	*Elites* who have power, and masses who do not.	*Multiple competing groups* (economic, racial, religious, ideological, etc.) that make demands upon government.
Structure of Power	*Hierarchial,* with power concentrated in a relatively small set of institutional leaders who make key social decisions.	*Polyarchal,* with power dispersed among multiple leadership groups who bargain and compromise over key societal decisions.
Interaction among Leaders	*Consensus over values and goals* for society, with disagreements largely limited to means of achieving common goals.	*Conflict and competition over values and goals* as well as means of achieving them.
Sources of Leadership	*Common backgrounds and experiences* in control of institutional resources; wealth, education, upper socioeconomic status; slow continuous absorption of persons who accept prevailing values.	*Diversity in backgrounds and experiences* and activism in organizations; continuous formation of new groups and organizations; skills in organizational activity and gaining access to government.
Principal Institutions of Power	Corporations, banks, investment firms, media giants, foundations, "think tanks," and other *private organizations, as well as government.*	Interest groups, parties, and the legislative executive, and judicial branches of *government.*
Principal Direction of Political Influence	*Downward* from elites to masses through mass media, education, civic, and cultural organizations.	*Upward* from masses to elites through interest groups, parties, elections, opinion polls, etc.
View of Public Policy	Public policy reflects *elite preferences,* as modified by both altruism and desire to preserve the political system from mass unrest; policy changes occur incrementally when elites redefine their own interests.	Public policy reflects *balance of competing interest groups;* policy changes occur when interest groups gain or lose influence, including mass support.
Principal Protection for Democratic Values	*Elite commitments* to individual liberty, free enterprise, and tolerance of diversity, and their desire to preserve the existing political system.	*Competition among groups:* counter veiling centers of power each checking the ambitions of others.

leaders. Instead, pluralists argue that leaders' decisions are a product of their role perceptions, institutional constraints, interest group pressures, public opinion, and so on. Elitism focuses on leadership consensus, asserting that elites differ more over the means than the ends of public policy. Pluralism focuses on elite conflict, asserting that elites differ on a wide variety of issues of vital importance to society.

Pluralism and elitism also differ over the nature and extent of mass influences over societal decision making. Elitism asserts that elites influence masses more than masses influence elites. Communication flows primarily downward from elites to masses. An enlightened elite may choose to consider the well-being of the masses in decision making, either out of ethical principles or a desire to avoid instability and revolution. But even when elites presume to act in the interests of the masses, the elites act on their own view of what is good for the masses, not what the masses decide for themselves. In contrast, pluralists, while acknowledging that elites rather than the masses make society's decisions, nonetheless assert that the masses influence policy through both their membership in organized interest groups and their participation in elections. Interest groups, parties, and elections, according to the pluralists, provide the means by which the masses can hold elites accountable for their decisions. But elite theory contends that the principal function of elections is not to provide policy mandates to elites, but rather to legitimize elite rule by providing symbolic reassurance that democratic elites govern on behalf of the masses.

In short, while elitism and pluralism share some common views on the preeminent role of elites in a democratic society, elitism differs from pluralism in several key respects, as summarized in Table 1.

★ *Elite and Mass Threats to Democracy*

It is the irony of democracy that the survival of democratic values—individual dignity, limited government, equality of opportunity, private property, freedom of speech and press, religious tolerance, and due process of law—depends on enlightened elites. The masses respond to the ideas and actions of elites. When elites abandon democratic principles or the masses lose confidence in elites, democracy is in peril.

Elite Distemper

Yet democratic elites do not always live up to their responsibilities to preserve the system and its values. Elite behavior is not always enlightened and farsighted, but is instead frequently shortsighted and narrowly self-serving. The relative autonomy of separate elites in a democracy—governmental, corporate, financial, media, legal, civic, and cultural—often encourages narrow visions of the common good and a willingness to sacrifice societal values for relative advantage.

Examples of narrowly self-serving elite behavior abound. Politicians resort to divisive, racial appeals or to class antagonisms—setting black against white or poor against rich—to win elections, even while knowing that these tactics undermine mass confidence in national leadership. Corporate officials sacrifice long-term economic growth for short-term, windfall, paper profits, knowing that the nation's competitive position in the world is undermined by shortsighted "bottom-line" policies. Elites move factories and jobs out of the United States in search of low-paid workers and higher profits. Global trade and unchecked immigration lower the real wages of American workers. Inequality in America increases, and elites and masses grow further apart. Members of Congress in pursuit of personal pay and perks as well as lifetime tenure cater to fat-cat political contributors and well-heeled interest groups. They devote more energy to running for office than to running the government. Bureaucrats, seeking to expand their powers and budgets, create a regulatory quagmire, disadvantaging the nation in global competition.

Politicians and bureaucrats have burdened future generations with enormous debts. Interest group leaders pursue their quest for special privilege, treatments, and exemptions from law, at the expense of the public interest. Network television executives "hype" both news and entertainment shows with violence, scandal, sex, corruption, and scares of various sorts, knowing that these stories undermine mass confidence in the nation's institutions. Lawyers and judges pervert the judicial process for personal advantage, drowning the nation in a sea of litigation, clogging the courts and delaying justice, reinterpreting laws and the Constitution to suit their purposes, and undermining mass respect for the law.

In short, elites do not always act with unity and purpose. They all too frequently put narrow interests ahead of broader, shared values. These behaviors grow out of the relative autonomy of various elites in a democracy. They are encouraged by the absence of any external checks on the power of elites in their various domains. The only effective check on irresponsible elite behavior is their own realization that the system itself will become endangered if such behavior continues unrestrained. So periodically elites undertake reforms, mutually agreeing to curb the most flagrant abuses of the system. The stimulus to reform is the restoration of mass confidence in elite government, and ultimately the preservation of the elite system itself. But reforms often succeed only in creating new opportunities for abuse, changing the rules but failing to restrain self-interested elites.

Mass Unrest

But mass politics can also threaten democratic values. Despite a superficial commitment to the symbols of democracy, the masses have surprisingly weak commitments to the principles of individual liberty, toleration of diversity, and freedom of expression when required to apply these principles to despised or obnoxious groups or individuals. In contrast, elites, and the better-educated groups from which they are recruited, are generally more willing than the masses to apply democratic values to specific situations and to protect the freedoms of unpopular groups.

Masses are dangerously vulnerable to demagogic appeals to intolerance, racial hatred, anti-intellectualism, class antagonisms, anti-Semitism, and violence. Counter-elites, or demagogues, are mass-oriented leaders who express hostility toward the established order and appeal to the mass sentiments. These counter-elites, whether they are on the left or right, are extremist and intolerant, impatient with due process, contemptuous of individual rights, eager to impose their views by sweeping measures and often willing to use violence and intimidation to do so. Right-wing counter-elites talk of "the will of the people," while left-wing radicals cry, "All power to the people." Both appeal to mass extremism: the notion that compromise and coalition-building, and working within the democratic system for change, is pointless or even immoral. Democratic politics is viewed with cynicism. Counter-elites frequently resort to conspiracy theories to incite the masses. The left charges that the capitalist conspiracy exploits and oppresses the people for its own profit and amusement; the right charges that the nation is falling prey to an international conspiracy whose goal is to deprive the American people of their liberty and property. The historian Richard Hofstadter refers to this popularity of conspiracy theories as "the paranoid style of politics."[14]

It is the irony of democracy that democratic values can survive only in the absence of mass political activism. Democratic values thrive best when the masses are absorbed in the problems of everyday life and involved in groups and activities that distract their attention from mass political movements. Political stability depends on mass involvement in work, family, neighborhood, trade union, hobby, church, group recreation, and other activities. When the masses become alienated from home, work, and community—when their ties to social organizations and institutions weaken—

Focus

The Unpolitics of College Students

For most college students, politics is *not* as interesting as football or basketball, or the sex lives of celebrities, or prime-time television sitcoms. When it comes to political issues, inattention, boredom, cynicism, and a sense of powerlessness are especially prevalent among college-age people today. The "baby boom" generation of students of the late 1960s and early 1970s were more active politically and more liberal in their views. This earlier generation of students confronted an unpopular war in Vietnam, the military draft, and the Watergate scandal and the forced resignation of a president.

This is the generation from which many current college instructors were recruited.

College students today are far less active politically than students a generation ago. Today's students are much more concerned with their financial futures and with raising a family than their predecessors. Students today are much less interested in "developing a meaningful philosophy of life." (See Table 2.)

It is not easy trying to develop an interest in politics on the campus today. Only 27 percent of students believe that "keeping up with political affairs" is important, and only 17 percent think that "influencing the political structure" is important. Only 14 percent even discussed politics in the last year! Why? One student replied: "I don't think our opinion matters in the grand scale of things," reflecting a widely shared feeling of powerlessness among young people.

they become vulnerable to the appeals of demagogues, and democratic values are endangered.

Mass activism inspires elite repression. Mass political movements, when they gain momentum and give rise to hatred, generate fear and insecurity among elites. They respond by limiting freedom and strengthening security, banning demonstrations, investigating and harassing opposition, arresting activists, and curtailing speech, writing, and broadcasting—usually under the guise of preserving law and order. Universities, once heralded as society's bastions of free thought and expression, impose "speech codes," "sensitivity training," and other repressive measures on students and faculty, in the paradoxical pursuit of tolerance and "diversity." Ironically, elites resort to these repressive actions out of a genuine belief that they are necessary to preserve democratic values.

Elite theory, then, recognizes multiple threats to democracy: *elite misdeeds*—shortsighted and self-interested behavior that undermines popular support for the political system; *mass activism*—extremist and intolerant political movements, led by counter-elites appealing to racial hatred, class antagonism, and personal fears; and *elite repression*—forced indoctrination in "political correctness"; limitations on dissent, speech, and assembly in the name of law and order; and the subversion of democratic values in a paradoxical effort to preserve the system.

TABLE 2 Survey of college freshmen in 1970 and 1998

Questions	*Percentage Who Responded Positively* 1970	1998
Objectives considered important in life:		
Being very well off financially	41	75
Raising a family	65	73
Developing a meaningful philosophy of life	71	41
Keeping up with political affairs	49	27
Influencing the political structure	41	17
Political activities in past year:		
Discussed politics	30	14
Worked in a campaign	12	8
Political views, self-described:		
Far left	2	3
Liberal	33	22
Middle of the road	48	55
Conservative	16	19
Far right	1	2
Policy positions, agree that:		
Abortion should be legal	83	54
Death penalty should be abolished	33	24
Marijuana should be legalized	47	35
Affirmative action in college admissions should be abolished	NA	50

Source. Selected questions from the American Council on Education Annual Survey of College Freshmen, as reported in the *Chronicle of Higher Education,* January 16, 1998.

★ An Elitist Theory of Democracy

All societies are governed by elites, even democratic societies. The elitist theory of democracy is not an attack upon democracy, but rather an aid in understanding the realities of democratic politics.

Elite theory is not an apology for elite rule; it is not defense of official misdeeds or repression. Rather, it is a realistic explanation of how democracy works, how democratic values are both preserved and threatened, how elites and masses interact, how public policy is actually determined, and whose interests generally prevail.

Critics of this elitist theory of democracy claim that it is "conservative," that it legitimizes elite rule, that it obstructs social progress of the masses. But elite theory neither endorses nor condemns elite governance, but rather seeks to expose and analyze the way in which elites function in a democracy.

Elite theory poses the central questions of American politics: Who governs the nation? How do people acquire power? How are economic and political power related? What interests shaped the U.S. Constitution? How have American elites changed over two centuries? How widely is power shared in the United States today? Are leaders in government, business, banking, the media, hew, foundations, interest groups, and cultural affairs separate, distinct, and competitive—or are they concentrated, interlocked, and consensual? Do elites or masses give greater support to democratic values? Are elites becoming ever more isolated from masses? Are masses losing confidence in the nation's elite, and if so, what does this mean for democracy? Can democracy long survive when most people are distrustful of government and cynical toward politics?

Are masses generally informed, sensible, and considerate—or are they largely ill informed, apathetic, and intolerant? Does public opinion shape elite behavior—or do elites shape public opinion through the mass media? How successful are media elites in molding mass opinion and influencing public debate? Are American political parties "responsible" instruments of popular control of government—or are they weakened oligarchies, dominated by ideologically motivated activists? Do elections serve as policy mandates from the people—or are they primarily an exercise in citizenship, choosing personnel, not policy? Are political campaigns designed to inform voters and assess their policy preferences—or are they expensive, commercial adventures in image making? How politically active, informed, knowledgeable, and consistent in their views are the American people? Do organized interest groups fairly represent the views of their members—or do they reflect the views and interests of leaders who are largely out of touch with the members? Does competition among interest groups create a reasonable balance in public policy—or do the special interests dominate policy making at the expense of the mass public?

How much influence do masses have over the actions of presidents, Congress, and courts? What role does the president play in America's elite system? What effect does the president's behavior have on the way the masses view their government? Does presidential popularity with the masses affect the power of the president? Is power shifting from elected officials to "faceless bureaucrats"? What are the sources of bureaucratic power, and can bureaucracy be restrained? Whom do members of Congress really represent?

Are members of Congress held accountable for their policy decisions by the voters back home—or are they free to pursue their personal interests in Washington, knowing that their constituents are generally unaware of their policy positions? Why are the nation's most important domestic policy questions usually decided by the most elitist branch of the government, the unelected, lifetime-tenured justices of the Supreme Court? Can political decentralization—decision making by sub-elites in states and communities—increase mass involvement in government? How do elites respond to mass protest movements? Do protest movements themselves become oligarchic over time and increasingly divorced from the views of the masses?

This text will address questions such as these from the perspective of elite theory. But it will also compare and evaluate the answers suggested by *pluralist* theory and *democratic* theory. The goal is a better understanding not only of American politics but also of elitism, pluralism, and democracy.

★ **Thomas R. Dye** *is Professor of Political Science at Florida State University.*

Endnotes

[1]Harold Lasswell and Abraham Keplan, *Power and Society* (New Haven, Conn.: Yale University Press, 1950), p. 219.

[2]Gaetano Mosca, *The Ruling Class* (New York: McGraw-Hill, 1939), p. 50.

[3]Roberto Michels, *Political Parties: A Sociological Study of the Oligarchical Tendencies of Modern Democracies* (1915; reprint, New York: Free Press, 1962), p. 70.

[4]Harold Lasswell and Daniel Lemer, *The Comparative Study of Elites* (Stanford, Calif: Stanford University Press, 1952), p.7.

[5]David Truman, "The American System in Crisis," *Political Science Quarterly* 74 (December 1959): 489.

[6]Richard Hofstadter, *The American Political Tradition* (New York: Knopf, 1948), p. viii.

[7]John Stuart Mill, *Representative Government* (New York: Dutton, Everyman's Library, 1962), p. 203.

[8]For a discussion of John Locke and the political philosophy underlying democracy, see George Sabine, *A History of Political Theory* (New York: Holt, Rinehart & Winston, 1950), pp. 517–541.

[9]James Madison, *The Federalist, Number 10* (New York: Modern Library, 1937).

[10]For a discussion of "Democracy in the States" and a list of states that allow initiative and referenda voting, see Thomas R. Dye, *Politics in States in Communities* (Upper Saddle River, N.J.: Prentice-Hall, 1997), Chapter 2.

[11]E. E. Schattschneider, *Two Hundred Americans in Search of a Government* (New York: Holt, Rinehart & Winston, 1969), p. 63.

[12]See Eva Etzioni-Halevy, *The Elite Connection* (Cambridge, Mass.: Polity Press, 1993).

[13]Peter Bachrach, *The Theory of Democratic Elitism: A Critique* (Boston: Little, Brown, 1967), p. xi.

[14]Richard Hofstadter, *The Paranoid Style of American Politics* (New York: Knopf 1965).

Selected Readings

Dahl, Robert A. *Pluralist Democracy in the United States: Conflict and Consensus.* Chicago: Rand McNally, 1967. Most of Dahl's important theoretical work was at the community level. This book extended pluralism to the national level.

Etzioni-Halevy, Eva. *The Elite Connection,* Cambridge, Mass.: Polity Press, 1993. A scholarly description of "democratic elite theory," with comparisons to classical liberalism, traditional European elite theory, and modern American pluralism. It argues that although Western democracy is not "government by the people," it preserves democratic values through competition among separate and relatively autonomous elites both within and outside the state.

Etzioni-Halevy, Eva. (Ed.) *Musses and Elites in Democracy.* New York: Garland Press, 1997. Advanced students may wish to read key selections from the scholarly literature on classes, elites, and democracy. This well-edited volume contains thirty-eight brief selections from the works of such writers as Karl Marx, Roberto Michels, Gaetano Mosca, Vilfredo Pareto, Joseph A. Schumpeter, C. Wright Mills, Robert A. Dahl, Samuel P. Huntington, and Seymour Martin Lipset.

Henry, William A., III. *In Defense of Elitism.* New York: Doubleday, 1994. A critical debunking of the myths that everyone is alike (or should be), that a just society will produce equal success for everyone, and that the common man is always right.

Michels, Roberto. *Political Parties: A Sociological Study of the Oligarchical Tendencies of Modern Democracies.* New York: Free Press, 1962. This classic book first appeared in 1911 in German. Michels was a disciple of Mosca. Like Mosca, he saw elitism as an outcome of social organization. Michels argued that the very fact of organization in society leads inevitably to an elite. His often-quoted thesis is, "Who says organization, says oligarchy." Political scientists have called this "the iron law of oligarchy."

Mosca, Gaetano. *The Ruling Class.* Edited by A. Livingston. New York: McGraw-Hill, 1939. This classic book was first published in 1896 in Italy. Mosca added to it in a 1923 edition that reflects the impact of World War I on his ideas. Along with the work of Vilfredo Pareto, Mosca's Ruling forms the basis of "classical elitism."

Pareto, Vilfredo. *The Mind and Society: Treatise of General Sociology*. New York: Harcourt, Brace & World, 1935 (originally published in 1915–1916 in four volumes). Pareto begins with a very broad definition of elite. He suggests that in any human activity, those who are the top practitioners are the elite in that activity. Thus he groups elites into two classes—the governing elite and the nongoverning elite—depending on whether the activity of which they are a top practitioner is important to government. Pareto also introduces psychological notions into his work. He speaks of "residues," which are human instincts, sentiments, or states of mind that remain constant over time and from state to state.

★ ★ ★ ★ ★

Questions

1. To what extent does elitism enable democracy?
2. How do elites exert influence in the political process?
3. Who are key members of America's elite today?
4. The original meaning of the Greek word "aristocracy" is "the best rule." The original meaning of the Greek word "oligarchy" is "the few rule." Would it be more honest to call our form of government aristocracy or oligarchy?
5. Do elites actually compete with each other, or do they silently conspire to serve their own interests?

☆ ☆ ☆

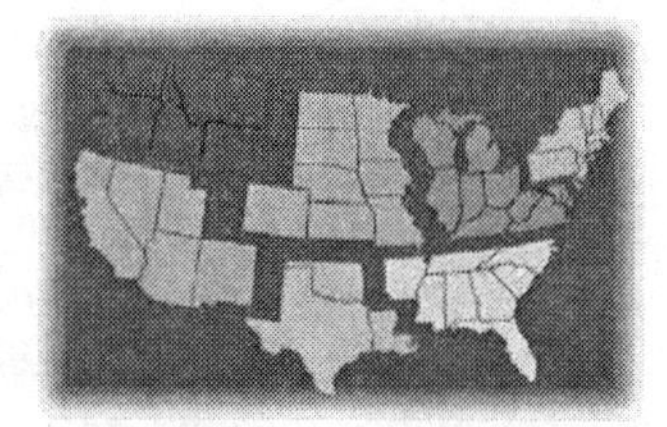

The State-Centered Theoretical Perspective

Department of Social Sciences, U.S. Military Academy

The theory of pluralism maintains that citizens govern through supporting interest groups that vie for influence in the areas of public policy with which they are most concerned. Elitism argues that the few, the rich, and the influential actually make public policy, even though they sometimes use groups or mass movements as their instruments. In this article West Point's political scientists present a third explanation for how political power works in American society. For state-centered theorists, it is government officials and institutions that play the definitive role in determining the course society takes. If there is a political elite in America, it is composed of elected and appointed officials at all levels of government.

Thus far in the course you have examined two theories that address "who governs" in the US political system. The first theory, pluralism, argues that changes in public policy occur when interest groups pressure major political institutions (i.e., Congress, the President, and bureaucracy). Because pluralism views institutions as neutral referees, government officials would be expected to craft public policy to reflect the strength, influence and competition of interest groups in America. The conclusion is that the people govern through interest group membership.

☆ ☆ ☆ ☆ ☆ ☆

Elite theory, in contrast, claims that, for the most part, common people don't matter as much as the ruling class. According to this theory, elites enact public policy to advance their own interests and maintain political stability. While pluralism views the major institutions as neutral referees, elite theory sees them as tools of the politically powerful. Once individuals attain elite status they move in and among the major pillars of society (government, business, media and the military), in a fashion often referred to as the "revolving door." Thus, elite theory, like pluralism, assumes that institutions implement an agenda promoted by external actors.

The third theory that we will introduce as you prepare for the institutions block of the course is state-centered theory. This theoretical approach fundamentally redefines the role of institutions. According to this approach, governmental actors *at all levels* and political rules and organizations are the predominate influence in the public policy making process. While interest groups and private sector elites, at times, influence political decisions, public policy is shaped primarily by those inside the government. Central to this argument is the claim that elected representatives, politically appointed officials, and career civil servants all come to their jobs with private agendas and work to enact them while responding to the three branches of government, other agencies, interest groups and business elites.

Moreover, this theory also contributes to a macro-political understanding of political behavior. *If you know the players and understand the rules, you can predict how the game will be played.* This theory allows us to understand the political infighting that often takes place in our system between the President, Congress, the bureaucracy and the Courts. The rules—Constitutional checks and balances—were designed to prevent the accumulation of power by any one player in our political system. Infighting is just the expected outcome of what James Madison called "Ambition to counteract ambition."[1]

★ A Brief History of State-Centered Analysis

Although the roots of analysis can be traced back to the Founding, this approach has been popular with sociologists, political scientists and economists who all seek to "bring the state back" into the study.[2] Today variants of this approach are referred to as "new institutionalism," or "new economics of organizations."

It is important to define institutions before we begin to explore this theory. Although you are familiar with the common use of "institutions" to mean a formal organization like USMA, political scientists have a broader concept of institutions. Political scientist Sven Steinmo says:

> In the broadest sense, institutions are simply rules. As such, they are the foundation of all political behavior. Some are formal (as in constitutional rules) some are informal (as in cultural norms), but without institutions there could be no organized politics. Simply attempt to consider a world in which there were no rules governing social or political behavior. In this Hobbesian hell there could be no political organization, indeed no social organization at all (North, 1990). Institutionalists are those that think theoretically about institutions and their impact on behavior and outcomes. Institutions structure politics because they: 1) define who is able to participate in the particular political arena, 2) shape the various actors' political strategies, and (more controversially) 3) influence what these actors believe to be both possible and desirable (i.e., their preferences).[3]

Some social scientists use politics to explain real-world outcomes. These "historical institutionalists" look at how political institutions shape, structure or otherwise determine political outcomes.[4] Others, using tools from economics, look at politics as a game played by rational actors. Institutions define the "rules of the game." This thread of institutions is called Rational Choice, Positive Theory of Institutions (PTI) or "new economics of organization."[5] A third theory of institutions, advanced by sociologists Meyer and Rowan, sees institutions as taking on a symbolic, legitimate or "myth"-like status.[6] While these branches of theory are all slightly different, they all emphasize the importance of institutions in political life.

★ A Look at the State-Centered Theory Framework

As with the other theories, in this section we outline the theory's approach to five basic questions:

- Who are the key actors?
- What is the role of the people? How is political participation viewed?
- What is political power and where does it reside?
- What is the importance and significance of institutions?
- How is public policy made?
- Who governs in this process?
- How democratic is the process and product of American politics in this theory?

★ Who Are the Key Actors?

The foundations of State-Centered Theory are the relationships between government agents and the people. In rational choice-based theory, this "principal-agent" relationship is not unlike a contract between a car owner and his mechanic. The car owner values the expertise of a trained mechanic, but is also wary of paying money for a service that he does not fully understand. Will the mechanic do a good job? Will he overcharge? The mechanic may have other concerns: Will he get paid? Can he economize on parts? The problems in this relationship can be explained by a *lack of information* and possible *divergent interests*. In the same way, the people *contract* for lawmaking when they elect members of Congress. The President also contracts for specific administrative functions when he appoints members of his Cabinet. As Terry Moe says:

> Politics is easily viewed in principal-agent terms. Citizens are principals, politicians are their agents. Politicians are principals, bureaucrats are their agents. Bureaucratic superiors are principals, bureaucratic subordinates are their agents. The whole of politics is therefore structured by a chain of principal-agent relationships, from citizen to politicians to bureaucratic superior to bureaucratic subordinate and on down the hierarchy of government to the lowest-level bureaucrats who actually deliver services directly to citizens.[7]

The key actors in state-centered theory are not groups or elites, but members of government institutions who serve as principals and agents. State-centered theory holds that institutions are the dominant force in politics and people within those institutions, each pursuing their own personal agendas, shape political activity. Politicians should not be viewed as loyal, objective representatives of the people; bureaucrats should not be viewed as detached administrators. Rather, these individuals have personal goals and preferences they seek to advance when creating, reviewing or administering policy.

★ What Is the Role of the People?

State-centered analysis views individual participation as important for determining society's desires. *The people matter because they legitimize government action by their consent.* Just as the car owner hires a mechanic, people "hire" a politician from the major political parties. Political participation is not viewed, as with pluralism, as an integral part of public policy development, but rather as a contract for services that will be carried out with a great deal of discretion on the part of the government officials. Nor is political participation symbolic as elite theory suggests, because governmental behavior outside the realm of acceptable behavior is often either terminated by investigation, impeachment, or failing to secure reelection. If people are not satisfied with the actions of a representative, they will simply refuse to "re-hire" him (e.g., reelection). In the case of a public servant or bureaucrat they will not "recommend him" for the next higher position, or will put conditions on his services (e.g., call for investigations).

In the sociological tradition, institutions respond to public perception of their proper or "legitimate" role, even when rules, positions or functions are not necessary to mission success. As an example, an organization with a personnel department or a research and development division is more likely to grow and be successful because the public deems these functions proper to a modern organization.[8] Citizen participation involves reinforcing those symbols, myths, and actions that make an agency or representative legitimate or not. This "legitimization," however, is certainly after the fact.

★ What Is Power?

The state-centered concept of power is the power to advance one's personal agenda as an agent of the people within the rules of the game. The power of the mechanic is his expertise with vehicles. Similarly, even low and mid-level bureaucrats (e.g., military leaders, FBI agents, U.S. Fish and Wildlife Service employees) can influence public policy development. Pluralism (and elite theory for that matter) would have trouble explaining an IRS agent's ability to exercise power. Certainly interest group activity didn't provide her power, and pluralism views institutions as "neutral." Further, one could hardly classify servants like IRS agents as elites, however influential they are.

State-centered theory treats power as a variable which waxes and wanes depending on one's ability to advance a personal agenda and influence others in government (according to the political rules), and also satisfy those outside of government. This power is derived from both formal and informal sources. It is not limited to position, but also includes leadership ability, organizing skills, ability to manipulate the structure, rules and norms of the institutions, media access and knowledge about an issue.

★ The Role of Institutions

Perhaps the biggest difference among the three theories is in their interpretations of the significance of institutions. As stated earlier, pluralism views institutions as neutral referees and elite theory views institutions as a tool of the top 1-2% of Americans. *However, state-centered theorists focus on institutions—those political bodies and rules—as the determinant variable in explaining "who governs."* The mechanic in our metaphor is constrained by state licensing, certifications, safety regulations, the Better Business Bureau and the threat of small claims court. If the car owner thinks that the mechanic will take advantage of him, the owner may specify the types of repairs authorized or pay in installments. These rules structure the relationship.

It is important to note that a consensus does not exist as to what constitutes an institution. In its narrowest interpretation, institutions include the Congress, the presidency, bureaucracy and the courts. But recent scholarship has expanded this definition to include other critical players on the political scene with quasi-governmental connection. Theda Skocpol and Martin Shefter, for example, broaden the concept to include political parties.[9] This is a key move for these theorists because it allows the approach to explain much more about "who governs" without significantly reducing its parsimony.

To Elmer E. Schattschneider who wrote the seminal work in party theory in the early 1960s, political parties are the key players in American politics.[10] Schattschneider does not subscribe to the pluralist theory that politicians neutrally enact the will of the people, but rather that they pick issues that will alter the balance of power in their favor.[11] It is these quasi-institutions that manage conflict and political issues in a way that maximizes their power and control of the system. But consistent with the theory, parties must compete to gain the "consent of the governed." That is, parties pick the issues they stress, create a position they hope will resonate with the voters, and then actively campaign for their support. When the American people vote, they choose among competing alternatives pertaining to not only *who should govern,* but also, *towards what end* government should be used. Thus, in an indirect manner, the people govern by deciding the winner among competing visions of proposed public policy choices. After elections the quasi-power of parties is transferred to the more formal institutions of Congress, the Presidency and bureaucracy to carry out the wishes of the people. When the formal institutions fail to carry out these wishes, Schattschneider claims that we become "semi-sovereign" people.[12]

★ Policymaking

Policymaking in theory is a direct reflection of the interests of the key actors. Did our hypothetical car owner end up with new tires and a few unnecessary parts? This theory explains why members of Congress tack seemingly unrelated projects onto legislation, why bureaucratic agencies resemble Frankenstein's monster, and why Supreme Court Justices stray ideologically from presidents who appointed them. Because policy is made by institutions and governmental actors pursuing their own agenda, while occasionally appeasing interest groups and private sector elites, changes in the direction of American politics can be profound or unexpected. Thomas L. McNaugher says that consensus-building explains the Bradley Fighting Vehicle's "strange combination of capabilities." McNaughter says,

> The Army started with two perfectly valid military needs—that for an infantry fighting vehicle and that for a mobile missile-carrying tank killer. In putting the two together, however, the service has to sacrifice the size of its infantry squads, while placing its TOW missiles on a vehicle that will travel far closer to the front lines than tank killers needed to be. Significantly, the vehicle's TOW capability was added after the project had entered development, despite serious resistance to the idea from among important elements within the service, and partly because of strong "support for the TOW, in particular in Congress and the Office of the Secretary of Defense."[13]

Other examples include cases where mid-level bureaucrats created or significantly alter public-policy such as, the daily decisions made by bureaucrats in the Environmental Protection Agency (EPA), and Occupational Safety and Health Administration (OSHA). The daily decisions made by these bureaucrats—some appointed, some career officials—impact the businesses, environment, food, and infrastructure of everyday life, all without a "democratic" mandate.

Therefore, state-centered theory explains policy-making by examining how the structure, rules, and norms of governmental institutions affect the behavior of individuals who make policy decisions, and vice versa. This approach can be insightful in explaining political events like the slowness of the US Congress to adopt affirmative action programs in the 1960s despite Democratic Party majorities in both houses and occupants in the White House sympathetic to the cause. The seniority system (rules) in place in Congress during the 1960s, allowed the conservative Southern Democrats, who held the key committee chairmanships, to block these initiatives, preventing them from ever making it out of their committees. After the significant Congressional reforms enacted throughout the 1970s, which changed these rules, affirmative action programs and welfare changes also promoted by the Democratic Party had an easier time becoming law.

Of course, there are times when the cause for a particular change in public policy may be over-determined. That is, there are many acceptable explanations for the change. For example, a president may favor a tax-cut in an election year because he is trying to win over voters, placate interest groups and get big dollar donations from private sector elites. In these cases, any number of theories, in varying degrees, may explain "who governs." But in a number of circumstances, state-centered theory provides a substantial, if not best, explanation for "who governs?"

★ What Is Politics?

The state-centered approach to politics stresses the importance of how both institutions, and members within those institutions, affect public policy development. It sees politics as the process that emerges from governmental actors and institutions attempting to accomplish their missions while advancing their own self interest. In this process, institutions and state actors will attempt to placate interest groups, the public, and private sector elites to maintain and increase their power. However, placating activities are secondary to the primary behavior of manipulation of the system to accomplish private agendas. Politics is not about interest group competition or about elites accommodating one other (which encompasses both private and public elites), but instead about how governmental officials manipulate conflict, manage issues and pursue policy agendas.

★ Assumptions about Democracy

In state-centered theory elected officials and government bureaucrats act as agents for the people. The people matter because, as we learned from the political philosophers earlier in the course, government legitimacy is derived from "the consent of the governed." Key to this understanding however, is interpretation of the word "consent." What is implied is that government acts with consent of the people, ***not*** that the people direct how policy will be made, reviewed or executed. That doesn't mean that the people don't influence the creation of public policy, only that it is primarily the job of government agents to create public policy that the people will accept while advancing their personal agendas and still retaining their jobs!

★ Problems with Theory

Pluralist theorists fundamentally disagree with the degree of independence that theorists ascribe to individual government actors in the policy making process. This is not surprising given their approach that stresses the importance of interest group pressure in causing political change. Elite theorists generally don't have a problem with an explanation that includes top-level governmental actors (e.g. the President and members of Congress), independently creating public policy. Their main criticism is with the handling of private sector influence, which elite theorists view as much more significant. Elite theorists critique the manner in which state-centered theory downplays the importance of economic and cultural institutions, most notably the media. To a degree, and depending on their definition of "elites," they also differ with the degree of influence that mid-level bureaucrats can play in the public policy-making process. Students of American politics can be their own judge of these points.

Endnotes

[1]Madison, *Federalist Paper # 51.*

[2]See Theda Skocpol★★★

[3]Sven Steinmo, "The New ism" in *The Encyclopedia of Democratic Thought,* Barry Clark and Joe Foweraker (eds.) London: Routledge (2001).

[4]Steinmo, 2001.

[5]Steinmo, 2001 and Moe, 1984.

[6]John W. Meyer and Brian Rowan, 1977. "Institutionalized" (*American Journal of Sociology*, Vol. 83, No. 2: 340-363).

[7]Terry M. Moe, 1984. "The New Economics of Organization" (*American Journal of Political Science* 4:765-766).

[8]Meyer and Rowan, 1977, p. 361.

[9]See Theda Skocpol, *Protecting Soldiers and Mothers* (Cambridge: Harvard University Press, 1992), and Martin Shefter, *Political Parties and the State.*

[10]Elmer E. Schattschneider, *The Semi-Sovereign People.* (Hinsdale, Illinois: The Dryden Press, 1975).

[11]*The Semisovereign People.* E. E. Schattschneider Review author: Malcolm E. Jewell *The Journal of Politics*, Vol. 24, No. 1. (Feb., 1962), pp. 203-204.

[12]Ibid.

[13]"Weapons Procurement: The Futility of Reform" (1987) Thomas L. McNaughen. *International Security*, Vol. 12, No. 2. (Autumn, 1987), p. 95. citing, Daniel J. Kaufmann, "Organizations, Technology, and Weapons Acquisition: The Development of the Infantry Fighting Vehicle" (Ph.D. Dissertation, MIT).

★ ★ ★ ★ ★

Questions

1. Why should anyone doubt that presidents, senators, commissioners, governors, representatives, and councilpersons actually make the policies that run America?
2. To what extent do elected and appointed officials lead rather than follow the people who are active in interest groups?
3. To what extent do elected and appointed officials lead rather than follow America's business and labor leaders?
4. To what extent do elected and appointed officials present citizens with the opportunity to circumvent the influence of elites and interest groups and govern directly?
5. To what extent are political institutions such as Congress or the Department of Agriculture independent of the interest groups and elites who try to influence them?

★ ★ ★

The Legislator as Delegate

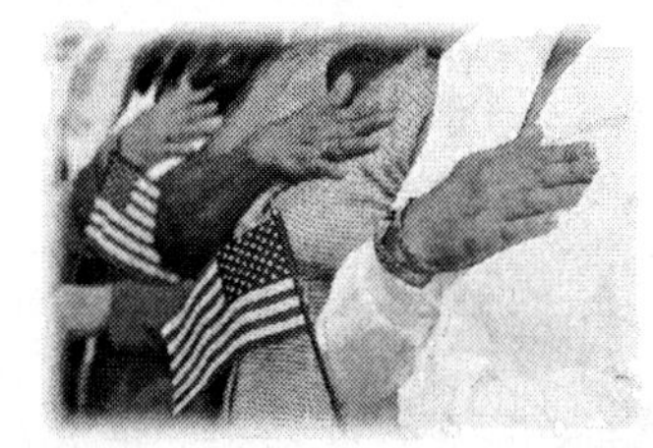

General Assembly of Virginia

For each vote taken, a legislator can act as either delegate or trustee. Delegates follow the instructions of voters who place them in office. Trustees vote according to their own best judgment of the issue in the ultimate interest of the electorate. Which course will a legislator take? Cynics insist that this distinction itself provides a pretext for personal interest. A legislator whose vote coincides with the will of the majority can claim to be the servant of the popular will. A legislator whose vote conflicts with the will of the majority can claim to be using his or her own best judgment in the long-term interest of the constituents. In this statement the legislators of the Virginia assembly insist they are the people's delegates, following precedent firmly established in British tradition.

There can be no doubt that the scheme of a representative republic was derived to our forefathers from the constitution of the English House of Commons; and that that branch of the English government . . . was in its origin, and in theory always has been, purely republican. It is certain, too, that the statesmen of America, in assuming that as the model of our own institutions, designed to adopt it here in its purest form, and with its strictest republican tenets and principles. It becomes, therefore, an inquiry of yet greater utility than curiosity, to ascertain the sound doctrines of the constitution of the English House of Commons in regard to this right of the constituent to instruct the representative. For the position may safely be assumed that the wise and virtuous men who framed our constitutions designed, that,

★ ★ ★ ★ ★ ★

"The Legislator as Delegate," Journal of the Senate, General Assembly of the Commonwealth of Virginia, 1812.

in the United States, the constituent should have at least as much, if not a great deal more, influence over the representative than was known to have existed from time immemorial in England. Let us then interrogate the history of the British nation; let us consult the opinions of their wise men.

Instances abound in parliamentary history of formal instructions from the constituent to the representative, of which . . . the following may suffice: In 1640, the knights of the shire for Dorset and Kent informed the commons *that they had in charge from their constituents* seven articles of grievances, which they accordingly laid before the House, where they were received and acted on. In the 33rd year of Charles II, the citizens of London instructed their members to insist on the bill for excluding the Duke of York (afterward King James II) from the succession to the throne; and their representative said "that his *duty* to his electors *obliged* him to vote the bill." At a subsequent election, in 1681, in many places, formal instructions were given to the members returned, to insist on the same exclusion bill; we know, from history, how uniformly and faithfully those instructions were obeyed. . . . In 1741, the citizens of London instructed their members to vote against standing armies, excise laws, the septennial bill, and a long train of evil measures, already felt, or anticipated; and expressly affirm their right of instruction— "We think it" (say they) "our *duty,* as it is *our undoubted right,* to acquaint you, with *what we desire and expect from you, in discharge of the great trust we repose in you,* and what we take to be *your duty as our representative,* etc." In the same year, instructions of a similar character were sent from all parts of England. In 1742, the cities of London, Bristol, Edinburgh, York, and many others, instructed their members in parliament to seek redress against certain individuals suspected to have betrayed and deserted the cause of the people. . . .

Instances also are on record of the deliberate formal knowledgement of the right of instruction by the House of Commons itself, especially in old times. Thus the commons hesitated to grant supplies to King Edward III *till they had the consent of their constituents,* and desired that a new parliament might be summoned, which might be *prepared with authority from their constituents.* . . .

"Instructions" (says a member of the House of Commons) "ought to be *followed implicitly,"* after the member has respectfully given his constituents *his opinion* of them: *"Far be it from me to oppose my judgment to that of 6000 of my fellow citizens."* "The practice" (says another) "of consulting our constituents was good. I wish it was continued. *We can discharge our duty no better, than in the direction of those who sent us hither. What the people choose is right, because they choose it."* . . .

Without referring to the minor political authors . . . who have maintained these positions (quoted from one of them)—"that the people have a right to instruct their representatives; that no man ought to be chosen that will not receive instructions; that the people understand enough of the interests of the country to give general instructions; that it was the custom formerly to instruct all the members; and the nature of deputation shows that the custom was well grounded"—it is proper to mention that the great constitutional lawyer Coke . . . says, "It is the *custom of parliament,* when any new device is moved for on the king's behalf, for his aid and the like, that the commons may answer, *they dare not agree to it without conference with their counties."* And Sydney . . . maintains "that members derive their power from those that choose them; that those who give power do not give an unreserved power; that many members, in all ages, and sometimes the whole body of the commons have refused to vote until they consulted with those who sent them; that the houses have often adjourned to give them time to do so and if this were done more frequently, or if cities, towns and counties had on some occasions given instructions to their deputies, matters would probably have gone better in parliament than they have done." . . . The celebrated Edmund Burke, a man, it must be admitted, of profound knowledge, deep foresight, and transcendent abilities, disobeyed the instructions of his constituents; yet, by placing his excuse on the ground that the instructions were but the clamour of the day, he seems to admit the authority of instructions soberly and deliberately given; for he agrees, "he ought to look to their opinions" (which he explains to mean their permanent settled opinions) "but not the flash of the day"; and he says elsewhere, that he could not bear to show himself "a representative, whose face did not reflect the face of his constituents—a face that did not joy in their joys and sorrow in their sorrows." It is remarkable that, notwithstanding a most splendid display of warm and touching eloquence, the people of Bristol would not reelect Mr. Burke, for this very offense of disobeying instructions . . .

It appears, therefore, that the right of the constituent to instruct the representative, is firmly established in England, on the broad basis of the nature of representation. The existence of that right, there, has been demonstrated by the only practicable evidence, by which the principles of an unwritten constitution can be ascertained—history and precedent.

To view the subject upon principle, the right of the constituent to instruct the representative, seems to result, clearly and conclusively, from the very nature of the representative system. Through means of that noble institution, the largest nation may, almost as conveniently as the smallest, enjoy all the advantages of a government by the people, without any of the evils of democracy—precipitation, confusion, turbulence, distraction from the ordinary and useful pursuits of industry. And it is only to avoid those and the like mischiefs, that representation is substituted for the direct suffrage of the people in the office of legislation. The representative, therefore, must in the nature of things, represent his own particular constituents only. He must, indeed, look to the general good of the nation, but he must look also, and especially to the interests of his particular constituents as concerned in the commonweal; because the general good is but the aggregate of individual happiness. He must legislate for the whole nation; but laws are expressions of the general will; and the general will is only the result of individual wills fairly collected and compared. In order . . . to express the general will . . . it is plain that the representative must express the will and speak the opinions of the constituents that depute him.

It cannot be pretended that a representative is to be the organ of his own will alone; for then, he would be so far despotic. He must be the organ of others—of whom? Not of the nation, for the nation deputes him not; but of his constituents, who alone know, alone have trusted, and can alone displace him. And if it be his province and his duty, in general, to express the will of his constituents, to the best of his knowledge, without being particularly informed thereof, it seems impossible to contend that he is not bound to do so when he is so especially informed and instructed.

The right of the constituent to instruct the representative, therefore, is an essential principle of the representative system. It may be remarked that wherever representation has been introduced, however unfavorable the circumstances under which it existed, however short its duration, however unimportant its functions, however dimly understood, the right of instruction has always been regarded as inseparably incidental to it. . . .

A representative has indeed a wide field of discretion left to him; and great is the confidence reposed in his integrity, fidelity, wisdom, zeal; but neither is the field of discretion boundless, nor the extent of confidence infinite; and the very discretion allowed him, and the very confidence he enjoys, is grounded on the supposition that he is charged with the will, acquainted with the opinions, and devoted to the interests of his constituents. . . .

Various objections have been urged to this claim of the constituent, of a right to instruct the representative, on which it may be proper to bestow some attention.

The first objection that comes to be considered . . . is grounded on the supposed impossibility of fairly ascertaining the sense of the constituent body. The *impossibility* is denied. It may often be a matter of great difficulty; but then the duty of obedience resolves itself into a question, not of principle, but of fact: whether the right of instruction has been exercised or not. The representative cannot be bound by an instruction that is not given; but that is no objection to the obligation of an instruction *actually given*. . . .

It has been urged that the representatives are not bound to obey the instructions of their constituents because the constituents do not hear the debates, and therefore, cannot be supposed judges of the matter to be voted.

If this objection has force enough to defeat the right of instruction, it ought to take away, also, the right of rejecting the representative at the subsequent election. For it might be equally urged on that occasion, as against the right of instruction, that the people heard not the debate that enlightened the representative's mind—the reasons that convinced his judgment and governed his conduct. . . . In other words, the principle that mankind is competent to self-government should be renounced. The truth is, that our institutions suppose that although the representative ought to be, and generally will be, elected for superior virtue and intelligence, yet a greater mass of wisdom and virtue still reside in the constituent body than the utmost portion allotted to any individual. . . .

Finally, it has been objected, that the instructions of the constituent are not obligatory on the representative because the obligation insisted on is fortified with no sanction—the representative cannot be punished for his disobedience, and his vote is valid notwithstanding his disobedience. It is true that there is no mode of legal punishment provided for this . . . default of duty and that the act of disobedience will not invalidate the vote. It is true, too, that a representative may perversely advocate a measure which he knows to be ruinous to his country; and that neither his vote will be invalidated by his depravity, nor can he be punished by law for his crime, heinous as it surely is. But it does not follow that the one representative is *not bound to obey the instructions* of his constituents any more than that the other is not bound to obey the dictates of his conscience. Both duties stand upon the same foundation, with almost all the great political and moral obligations. The noblest duties of man are without any legal sanction: the great mass of social duties . . . , our duties to our parents, to our children, to our wives, to our families, to our neighbor, to our country, our duties to God, are, for the most part, without legal sanction, yet surely not without the strongest obligation. The duty of the *representative* to obey the instructions of the constituent body cannot be placed on higher ground.

Such are the opinions of the General Assembly of Virginia, on the subject of this great right of instruction, and such the general reasons on which those opinions are founded. . . .

✯ ✯ ✯ ✯ ✯

Questions

1. To what extent do legislators have a moral obligation to directly express the will of the people in each vote they take?
2. To what extent is it possible for legislators to directly express the will of the people in all of votes they take?
3. In America legislators are elected either by states or by districts. How frequently are legislators faced with a conflict between what is good for their state or district and what is good for the country as a whole?
4. To what extent do campaign contributions make it difficult for legislators to act as faithful delegates?
5. Should a legislator act as a delegate to the fullest extent possible, contradicting the popular will only when absolutely necessary?

☆ ☆ ☆

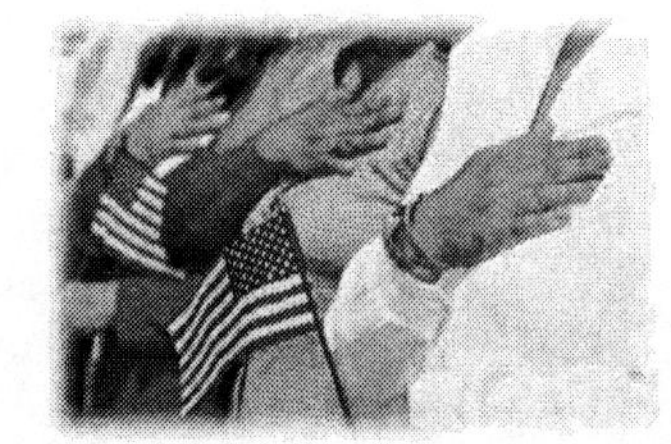

The Legislator as Trustee

John F. Kennedy

Senator John F. Kennedy was extraordinarily articulate long before his election to the presidency, as this statement on the delegate-trustee issue demonstrates. For Kennedy each senator has not only desire but also incentives to represent as accurately and often as possible the will of the people who elected him. When examined with a broader perspective, however, the inherent conflicts between state and national needs make the role of trustee, at least for senators, imperative. With typical eloquence Kennedy asserts: "Of course, we should not ignore the needs of our area—nor could we easily as products of that area—but none could be found to look out for the national interest if local interests wholly dominated the role of each of us."

The primary responsibility of a senator, most people assume, is to represent the views of his state. Ours is a federal system—a union of relatively sovereign states whose needs differ greatly—and my constitutional obligations as senator would thus appear to require me to represent the interests of my state. Who will speak for Massachusetts if her own senators do not? Her rights and even her identity become submerged. Her equal representation in Congress is lost. Her aspirations, however much they may from time to time be in the minority, are denied that equal opportunity to be heard to which all minority views are entitled.

Any senator need not look very long to realize that his colleagues are representing *their* local interests. And if such interests are ever to be abandoned in favor of the national good, let the constituents—not the senator—decide when and to what extent. For he is their agent in Washington, the

☆ ☆ ☆ ☆ ☆ ☆

"The Legislator as Trustee," by John F. Kennedy, reprinted from *Profiles in Courage*, HarperCollins, 1955.

protector of their rights, recognized by the vice president in the Senate Chamber as "the senator from Massachusetts" or "the senator from Texas."

But when all of this is said and admitted, we have not yet told the full story. For in Washington we are "United States senators" and members of the Senate of the United States as well as senators from Massachusetts and Texas. Our oath of office is administered by the vice president, not by the governors of our respective states; and we come to Washington, to paraphrase Edmund Burke, not as hostile ambassadors or special pleaders for our state or section, in opposition to advocates and agents of other areas, but as members of the deliberative assembly of one nation with one interest. Of course, we should not ignore the needs of our area—nor could we easily as products of that area—but none could be found to look out for the national interest if local interests wholly dominated the role of each of us.

There are other obligations in addition to those of state and region—the obligations of the party. . . . Even if I can disregard those pressures, do I not have an obligation to go along with the party that placed me in office? We believe in this country in the principle of party responsibility, and we recognize the necessity of adhering to party platforms—if the party label is to mean anything to the voters. Only in this way can our basically two-party nation avoid the pitfalls of multiple splinter parties, whose purity and rigidity of principle, I might add—if I may suggest a sort of Gresham's Law of politics—increase inversely with the size of their membership.

And yet we cannot permit the pressures of party responsibility to submerge on every issue the call of personal responsibility. For the party which, in its drive for unity, discipline and success, ever decides to exclude new ideas, independent conduct or insurgent members, is in danger. . . .

Of course, both major parties today seek to serve the national interest. They would do so in order to obtain the broadest base of support, if for no nobler reason. But when party and officeholder differ as to how the national interest is to be served, we must place first the responsibility we owe not to our party or even to our constituents but to our individual consciences.

But it is a little easier to dismiss one's obligations to local interests and party ties to face squarely the problem of one's responsibility to the will of his constituents. A senator who avoids this responsibility would appear to be accountable to no one, and the basic safeguards of our democratic system would thus have vanished. He is no longer representative in the true sense, he has violated his public trust, he has betrayed the confidence demonstrated by those who voted for him to carry out their views. "Is the creature," as John Tyler asked the House of Representatives in his maiden speech, "to set himself in opposition to his Creator? Is the servant to disobey the wishes of his master?"

How can he be regarded as representing the people when he speaks, not their language, but his own? He ceases to be their representative when he does so, and represents himself alone.

In short, according to this school of thought, if I am to be properly responsive to the will of my constituents, it is my duty to place their principles, not mine, above all else. This may not always be easy, but it nevertheless is the essence of democracy, faith in the wisdom of the people and their views. To be sure, the people will make mistakes—they will get no better government than they deserve—but that is far better than the representative of the people arrogating for himself the right to say he knows better than they what is good for them. Is he not chosen, the argument closes, to vote as they would vote were they in his place?

It is difficult to accept such a narrow view of the role of a United States senator—a view that assumes the people of Massachusetts sent me to Washington to serve merely as a seismograph to record shifts in popular opinion. I reject this view not because I lack faith in the "wisdom of the people," but because this concept of democracy actually puts too little faith in the people. Those who would deny the obligation of the representative to be bound by every impulse of the electorate—regardless of the conclusions his own deliberations direct—do trust in the wisdom of the people. They have faith in their ultimate sense of justice, faith in their ability to honor courage and respect judgment, and faith that in the long run they will act unselfishly for the good of the nation. It is that kind of faith on which democracy is based, not simply the often frustrated hope that public opinion will at all times under all circumstances promptly identify itself with the public interest.

The voters selected us, in short, because they had confidence in our judgment and our ability to exercise that judgment from a position where we could determine what were their own best interests, as a part of the nation's interests. This may mean that we must on occasion lead, inform, correct and sometimes even ignore constituent opinion, if we are to exercise fully that judgment for which we were elected. But acting without selfish motive or private bias, those who follow the dictates of an intelligent conscience are not aristocrats, demagogues, eccentrics, or callous politicians insensitive to the feelings of the public. They expect—and not without considerable trepidation—their constituents to be the final judges of the wisdom of their course; but they have faith that those constituents—today, tomorrow, or even in another generation—will at least respect the principles that motivated their independent stand.

If their careers are temporarily or even permanently buried under an avalanche of abusive editorials, poison-pen letters, and opposition votes at the polls—as they sometimes are, for that is the risk they take—they await the future with hope and confidence, aware of the fact that the voting public frequently suffers from what ex-Congressman T. V. Smith called the lag "between our way of thought and our way of life." . . .

Moreover, I question whether any senator, before we vote on a measure, can state with certainty exactly how the majority of his constituents feel on the issue as it is presented to the Senate. All of us in the Senate live in an iron lung—the iron lung of politics, and it is no easy task to emerge from that rarefied atmosphere in order to breathe the same fresh air our constituents breathe. It is difficult, too, to see in person an appreciable number of voters besides those professional hangers-on and vocal elements who gather about the politician on a trip home. In Washington I frequently find myself believing that forty or fifty letters, six visits from professional politicians and lobbyists, and three editorials in Massachusetts newspapers constitute public opinion on a given issue. Yet in truth I rarely know how the great majority of the voters feel, or even how much they know of the issues that seem so burning in Washington.

Today the challenge of political courage looms larger than ever before. For our everyday life is becoming so saturated with the tremendous power of mass communications that any unpopular or unorthodox course arouses a storm of protests. . . . Our political life is becoming so expensive, so mechanized, and so dominated by professional politicians and public relations men that the idealist who dreams of independent statesmanship is rudely awakened by the necessities of election and accomplishment. . . .

And thus, in the days ahead, only the very courageous will be able to take the hard and unpopular decisions necessary for our survival. . . .

★ **President Kennedy** *was, with Jefferson, Lincoln and Franklin Roosevelt, one of the best writers to inhabit the White House.*

Questions

1. To what extent do legislators have a moral obligation to give priority to the interests of the nation as a whole?
2. To what extent is the judgment of legislators normally superior to the collective judgment of the people who elect them?
3. In practical terms, how common are local-national conflicts of interest?

4. To what extent do campaign contributions make it difficult for legislators to act as faithful trustees?
5. Which kind of legislator is more likely to be re-elected, the delegate or the trustee?

★ ★ ★

Congress: The Electoral Connection

David Mayhew

Imagine a member of the U.S. House of Representatives on the witness stand. The prosecutor says to her: "Congressperson, you have killed the Republic. In your desperate preoccupation with reelection you have neglected the vital interests of the nation!" The Congressperson, like a caricature from a courtroom novel, points to the judge, jury, and visitors and shouts: "You made me do it!" Unfortunately, no such drama unfolds in this article. Political scientist David Mayhew, assuming the guilt of the accused, scrutinizes the three reelection activities that consume so much of every Congressperson's time: advertising, credit claiming, and position taking. Mayhew's analysis does, however, provide some interesting, ironic clues as to where the responsibility actually rests.

Whether they are safe or marginal, cautious or audacious, congressmen must constantly engage in activities related to reelection. There will be differences in emphasis, but all members share the root need to do things—indeed, to do things day in and day out during their terms. The next step here is to present a typology, a short list of the *kinds* of activities congressmen find it electorally useful to engage in. The case will be that there are three basic kinds of activities. . . .

One activity is *advertising,* defined here as any effort to disseminate one's name among constituents in such a fashion as to create a favorable image but in messages having little or no issue content. A successful congressman builds what amounts to a brand name, which may have a generalized electoral value

★ ★ ★ ★ ★ ★

for other politicians in the same family. The personal qualities to emphasize are experience, knowledge, responsiveness, concern, sincerity, independence, and the like. Just getting one's name across is difficult enough; only about half the electorate, if asked, can supply their House members' names. It helps a congressman to be known. "In the main, recognition carries a positive valence; to be perceived at all is to be perceived favorably." A vital advantage enjoyed by House incumbents is that they are much better known among voters than their November challengers. They are better known because they spend a great deal of time, energy, and money trying to make themselves better known. There are standard routines—frequent visits to the constituency, nonpolitical speeches to home audiences, the sending out of infant care booklets and letters of condolence and congratulation. . . .

. . . There are some differences between House and Senate members in the ways they go about getting their names across. House members are free to blanket their constituencies with mailings for all boxholders; senators are not. But senators find it easier to appear on national television—for example, in short reaction statements on the nightly news shows. Advertising is a staple congressional activity, and there is no end to it. For each member there are always new voters to be apprised of his worthiness and old voters to be reminded of it.

A second activity may be called *credit claiming,* defined here as acting so as to generate a belief in a relevant political actor (or actors) that one is personally responsible for causing the government, or some unit thereof, to do something that the actor (or actors) considers desirable. The political logic of this, from the congressman's point of view, is that an actor who believes that a member can make pleasing things happen will no doubt wish to keep him in office so that he can make pleasing things happen in the future. The emphasis here is on individual accomplishment (rather than, say, party or governmental accomplishment) and on the congressman as doer (rather than as, say, expounder of constituent views). Credit claiming is highly important to congressmen, with the consequence that much of congressional life is a relentless search for opportunities to engage in it.

Where can credit be found? If there were only one congressman rather than 535, the answer would in principle be simple enough. Credit (or blame) would attach in Downsian fashion to the doings of the government as a whole. But there are 535. Hence it becomes necessary for each congressman to try to peel off pieces of governmental accomplishment for which he can believably generate a sense of responsibility. For the average congressman the staple way of doing this is to traffic in what may be called "particularized benefits." Particularized governmental benefits, as the term will be used here, have two properties: (1) Each benefit is given out to a specific individual, group, or geographical constituency, the recipient unit being of a scale that allows a single congressman to be recognized (by relevant political actors and other congressmen) as the claimant for the benefit (other congressmen being perceived as indifferent or hostile). (2) Each benefit is given out in apparently ad hoc fashion (unlike, say, social security checks) with a congressman apparently having a hand in the allocation. A particularized benefit can normally be regarded as a member of a class. That is, a benefit given out to an individual, group, or constituency can normally be looked upon by congressmen as one of a class of similar benefits given out to sizable numbers of individuals, groups, or constituencies. Hence the impression can arise that a congressman is getting "his share" of whatever it is the government is offering. . . .

In sheer volume the bulk of particularized benefits come under the heading of "casework"—the thousands of favors congressional offices perform for supplicants in ways that normally do not require legislative action. High school students ask for essay materials, soldiers for emergency leaves, pensioners for location of missing checks, local governments for grant information, and on and on. Each office has skilled professionals who can play the bureaucracy like an organ—pushing the right pedals to produce the desired effects.

But many benefits require new legislation, or at least they require important allocative decisions on matters covered by existent legislation. Here the congressman fills the traditional role of supplier of goods to the home district. It is a believable role; when a member claims credit for a benefit on the order of a dam, he may well receive it. Shiny construction projects seem especially useful. . . .

How much particularized benefits count for at the polls is extraordinarily difficult to say. But it would be hard to find a congressman who thinks he can afford to wait around until precise information is available. The lore is that they count—furthermore, given home expectations, that they must be supplied in regular quantities for a member to stay electorally even with the board. Awareness of favors may spread beyond their recipients, building for a member a general reputation as a good provider. . . .

The third activity congressmen engage in may be called *position taking,* defined here as the public enunciation of a judgmental statement on anything likely to be of interest to political actors. The statement may take the form of a roll call vote. The most important classes of judgmental statements are those prescribing American governmental ends (a vote cast against the war; a statement that "the war should be ended immediately") or governmental means (a statement that "the way to end the war is to take it to the United Nations"). The judgments may be implicit rather than explicit, as in: "I will support the president on this matter." . . . The congressman as position taker is a speaker rather than a doer. The electoral requirement is not that he make pleasing things happen but that he make pleasing judgmental statements. The position itself is the political commodity. Especially on matters where governmental responsibility is widely diffused it is not surprising that political actors should fall back on positions as tests of incumbent virtue. For voters ignorant of congressional processes the recourse is an easy one. . . .

The ways in which positions can be registered are numerous and often imaginative. There are floor addresses ranging from weighty orations to mass-produced "nationality day statements." There are speeches before home groups, television appearances, letters, newsletters, press releases, ghostwritten books, *Playboy* articles, even interviews with political scientists. On occasion congressmen generate what amount to petitions; whether or not to sign the 1956 Southern Manifesto defying school desegregation rulings was an important decision for southern members. Outside the roll call process the congressman is usually able to tailor his positions to suit his audiences. . . .

. . . On a controversial issue a Capitol Hill office normally prepares two form letters to send out to constituent letter writers—one for the pros and one (not directly contradictory) for the antis. Handling discrete audiences in person requires simple agility. . . .

> "You may find this difficult to understand," said Democrat Edward R. Roybal, the Mexican-American representative from California's thirtieth district, "but sometimes I wind up making a patriotic speech one afternoon and later on that same day an anti-war speech. In the patriotic speech I speak of past wars but I also speak of the need to prevent more wars. My positions are not inconsistent; I just approach different people differently."

Roybal went on to depict the diversity of crowds he speaks to: one afternoon he is surrounded by balding men wearing Veterans' caps and holding American flags; a few hours later he speaks to a crowd of Chicano youths, angry over American involvement in Vietnam. Such a diverse constituency, Roybal believes, calls for different methods of expressing one's convictions.

Indeed it does. Versatility of this sort is occasionally possible in roll call voting. For example a congressman may vote one way on committal and the other on final passage leaving it unclear just how he stands on a bill. Members who cast identical votes on a measure may give different reasons for having done so. Yet it is on roll calls that the crunch comes; there is no way for a member to avoid making a record on hundreds of issues, some of which are controversial in the home constituencies. Of course, most roll call positions considered in isolation are not likely to cause much of a ripple at home. But broad voting patterns can and do; member "ratings" calculated by the Americans for Democratic Action, Americans for Constitutional Action, and other outfits are used as guidelines in the deploying of electoral resources. And particular issues often have their alert publics. . . .

Probably the best position-taking strategy for most congressmen at most times is to be conservative—to cling to their own positions of the past where possible and to reach for new ones with great caution where necessary. . . .

There can be no doubt that congressmen believe that positions make a difference. An important consequence of this belief is their custom of watching each other's elections to try to figure out what positions are salable. Nothing is more important in Capitol Hill politics than the shared conviction that election returns have proven a point. Thus the 1950 returns were read not only as a rejection of health insurance but as a ratification of McCarthyism. When two North Carolina nonsigners of the 1956 Southern Manifesto immediately lost their primaries, the message was clear to southern members that there could be no straying from a hard line on the school desegregation issue. . . .

These, then, are the three kinds of electorally oriented activities congressmen engage in—advertising, credit claiming, and position taking. . . . No deterministic statements can be made; within limits each member has freedom to build his own electoral coalition and hence freedom to choose the means of doing it. Yet there are broad patterns. For one thing senators, with their access to the media, seem to put more emphasis on position taking than House members; probably House members rely more heavily on particularized benefits. But there are important differences among House members. Congressmen from the traditional parts of old machine cities rarely advertise and seldom take positions on anything (except on roll calls), but devote a great deal of time and energy to the distribution of benefits. In fact they use their office resources to plug themselves into their local party organizations. . . .

Another kind of difference appears if the initial assumption of a reelection quest is relaxed to take into account the "progressive" ambitions of some members—the aspirations of some to move up to higher electoral offices rather than keep the ones they have. There are two important subsets of climbers in the Congress—House members who would like to be senators (over the years about a quarter of the senators have come up directly from the House), and senators who would like to be presidents or vice presidents (in the Ninety-third Congress about a quarter of the senators had at one time or another run for these offices or been seriously "mentioned" for them). In both cases higher aspirations seem to produce the same distinctive mix of activities. For one thing credit claiming is all but useless. It does little good to talk about the bacon you have brought back to a district you are trying to abandon. And, as Lyndon Johnson found in 1960, claiming credit on legislative maneuvers is no way to reach a new mass audience; it baffles rather than persuades. Office advancement seems to require a judicious mixture of advertising and position taking. Thus a House member aiming for the Senate heralds his quest with press releases; there must be a new "image," sometimes an ideological overhaul to make ready for the new constituency. Senators aiming for the White House do more or less the same thing.

★ **David Mayhew** *is Sterling Professor of Political Science at Yale University.*

★ ★ ★ ★ ★

Questions

1. What does Mayhew mean by advertising? What does it include?
2. What does Mayhew mean by credit claiming? When is it successfully accomplished?
3. What does Mayhew mean by position taking?
4. To what extent is position taking normally controlled by a desire to get reelected?
5. Would term limits increase or decrease the preoccupation with reelection?

★ ★ ★

Political Change and the Character of the Contemporary Congress

Nelson W. Polsby

At first glance Congress appears a static institution, functioning in a basically consistent manner for more than two centuries. Political scientist Nelson Polsby suggests, however, that if we take a closer look we will discover that, within the last half century, "meaningful change has come . . . even to that seemingly rock-solid fortress of continuity and stasis, the U.S. Congress." In this chapter of The New American Political System *Polsby examines the dynamics of the alternating periods of congressional innovation, stalemate, and retrenchment.*

The purpose of this chapter is to describe the main characteristics of the contemporary Congress, especially as they have emerged from slightly less contemporary features of the political landscape. In a world of change, Americans have been able to rely upon great stability in their political institutions. They have been deprived of the stimulus of occupying armies, or the refreshment of an internal revolution, or some other constitutional upheaval leading to a wholly new and different political order. Such upheavals have frequently emerged in the modern world over the past half-century, transforming the governments under which large chunks of world's population

★ ★ ★ ★ ★ ★

exist. Nevertheless, I shall argue that meaningful change has come to the American political system within living memory, and even to that seemingly rock-solid fortress of continuity and stasis, the U.S. Congress.

★ Continuity and Change—An Overview

As we look at the past half-century of Congress as a historical whole, it is possible to discern an alternating and somewhat overlapping pattern of activity and retrenchment, of focus and stalemate in congressional affairs. Three times during the fifty-year period, Congress has gone through episodes of high productivity and strong coordination; and through three somewhat longer episodes, Congress has more or less ridden at anchor in the political system at large. Neither one mode nor the other is exclusively "natural" to Congress. Although the legitimacy of congressional behavior in either mode is frequently the subject of hot dispute, both roles are historically characteristic of Congress, and both fully express the powers of Congress as contemplated in the overall constitutional design. This design confides to Congress two complementary assignments: to represent the American people in at least some approximation of their variety and diversity and to provide a forum for the taking of significant policy initiatives. When there are great variation and disparity in the opinions of Americans about public policy, this fact is bound to be recognized in pulling and hauling on Capitol Hill; when there are unanimity and resolution, Congress moves its business with dispatch.

I will be brief and schematic in identifying episodes of concentrated congressional activity over the past fifty years. In these historical moments, Congress initiates or ratifies sizable expansions of federal activity, focuses its energies effectively, and undertakes policy innovation. The first of these moments was the enactment of the New Deal (1933-1936) in which the political innovations of Franklin Roosevelt's first 100 days occurred, including the revision of banking laws, the formation of the Securities and Exchange Commission, the establishment of a social security system, and the passage of the Wagner Act, among other events.[1] The second moment was the creation of wartime agencies in Washington (1939-1946), which greatly increased the administrative capacities of central government and broke through congressional resistance to governmental economic forecasting and planning and to an administratively augmented presidency. This episode included, among others, the Budget Act of 1939; the establishment of the Office of War Mobilization and (later) Reconversion; the Employment Act of 1946, which created, among other things, a Council of Economic Advisers; the consolidation of civilian control of the armed services into a Defense Department; and the establishment of the Central Intelligence Agency, the Atomic Energy Commission, and the National Science Foundation.[2] The third moment was the New Frontier Great Society (1963-1969). This period saw the completion of the New Deal: the enactment of Medicare and civil rights laws and the creation or enhancement of federal bureaucracies (such as the Department of Housing and Urban Development) dedicated to less-advantaged clientele.[3]

Interspersed with these episodes of innovation have been episodes of stalemate and retrenchment. We remember, for example, the thwarting of the later New Deal (1937-1941), in which President Roosevelt attempted, and failed, to pack the Supreme Court after the Court found many early New Deal measures unconstitutional. Roosevelt then attempted, and failed, to defeat conservative Democratic members of Congress in the 1938 election, and Congress no longer produced a cornucopia of new legislation. In time, "Doctor New Deal" gave way to "Doctor Win-the-War." Then, from roughly 1950, when the Truman administration began to be bogged down in loyalty-security issues, and all through the Eisenhower administration, when the threat of a presidential veto prevented all but the most consensual of congressional initiatives, on into most of the Kennedy presidency, in which the dominance of conservative committee chairmen in Congress narrowed the president's agenda (1950-1963). Congress and the presidency existed in a sort of equilibrium described by one liberal commentator as a "deadlock of democracy."[4] Since 1968, there has been a period of consolidation in reaction to the most recent set of policy innovations, and during most of this time Congress has been in Democratic while the presidency has been in Republican hands. During most of these three periods, political innovation has been resisted or at a stalemate, and little or no consensus has existed favoring new departures in governmental policy. Private authority has been preferred to the authority of central government.

That periods of stalemate should last, on average, about twice as long as periods of innovation ought not greatly to surprise even the most casual student of human nature. In important respects, the U.S. population resembles the population that attempted to build the Tower of Babel. The point of that Biblical fable is perfectly straightforward: to undertake great public works, it helps if everyone speaks the same language. Finding that language in the expression of common goals and organizing concerted strategies toward those goals are not trivial tasks when formal power and autonomy are dispersed and it is necessary to mobilize the consent of majorities several times over—first in subcommittees, then in committees, and then on the floor of each of two legislative chambers. The most prevalent alternative form of coordination—dictatorship—is scarcely relevant to the politics of a

TABLE 1 Periods of Congressional Innovation and Stalemate, 1933–1989

Innovation	Stalemate
New Deal (1933-37)	1937-41
Wartime (1939-46)	1947-63
Great Society (1964-68)	1969-89

Source: Author.

free and self-governing people. Far more relevant is the simple fact, illustrated in Table 1, that it takes time to gather up the consensus necessary to move a bicameral representative body that exists independently within a constitutional separation of powers.

Crises of various sorts—notably, a depression, a war, and a presidential assassination—have done a great deal to press Congress toward bouts of innovative activity.[5] In contrast, reforms of congressional procedures have played little or no role in galvanizing forward motion on the policy front. The era's most comprehensive overhaul of procedures, the reform of the committee system in 1946, came at the start of a long period of stalemate.[6] Other important institutional changes included Lyndon Johnson's redesign of the seniority rules for assigning Democratic senators to committees, which occurred during the Eisenhower lull, the 1961 packing of the House Rules Committee, and various reorganizations and reforms of the House in the mid-1970s.[7] All these changes were significant in creating institutionalized settings for a more successful and better coordinated deployment of the resources of the majority party in Congress, but none was sufficient in and of itself to create an avalanche of new and innovative public policies. Avalanches require the cooperation of the president. Even so, the most important facts about the capacity of Congress to respond—to presidential leadership or to leadership within Congress itself—are encoded in Congress's own organizational structure and in the ways in which the changing composition of Congress makes an impact upon congressional organization.

★ *The Contemporary Senate*

The chief changes that have overtaken the U.S. Senate in the past half-century can be compactly described. It has become a more national and outward-looking and a less state-oriented and inward-looking institution.[8] Now, as a matter of course, senators interest themselves in constituencies beyond those mobilized exclusively in their home states and seek to influence national policy on the assumption that it is politically useful to them to achieve national recognition and national resonance in their work. This sea change in the expectations of senators and in the way they do their work, and therefore in the role of the Senate in the political system, I believe has been driven, in large part, by a fundamental change in the career prospects of U.S. senators that occurred in the early 1950s as the result of the arrival on the scene of national television.

We are fortunate in having a superb baseline from which to measure the transformation of the Senate. In 1957 William S. White, congressional correspondent of the *New York Times,* published a book, *Citadel,* which admirably captures the spirit of the place—the prevailing institutional ideology, in effect—as it had been handed down and as he experienced it.[9] What he described was a rather stuffy and comfortable club, complete with leather chairs, snoozing members, obsequious attendants, cigar smoke, and bourbon, and run more or less exclusively for the benefit of a small number of elderly and important men. Internal norms of "clubability" were what mattered, White explained. Ideology did not matter, although it seemed to be coincidentally the case that the most significant people in the place, the old bulls who constituted the "inner club," as White called it, just so happened to be themselves conservative, mostly southern, and ill-disposed toward much of the New Deal, though not the part, presumably, that sent resources to southern farmers, or invented tax breaks for the oil industry. And they tended to be against the advance of civil rights, sometimes immoderately so, even though the institution was alleged to prize moderation. White made the claim that the more progressive senators tended to give offense primarily because of their lack of deference to the collegial norms of the place and not because of the substance of their views. One could not do well in the Senate by seeking publicity, he argued, or by running for "other" offices—presumably the presidency.

White argued that in its essence the Senate of those days was fulfilling its historic constitutional purpose of "cooling the legislative tea" by providing a calm, skeptical, and carefully deliberative counterweight to an allegedly more impulsive House of Representatives and a demonstrably more innovative and demanding presidency. What he described, however, was in large measure the very successful pursuit of parochial interest, sometimes clothed in statesmanship, sometimes not. The southerners who ran the place, insofar as they actually did so, attended with great care to the local prejudices of the small and lily-white electorates that sent them to Washington. No doubt they were obliged to do so to stay in the Senate, but nevertheless this was a clear prerequisite that allowed the more able among them to adopt an interest in broader concerns, such as foreign or military affairs or health care.[10]

There were some questions about the descriptive accuracy of White's portrait by the time it reached print. On the whole, it was accepted by a great many of those journalists and biographers who wrote about the Senate during the 1960s and even thereafter. It is common to find in magazine profiles of senators of that era, for example, some attempt to assess whether the subject was "in" or "outside" the "inner club," and one writer once went so far as to publish what he advertised as a guess at a comprehensive listing of the club's members.[11] This suggests that White captured something about the Senate that had high credibility among observers.

By the time *Citadel* was published, however, two forces were transforming the Senate radically. One was television, as I have mentioned, and the other was Lyndon Johnson. Television, it appears, happened very suddenly indeed to the U.S. Senate. In March 1951, a senator who had not much weight in the institution, Estes Kefauver of Tennessee, became an overnight media star as the result of the daytime broadcast of hearings of his committee's investigation of organized crime. Kefauver went on to run in the 1952 presidential primary elections—very successfully—and more or less on the strength of his lucky burst of publicity, he became a factor in the presidential nominating politics of the Democratic party for the rest of his life.[12]

From the 1950s onward, senators in wholesale lots, if they could manage it, began to maneuver themselves toward active roles in presidential nominating politics. Some of them simply used the Senate as a publicity springboard from which they could launch themselves. Kefauver and, more successfully, John Kennedy pursued that strategy. Others, following the early lead of Arthur Vandenberg and Robert A. Taft and, notably Hubert Humphrey sought to use their position in the Senate to pursue national policy goals in a way that would commend themselves to the party leaders who in those days controlled the presidential nominating process. In short, they began to invent the Senate as an arena within which, and not merely from which, one could launch a presidential bid.

Lyndon Johnson's ambitions led him to the latter strategy. Under the patronage of elders of the old inner club, he became the Democratic leader of the Senate mid-way through his first term as senator. He managed the business of his party in the Senate in part with an eye toward national office—refusing, for example, to join the southerners who put him into the leadership in overtly opposing civil rights initiatives.

Johnson's leadership of the Senate also greatly changed the institution itself. Decisions by consensus of senior members were replaced by the accretion of powers, large and small, in Johnson's own hands. Ralph Huitt, Joseph Clark, and others have left us a picture of a body that was being explicitly managed by an assiduous, indeed a compulsively driven, leader anxious to make a record and advance his career by coordinating as many different things as he could reach within the institution.[13]

By the time Johnson ascended to the vice presidency in 1961, the old citadel had largely disappeared. Senators were in no mood to continue the highly centralized pattern of leadership that Johnson had imposed on the institution. It was a great virtue that Mike Mansfield, Johnson's successor, vastly preferred a lighter touch on the reins.[14] But the Senate did not return to the collegial pattern of the old inner club. In the meantime the goals of senators had shifted perceptibly. A senator was in the White House—the first one originally elected to the presidency since Warren G. Harding. He had beaten a former member of the Senate in the general election as well as several in the prenomination period to get there. And a senator was vice president. At least ten senators—Russell, Kerr, Lodge, Johnson, Kefauver, Kennedy, Taft, Vandenberg, Symington, and Humphrey—had been serious contenders for the presidency over the past couple of nomination cycles.

In the 1930s and 1940s, it was unusual for senators to run for president, to cultivate national constituencies in the pursuit of policy initiatives, or to go out of their way to court publicity. Now all these activities are usual. Indeed, for a senator not to do so nowadays may even occasion comment.[15] These changes in the way individual senators conduct their jobs—facilitated by an enormous increase in staff, space, and equipment—have also wrought changes in the Senate's role as a corporate entity in the political system. As it has become a less collegial and reactive body, it has become more enterprising and innovative with respect to public policy. The Senate is now a place in which public policy ideas are tried out, floated, deliberated, and sometimes parked as they await the proper constellation of forces leading to eventual enactment. The careers of senators, and of the staffs of senators, depend far more on engagement with the new and far less upon the preservation of the old than was true forty or fifty years ago,

★ *The Contemporary House of Representatives*

As recently as twenty years ago, an observer might have said that, of all of the institutions of American government, the House of Representatives had been least touched by change since the creation of most of the institutions of modern America in the early years of the twentieth century. Not since 1919 had an ongoing committee assignment in the House violated the criterion of seniority.[16] New committee assignments were doled out by committees of each party, much influenced by the leaders of key state delegations.[17] Committee chairmen—those most senior in committee service in the House majority party—dominated the policy-making process within their respective domains, sometimes collaborating with ranking minority members, sometimes not. The Republican conference—the assembly of all Republican members—was considerably more influential than its counterpart body, the House Democratic caucus, in expressing a party mainstream ideological position. This was understandable in light of the fact that Republicans in the House were, on the whole, far more ideologically united.[18] For the most part, both the conference and the caucus were moribund, meeting to do serious business only once in every two years, to nominate and elect party leaders and to ratify the work of their respective committees on committees. For the rest of the time, party leaders—the Speaker, majority and minority leaders, and party whips—had custody of all the routines and schedules that are at the heart of the management of a complex legislative body, but they were constrained to exercise their power more or less in the fashion of tugboats urging a gigantic ocean liner along a course it intends to pursue anyway.

In recent years, however, change has finally come to the House of Representatives. Its main outlines are these: committee chairmen, once beyond reach, have been deposed and threatened with removal on several occasions since 1950, mainly for being out of step with mainstream sentiment among the Democratic members of the caucus; committees on committees have been reconstituted to give party leaders much more power, including the power unilaterally to appoint members to the key scheduling committee, the Rules Committee; and uniform rules of committee conduct have been written so as to spread power downward and outward to subcommittees and their chairmen. As subcommittees have gained autonomy and party leaders have gained responsibilities, power has slipped away from the chairmen of full committees who have been the major losers in the transformation that have taken place.[19]

The main engine of change has been the House Democratic caucus. Because the House has been firmly in the hands of a Democratic majority since 1954, what has happened to the Democrats is of paramount concern in following developments in the House. From 1937 until quite recently, the divisions within the caucus were sufficient to neutralize any attempts to use the caucus to coordinate the majority party. Southern Democrats—about 100 strong during most of the period, and virtually all of them from safe seats—made up almost half the Democratic members of the House—sometimes a little less, depending on Democratic electoral fortunes in the rest of the country. And about two-thirds of the southern Democrats were Dixiecrats, which meant that they were opposed to Democrats from the rest of the country on most issues of public policy and were perfectly willing to make coalitions with House Republicans to stop liberal legislation. So the actual ideological division in the House as a whole was frequently closely balanced when conservatives were not slightly in the lead. This made the

House the graveyard of many liberal proposals during the Truman and Kennedy presidencies.[20]

From time to time, House members closer to the mainstream of the national party would become restive. A small uprising of the peasants took place after the 1958 election, for example, when a flood of newly elected liberal Democrats descended on the House. As Speaker Rayburn saw all too clearly, this was bound to have no legislative consequences over the short run, since liberal initiatives could not in any event survive an Eisenhower veto. In their impatience a few young leaders of the party in the House—notably Eugene McCarthy, Lee Metcalf, and Frank Thompson—organized what in time became a programmatically oriented substitute for the caucus, the Democratic Study Group.[21] This group soon embraced most ideologically mainstream Democratic members. It took more than a few years for the House Democratic leadership to become comfortable with the study group, which at its most effective acted as the sort of communications system and rallying-point that the official Democratic whip system could not provide, because of its obligation to serve all Democratic members, whatever their ideological stripe.

By the 1970s, the caucus had aborted many of these functions of the study group and had revived as an instrument of House leadership after a fifty-year period of quiescence. What had happened was this: slightly more than a score of Dixiecrats had disappeared from the House, and they had been replaced by Republicans. It is not altogether intuitively obvious that a gain of about twenty-five Republican seats in the House would be a proximate cause of the liberalization of the House, but this, more or less, is what happened. It was, to be sure, not the new Republican members themselves, most of whom were ferociously conservative, who were the instruments of change but rather the drastic change in the make-up of the Democratic caucus that did the job, enabling the caucus to take initiatives that only a few years earlier would have torn it apart.

Indirectly, of course, these changes were the product of the nationalization of the South, of demographic changes that made the South more like the rest of the country, and of the party realignments that made it possible for southern Republicans to run for House seats and win. Promiscuous and ill-founded claims of party realignment at the national level have given the whole idea of realignment a bad name among careful analysis. If there has been a party realignment anywhere in America these past fifty years, however, it has occurred in the South, and it has led to liberalization in the House of Representatives.

Endnotes

[1]For discussion of these various achievements, see E. Pendleton Herring, *Presidential Leadership* (New York: Farrar and Rhinehart, 1940); and James T. Patterson, *Congressional Conservatism and the New Deal* (Lexington: University of Kentucky Press, 1967).

[2]See Herman Somers, *Presidential Agency* (Cambridge, Mass.: Harvard University Press, 1950); Stephen K. Bailey, *Congress Makes a Law: The Story Behind the Employment Act of 1946* (New York: Columbia University Press, 1950); Nelson W. Polsby, *Political Innovation in America* (New Haven, Conn.: Yale University Press, 1984); and Paul Hammond, *Organizing for Defense* (Princeton, N.J.: Princeton University Press, 1961).

[3]Much of this legislation passed in the 89th Congress. See *Congressional Quarterly Almanac, 89th Congress, 1st Session, 1965,* vol. 21 (Washington, D.C.: Congressional Quarterly Service, 1966), pp. 65-122; and *Congressional Quarterly Almanac, 89th Congress, 2nd Session, 1966,* vol. 22 (Washington, D.C.: Congressional Quarterly Service, 1967), pp. 69–94, 99–115.

[4]James McGregor Burns, *The Deadlock of Democracy: Four Party Politics in America* (Englewood, Cliffs, N.J.: Prentice-Hall, 1963).

[5]On crisis and its effects on innovation, see Polsby, *Political Innovation,* pp. 167–72.

[6]For authoritative commentary on the Legislative Reorganization Act of 1946, see George Galloway, *Congress at the Crossroads* (New York: Crowell, 1946).

[7]On Johnson, see Ralph K. Huitt, "Democratic Party Leadership in the Senate," *American Political Science Review,* vol. 55 (June 1961), pp. 331–44. On the packing of the Rules Committee, see Neil MacNeil, *Forge of Democracy: The House of Representatives* (New York: McKay, 1963), pp. 412-47; and William MacKaye, *A New Coalition Takes Control; The House Rules Committee Fight of 1961* (New Yok: McGraw Hill, 1963). On recent reforms of the House, see Norman Ornstein, "The Democrats Reform Power in the House of Representaives, 1969–1975," in Allan Sindler, ed., *America in the Seventies: Problems, Policies, and Politic* (Boston, Mass.: Little, Brown, 1977), pp. 2–48.

[8]See Polsby, *Congress and the Presidency* (Englewood Cliffs, N.J.: Prentice-Hall, 1986). pp. 85–113; and "What Hubert Humphrey Wrought," *Commentary,* vol. 78 (November 1984), pp. 47–50. Also see Alan Ehrenhalt, "In the Senate of the 80s Team Spirit Has Given Way to the Role of Individuals," *Congressional Quarterly,* September 4, 1982, pp. 2175–82.

[9]William S. White, *Citadel* (New York: Harper and Row, 1956). See also Joseph S. Clark, *Congress: The Sapless Branch* (New York: Harper and Row, 1964); and Ralph K. Huitt, "The Outsider in the Senate: An Alternative Role," *American Political Science Review,* vol. 55 (June 1961), pp. 556–75.

[10]See, for example, Virginia Van der Veer Hamilton's biography of a highly influential and constructive southern senator, *Lister Hill: Statesman from the South* (Chapel Hill, N.C.: University of North Carolina Press, 1987).

[11]Clayton Fritchey, "Who Belongs to the Senate's Inner Club?" *Harper's* (May 1967), pp. 104–10.

[12]Joseph B. Gorman, *Kefauver: A Political Biography* (New York: Oxford University Press, 1971).

[13]See Huitt, "Democratic Leadership in the Senate"; Clark, *Congress: The Sapless Branch;* Doris Kearns, *Lyndon Johnson and the American Dream* (New York: Harper and Row, 1976), pp. 72–159; and Rowland Evans and Robert Novak, *Lyndon B. Johnson: The Exercise of Power* (New York: New American Library, 1966), pp. 50–224.

[14]See John G. Stewart, "Two Strategies of Leadership: Johnson and Mansfield," in Nelson W. Polsby, ed., *Congressional Behavior* (New York: Random House, 1971), pp. 61–92.

[15]See, for example, Jeffrey H. Birnbum, "Nevada Senator Hecht, a Barrel of Gaffes, Staves off Spotlight," *Wall Street Journal,* August 11, 1988.

[16]See Nelson W. Polsby, Miriam Gallaher, and Barry Spencer Rundquist, "The Growth of the Seniority System in the U.S. House of Representatives," *American Political Science Review,* vol. 63 (September 1969), pp. 787–807.

[17]Nicholas Masters, "Committee Assignments in the House of Representatives," *American Political Science Review,* vol. 55 (June 1961), pp. 345–57.

[18]See Barbara Deckard Sinclair, "Determinants of Aggregate Party Cohesion in the U.S. House of Representatives, 1901–1956," *Legislative Studies Quarterly,* vol. 2 (May 1977), pp. 155–75, esp. p. 160; and Barbara Deckard and John Stanley, "Party Decomposition and Region: The House of Representatives, 1945–1970," *Western Political Quarterly,* vol. 27 (June 1974), pp. 249–64, esp. pp. 250, 257. Also see Julius Turner and Edward V. Schneier, Jr., *Party and Constituency: Pressures on Congress* (Baltimore, Md.: Johns Hopkins Press, 1970), pp. 41–106 and 165–89.

[19]See Thomas Mann and Norman Ornstein, eds., *The New Congress* (Washington, D.C.: American Enterprise Institute, 1981), especially chapters by Roger Davidson and Michael Malbin, pp. 99–177; Leroy Rieselbach, *Congressional Reform in the Seventies* (Morristown, N.J.: General Learning Press, 1977); and Ornstein, "The Democrats Reform Power."

[20]See Clem Miller, in John Baker, ed., *Member of the House* (New York: Scribner's, 1962), pp. 116–31.

[21]See Mark Ferber, *The Democratic Study Group: A Study of IntraParty Organization in the House of Representatives* (Ph.D. diss., University of California at Los Angeles, 1964.)

★ **Nelson W. Polsby** *is Heller Professor of Political Science at the University of California at Berkeley.*

★ ★ ★ ★ ★

Questions

1. To what extent is Congressional stability essential to the continued vitality of the nation?
2. What are the key factors that determine the extent of Congressional innovation?
3. What causes retrenchment?
4. To what extent is occasional retrenchment desirable?
5. To what extent does a predictable cycle of innovation, stalemate, and retrenchment provide the kind of continuity that the nation needs?

☆ ☆ ☆

An Introduction to Presidential-Congressional Rivalry

James H. Thurber

Counseling psychologists have long noted how many marriages evince an unspoken role assignment: typically, in such a marriage, one spouse actively initiates while the other passively responds. Many observers of Congress have similarly noted that, most of the time, the president proposes while Congress disposes, and certainly an organization of 535 members is generally in a better position to respond and reflect that to initiate. In this thoughtful study, however, James Thurber looks more deeply into the subject, identifying seven basic factors that determine much of the character and substance of presidential-congressional relations: constitutional design, differing constituencies, varying terms of office, weakness of political parties, divided party control, competition for power, and pluralism.

The 1994 midterm congressional election reversed a generation of Democratic dominance in the House, brought divided party control of government again, and dramatically reshaped the rivalry between the president and Congress. The 1994 election not only brought an overwhelming victory for the Republican party and major changes in the policy agenda and the structure of Congress, but it also dramatically changed the balance of power between the president and Congress. Having received an electoral mandate to implement their legislative program of cutbacks, devolution, and

☆ ☆ ☆ ☆ ☆ ☆

deregulation, Republicans in Congress boldly set about dictating the policy agenda. In contrast, President Clinton found that his negotiating power had been significantly diminished. The centralized decision-making system in the House of Representatives also limited the president's ability to influence Congress.

After the historic 1994 midterm election, President Clinton was impelled to reach out to the new Republican leadership in the House and the Senate. After Speaker Newt Gingrich, R-Ga., received a boost in power from a highly unified House Republican Conference and the structural reforms that it imposed upon the House, President Clinton's activist agenda during the 103d Congress was overshadowed by the Contract with America and the GOP-led drive to balance the budget and cut back the federal government. However, ultimately, neither President Clinton nor the new Republican leadership could govern effectively without the cooperation of the other. Elections have an impact on presidential and congressional relations, as shown so clearly in the shift in political mood and policy from 1992 to 1994.

The 1992 presidential election brought a Democrat to the White House and unified party control of government for the first time in twelve years. At the heart of the 1992 presidential campaign was President Clinton's promise to fix the economy and to use the presidency to do so. He believed in an activist role for the federal government. The election produced the largest turnover of membership in the House of Representatives in more than forty years; 110 new members took office in January 1993. Although President Clinton had a majority of Democrats in the House and Senate, unified party control of government, and many new members of Congress who wanted change, he found out quickly that 43 percent support in the election (all but four House members ran ahead of him in absolute votes) did not translate into a mandate or easy coalition to push his activist agenda. Clinton sent strong signals to the Hill that he wanted to cooperate with Congress as a "New Democrat" with a policy agenda along centrist lines. However, it was difficult for the president to find common ground for his centrist agenda with the Republicans and liberal Democrats.

Unified party control of government did not bring an end to the rivalry between the president and Congress. Within a few months, bitter struggles had broken out pitting the president not only against Republicans in Congress, but also against important congressional leaders within the Democratic party. Although President Clinton presented himself as a moderate, pragmatic president, he had to work with the majority of House Democrats, whose center of gravity had moved to the left on the political spectrum and who, as a result, frequently opposed the president's policies. For example, eleven Democratic House subcommittee chairs voted against President Clinton's economic package in May 1993, and the president's program barely survived. In a clear indication of the lack of discipline in the Democratic party, a subsequent demand by some House members, especially freshmen, that the eleven be stripped of their chairmanships was rejected by the House leadership. Clinton also had to build cross-party coalitions with more conservative Republican leaders to pass several major bills on his agenda, such as the North American Free Trade Agreement (NAFTA) and the General Agreement on Tariffs and Trade (GATT). Many of President Clinton's initiatives were stopped or amended so thoroughly that they bore little resemblance to his original proposals. Unified government did not guarantee presidential dominance in Clinton's relationship with Congress.

President George Bush had similar "problems" with Congress. Immediately after his inauguration, President Bush, also in a gesture of good will, praised Congress: "To the Members of the Congress, to the institution of the House of Representatives and the Senate of the United States, may they flourish and may they prosper." In response to President Bush's efforts to build better relations with Congress, Thomas S. Foley, D-Wash., then House majority leader, said, "That's another example of President Bush reaching out. We're going to respond very positively to that." President Bush went on to have one of the lowest records of support for his policy initiatives in Congress in the last fifty years. Presidents Clinton and Bush had every good intention to work with broad bipartisan coalitions in Congress, but whether unified or divided party control of government, it did not work out that way.

Good will does not generally characterize the institutional relationship between Congress and the president. President Clinton earned some of the highest presidential support scores (the percentage of presidential proposals that are approved by Congress, calculated annually by *Congressional Quarterly Weekly Report*) in his first two years of office, but never rose over 50 percent in the national public opinion polls. He is popularly known as a president that did not get his agenda through Congress—health care reform and welfare reform in particular. However, he did continue to reduce the federal budget deficit, built bipartisan support for successful passage of NAFTA and GATT, and passed the family and medical leave law. In his first year in office, President Bush fared worse than any other president elected in the postwar era, winning only 63 percent of the roll-call votes on which he took an unambiguous position. Despite Bush's popularity with the American people during Desert Storm (the highest in the polls of any postwar president at the end of his first year) and his sincere efforts to build bridges between the White House and Capitol Hill, executive-legislative relations during his presidency remained deeply rooted in political and institutional divisions. These divisions did not evaporate for President Clinton with unified government in 1993-1994, and they were clearly revealed in Clinton's relationship with Congress after the 1994 election. What are the roots of the rivalry between the president and Congress?

★ The Roots of Presidential-Congressional Rivalry

In this introduction I will examine seven root causes of the rivalry between the president and Congress: constitutional design, different constituencies, varying terms of office, weak political parties, divided party control of government, ongoing competition for power, and pluralism.

Constitutional Design

The Framers of the Constitution bequeathed to us one of the most enduring rivalries in government, that between the presidency and Congress. The Constitution separates the three branches of government (legislative, executive, and judicial) but combines their functions, creating conflict and shared powers. The president and the Congress are organized differently, and they are jealous of their constitutional prerogatives.

The Constitution invests Congress with "all legislative Powers," but it also authorizes the president to recommend and to veto legislation. If the president vetoes a bill, it shall be repassed by two thirds of the Senate and the House of Representatives" (Article I, section 7). Because it is so difficult for Congress to gain a two-thirds' vote, presidential vetoes are usually sustained. Through 1994 presidents had used the veto 2,515 times; 1,065 of these were "pocket vetoes" not subject to congressional override. Congress overrode presidential vetoes slightly more than 7 percent of the time (104 times) when it had the opportunity to vote on them. Thus, the threat of a veto in the legislative process gives the president an important bargaining tool, however, President Clinton did not use this tool until 1995, when he vetoed a $16 billion rescission bill. Clinton also used the veto in his confrontation with the Republican-led Congress over the cuts in Medicaid, Medicare, welfare, education, and federal environmental programs in the fiscal year 1996 federal budget. The greatest power of the president in divided government is often the power to say no. President Clinton embraced that notion in the budget battle when he said: ". . . this is one of those moments in history when I'm grateful for the wisdom of our Founding Fathers. The Congress gets to propose, but the president has to sign or veto, and that Constitution gave me that authority and one of the reasons for the veto is to prevent excess. They knew what they were doing and we're going to use the Constitution they gave us to stand up for what's right."

Congress is given a broad list of powers in Article I, section 8, of the Constitution, but the greatest power of Congress is its authority to pass laws directly binding upon all citizens. Also of great importance is the power of the purse. Congress must authorize and appropriate funds for the president and the executive branch agencies. Presidents may propose budgets for the federal government, but Congress has the final say on spending, bringing automatic rivalry and conflict over spending priorities. Congress also has the power to levy and collect taxes, to borrow and coin money, and to regulate foreign and interstate commerce. A central element of the rivalry between the president and Congress has been battles over tax and trade policy. The powers to declare war, to provide for a militia, and to adopt laws concerning bankrupt, naturalization, patents, and copyrights are also bestowed on Congress. The interpretation of presidential and congressional war power has changed over time and is another contemporary source of conflict. Congress has the authority to establish or eliminate executive branch agencies and departments and to oversee their operations. The Senate must approve cabinet nominees, ambassadors, and Supreme Court and federal judicial appointees before they can take office. A president cannot enter into a binding treaty with a foreign government without a two-thirds' vote of the Senate, nor can the president "declare war," a power the Constitution purposely gives to Congress. All of these constitutional congressional and presidential powers force both institutions to confront each other in governance, which more often than not creates rivalry and conflict.

A dramatic but rarely employed check on the president is impeachment. Executive branch officials can be impeached (formally accused) by a majority vote in the House and tried in the Senate. If two-thirds of the senators vote to convict, the official is removed from office. Only President Andrew Johnson has been tried on impeachment charges; the vote fell one short of the number required to convict him. The House Judiciary Committee recommended that Richard M. Nixon be impeached for transgressions in connection with the Watergate burglary of the offices of the Democratic National Committee—and the ensuing cover-up. Nixon, however, resigned the presidency before a full session of the House could vote on the impeachment issue. The threat of impeachment establishes an important check on the president and executive branch.

The Framers of the Constitution deliberately fragmented power between the national government and the states and among the executive, legislative, and judicial branches. They also divided legislative powers by creating two coequal houses, a bicameral Congress, which further magnifies rivalry and conflict. Although divided, Congress was designed to be independent and powerful, able to check the power of the executive and to be directly linked with the people through popular, periodic elections. The Framers wanted an effective and powerful federal government, but they wanted to limit its power in order to protect personal and property rights. Having experienced the abuses of English monarchs and their colonial governors, the men who wrote the Constitution were wary of excessive authority in an executive. They also feared "elective despotism," or excessive legislative power, something the Articles of Confederation had given their own state legislatures.

Therefore, the Framers created three branches of government with none having a monopoly. This separation of powers restricted the power of any one branch, and it required cooperation among the three in order for them to govern effectively. Today, as then, political action requires cooperation between the president and Congress. Yet the Constitution, in the way it divided power between the two branches, created an open invitation for conflict. In sum, in creating a separated presidency and two equal legislative chambers, the Framers guaranteed on ongoing rivalry between the president and Congress.

Different Constituencies

The U.S. system of government, unlike parliamentary systems throughout the world, elects the executive and members of the legislature independently. The president is elected from vastly broader electoral coalitions than are representatives and senators, who have narrow constituencies in districts or states. Members of Congress, even those who belong to the president's party or hail from his home state, represent specific interests that can conflict with the interests of the president, who represents the nation as a whole. James Madison well understood this dichotomy of interests as an important source of conflict between the president and Congress: "The members of the federal legislature will be likely to attach themselves too much to local objects. . . . Measures will too often be decided according to their probable effect, not on the national prosperity and happiness, but on the prejudices, interests, and pursuits of the governments and the people of the individual States."

Varying Terms of Office

The interaction of Congress and the president is shaped not only by their different constituencies but also by their different terms of office. The constitutional structure of U.S. government, which separates the Congress and the president, sets different terms of office for representatives, senators, and the president, and ensures they will be chosen from different constituency bases.

House members are elected every two years; senators, every six. Presidents have only four years, possibly eight, in which to establish their programs. They are expected to set the national policy agenda and usually move rapidly in the first year before the traditional decline in their popularity. Presidents are not concerned about reelection after the first four years of office; establishing good public policy and an honored place in history is their first priority. Other interests are certainly operative, but reelection concerns for members of Congress are most important, even for new members who support term limits. Legislators, then, are often reluctant to allow their workload and policy agenda to be dictated by a president who has no electoral mandate to do so.

Congress moves more slowly than the president; it is deliberative and inefficient primarily because it represents a vast array of local interests. Congress passes new laws slowly and reviews old ones carefully. The House of Representatives of the 104th Congress had centralized power and was more efficient than the House of any other modern Congress, but this too caused conflict with President Clinton's agenda. The decision-making pace of Congress and of the president is not the same because of their different terms of office, electoral base, and perceived constituent mandates. The result of these differences is rivalry, conflict, and often deadlock.

Weak Political Parties

The federal system of state-based political parties contributes to the independence of members of Congress from the president. The president must work with weak, decentralized political parties that exercise little discipline and even less leverage over members. Senators and representatives usually run their own races with their own financing. The way they respond to local conditions has little to do with national party platforms or presidential politics. Members freely pursue their own interests without fear of discipline from the president.

Independence from political parties and the president allows legislators to seek benefits for their own constituents and to serve specialized interests. Thomas Mann argues further that:

> [t]he changes that swept through the political system during the 1960s and 1970s—the increase in split-ticket voting, the growing cost of campaigns and reliance on contributions from special interests, the rise of television, the expansion and growing political sophistication of interest groups in Washington, and the democratization and decentralization of Congress—may well have weakened

the classic iron triangles, but they also heightened the sensitivity of politicians to all forms of outside pressure.

For Republican members of the House, the 1994 election deviated from the normal individualistic election. The Contract with America, signed by three hundred Republican candidates for the House, "nationalized" the campaign for most of those candidates. No incumbent Republican House member lost in the 1994 election. Republicans earned a net gain of seventeen in the fifty-two open-seat House contests and lost only four Republican-controlled House open seats to the Democrats. Thirty-five House incumbent Democrats lost. With the Democrats losing fifty-two seats in the House and eight Senate seats, the mandate of the new Republicans was to be loyal to the contract, to the House Republican leadership, and to the reduction of individualism in the House. Party discipline came from the congressional party leaders, not from the grass-roots party organizations throughout the United States. This was unique in modern congressional elections and created the basis of conflict with President Clinton.

Divided Party Control of Government

Another electorally based impediment to legislative-executive cooperation is divided government, as shown by the dramatic election of 1994, which left a Democrat in the White House working with Republican majorities in the House and Senate. There are two varieties of divided government (the condition that exists when the majority party in either or both houses of Congress differs from the party of the president): divided party control of Congress and split control of Congress and the White House. Opposing parties have controlled the presidency and one or both houses of Congress in twenty-two of the past twenty-eight years (79 percent of the time from 1969 through 1996), with the Republicans mainly controlling the White House and the Democrats controlling Congress. From 1887 to 1954, divided party control of government occurred only eight years (14 percent of the time), but from President Dwight D. Eisenhower's first year (1953) through President Clinton's fourth year in office (1996), it occurred twenty-eight years (56 percent of the time) (see Table 1). Therefore, divided party control of government at the federal level has been the norm in modern U.S. politics.

The trend toward ticket splitting between presidential and congressional candidates further exacerbates already strained relations. Election returns for Congress have increasingly diverged from national presidential returns; "the range in the . . . variance, which measures the extent to which changes in

Table 1 Unified and Divided Party Control of Government, 1901–1996

Year	*President*	*Senate*	*House*
1901-1903	R	R	R
1903-1905	R	R	R
1905-1907	R	R	R
1907-1909	R	R	R
1909-1911	R	R	R
1911-1913	Divided party control		
1913-1915	D	D	D
1915-1917	D	D	D
1917-1919	D	D	D
1919-1923	Divided park control		
1921-1923	R	R	R
1923-1925	R	R	R
1925-1927	R	R	R
1927-1929	R	R	R
1929-1931	R	R	R
1931-1933	Divided party control		
1933-1935	D	D	D
1935-1937	D	D	D
1937-1939	D	D	D
1939-1941	D	D	D
1941-1943	D	D	D
1943-1945	D	D	D
1945-1947	D	D	D
1947-1949	Divided party control		
1949-1951	D	D	D
1951-1953	D	D	D
1953-1955	R	R	R
1955-1961	Divided party control		
1961-1963	D	D	D
1963-1965	D	D	D
1965-1967	D	D	D
1967-1969	D	D	D
1969-1977	Divided party control		
1977-1979	D	D	D
1979-1981	D	D	D
1981-1993	Divided party control		
1993-1995	D	D	D

Source: "Political Party Affiliations in Congress and the Presidency, 1789-1991," *Congressional Quarterly's Guide to Congress,* 4th ed. (Washington, D.C.: Congressional Quarterly Inc., 1991), 93-A and 94-A.

local returns differ from the change in national returns, has more than doubled." During the past thirty years, as the power of political parties has declined significantly, there has been a corresponding rise in individualistic candidacies for the presidency, the Senate, and the House. Fewer and fewer members of Congress ride into office on the electoral "coattails" of the president. This has led to the election of presidents who find it difficult to translate electoral support into governing support. The scarcity of presidential coattails by Bush in 1988 and Clinton in 1992 brings the conclusion that "the emperor has no coat." Bush was the first candidate since John F. Kennedy to win the White House while his party lost seats in the House. Clinton ran behind all but four members of the House. With the decline of presidential coattails, strong-willed members of Congress are largely beyond the president's control. They are often more responsive to district and specialized interests than to the national agenda of the president.

Unified party control of government does not mean the two branches will work closely together. Divided government does not mean that the two branches will fight. David Mayhew found that when it comes to passing major legislation or conducting investigations, it "does not seem to make all that much difference whether party control of the American government happens to be unified or divided." However, we do know that it was generally easier for presidents to govern during periods of unified government such as the early days of the New Deal (1933-1937), during World War II (1941-1945), and during the Great Society (1964-1965)—than in periods of divided government (especially since 1981, Reagan's first year in office).

Ongoing Competition for Power

The balance of power between and within the institutions of Congress and the presidency is dynamic and conflict is inevitable, another root cause of the rivalry between the president and Congress. The 1994 election brought the most centralized power structure in the House since Republican Speaker Joseph G. "Czar" Cannon, who served from 1903 to 1911. Just one year before, the 103d Congress under Speaker Thomas Foley was decentralized and fragmented. What the public expects from each institution varies over time, as dramatically shown by the differences between the 103d and 104th Congresses. For two hundred years Congress has continued to represent local interests and to respond (some think too much) to political preferences and public pressures. Nevertheless, the institution has changed dramatically. The reforms of the past two decades have made Congress even more representative and accountable and, in the 104th Congress, more centralized. The reforms of the last twenty years have changed the way it makes laws, passes budgets, oversees the executive branch, and confronts the president.

As the congressional leadership is centralized and made more effective by one party, the power of the president is often diminished, as we have seen in the 104th Congress. This creates more tension between the two branches, with a clash between the president's national policy agenda and the agenda of Congress. President Clinton's legislative successes during the 103d Congress (1993-1995) were impressive, with a remarkable 86.4 percent win record on the votes on which he took a position. The 1994 election changed his success and the competitive environment with Congress; he was overshadowed by the Contract with America, the leadership of Speaker Newt Gingrich, and the Republican drive to balance the budget. Unified government and a decentralized Congress helped his legislative successes in 1993 and 1994; a massive loss in the midterm elections to the Republicans created conflict and deadlock between the two branches. If the president is popular with the American public, he has electoral coattails bringing many new members into Congress that are beholden to him, and if he has a well-organized and well-run White House and administration, he is more able to control the national policy agenda. An example of a president meeting these criteria is President Lyndon Baines Johnson during his first two years of office, before the war in Vietnam undermined his influence in Congress and popularity with the American voters. His central core of authority in dealing with the Congress reduced conflict between the two branches. Structural reforms within the presidency (for example, the establishment of the Bureau of the Budget and, later, the creation of the Office of Management and Budget and the expansion of the post-World War II White House staff) and change in Congress (for example, the centralization of power by the Republican party congressional leadership and increased party unity in the 104th Congress) have direct impacts on the ability of the president to dominate the legislative agenda and for the Congress to act independently from the president. Thus, cooperation and conflict between the two branches are the norm.

Pressure to check the power of the president through the War Powers Resolution of 1973 and the Budget and Impoundment Control Act of 1974 brought changes that helped Congress reclaim some of the power it had lost to the president during the previous decades. Many institutional reforms of the 1970s, however, resulted in decentralization, which made Congress more democratic but also less efficient. With the new openness came greater accountability and responsiveness but at the price of efficiency and effectiveness as a lawmaking body. Modern presidents find Congress harder to influence than did their predecessors in the White House.

Members of Congress are more independent. And with the weakening of strict seniority rules wielded by strong parties, coordinating the legislative process was more difficult for congressional party leaders until the House reforms of the 104th Congress that centralized power with the Republican leadership.

Although Congress created new ways of checking presidential power in the 1970s, ultimately legislative-executive relationships are not zero-sum games. If one branch gains power, the other does not necessarily lose it. The expansion of the federal government since World War II has given vast new power to both branches. Events and public policy issues contribute to the policy-making power of both the president and Congress. The war on drugs, environmental concerns, the savings and loan crisis, Desert Storm, and continuing budget deficits have led to new administrative (and legislative) powers expanding the scope of both branches. Even these crises, however, are not enough to reduce the rivalry between the two institutions.

The decentralization and fragmentation of power within Congress was dramatically altered as a result of the 1994 election. The Speaker, the only structural feature of the House dictated by the Constitution, had significant power before Speaker Gingrich expanded that power even more. Gingrich appointed the committee chairs and increased his influence over committee assignments, placing freshmen on the Ways and Means, Appropriations, Rules, and Commerce Committees. Of the eleven Republican openings on the Appropriations Committee, Speaker Gingrich appointed nine freshmen, thus assuring cohesion and loyalty from the new Republicans in the House. Gingrich's control over committee assignments for freshmen and over the selection of chairs was a dramatic break from the decentralized and more democratic House of the last twenty years. He abolished proxy voting in committees, thus limiting the power of committee chairs. He reduced committee staffing, abolished independent subcommittee staff, and placed six-year term limits on committee chairs, thus reducing the power of the chairs and increasing the power of the leadership. Gingrich, with the support of the Republican Conference, also limited committee assignments and restructured the committee system generally. All of these reforms helped to centralize power in the Speakership. Under the reformed House of Representatives, Speaker Gingrich gained substantial power to control the policy agenda using key provisions in the GOP Contract with America. He was able to overshadow President Clinton (and the Senate) and pass far-reaching legislation that projected a balanced budget in seven years, cut taxes, cut back spending on Medicare, Medicaid, and welfare, and decentralized federal government, sending more programs and money to the states. Not only the Republican party dominance of the House and Senate, but also the internal change in the House power structure changed fundamentally the relationship with the president in 1995.

Pluralism

Pluralism, group-based politics, limits the power of the president and Congress to pursue their own agendas and thereby increases the competition between them. Policy-making gridlock often comes from competition among organized interests in society, not from divided party control of government. As more people are organized, as the political process is opened to more groups and classes than ever before, and as the demands and needs of those competing interests are weighed and mediated in the political process, the power of the president and Congress to control the policy agenda is reduced. The constitutional First Amendment rights, especially freedom of speech, freedom of assembly, freedom of the press, and freedom to petition government for grievances, are the foundation of pluralism in U.S. politics. The decay of political party organizations in the last thirty years in the United States has helped the growth of pluralism. As political parties have lost power to recruit and elect candidates that are loyal to party leaders in government, interest groups have gained political power. The United States is experiencing "hyperpluralism," or extreme competition among groups that makes it almost impossible to define the public good in terms of anything other than the collection of special narrow interests. Hyperpluralism contributes fundamentally to the rivalry between the president and Congress and often leads to deadlock between the two branches of government (as with the fiscal year 1996 budget) by making it difficult to make the necessary compromises between the national interests of the president and the parochial interests of members of Congress.

Conclusion

Organization theorists suggest that conflict produces incentives for organizations to centralize decision-making power. When an organization is threatened, a premium is placed on efficiency, effectiveness, and cohesiveness in setting strategy. After forty years of Democratic control and two years of conflict from the Clinton White House, the House Republicans centralized their decision-making power structure in unprecedented ways. The House Republican centralization of decision making in the 104th Congress reduced individualism and brought about a more efficient and cohesive institution in its battle with President Clinton. Threatened by a unified Republican House, President Clinton reorganized and centralized his White House staff through Leon Panetta, his chief of staff. He simplified his policy agenda and built a more tightly knit and effective legislative affairs operation. Faced with a Democratic majority in the House in the 1980s, then-Minority Whip Newt Gingrich helped to build a cohesive, centralized, and efficient opposition that was eventually used as a majority party organization against President Clinton and the congressional Democrats in 1995.

Intense rivalry between the president and Congress is inevitable in an electoral system that can produce divided party control of the two branches. Cooperation may be more likely when both the president and Congress are of the same party. Even so, because of the wide range of views within a party, unified government is no safeguard against conflict, as was shown with President Clinton and the congressional Democratic party in 1993 and 1994. Partisanship may also serve to move legislation. For example, the 1986 tax reform law benefited from the battle between the Democrats and Republicans because both sides saw political advantage in moving the bill or disadvantage in being seen as obstructionist. The give-and-take between national and local representation, deliberation and efficiency, openness and accountability, specific interests and the "public good" ensures a certain amount of confrontation between Congress and the president. As we have seen, their relations are shaped by an amalgam of factors: constitutional design, different constituencies, different terms of office, weak political parties, divided party control of government, ongoing competition for power, and pluralism. Although the rivalry and conflict between Congress and the president are inherent in our system of government, presidents must find support in Congress and members must seek assistance from the White House. To succeed in office every president must surmount the constitutional and political obstacles to pass their legislative program and establish a working relationship with Congress.

Separation of powers and the division of political control between presidents and congresses do not present an insurmountable barrier to good public policy making. Presidents need to lead both public opinion and a consensus among the policy communities in Congress to solve the problems that are so readily visible. Overcoming divided government, changing public opinion, building consensus, and establishing the nation's policy priorities calls for leadership from the president or from inside Congress. Congress and the president must work together. Unified partisan control of both branches of government does not guarantee cooperation. Divided government does not guarantee conflict. Governing calls for bargaining, accommodation, and compromise by Congress and the president, the basis of our "separated" system of government.

★ **James Thurber** *is Director of the Center for Congressional and Presidential Studies and the Campaign Management and Public Affairs/Lobbying Institutes at American University in Washington, D.C.*

★ ★ ★ ★ ★

Questions

1. To what extent should Congress, under normal conditions, be satisfied with responding to presidential initiatives?
2. The Founding Fathers symbolically placed their description of the legislature in Article 1 of the Constitution, implying Congressional primacy among equal branches. To what extent did their design of Congress, to the contrary, make the presidency the governmental prime mover?
3. Of the factors that Thurber mentions, which are the most important in determining the quality of presidential-congressional relations?
4. Should the power of Congress, with respect to the presidency, be strengthened?
5. To what extent is continuously strong presidential leadership desirable?

☆ ☆ ☆

The War Power

Although the Constitution declares that Congress shall have the power to declare war, technology has effectively and necessarily transferred the authority to initiate external conflict from Congress to the president. How did this happen? What has been done about it? These questions are answered in this selection. Starting with the causes, stipulations, and effects of the War Powers Resolution of 1973, the authors examine the history of military conflicts from President Ford to President Clinton within the context of congressional-presidential relations, emphasizing the importance of cross-branch cooperation and accommodation.

☆ The War Powers Resolution of 1973

After decades of debate, Congress passed legislation in 1973 to limit war-making actions by the President. The statute calls for "collective judgment" by Congress and the President before U.S. forces are sent into combat, especially for long-term military engagements. The War Powers Resolution permits the President to act unilaterally for up to ninety days, but congressional approval is required after that. For reasons to be explained, that particular provision has never worked as intended. The statute also provides for reports to Congress and encourages the President to consult with Congress before taking action.

Given the political environment at the time the War Powers Resolution was passed, it is natural to view it solely within the context of the Vietnam War. Indeed the legislative history is replete with partisan attacks on Richard Nixon and even includes motivations to retaliate against the policies of Lyndon Johnson. However, the War Powers Resolution represents something more than a mix of partisan and personal politics. It reflects almost four decades of bipartisan effort to recapture legislative authority that had drifted to the President.

☆ ☆ ☆ ☆ ☆ ☆

When the Pendulum Stopped Swinging

Executive-legislative conflicts from President George Washington to the 1930s were characterized by a cycle—strong Presidents, (Jefferson, Jackson, Lincoln, and Wilson, among others) followed by a resurgent Congress. Power did not remain lodged in a single branch for very long. The system of checks and balances functioned in a way to disperse power and block institutional ambition. Even after major military conflicts, such as the Civil War and World War I, Congress was able to restore its place as a coequal branch.

Something different happened in the 1930s. The powers transferred to President Franklin D. Roosevelt during the Great Depression and later during World War II did not return to Congress. What had been a temporary disequilibrium in earlier periods, quickly righted to begin a new cycle, now became a permanent fixture of executive-legislative relations. Congress recognized the radical nature of this transformation and made concerted efforts, after World War II, to regain its stature.

After his election in 1932, President Roosevelt sought, and obtained, major grants of emergency authority from Congress. In his inaugural address in 1933, Roosevelt drew an analogy between the Great Depression and a time of war, urging the country to move forward "as a trained and loyal army." He hoped that the normal balance of executive and legislative authority would be sufficient to meet the crisis, but "it may be that an unprecedented demand and need for undelayed action may call for temporary departure from that normal balance of public procedure." This temporary departure became a permanent condition, in part through Roosevelt's initiatives, in part through forces beyond his control.

The pendulum seemed ready to swing back toward Congress after Roosevelt's reelection victory in 1936. He had badly miscalculated in his effort to pack the Supreme Court and seize additional executive authority. Congress was clearly poised to recapture power that had slipped to the President. The normal swings of presidential and congressional dominance were about to resume. At that very moment, however, rumblings in Europe and the Far East set the stage for World War II and continued executive dominance.

With the United States in the midst of hostilities, Roosevelt warned Congress in 1942 that he would act with or without statutory authority. He gave Congress a deadline and said that in the event that Congress "should fail to act, and act adequately, I shall accept the responsibility, and I will act." In that same address, he claimed that when "the war is won, the powers under which I act automatically revert to the people—to whom they belong."[1]

In fact, after the war was won, presidential powers did not revert either to Congress or to the people. President Harry Truman announced the end of the war in Europe on May 8, 1945, and the surrender of Japan on August 14, 1945, and yet he did not proclaim the "termination of hostilities" until December 31, 1946. Furthermore, he retained a number of emergency powers by claiming that "a state of war still exists."[2] On April 28,1952, he finally signed a statement ending the state of war with Japan and terminating the national emergencies that Roosevelt had proclaimed in 1939 and 1941. Although actual hostilities had lasted for less then four years, Roosevelt and Truman exercised emergency and war powers for more than twelve years.

Truman's initiative in sending troops to Korea in 1950 dramatized the growth of executive power. The legality of his action has been debated for decades. What is not debatable is that the President, for the first time, had committed U.S. troops abroad into a major conflict on his own authority. He acted without a declaration of war or specific authorization from Congress. Significantly, the President's critics at that time were conservative Republicans; liberal Democrats had rushed to his defense.[3]

In 1951 Truman announced his intention to send ground forces to Europe without seeking congressional approval, possibly triggering military conflict with the Soviet Union. His action precipitated a major confrontation with Congress. In an extremely powerful floor statement, the leading conservative of the time, Senator Robert ("Mr. Republican") Taft, delivered a 10,000-word speech urging Congress to defend its prerogatives. Taft insisted that Congress had "a constitutional obligation to reexamine constantly and discuss the foreign policy of the United States." The trend toward secrecy on the part of recent administrations, combined with the failure to consult Congress and seek its advice, deprived members of Congress "of the substance of the powers conferred on them by the Constitution."[4] He concluded: "The policy we adopt must be approved by Congress and the people after full and free discussion. The commitment of a land army to Europe is a program never approved by Congress, into which we should not drift. The policy of secret executive agreements has brought us to danger and disaster. It threatens the liberties of our people."[5]

For three months in 1951 the Senate engaged in the "Great Debate" on the relative prerogatives of Congress and the President in exercising the war power. Taft believed that Congress had the power to prevent the President from sending troops anywhere in the world to involve the United States in war. In what could be read as a precursor to the War Powers Resolution, he urged Congress to assert its powers in the form of a joint resolution.[6] Senator John McClellan offered an amendment requiring congressional approval of future plans to send troops abroad. Although the amendment was initially rejected, 44 to 46, it was later accepted.[7] The Senate passed the resolution by a vote of 69 to 21, expressing its approval of Truman's sending four divisions to Europe but stating that "in the interests of sound constitutional processes, and of national unity and understanding, congressional approval should be obtained of any policy requiring the assignment of American troops abroad when such assignment is in implementation of article 3 of the North Atlantic Treaty" and that no ground troops in addition to the four divisions should be sent "without further congressional approval."[8] As a Senate resolution, the measure was not legally binding. It merely expressed the sense of the Senate on constitutional processes, although the debate and the votes are highly significant.

Eisenhower's Philosophy of Joint Action

The destructive collisions between President Truman and Congress convinced President Dwight D. Eisenhower to avoid unilateral executive actions in dispatching troops abroad. Instead, he sought the enactment of area resolutions that would delegate congressional authority to the President. In 1955 he urged Congress to pass the Formosa Resolution, which recognized the security risks in Formosa and the Pescadores and authorized the President to use military force "as he deems necessary." Although Eisenhower believed that he possessed some independent constitutional powers as Commander in Chief, he thought it far more prudent for the two branches to act in concert.[9]

Eisenhower repeated this approach in 1957, asking Congress to pass a joint resolution authorizing him to employ armed forces in the Middle East. Congress debated the proposal carefully and added a section that permitted that body to terminate the authority by passing a concurrent resolution, requiring action by both Houses but eliminating the President's opportunity for a veto. Eisenhower was committed to the importance of executive-legislative coordination: "I deem it necessary to seek the cooperation of the Congress. Only with that cooperation can we give the reassurance needed to deter aggression."[10]

In his memoirs, Eisenhower discussed the choice between using executive prerogatives or seeking congressional approval. On New Year's Day in 1957 he met with Secretary of State John Foster Dulles and congressional leaders of both parties, requesting their support for the Middle East Resolution. House Majority Leader John McCormack asked Eisenhower whether he, as Commander in Chief, already possessed power to dispatch troops without congressional authorization. Eisenhower acknowledged the existence of those powers but explained that "greater effect could be had from a consensus of Executive and Legislative opinion, and I spoke earnestly of the desire of the Middle East countries to have reassurance now that the United States would stand ready to help. . . . Near the end of the meeting I reminded the legislators that the Constitution assumes that our two branches of government should get along together."[11]

Eisenhower's position was sound but short-lived. President John F. Kennedy made it clear during the Cuban missile crisis that he was prepared to act solely on his own constitutional authority as Commander in Chief.[12] Congress passed another area resolution, the Cuba Resolution, but it did not authorize presidential action. It merely expressed the sentiments of Congress and omitted the procedure for terminating the President's authority by passing a concurrent resolution.[13] When Kennedy later acted to interdict weapons being delivered to Cuba, he acted on what he considered to be his constitutional powers.[14] The next area resolution, the fateful Southeast Asia Resolution, shot through Congress with little debate and no time taken for independent legislative judgment. The Senate Foreign Relations Committee, which reported the Tonkin Gulf Resolution favorably, later admitted that it had abdicated its institutional duties by assuming that President Johnson would not abuse the authority delegated to him.[15]

From 1969 to 1973, Congress retraced the arguments made during the Great Debate of 1951 and concluded that commitments abroad required the concerted action of both branches. The National Commitments Resolution of 1969, which passed the Senate 70 to 16, declared that the commitment of armed forces to a foreign territory or the promise of financial assistance could result "only from affirmative action taken by the executive and legislative branches of the United States by means of a treaty, statute, or concurrent resolution of both Houses of Congress specifically providing for such commitment."[16] The resolution, which was not legally binding because it expressed the sentiments of only one House and was not presented to the President, won the backing of both parties. The Democrats supported it, 43 to 3; the Republicans favored it, 27 to 13.

The War Powers Resolution

In 1970 the House of Representatives conceded a measure of war prerogatives to the President. A War Powers Resolution, passed by a vote of 289 to 39, recognized that the President "in certain extraordinary and emergency circumstances has the authority to defend the United States and its citizens without specific prior authorization by the Congress." Instead of trying to define the precise conditions under which Presidents may act, the House relied on procedural safeguards. The President would be required, "whenever feasible," to consult with Congress before sending American forces into armed conflict. He was also to report the circumstances necessitating the action; the constitutional, legislative, and treaty provisions authorizing the action, together with his reasons for not seeking specific prior congressional authorization; and the estimated scope of activities.[17] The Senate did not act on the measure.

Both Houses later passed War Powers Resolutions that went beyond mere reporting requirements. The House of Representatives, following its earlier example, did not try to define or codify presidential war powers. It directed the President "in every possible instance" to consult with Congress before sending forces into hostilities or situations where hostilities might be imminent. If unable to do so, he was to report to Congress within seventy-two hours, setting forth the circumstances and details of his action. Unless Congress declared war within 120 days or specifically authorized the use of force, the President had to terminate the commitment and remove the troops. Congress could also direct disengagement at any time during the 120-day period by passing a concurrent resolution.[18]

The Senate attempted to spell out the conditions under which Presidents could take unilateral action. Armed force could be used in three situations: (1) to repel an armed attack upon the United States, its territories and possessions, retaliate in the event of such an attack, and forestall the direct and imminent threat of such an attack; (2) to repel an armed attack against U.S. armed forces located outside the United States, its territories and possessions, and forestall the direct and imminent threat of such an attack; and (3) to rescue endangered American citizens and nationals in foreign countries or at sea. The first situation (except for the final clause) conforms to the understanding developed at the Philadelphia convention. The other situations reflect the changes that have occurred in the concept of defensive war and life-and-property actions.

The Senate bid required the President to cease military action unless Congress, within thirty days, specifically authorized the President to continue. A separate provision allowed him to sustain military operations beyond the thirty-day limit if he determined that "unavoidable military necessity respecting the safety" of the armed forces required their continued use for purposes of "bringing about a prompt disengagement."[19] This effort to codify presidential war powers carried a number of risks. Because of ambiguities in the language, legislation might widen presidential power instead of restricting it. Executive officials could interpret in broad fashion such terms as "necessary and appropriate retaliatory actions," "imminent threat," and "endangered citizens."

The two Houses presented a compromise measure to President Nixon. He vetoed the bill primarily because he regarded it as impractical and dangerous to fix in a statute the procedure by which President and Congress should share the war power. He also believed that the legislation encroached upon the President's constitutional responsibilities as Commander in Chief. He reminded Congress that the "only way in which the constitutional powers of a branch of the Government can be altered is by amending the Constitution—and any attempt to make such alterations by legislation alone is clearly without force."[20] Both Houses mustered a two-thirds majority to override the veto: the House narrowly (284 to 135), the Senate by a more comfortable margin (75 to 18).[21]

Although the War Powers Resolution of 1973 overcame a veto, it did not survive doubts about its quality and motivation. Some of the congressional support for the resolution was based on party politics and the resolution's symbolic value rather than its contents. Consider the voting record of fifteen members of the House.[22] After voting against the House bill and the conference version, they inconsistently voted to override the veto. If they opposed the legislation because they considered it inadequate or unsound, why vote to make it public law?

This reversal occurred in part because of fear that a vote to sustain might lend credence to the views advanced in Nixon's veto message. Despite serious misgivings about the quality of the bill, some legislators concluded that congressional inaction could be interpreted as a concession in the constitutional claims of Nixon (and Johnson). Other legislators used the override to propel the House toward impeaching Nixon. One of those who voted against the House resolution and the conference version but then in favor of overriding the veto—Democrat Bella Abzug of New York—advised her colleagues that "this could be a turning point in the struggle to control an administration that has run amuck. It could accelerate the demand for the impeachment of the President."[23]

Another factor was that Democrats were anxious to override a Nixon veto. Eight times during the 93rd Congress he had vetoed legislation; eight times Congress came up short on the override. A number of members looked upon the War Powers Resolution as a vehicle to test congressional power.[24] This attitude was especially tempting in the wake of the Watergate scandals. The "Saturday Night Massacre," which sent Special Prosecutor Archibald Cox, Attorney General Elliot Richardson, and Deputy Attorney General William Ruckelshaus out of the government, occurred just four days before Nixon's veto of the War Powers Resolution. Ten days before the Saturday Night Massacre, Spiro Agnew had heightened the politicized climate by resigning as Vice President.

Analysis of the Bill

The War Powers Resolution sets forth three main procedures: presidential consultation with Congress, presidential reports to Congress, and congressional termination of military action. The purpose of the resolution, according to Section 2(a), is "to insure that the collective judgment" of both branches will apply to the introduction of U.S. forces into hostilities. Yet an examination of other sections, together with executive interpretations and congressional behavior, supplies ample evidence that collective judgment is by no means assured.

The President is to consult with Congress "in every possible instance." This language obviously leaves considerable discretion to the President as to the form and timing of consultation. The Carter administration noted that the President's responsibilities under the sections involving consultation and reporting "have not been delegated, so that the final decision as to whether consultation is possible and as to the manner in which consultations be undertaken or reports submitted rests with the President."[25]

The authors of the resolution did not expect the President to consult with 535 legislators. But whom should he contact? The leadership? The chairmen and ranking members of designated committees? Selected advisers? Should they merely be briefed or does consultation mean a more active role for Congress? The legislative history makes clear that consultation goes beyond simply being informed of a decision. Consultation means that "a decision is pending on a problem and that Members of Congress are being asked by the President for their advice and opinions and, in appropriate circumstances, their approval of action contemplated."[26]

The War Powers Resolution requires that the President, after introducing forces into hostilities, report to Congress within forty-eight hours. Precisely what conditions require a report is unclear from the legislation. If the report is delayed for any reason, so are the mechanisms for congressional control. The President may extend the period of sixty days by an additional thirty days if he determines that it is necessary to protect and remove American troops. Congress provided two means of legislative control: a decision not to support the President during the sixty to ninety days or passage of a concurrent resolution at any time to direct the President to remove forces engaged in hostilities.

The problem with the "deadlines" is that the clock does not start ticking for the sixty-to-ninety-day limit unless the President reports under a very specific section: Section 4(a)(1). For obvious reasons, Presidents do not submit reports under that section. Only twice has the clock begun. President Ford reported under Section 4(a)(1) after the *Mayaguez* was captured, but by the time he did so, the military operation was already completed. Congress started the clock again through the regular legislative process by passing the Lebanon Resolution on October 12, 1983, which declared that Section 4(a)(1) had been activated on August 29, 1983. The resolution, however, authorized President Reagan to keep troops in Lebanon for up to *eighteen* months, although Reagan removed most of the Marines in February 1984.[27]

The second form of legislative control—passage of a concurrent resolution—is also of questionable potency. The Legal Adviser to the State Department told a House committee in 1975 that if the President has the power to put men into combat, "that power could not be taken away by concurrent resolution because the power is constitutional in nature."[28] That position seemed to be reinforced in 1983 when the Supreme Court, in *INS v. Chadha,* struck down the legislative veto as unconstitutional. The Court said that whenever Congress wanted to control the executive branch it had to act not merely by both Houses but in a bill or joint resolution that is presented to the President.

In response to *Chadha,* Senator Robert Byrd offered an amendment to the State Department authorization bill to conform the provisions of the War Powers Resolution to the Court's decision. In place of the concurrent resolution, Congress would have to act by joint resolution or bill. His amendment passed the Senate, but, altered in conference, it did not amend the War Powers Resolution. Instead, it was enacted as a freestanding, expedited procedure to require the President to withdraw troops.[29]

During hearings in 1988, the Legal Adviser to the State Department testified that the concurrent resolution was "clearly" unconstitutional and should be repealed.[30] In a committee report in 1987, the Senate Foreign Relations Committee had also stated that the concurrent resolution in the War Powers Resolution "has been effectively nullified" by *Chadha.*[31]

Should the concurrent resolution be replaced by a joint resolution to comply with *Chadha*'s requirements for bicameralism and presentment? That would be both unnecessary and undesirable. The term "legislative veto" should be defined strictly to mean a condition placed on delegated power, such as the one-House veto that accompanied the delegation of reorganization authority to the President, or the two-House veto attached to rulemaking authority for the Federal Trade Commission. In the case of the War Powers Resolution, no power was delegated. No one argued that the war power belongs exclusively to the legislative branch and was being delegated to the President in the War Powers Resolution on the condition that Congress retain control by passing a concurrent resolution. Section 8(d)(2) expressly states that nothing in the War Powers Resolution "shall be construed as granting any authority to the President with respect to the introduction of United States Armed Forces into hostilities or into situations wherein involvement in hostilities is clearly indicated by the circumstances which authority he would not have had in the absence of this joint resolution."

The constitutional case for the concurrent resolution in the War Powers Resolution thus rests on fundamentally different grounds than the legislative vetoes invalidated in *Code.* The disadvantages of replacing the concurrent resolution by a joint resolution are obvious. If Congress passed a joint resolution ordering the President to withdraw troops, the President could veto the measure and Congress could enforce its policy only by locating a two-thirds majority in each House to override the President. In other words, the President could continue in the face of majority apposition in both Houses simply by securing the support of one-third plus one in a single House.

To make this issue concrete, consider the effort by Congress to use its power of the purse to end the war in Vietnam. In 1973 Congress added language to an appropriations bill forbidding the use of any funds to support combat activities in Cambodia or Laos. The language covered not only the supplemental funds in the bill but also funds made available by previous appropriations. President Nixon vetoed the bill, and Congress was unable to muster a two-thirds majority in each House for the override. As a result, the bill had to be revised to delay the cutoff of funds from June 30 to August 15, 1973, giving Nixon forty-five additional days to bomb Cambodia.

Congresswoman Elizabeth Holtzman filed a suit in New York, asking a federal court to determine that the President could not engage in combat operations in Southeast Asia without congressional authorization. U.S. District Judge Orrin G. Judd held that Congress had not authorized the bombing of Cambodia. Furthermore, the inability of Congress to override Nixon's veto could not be interpreted as an affirmative grant of authority. As Judd observed, "It cannot be the rule that the President needs a vote of only one-third plus one of either House in order to conduct a war, but this would be the consequence of holding that Congress must override a Presidential veto in order to terminate hostilities which it has not authorized."[32] Judd's order was stayed by the Supreme Court because the August 15 compromise agreed to by Congress had broken the impasse between the two branches.[33] Eventually, Judd's decision was reversed by the Second Circuit, which treated the dispute as a political question.[34]

Converting the concurrent resolution to a joint resolution would not entirely solve the constitutional dispute, even if it might satisfy the Court's test in *Chadha*. It has been argued within Congress and the executive branch that Congress cannot order the President to remove troops even by joint resolution. The claim is that the President has plenary power as Commander in Chief to move and remove troops. If Congress could not act by concurrent or joint resolution, the next step in constraining the President is to amend the Constitution.[35] That might resolve all of the legal niceties, but such a proposal is impractical and unwieldy.

The concurrent resolution in the War Powers Resolution remains a useful and appropriate means for expressing congressional policy. If Congress were to pass such a resolution, the President could argue that it had no legally binding effect because of *Chadha*. However, such reasoning would also publicize the President's determination to keep U.S. forces engaged in hostilities despite the opposition of a majority of both Houses of Congress.

Politically, if not constitutionally, that is not a tenable position for the President. It is constitutionally repugnant for a President to initiate and continue a war with only the backing of one-third plus one in a single House. Congress should not have to regain control by securing a two-thirds majority in both Houses. Under these conditions, and confining *Chadha* as it should be to questions of delegated authority, the concurrent resolution remains an appropriate vehicle.

Military Initiatives from Ford to Clinton

Presidents have submitted a number of reports under the War Powers Resolution, but the manner of the reports and the response by Congress underscore the fact that the resolution is simply a framework for executive-legislative relations. The actual outcome in every case depends on a spirit of comity, good-faith efforts by the President and members of Congress, and a willingness by Congress to assert itself to control unilateral presidential actions.

On three occasions in April 1975, President Ford reported to Congress the use of military forces to evacuate U.S. citizens and refugees from Vietnam and Cambodia. Typical of these reports under the War Powers Resolution, Ford cited his constitutional authority as Chief Executive and Commander in Chief rather then statutory sources of authority. After the evacuations, the War Powers Resolution was put to a more severe test the following month. The U.S. merchant ship *Mayaguez,* traveling from Hong Kong to Sattahip, Thailand, was seized by Cambodians. Two days later the United Stares recovered the vessel and its crew, but only after President Ford had ordered air strikes against Cambodia and called upon Marine ground forces. Weeks and months would pass before Congress had an adequate picture of what had taken place.

Nevertheless, on the very day of the recovery, members of Congress rushed forward with glowing words of praise. A spirit of jingoism filled the air. The episode became a "proud new chapter in our history." Members expressed pride in their country and in their President, exclaiming with youthful enthusiasm that it was "great to be an American."[36] A few members reserved judgment, which was sensible, for no one knew exactly what had happened or why. A legislator could have announced: "I am happy that the crew is back. Unfortunately, many lives were lost in the effort. It is still too early, the facts still to incomplete, for us to make a judgment." Most members, however, felt compelled to outdo one another with words of commendation and jubilation.

As details of the capture trickled in, Ford's action looked less and less appealing. Approximately forty-one Americans lost their lives trying to rescue thirty-nine crewmen. The administration spent little effort probing diplomatic avenues before resorting to force. The quality of military intelligence was not reassuring. The Marines suffered heavy casualties during the assault on Koh Tang Island, under the erroneous impression that the crewmen were detained there. A punitive spirit seemed to infuse the operations. The United States bombed the Cambodian mainland *after* the crew had been released. A 15,000-pound bomb—the largest conventional bomb in America's arsenal—was dropped on a Cambodian island that measured just a few square miles.[37]

Administration leaders suggested that this use of force contained valuable lessons regarding America's determination to meet its international commitments, but the application of that event to future contingencies was hard to envision. Anthony Lewis of the *New York Times* said that for "all the bluster and righteous talk of principle, it is impossible to imagine the United States behaving that way toward anyone other than a weak, ruined country of little yellow people who have frustrated us."[38] An editorial in the *Washington Post* noted with alarm that the use of force by the greatest power in the world against a small country could serve as such a tonic in the nation's capital: "That anyone could find the Mayaguez affair a valid or meaningful guide to the requirements of post-Vietnam foreign policy at other times and places defies common sense."[39]

It is difficult to believe that one month after the costly disengagement from Southeast Asia, after the United States had finally broken free from a lengthy and violent war that had racked the country, there could be such a celebration of force. What happened to the "deliberative process" of Congress? The independent legislative capability? The promise of closer scrutiny of executive actions? Unless members take the time personally to analyze a President's decision, Congress cannot expect a coequal status or a share in "collective judgment." Instead, legislators will become prematurely associated with a policy they may later find unworthy of support.[40]

In 1980 President Carter reported to Congress on the use of military force in an unsuccessful attempt to rescue American hostages in Iran. In reporting "consistent" with the War Powers Resolution, he relied on the President's authority as Chief Executive and Commander in Chief. Although Carter's effort to consult with Congress was no better than Ford's, there was little criticism from legislators. However, Secretary of State Cyrus Vance resigned to protest the rescue operation.[41]

Military initiatives by President Reagan in 1982 and 1983 in Lebanon highlighted another weakness of the War Powers Resolution. Although hostilities were not merely "imminent" but actual, Reagan sent in troops without reporting under Section 4(a)(1) of the War Powers Resolution. By merely reporting "consistent" with the resolution, he did not set in motion the clock that would have limited military action to sixty to ninety days unless Congress specifically authorized an extension. Rather than acting under the procedures of the resolution, Reagan deployed troops pursuant to the President's "constitutional authority with respect to the conduct of foreign relations and as Commander-in-Chief of the United States Armed Forces."[42]

Reagan's refusal to trigger the clock meant that Congress had to pass legislation to invoke Section 4(a)(1). In passing this legislation in the fall of 1983, Congress gave the administration authority for eighteen months, deliberately allowing military forces to remain in Lebanon throughout the election year of 1984 without further legislative action. Members supported this massive delegation by reasoning that Reagan, upon signing the bid, would concede the legitimacy of the process established by the War Powers Resolution. Instead, Reagan made it clear that he might continue military operations beyond the eighteen-month period without reauthorization by Congress.[43]

The choice of eighteen months reflected the decision by both branches to remove Lebanon from the political calendar for 1984. Neither Congress nor the President wanted to risk trying to reauthorize a shorter period in the midst of a national election. But after members of Congress adjourned for the remainder of 1983, they recognized that the grant of authority for eighteen months was a mistake. Reagan also realized that public opinion would not sustain military operations over that period. By the spring of 1984 he had withdrawn the Marines from Lebanon. Nevertheless, the events of 1983 illustrated that Congress was willing, in return for short-term political advantages, to forfeit long-term institutional interests and act contrary to a fundamental goal of the War Powers Resolution. The purpose of that statute was to make Congress a coequal partner both in the initiation and continuation of military force.

In 1986 President Reagan ordered bombing strikes on facilities and military installations in Libya. There were no meaningful consultations with Congress on this use of force. Reagan advised Congress that he had taken the actions pursuant to his authority as Commander in Chief.[44] He defended the air strikes against Libya as an act of "self-defense" and a preemptive strike designed to "deter acts of terrorism by Libya."[45]

On four occasions during the 1980s, members of Congress went to court to charge that President Reagan had violated the War Powers Resolution. In the case of El Salvador, President Reagan did not report under any provision of the War Powers Resolution when he sent military advisers to that country in 1981. The State Department claimed that no report was necessary because the Americans were not being introduced into hostility or imminent hostilities. Several members of Congress filed a suit claiming that Reagan had violated the War Powers Resolution by sending the advisers. Eventually twenty-nine members of the House of Representatives joined the action against Reagan. Arrayed on the opposite side were sixteen Senators and twelve Representatives who supported Reagan and urged that the case be dismissed. The federal judge, confronted by two congressional factions, refused to do the fact-finding that would have been necessary to determine whether hostilities or imminent hostilities existed. The judge pointed out that Congress had failed to act legislatively to restrain Reagan.[46]

In a similar case, eleven members of Congress brought action against President Reagan for his invasion of Grenada in 1983, contending that he had violated the power of Congress to declare War. The judiciary declined to exercise its jurisdiction because of the relief available to members through the regular legislative process. The message was clear: If Congress wants to confront the President, it must do so by exerting legislative powers, not by turning to the courts.[47] Another suit involving the administration's activities in Nicaragua was avoided by the courts on similar grounds.[48] Also unsuccessful was a case brought by members of Congress who claimed that Reagan's use of military force in the Persian Gulf in 1987 had not followed the procedures of the War Powers Resolution. The advice from the court was familiar: If Congress fails to defend its prerogatives, it cannot expect to be bailed out by the courts.[49]

On December 20, 1989, President George Bush ordered U.S. military forces into Panama, citing five justifications: to protect the lives of American citizens there, to defend democracy in Panama, to combat drug trafficking, to protect the integrity of the Panama Canal Treaty, and to bring the Panamanian strongman General Manuel Noriega "to justice in the United States."[50] The idea of invading another country, particularly one in Central America, and toppling its government for the reasons Bush gave seemed a throwback to nineteenth-century American adventurism. It was inconceivable—or so many observers hoped—that the United States would use those justifications to invade other nations in the Southern Hemisphere. On February 7, 1990, the House of Representatives passed a resolution stating that the U.S. action in Panama "was a response to a unique set of circumstances, and does not undermine the commitment of the government of the United States to the principle of nonintervention in the internal affairs of other countries."[51]

In August 1990, President Bush sent U.S. troops to Saudi Arabia and neighboring countries after Iraq invaded Kuwait. The administration's justifications were numerous: protection of Saudi and Kuwaiti sovereignty, deterrence of Iraqi aggression, maintaining security and stability in the Persian Gulf, protection of American citizens abroad, and regaining access to Middle East oil. President Bush claimed that he did not need congressional authorization to take offensive action against Iraq, but under the Constitution the President has limited authority to take unilateral military action. Such actions may be taken for defensive, non-offensive, purposes. On January 8, 1991, President Bush asked Congress to pass legislation authorizing military action against Iraq. Congress enacted that legislation four days later after extensive debate.

In two decisions on December 13, 1990, U.S. district courts rejected legal challenges to the sending of troops to Saudi Arabia. In *Ange v. Bush,* it was held that the President's deployment order presented non-justiciable political questions.[52] In *Dellums v. Bush,* the court ruled that the issue was not ready for judicial determination but also rejected many of the sweeping claims for presidential war-making prerogatives presented by the Justice Department. The court concluded that if Congress confronted the President and the President refused to accept a statutory restriction, the issue might be ripe for the courts.[53]

The most striking transformation of the war-making power in the last fifty years has been the extent to which Presidents seek authority not from Congress but from international and regional institutions, particularly the United Nations and the North Atlantic Council. Truman in Korea, Bush in Iraq, Clinton in Haiti and Bosnia—in each case these Presidents circumvented Congress by going either to the UN or to NATO. Only at the eleventh hour did President Bush turn to Congress and obtain statutory authority for the war against Iraq.

Truman's action was the most damaging, became his decision to go to the UN Security Council rather than Congress was flatly contrary to the legislative history of the UN and the plain language of the UN Participation Act of 1945, which anticipated that before the President could enter into military activities with the UN he would first have to obtain specific statutory authority from Congress.[54] President Bush followed Truman's precedent by seeking a resolution from the Security Council and regarding that as sufficient legal backing for acting militarily against Iraq.[55]

In 1994, President Clinton threatened to invade Haiti after the Security Council adopted a resolution "inviting" all states, particularly those in the region of Haiti, to use "all necessary means" to remove the military leadership on that island. At a news conference on August 3, he denied that he needed authority from Congress to invade Haiti: "Like my predecessors of both parties, I have not agreed that I was constitutionally mandated" to obtain the support of Congress.[56] In a nationwide televised address on September 15, he told the American public that he was prepared to use military force to invade Haiti, referring to the UN resolution and his willingness to lead a multinational force to "carry out the will of the United Nations."[57] Because of negotiations by former President Jimmy Carter, an invasion was not necessary.

In Bosnia, Clinton relied on a combination of Security Council resolutions and NATO decisions to carry out air strikes against Serb positions. These bombings began in February 1994 and carried through to August 1995. At that point he contemplated sending in U.S. ground troops to help implement a Bosnian peace accord he had orchestrated. At a news conference on October 19, 1995, he was asked whether he would send the troops if Congress disapproved. His response: "I am not going to lay down any of my constitutional prerogatives here today."[58] By the end of the year he ordered the deployment of 20,000 American ground troops to Bosnia without obtaining authority from Congress.

The history of the War Powers Resolution has been disappointing to its authors and supporters, but the resolution was never more than a set of procedures to encourage greater collective judgment between Congress and the President. The sixty-to-ninety-day window for presidential initiatives is a conspicuous contradiction to the principle of collective judgment. For the most part, military actions taken by Presidents after 1973 have been short-term: Grenada, Libya, Panama, and the like. Although the sixty-day clock did not run legally, executive officials behaved as though it did. The war against Iraq seemed to signal that long-term military actions require joint action by both branches, and yet Congress did not effectively challenge the military initiatives taken by President Clinton, including substantial commitments in Haiti and Bosnia.

★ *The Politics of Comity*

The post-Vietnam years underscore the need for the President to reach an accommodation with Congress in foreign policy and national defense. Unilateral actions by the President eventually become counterproductive. To sustain a successful policy, the executive branch must at some point secure the support and cooperation of Congress. As Secretary of State Henry Kissinger noted in 1975: "Comity between the executive and legislative branches is the only possible basis for national action. The decade-long struggle in this country over executive dominance in foreign affairs is over. The recognition that the Congress is a coequal branch of government is the dominant fact of national politics today. The executive accepts that the Congress must have both the sense and the reality of participation: foreign policy must be a shared enterprise."[59]

The President is not the sole voice in foreign affairs. He cannot, or should not, isolate himself from Congress and the general public, dismissing their contributions as narrow, local, or parochial. Patsy T. Mink, after dual careers in Congress and the State Department, warned that it "is folly to believe, as many in the top echelons of State and White House staff sincerely do, that good foreign policy necessarily stands above the pressures of domestic politics and constituent interests. Politics is the art of reconciling and educating, not of avoiding, those interests."[60] For that task the President needs members of Congress to develop and support effective international policies.

Secretary of Defense Caspar Weinberger, a strong defender of presidential power, recognized that combat troops should not be sent abroad unless there is congressional and public support. In an important address in 1984, he identified six major tests to be applied in cases of military force. One of the tests adds this caveat: "Before the U.S. commits combat forces abroad, there must be some reasonable assurance we will have the support of the American people and their elected Representatives in Congress. This support cannot be achieved unless we are candid in making clear the threats we face; the support cannot be sustained without continuing and close consultation. We cannot fight a battle with the Congress at home while asking our troops to win a war overseas."[61]

In testimony before the Senate Foreign Relations Committee in 1988, Abraham D. Sofaer, Legal Adviser to the State Department, offered a similar perspective: "This administration recognizes that Congress has a crucial role to play in the determination of the circumstances under which the United States should commit its forces to actual or potential hostilities. No Executive policy or activity in this area can have any hope of success in the long term unless Congress and the American people concur in it and are willing to support its execution."[62]

Congress's influence depends on its willingness to act and take responsibility. A failure to act creates a vacuum into which Presidents can enter. As Justice Jackson noted in the Steel Seizure Case of 1952, presidential authority reaches its highest level when the President acts pursuant to congressional authorization. His power is at its "lowest ebb" when he takes measures incompatible with the will of Congress. But in between those two categories lies a "zone of twilight" in which Congress neither grants nor denies authority. In such circumstances, "congressional inertia, indifference or quiescence may sometimes, at least as a practical matter, enable, if not invite, measures on independent presidential responsibility."[63]

President Carter's termination of the Taiwan defense treaty was not met by an effective challenge from Congress. Justice Powell noted that if Congress "chooses not to confront the President, it is not our task to do so."[64] Carter's actions against Iran, including his freezing of assets and the suspension of claims pending in American courts, was upheld in the courts partly because of congressional acquiescence. Presidents have a freer hand in foreign affairs "where there is no contrary indication of legislative intent and when, as here, there is a history of congressional acquiescence in conduct of the sort engaged in by the President."[65]

It has been argued that the War Powers Resolution and other statutory provisions have created uncertainty in the international arena, preventing the President from negotiating effectively with other nations. Foreign leaders supposedly see these legislative constraints as impediments in entering into long-term commitments. But it would be worse for the President to go it alone, acting in isolation without the backing of Congress and the public. Other nations should feel more secure knowing that the President has consulted closely with congressional leaders in hammering out a policy that finds support in both branches.

Endnotes

[1]11 Public Papers and Addresses of Franklin D. Roosevelt 364-65 (1950).

[2]Public Papers of the Presidents, 1946, at 512-13.

[3]Louis Fisher, "The Korean War: On What Legal Basis Did Truman Act?" 89 Am J. Int'l I. 21 (1995).

[4]97 Cong. Rec. 55 (1951).

[5]Id. at 61.

[6]Id. at 2987.

[7]Id. at 3082-83, 3096.

[8]Id. at 3283 (para. 6).

[9]Public Papers of the Presidents, 1955, at 209-10; 69 Stat. 7(1955).

[10]Public Papers of the Presidents, 1957, at 11; 71 Stat. 4 (1957).

[11]Dwight D Eisenhower, Waging Peace 179 (1965).

[12]Public Papers of the Presidents, 1962, at 674, 679.

[13]76 Stat. 697 (1962).

[14]Public Papers of the Presidents, 1962, at 810.

[15]S.Rept. No. 129, 91st Cong. 1st Sess. 23 (1969).

[16]115 Cong. Rec. 17245 (1969).

[17]116 Cong. Rec. 37398-408 (1970). Passed again the next year under suspension of the rules (requiring two-thirds support), 117 Cong. Rec. 28870-78 (1971).

[18]119 Cong. Rec. 24653-708 (1973).

[19]Id. at 25051-120.

[20]Public Papers of the Presidents, 1973, at 893.

[21]87 Stat. 555 (1973).

[22]Representatives Abzug, Drinan, Duncan, Flynt, Harsah, Hechler (W. Va), Holtzman, Hungate, Landrum, Lott, Maraziti, Milford, Narcher, Stubblefield, and Whitten.

[23]119 Cong. Rec. 36221 (1973).

[24]See Thomas F. Eagleton, War and Presidential Powers 213-20 (1974).

[25]123 Cong. Rec. 21898 (1977).

[26]H. Rept. No. 287, 93d Cong., 1st Sess. 6-7 (1973).

[27]97 Stat. 805 (1983).

[28]"War Powers: A Test of Compliance," hearings before the House Committee on International Relations, 94th Cong., 1st Sess. 91 (1975).

[29]129 Cong. Rec. 28406-8, 28673-74, 28683-84, 28686-89, 33385, 33395-6 (1983); 97 Stat. 1062-63, sec. 1013 (1983); 50 U.S.C. 1546a (1994).

[30]"The War Power After 200 Years," hearings before the Senate Committee on Foreign Relations, 100th Cong., 2d Sess. 1061 (1988).

[31]S. Rept. No. 100-106, 100th Cong., 1st Sess. 6 (1987).

[32]Holtzman v. Schlesinger, 361 F.Supp. 553, 565 (E.D. N.Y. 1973).

[33]Holtzman v. Schlesinger, 414 U.S. 1304, 1316, 1321 (1973).

[34]Holtzman v. Schlesinger, 484 F.2d 1307 (2d Cir. 1973), cert. denied, 416 U.S. 936 (1974).

[35]For example, the position of Senator Barry Goldwater at 129 Cong. Rec. 28686-87 (1983) and testimony by the executive branch in "War Powers: A Test of Compliance," hearings before the House Committee on International Relations, 94th Cong., 1st Sess. 90-91 (1975).

[36]See especially the Congressional Record of May 15, 1975.

[37]"War Powers: A Test of Compliance"; "Seizure of the Mayaguez," hearings before the House Committee on International Relations, 94th Cong., 1st Sess. (1975); and statement by Senator Javits, 121 Cong. Rec. 18312-13 (1975). See also Jordan J. Paust, "The Seizure and Recovery of the Mayaguez," 85 Yale L. J. 774 (1976).

[38]New York Times, May 19, 1975, at 29.

[39]Washington Post, May 16, 1975, at A26.

[40]See Robert Zutz, "The Recapture of the S.S. Mayaguez: Failure of the Consultation Clause of the War Powers Resolution," 8 N.Y.U. J. Int'l L. & Pol. 457 (1976). In 1980 a federal district judge upheld Ford's action in *Mayaguez* as immune from judicial scrutiny under the political question doctrine; Rappenecker v. United States, 509 F.Supp. 1024 (N.D. Cal. 1980).

[41]Cong. Q. Wkly Rept., May 3, 1980, at 1200.

[42]Poetic Papers of the President, 1982 (II), at 1238.

[43]Public Papers of the President, 1983 (II), 1367-68, 1444-45.

[44]Public Papers of the President, 1986 (I), at 407.

[45]Id. at 478.

[46]Crockett v. Reagan, 558 F.Supp. 893 (D.D.C 1982), aff'd, Crockett v. Reagan, 720 F.2d 1355 (D.C. Cir. 1983).

[47]Conyers v. Reagan, 578 F.Supp. 324 (D.D.C 1984), dismissed as moot, Conyers v. Reagan, 765 F.2d 1124 (D.C. Cir. 1985).

[48]Sanchez-Espinoza v. Reagan, 568 F.Supp. 596 (D.D.C. 1983), aff'd, Sanchez-Espinoza v. Reagan, 770 F.2d 202 (D.C. Cir. 1985).

[49]Lowry v. Reagan, 676 F.Supp. 333 (D.D.C. 1987), aff'd, No. 87-5426 (D.C. Cir. 1988).

[50]Public Papers of the President, 1989 (II), 1722-23.

[51]136 Cong. Rec. 1507 (1990).

[52]Ange v. Bush, 752 F.Supp. 509 (D.D.C. 1990).

[53]Dellums v. Bush, 752 F.Supp. 1141 (D.D.C. 1990).

[54]Fisher, Presidential War Power, at 70-84.

[55]Id. at 148-51.

[56]30 Wkly Comp. Pres. Doc. 1616 (1994).

[57]Id. at 1780.

[58]31 Wkly Comp. Pres. Doc. 1878 (1995). See Louis Fisher, "President Clinton as Commander in Chief," in James A. Thurber, ed., Rival for Power: Presidential-Congressional Relations 214-31 (1996).

[59]72 Dept. of State Bull. 562 (1975).

[60]Thomas M. Franck, ed., The Tethered Presidency 74 (1981).

[61]Statement made by Casper Weinberger, Secretary of Defense, news release, Office of the Assistant Secretary of Defense (Public Affairs), November 28, 1984.

[62]"The War Power After 200 Years," hearings before the Senate Committee on Foreign Affairs, 100th Cong., 2d Sess. 144 (1988).

[63]Youngstown Co. v. Sawyer, 343 U.S. 579, 637 (1952).

[64]Goldwater v. Carter, 444 U.S. 996, 998 (1979).

[65]Dames & Moore v. Regan, 453 U.S. 654, 678-79 (1981).

★ ★ ★ ★ ★

Questions

1. Why did the Founding Fathers stipulate that Congress have the power to declare war?

2. In view of the fact that technology necessitates capacity for quick response, should war declaration authority be formally transferred to the presidency?

3. To what extent does the War Powers Resolution of 1973 represent a viable accommodation of congressional and presidential power?
4. To what extent is the U.S. at a disadvantage in international negotiations because the president must get congressional approval?
5. Has the War Powers Resolution of 1973 had a real effect on presidential actions in the thirty years since it was passed?

★ ★ ★

Presidential Power

Richard Neustadt

Thanks to Columbia University presidential scholar Richard Neustadt, Harry Truman's musings about his successor are among the best known presidential utterances: "He'll sit there and he'll say, 'Do this! Do that!' And nothing will happen." With this introduction Neustadt convincingly argues that presidential power derives primarily neither from constitutional sanction nor from the prerogatives of military command, but from the president's personal ability to persuade people to do what he wants. Neustadt goes on to demonstrate how both the limits of command and the opportunities for influence that define presidential power are inherent in the system itself.

In the early summer of 1952, before the heat of the campaign, President [Harry] Truman used to contemplate the problems of the general-become-President should Dwight David Eisenhower win the forthcoming election. "He'll sit here," Truman would remark (tapping his desk for emphasis), "and he'll say, 'Do this! Do that!' *And nothing will happen.* Poor Ike—it won't be a bit like the Army. He'll find it very frustrating."

Eisenhower evidently found it so. "In the face of the continuing dissidence and disunity, the President sometimes simply exploded with exasperation," wrote Robert Donovan in comment on the early months of Eisenhower's first term. "What was the use, he demanded to know, of his trying to lead the Republican Party. . . ." And this reaction was not limited to early months alone, or to his party only. "The President still feels," an Eisenhower aide remarked to me in 1958, "that when he's decided something, that ought to be the end of it . . . and when it bounces back undone or

★ ★ ★ ★ ★ ★

"Presidential Power," by Richard Neustadt, reprinted from *Presidential Power and the Modern Presidents: The Politics of Leadership, from Roosevelt to Reagan,* Simon & Schuster, 1990.

done wrong, he tends to react with shocked surprise." Truman knew whereof he spoke. With "resignation" in the place of "shocked surprise," the aide's description would have fitted Truman. The former senator may have been less shocked than the former general, but he was no less subjected to that painful and repetitive experience: "Do this, do that, and nothing will happen." Long before he came to talk of Eisenhower he had put his own experience in other words: "I sit here all day trying to persuade people to do the things they ought to have sense enough to do without my persuading them. . . . That's all the powers of the President amount to."

In these words of a President, spoken on the job, one finds the essence of the problem now before us: "powers" are no guarantee of power; clerkship is no guarantee of leadership. The President of the United States has an extraordinary range of formal powers, of authority in statute law and in the Constitution. Here is testimony that despite his "powers" he does not obtain results by giving orders—or not, at any rate, merely by giving orders. He also has extraordinary status, ex officio, according to the customs of our government and politics. Here is testimony that despite his status he does not get action without argument. Presidential power is the power to persuade. . . .

The limits on command suggest the structure of our government. The Constitutional Convention of 1787 is supposed to have created a government of "separated powers." It did nothing of the sort. Rather, it created a government of separated institutions *sharing* powers. "I am part of the legislative process," Eisenhower often said in 1959 as a reminder of his veto. Congress, the dispenser of authority and funds, is no less part of the administrative process. Federalism adds another set of separated institutions. The Bill of Rights adds others. Many public purposes can only be achieved by voluntary acts of private institutions; the press, for one, in Douglass Cater's phrase, is a "fourth branch of government." And with the coming of alliances abroad, the separate institutions of a London, or a Bonn, share in the making of American public policy.

What the Constitution separates our political parties do not combine. The parties are themselves composed of separated organizations sharing public authority. The authority consists of nominating powers. Our national parties are confederations of state and local party institutions, with a headquarters that represents the White House, more or less, if the party has a President in office. These confederacies manage presidential nominations. All other public offices depend upon electorates confined within the states. All other nominations are controlled within the states. The President and congressmen who bear one party's label are divided by dependence upon different sets of voters. The differences are sharpest at the stage of nomination. The White House has too small a share in nominating congressmen, and

Congress has too little weight in nominating presidents for party to erase their constitutional separation. Party links are stronger than is frequently supposed, but nominating processes assure the separation.

The separateness of institutions and the sharing of authority prescribe the terms on which a President persuades. When one man shares authority with another, but does not gain or lose his job upon the other's whim, his willingness to act upon the urging of the other turns on whether he conceives the action right for him. The essence of a President's persuasive task is to convince such men that what the White House wants of them is what they ought to do for their sake and on their authority. (Sex matters not at all; for *man* read *woman.)*

Persuasive power, thus defined, amounts to more than charm or reasoned argument. These have their uses for a President, but these are not the whole of his resources. For the individuals he would induce to do what he wants done on their own responsibility will need or fear some acts by him on his responsibility. If they share his authority, he has some share in theirs. Presidential "Powers" may be inconclusive when a President commands, but always remain relevant as he persuades. The status and authority inherent in his office reinforce his logic and his charm. . . .

A President's authority and status give him great advantages in dealing with the men he would persuade. Each "power" is a vantage point for him in the degree that other men have use for his authority. From the veto to appointments, from publicity to budgeting, and so down a long list, the White House now controls the most encompassing array of vantage points in the American political system. With hardly an exception, those who share in governing this country are aware that at some time, in some degree, the doing of *their* jobs, the furthering of *their* ambitions, may depend upon the President of the United States. Their need for presidential action, or their fear of it, is bound to be recurrent if not actually continuous. Their need or fear is his advantage.

A President's advantages are greater than mere listing of his "powers" might suggest. Those with whom he deals must deal with him until the last day of his term. Because they have continuing relationships with him, his future, while it lasts, supports his present influence. Even though there is no need or fear of him today, what he could do tomorrow may supply today's advantage. Continuing relationships may convert any "power," any aspect of his status, into vantage points in almost any case. When he induces other people to do what he wants done, a President can trade on their dependence now and later.

The President's advantages are checked by the advantages of others. Continuing relationships will pull in both directions. These are relationships of mutual dependence. A President depends upon the persons whom he would persuade; he has to reckon with his need or fear of them. They too will possess status, or authority, or both, else they would be of little use to him. Their vantage points confront his own; their power tempers his. . . .

The power to persuade is the power to bargain. Status and authority yield bargaining advantages. But in a government of "separated institutions sharing powers" they yield them to all sides. With the array of vantage points at his disposal, a President may be far more persuasive than his logic or his charm could make him. But outcomes are not guaranteed by his advantages. There remain the counter pressures those whom he would influence can bring to bear on him from vantage points at their disposal. Command has limited utility; persuasion becomes give-and-take. It is well that the White House holds the vantage points it does. In such a business any President may need them all—and more. . . .

When a President confronts divergent policy advisers, disputing experts, conflicting data, and uncertain outlooks, yet must choose, there plainly *are* some other things he can do for himself besides consulting his own power stakes. But there is a proviso—provided he has done that first and keeps clear in his mind how much his prospects may depend on his authority, how much on reputation, how much on public standing. In the world Reagan inhabited where reputation and prestige are far more intertwined than they had been in Truman's time, or even LBJ's, this proviso is no easy test of presidential expertise. It calls for a good ear and a fine eye. . . .

But when a President turns to others, regardless of the mode, he is dependent on their knowledge, judgment, and good will. If he turns essentially to one, alone, he puts a heavy burden on that other's knowledge. If he chooses not to read or hear details, he puts an even greater burden on the other's judgment. If he consents, besides, to secrecy from everyone whose task in life is to protect his flanks, he courts deep trouble. Good will should not be stretched beyond endurance. In a system characterized by separated institutions sharing powers, where presidential interests will diverge in some degree from those of almost everybody else, that suggests not stretching very far. . . .

Personally, I prefer President. . . . more skeptical than trustful, more curious than committed, more nearly Roosevelts than Reagans. I think the former energize our governmental system better and bring out its defects less than do the latter. Reagan's years did not persuade me otherwise, in spite of his appeal on other scores. Every scandal in his wake, for instance, must owe something to the narrow range of his convictions and the breadth of his incuriosity, along with all that trust. A President cannot abolish bad behavior, but he sets a tone, and if he is alert to possibilities he can set traps, and with them limits. Reagan's tone, apparently, was heard by all too many as "enrich yourselves," while those few traps deregulation spared appear to have been sprung and left unbaited for the most part. But this book has not been written to expound my personal preferences. Rather it endeavors to expose the problem for a President of either sort who seeks to buttress prospects for his future influence while making present choices—"looking toward tomorrow from today," as I wrote at the start. For me that remains a crucial enterprise. It is not, of course, the only thing a President should put his mind to, but it is the subject to which I have put my own throughout this book. It remains crucial, in my view, not simply for the purposes of Presidents, but also for the products of the system, whether effective policy, or flawed or none. Thus it becomes crucial for us all.

We now stand on the threshold of a time in which those separated institutions, Congress and the President, share powers fully and uncomfortably across the board of policy, the foreign and domestic. From the 1940s through the 1960s—"midcentury" in this book's terms—Congress, having been embarrassed at Pearl Harbor by the isolationism it displayed beforehand, gave successive Presidents more scope in defense budgeting and in the conduct of diplomacy toward Europe and Japan than was the norm between the two world wars. Once the Cold War had gotten under way, and then been largely militarized after Korea, that scope widened. With the onset of the missile age it deepened. Should nuclear war impend, the President became the system's final arbiter. Thus I characterized JFK against the background of the Cuban missile crisis. But by 1975 the denouement of Watergate and that of Vietnam, eight months apart, had put a period to what remained of congressional reticence left over from Pearl Harbor. And the closing of the Cold War, now in sight though by no means achieved, promises an end to nuclear danger as between the Soviet Union and the United States. Threats of nuclear attack could well remain, from Third World dictators or terrorists, but not destruction of the Northern Hemisphere. So in the realm of military preparation—even, indeed, covert actions—the congressional role waxes as the Cold War wanes, returning toward normality as understood in Franklin Roosevelt's first two terms.

In a multipolar world, crisscrossed by transnational relations, with economic and environmental issues paramount, and issues of security reshaped on regional lines, our Presidents will less and less have reason to seek solace in foreign relations from the piled-up frustrations of home affairs. Their foreign frustrations will be piled high too.

Since FDR in wartime, every President including Bush has found the role of superpower sovereign beguiling: personal responsibility at once direct and high, issues at once gripping and arcane, opposite numbers frequently intriguing and well-mannered, acclaim by foreign audiences echoing well at home, foreign travel relatively glamorous, compared with home, interest groups less clamorous, excepting special cases, authority always stronger, Congress often tamer. But the distinctions lessen—compare Bush's time with Nixon's to say nothing of Eisenhower's—and we should expect that they will lessen further. Telecommunications, trade, aid, banking and stock markets combined with AIDS and birth control and hunger, topped off by toxic waste and global warming—these are not the stuff of which the Congress of Vienna[1] was made, much less the summits of yore. Moreover, Europeans ten years hence, as well as Japanese, may not resemble much the relatively acquiescent "middle powers" we grew used to in the 1960s and 1970s. Cooperating with them may come to seem to Presidents no easier than cooperating with Congress. Our friends abroad will see it quite the other way around: How are they to cooperate with our peculiar mix of separated institutions sharing powers? Theirs are ordered governments, ours a rat race. Complaints of us by others in these terms are nothing new. They have been rife throughout this century. But by the next, some of the chief complainants may have fewer needs of us, while ours of them grow relatively greater, than at any other time since World War II. In that case foreign policy could cease to be a source of pleasure for a President. By the same token, he or she would have to do abroad as on the Hill and in Peoria: Check carefully the possible effects of present choices on prospective reputation and prestige—thinking of other governments and publics quite as hard as those at home. It is not just our accustomed NATO and Pacific allies who may force the pace here, but the Soviet Union, if it holds together, and potentially great powers—China, India, perhaps Brazil—as well as our neighbors, north and south.

From the multicentered, interdependent world now coming into being, environmentally endangered as it is, Presidents may look back on the Cold War as an era of stability, authority, and glamour. They may yearn for the simplicity they see in retrospect, and also for the solace. Too bad. The job of being President is tougher when incumbents have to struggle for effective influence in foreign and domestic spheres at once, with their command of nuclear forces losing immediate relevance, and the American economy shorn of its former clout. There are, however, compensations, one in particular. If we outlive the Cold War,[2] the personal responsibility attached to nuclear weapons should become less burdensome for Presidents themselves, while contemplation of their mere humanity becomes less haunting for the rest of us. To me that seems a fair exchange.

★ **Richard Neustadt** *is Professor of Political Science at Columbia University.*

Endnotes

[1]After the 1814 defeat of the French leader Napoleon by Russia, Prussia, Austria, and Britain, these great powers met in Vienna, Austria, to ensure that the future of Europe would be peaceful. At the Congress of Vienna, they created a "balance of power" system, so that no single European nation could dominate the continent.—EDS.

[2]The Cold War refers to the hostility that existed between the United States and the Soviet Union from the end of World War II until recent times. The Cold War involved many forms of hostility: democracy versus communism; America's NATO allies versus the Soviet Union's Warsaw Pact military partners; the threat of nuclear war; economic competition; the dividing of Third World nations into pro-U.S. and pro-Soviet camps. With the demise of communism in Eastern Europe and the disintegration of the Soviet Union, the Cold War era has ended.—EDS.

★ ★ ★ ★ ★

Questions

1. What is presidential power?
2. If persuasion is important, what makes a president more influential, style or substance?
3. Of the people the president must persuade (Congress, courts, general public, etc.) who are the most important?
4. In the 1980 presidential election, what made Ronald Reagan more persuasive than Jimmy Carter?
5. Does the increase in information available to the public from the Internet and other sources make it more or less difficult for the president to be persuasive?

★ ★ ★

The Imperial Presidency

Arthur M. Schlesinger, Jr.

While many Americans insist they are neither Democrats nor Republicans, most, since the Revolution, consider themselves democrats and republicans, at least in contrast to aristocrats and monarchists, and for this reason the Constitution forbids granting titles of nobility. Why, however, should a president need a title of nobility when he has more power, prestige, and prerogatives than Caesar, let alone the Duke of Milan, ever dreamed of? Perhaps it's not formal White House dinners catered with an army of smartly dressed stewards that is the problem. Perhaps the real problem lies in the willingness of Americans and their elected congressional representatives to sanctify the office of the executive and abandon their own responsibilities. The imperial presidency, in which the chief executive arrogates power to himself, to the detriment of the nation, is the result. While Richard Nixon may be the chief culprit, others have too often succumbed to the same temptation.

In the last years, presidential primary, so indispensable to the political order, has turned into presidential supremacy. The constitutional Presidency—as events so apparently disparate as the Indochina War and the Watergate affair showed—has become the imperial Presidency and threatens to be the revolutionary Presidency.

This book . . . deals essentially with the shift in the *constitutional* balance—with, that is, the appropriation by the Presidency, and particularly by the contemporary Presidency, of powers reserved by the Constitution and by long historical practice to Congress.

★ ★ ★ ★ ★ ★

This process of appropriation took place in both foreign and domestic affairs. Especially in the twentieth century, the circumstances of an increasingly perilous world as well as of an increasingly interdependent economy and society seemed to compel a larger concentration of authority in the President. It must be said that historians and political scientists, this writer among them, contributed to the rise of the presidential mystique. But the imperial President received its decisive impetus, I believe, from foreign policy; above all, from the capture by the Presidency of the most vital of national decisions, the decision to go to war.

This book consequently devotes special attention to the history of the war-making power. The assumption of that power by the President was gradual and usually under the demand or pretext of emergency. It was as much a matter of congressional abdication as of presidential usurpation. . . .

The imperial President was essentially the creation of foreign policy. A combination of doctrines and emotions—belief in permanent and universal crisis, fear of communism, faith in the duty and the right of the United States to intervene swiftly in every part of the world—had brought about the unprecedented centralization of decisions over war and peace in the Presidency. With this there came an unprecedented exclusion of the rest of the executive branch, of Congress, of the press and of public opinion in general from these decisions. Prolonged war in Vietnam strengthened the tendencies toward both centralization and exclusion. So the imperial Presidency grew at the expense of the constitutional order. Like the cowbird, it hatched its own eggs and pushed the others out of the nest. And, as it overwhelmed the traditional separation of powers in foreign affairs, it began to aspire toward an equivalent centralization of power in the domestic polity.

We saw in the case of Franklin D. Roosevelt and the New Deal that extraordinary power flowing into the Presidency to meet domestic problems by no means enlarged presidential authority in foreign affairs. But we also saw in the case of FDR and the Second World War and Harry S. Truman and the steel seizure that extraordinary power flowing into the Presidency to meet international problems could easily encourage Presidents to extend their unilateral claims at home. . . . Twenty years later, the spillover effect from Vietnam coincided with indigenous developments that were quite separately carrying new power to the President. For domestic as well as for international reasons, the imperial President was sinking roots deep into the national society itself.

One such development was the decay of the traditional party system. . . . For much of American history the party has been the ultimate vehicle of political expression. Voters inherited their politics as they did their religion. . . . By the 1970s ticket-splitting had become common. Independent voting was spreading everywhere, especially among the young. Never had party loyalties been so weak, party affiliations so fluid, party organizations so irrelevant.

Many factors contributed to the decline of parties. The old political organizations had lost many of their functions. The waning of immigration, for example, had deprived the city machine of its classical clientele. The rise of civil service had cut off the machine's patronage. The New Deal had taken over the machine's social welfare role. Above all, the electronic revolution was drastically modifying the political environment. Two electronic devices had a particularly devastating impact on the traditional structure of politics—television and the computer. . . .

As the parties wasted away, the President stood out in solitary majesty as the central focus of political emotion, the ever more potent symbol of national community . . .

At the same time, the economic changes of the twentieth century had conferred vast new powers not just on the national government but more particularly on the Presidency . . .

. . . The managed economy, in short, offered new forms of unilateral power to the President who was bold enough to take action on his own. . . .

. . . The imperial president, born in the 1940s and 1950s to save the outer world from perdition, thus began in the 1960s and 1970s to find nurture at home. Foreign policy had given the President the command of peace and war. Now the decay of the parties left him in command of the political scene, and the Keynesian revelation placed him in command of the economy. At this extraordinary historical moment, when foreign and domestic lines of force converged, much depended on whether the occupant of the White House was moved to ride the new tendencies of power or to resist them.

For the American President was a peculiarly personal institution. It remained, of course, an agency of government, subject to unvarying demands and duties no matter who was President. But, more than most agencies of government, it changed shape, intensity and ethos according to the man in charge. . . . The management of the great foreign policy crisis of the Kennedy years—the Soviet attempt to install nuclear missiles in Cuba—came as if in proof of the proposition that the nuclear age left no alternative to unilateral presidential decision. . . .

Time was short, because something had to be done before the bases became operational. Secrecy was imperative. Kennedy took the decision into his own hands, but it is to be noted that he did not make it in imperial solitude. The celebrated Executive Committee became a forum for exceedingly vigorous and intensive debate. Major alternatives received strong, even vehement, expression. Though there was no legislative consultation, there was most effective executive consultation. . . . But, even in retrospect, the missile crisis seems an emergency so acute in its nature and so peculiar in its structure that it did in fact require unilateral executive decision.

Yet this very acuteness and peculiarity disabled Kennedy's action in October 1962 as a precedent for future Presidents in situations less acute and less peculiar. For the missile crisis was unique in the postwar years in that it really combined all those pressures of threat, secrecy and time that the foreign policy establishment had claimed as characteristic of decisions in the nuclear age. Where the threat was less grave, the need for secrecy less urgent, the time for debate less restricted—i.e., in all other cases—the argument for independent and unilateral presidential action was notably less compelling.

Alas, Kennedy's action, which should have been celebrated as an exception, was instead enshrined as a rule. This was in great part because it so beautifully fulfilled both the romantic ideal of the strong President and the prophecy of split-second presidential decision in the nuclear age. The very brilliance of Kennedy's performance appeared to vindicate the idea that the President must take unto himself the final judgments of war and peace. The missile crisis, I believe, was superbly handled, and could not have been handled so well in any other way. But one of its legacies was the imperial conception of the President that brought the republic so low in Vietnam. . . .

. . . Johnson talked to, even if he too seldom listened to, an endless stream of members of Congress and the press. He unquestionably denied himself for a reality long time, especially when it came to Vietnam. But in the end reality broke through, forcing him to accept unpleasant truths he did not wish to hear. Johnson's personality was far closer than Truman's to imperial specifications. But the fit was by no means perfect. . . .

Every President reconstructs the Presidency to meet his own psychological needs. Nixon displayed more monarchical yearnings than any of his predecessors. He plainly reveled in the ritual of the office, only regretting that it could not be more elaborate. What previous President, for example, would have dreamed of ceremonial trumpets or of putting the White House security force in costumes to rival the Guards at Buckingham Palace? Public ridicule stopped this. But Nixon saw no problem about using federal money, under the pretext of national security, to adorn his California and Florida estates with redwood fences, golf carts, heaters and wind screens for the swimming pool, beach cabanas, roof tiling, carpets, furniture, trees and shrubbery . . . Nixon's fatal error was to institute within the White House itself a centralization even more total than that he contemplated for the executive branch. He rarely saw most of his so-called personal assistants. If an aide telephoned the President on a domestic matter, his call was switched to Haldeman's office.[1] If he sent the President a memorandum, Haldeman decided whether or not the President would see it. "Rather than the President telling someone to do something," Haldeman explained in 1971, "I'll tell the guy, If he wants to find out something from somebody, I'll do it."

Presidents like Roosevelt and Kennedy understood that, if the man at the top confined himself to a single information system, he became the prisoner of that system. Therefore they pitted sources of their own against the information delivered to them through official channels. They understood that contention was an indispensable means of government. But Nixon, instead of exposing himself to the chastening influence of debate, organized the executive branch and the White House in order to shield himself as far as humanly possible from direct question or challenge—i.e., from reality. . . .

As one examined the impressive range of Nixon's initiatives—from his appropriation of the war-making power to his interpretation of the appointing power, from his unilateral determination of social priorities to his unilateral abolition of statutory programs, from his attack on legislative privilege to his enlargement of executive privilege, from his theory of impoundment to his theory of the pocket veto, from his calculated disparagement of the cabinet and his calculated discrediting of the press to his carefully organized concentration of federal management in the White House—from all this a larger design ineluctably emerged. It was hard to know whether Nixon, whose style was banality, understood consciously where he was heading. He was not a man given to political philosophizing. But he was heading toward a new balance of constitutional powers, an audacious and imaginative reconstruction of the American Constitution. He did indeed contemplate, as he said in 1971 State of the Union message, a New American Revolution. But the essence of this revolution was not, as he said at the time, power to the people. The essence was power to the Presidency . . . His purpose was probably more unconscious than conscious; and his revolution took direction and color not just from the external circumstances pressing new powers on the President but from the needs and drives of his own agitated psyche. This was the fatal flaw in the revolutionary design. For everywhere he looked he saw around him hideous threats to the national security—threats that, even though he would not describe them to Congress or the people, kept his White House in constant uproar and warranted in his own mind a clandestine presidential response of spectacular and historic illegality. If his public actions led toward a scheme of presidential supremacy under a considerably debilitated Constitution, his private obsessions pushed him toward the view that the President could set itself, at will, above the Constitution. It was this theory that led straight to Watergate . . .

Secrecy seemed to promise government three inestimable advantages: the power to withhold, the power to leak and the power to lie. . . .

The power to withhold held out the hope of denying the public the knowledge that would make possible an independent judgment on executive policy. The mystique of inside information—"if you only knew what we know"—was a most effective way to defend the national-security monopoly and prevent democratic control of foreign policy. . . .

The power to leak meant the power to tell the people what it served the government's purpose that they should know. . . .

The power to withhold and the power to leak led on inexorably to the power to lie. The secrecy system instilled in the executive branch the idea that foreign policy was no one's business save its own, and uncontrolled secrecy made it easy for lying to become routine. It was in this spirit that the Eisenhower administration concealed the CIA operations it was mounting against governments around the world. It was in this spirit that the Kennedy administration stealthily sent the Cuban brigade to the Bay of Pigs[2] and stealthily enlarged American involvement in Vietnam. It was in this spirit that the Johnson administration Americanized the Vietnam War, misrepresenting one episode after another to Congress and the people—Tonkin Gulf, the first American ground force commitment, the bombing of North Vietnam, My Lai and the rest.[3]

The longer the secrecy system dominated government, the more government assumed the *right* to lie . . .

God, it has been well said, looks after drunks, children and the United States of America. However, given the number, the brazen presumption and the clownish ineptitude of the conspirators, if it had not been Watergate, it would surely have been something else. For Watergate was a symptom, not a cause. Nixon's supporters complained that his critics were blowing up a petty incident out of all proportion to its importance. No doubt a burglary at Democratic headquarters was trivial next to a mission to Peking. But Watergate's importance was not simply in itself. Its importance was in the way it brought to the surface, symbolized and made politically accessible the great question posed by the Nixon administration in every sector—the question of presidential power. The unwarranted and unprecedented expansion of presidential power, because it ran through the whole Nixon system, was bound, if repressed at one point, to break out at another. This, not Watergate, was the central issue. . . . Watergate did stop the revolutionary Presidency in its tracks. It blew away the mystique of the mandate and reinvigorated the constitutional separation of powers. If the independent judiciary, the free press, Congress and the executive agencies could not really claim too much credit as institutions for work performed within them by brave individuals, nonetheless they all drew new confidence as institutions from the exercise of power they had forgotten they possessed. The result could only be to brace and strengthen the inner balance of American democracy. . . .

If the Nixon White House escaped the legal consequences of its illegal behavior, why would future Presidents and their associates not suppose themselves entitled to do what the Nixon White House had done? Only condign punishment would restore popular faith in the Presidency and deter future Presidents from illegal conduct—so long, at least, as Watergate remained a vivid memory. We have noted that corruption appears to visit the White House in fifty-year cycles. This suggests that exposure and retribution inoculate the Presidency against its latent criminal impulses for about half a century. Around the year 2023 the American people would be well advised to go on the alert and start nailing down everything in sight.

Endnotes

[1]Robert Haldeman headed Richard Nixon's White House staff. He was a stern gatekeeper (the president wished it so) before his resignation in the face of the exploding Watergate scandals during the spring of 1973. He was subsequently convicted of criminal charges and imprisoned for his role in Watergate.-EDS.

[2]In 1961, President John F. Kennedy accepted responsibility for the disaster at the Bay of Pigs in Cuba. Over a thousand Cuban exiles, trained by the U.S. Central Intelligence Agency (CIA), tried to land in Cuba to overthrow the communist government of Fidel Castro. The invasion was a complete failure, forcing Kennedy to reassess his foreign policy approach, especially toward Latin America -EDS.

[3]The Tonkin Gulf incident involved two alleged attacks on American ships in the waters off the coast of Vietnam in 1964. President Lyndon Johnson may have exaggerated the extent of the attacks to gain support for widening the war. In response to the incident, the Senate voted 88 to 2 and the House of Representatives 416 to 0 to allow the president significant latitude in the use of American forces in Vietnam. No formal declaration of war was ever made concerning Vietnam, but the Gulf of Tonkin Resolution became the executive branch's "blank check" to expand the conflict. The 1968 My Lai massacre was a turning point in American public opinion concerning the Vietnam War. U.S. soldiers killed over a hundred Vietnamese villagers. One lieutenant was tried and convicted for the slaughter that had happened because of the inability of American troops to distinguish between enemy-soldiers and civilians. Some Americans believed that those higher up in the military, not just Lieutenant William Calley, should have been prosecuted for the massacre.-EDS.

★ *Prolific chronicler of the New Deal and Kennedy eras in American political history,* **Arthur Schlesinger** *is Professor Emeritus in the Humanities at the Graduate Center of the City University of New York.*

★ ★ ★ ★ ★

Questions

1. What does Schlesinger mean by the "imperial" presidency?
2. Is the imperial presidency the result of the Constitution or of tendencies in American culture?
3. To what extent is Schlesinger's portrayal of the imperial tendencies of the presidents accurate?
4. Have succeeding presidents learned lessons from Nixon's mistakes?
5. To what extent is the presidency of George W. Bush "imperial"?

☆ ☆ ☆

The Bureaucratic Politics Approach: The Evolution of the Paradigm

David C. Kozak, Ph.D.

"Bureaucratic politics"—a phrase that leaves you wondering whether to yawn or bristle, for it is hard to do both at the same time. The bureaucratic politics model of public administration is, however, a provocative illustration of the maxim that appearances may be deceiving, for it provides a substantial collection of insights on how public service operates and how public servants may be more effective. The bureaucratic politics model refutes the politics-administration dichotomy prevalent before World War II by demonstrating the creative potential of political-administrative interactions, and this article applies the lessons of the model to national security issues in particular.

Public administration as a learned discipline and academic field of study has been described as both science and art, comprising an amalgam of various approaches and schools.[1] It is science in that it attempts to explain the reality of the public sector: how it is structured, how and why it does its business as it does, how processes actually work and actors actually behave. It is also art in that it aspires to prepare practitioners for service in the public bureaucracy by enhancing their understanding, increasing their sophistication, and prescribing for them a methodology for better statecraft.

The polymorphic nature[2] of public administration is readily apparent to those familiar with its literature. Those studying organizational structure and

☆ ☆ ☆ ☆ ☆ ☆

formalism, managerial ideology, bureaucracy as a social system, decision-making, policy process and policy analysis, and broader environmental contexts have made important contributions. But, perhaps the most illuminating insights are those emanating from what has come to be known as the bureaucratic politics school.

The bureaucratic politics approach provides some very sophisticated notions of public bureaucracy that are most relevant to studies of U.S. national security and defense policy. The purpose of this article is to trace the evolution of the bureaucratic politics paradigms, to specify its major concepts for understanding public bureaucracy, and to identify the relevance of these concepts to the study of U.S. national security.

★ Bureaucratic Politics: Reactions Against the Politics/Administration Dichotomy

Bureaucratic politics as an approach to learning has its origins in the adverse reaction of modern, post-World War II public administration to what has come to be known as the politics/administration dichotomy.[3] The politics/administration dichotomy was the dogma that dominated early twentieth-century administration. Essentially, it depicted politics (or policy-making) and administration as two separate realms. Politics was the domain of the elected office holder and policymaker. Administration—considered to be the mechanical execution of decreed policy—was the proper province of the professional public servant.

Classic statements of this older view are found in the writings of the political scientist Woodrow Wilson and German sociologist Max Weber. Although many others also subscribed to those arguments—most notably Frank Goodman (1900) and W. F. Wiloughby (1927)—the works of Wilson and Weber have remained the most influential.[4] Writing in 1887, Wilson states that ". . . administration lies outside the proper sphere of politics."[5] To Wilson, "the field of administration is a field of business. It is removed from the hurry and strife of politics . . . It is a part of political life only as the methods of the counting-house are a part of the life of society; only as machinery is part of the manufactured product."[6] Max Weber also depicts an apolitical bureaucracy. As he writes in his remarks first published in 1922,

> To take a stand, to be passionate . . . is the politician's element . . . indeed, exactly the opposite principle of responsibility from that of the civil servant. The honor of the civil servant is vested in his ability to execute conscientiously the order of the superior authorities . . . Without this moral discipline and self-denial, in the highest sense, the whole apparatus would fall to pieces.[7]

The important thing to emphasize with regard to the writings of Wilson and Weber and the politics/administration dichotomy they fashion is that they each offer both descriptive and prescriptive propositions. To them not only are politics and administration in reality separate endeavors, but continued separation is a preferred arrangement. In other words, according to proponents of the dichotomy, not only never the twain meet, but never the twain should meet. The professional practice of public administration requires differentiation from politics and policymaking. The two functions are best handled by different institutions.

Notions of a politics/administration disjunction have not been confined to mere academic debate. For many years these ideas dominated thinking not just in academe but among practitioners as well, fostering what many have dubbed "the high noon of orthodoxy."[8] Nonpartisanship, hierarchical and mechanistic conceptions of public bureaucracy, emphases on unity of command and executive control and civil service, and preoccupation with efficiency and effectiveness—all of these flourished in an era of administration predicated on the independence of policymaking from policy execution. The Brownlow Committee (1937), The Hatch Act (1939), and the Hoover Commissions (1949, 1955) enacted into law the tenets of Wilson and Weber.

World War II produced the first significant stirring of skepticism concerning the validity of the politics/administration dichotomy. During that time of doubt, a generation of public administration scholars were educated by their experiences in government. Their service and the many insights it provided taught the inadequacies of an approach stressing a separation of politics and administration. For many, the dichotomy simply did not accurately grasp the reality of public administration as they had experienced and practiced it.[9] As Sayre stated in his 1958 review of the literature, ". . . to them, all administrative agencies and their staffs seemed to be involved in politics."[10] It was out of this adverse reaction to the politics/administration dichotomy—a reaction with a new emphasis on the involvement of administrators and administrative agencies in policy formation, the use of discretionary power, and the broader political process—that the bureaucratic politics paradigm was born.

★ Bureaucratic Politics: Classical Statements

If there is a consensus on any one item in modern, post-World War II public administration, it is the inadequacy of the politics/administration dichotomy as an accurate and valid description of the reality of the administrative process. From the seeds of post-war discontent, public administration scholars developed forty years of sophisticated debunking that has yielded many insights into the real world of government business. Pioneered by George Appleby and Norton Long in the 1940s and the 1950s, developed in the 1960s by Aaron Wildavsky and Francis Rourke, and refined in the 1970s and 1980s by Graham Allison, Morton Halperin, and Guy Peters, the bureaucratic politics approach emphasizes the political roles and relationships of bureaucracies, agencies and departments, and those who manage them. The scholars listed above and others make twelve major substantive points.

1. **Bureaucracy makes policy through the exercise of discretion.** To bureaucratic politics theorists, bureaucracy is anything but the mechanical and neutral implementation of policy. Although policy formulation and execution involve somewhat different roles and even dissimilar work cultures, responsibilities frequently blur. As many modern studies of public administration argue, bureaucrats make policy when exercising discretion and giving advice. Paul Appleby stated in his 1949 treatise that the essence of bureaucratic power is delegated power. In his words, "with a great increase in numbers of affairs handled, and with the increased complexity of those affairs, both the Congress and the President have had to resort to delegation."[11] Legislation cannot anticipate every eventuality. For reasons of either necessity or expediency, many blanks and much fine print are left to bureaucracy. In filling in the details, government agencies exercise discretion, thus making policy and giving administration a definite political character.

2. **Administration is the eighth political process.** Appleby in the same 1949 piece states a theme that will be echoed numerous times: "The administrative or executive process, involving everything done by agencies other than legislative and judicial ones" is influenced by politics,[12] "by citizen sentiment, by agitation, by the prospect of elections and by the actuality of elections already held, by what takes place in or what can take place in nominating procedures."[13] No doubt some of the redefinition of administration as politics can be attributed to modern definitions of politics as more behavioral and analytical in nature, something more than electioneering. Harold Lasswell's definition of politic as "power,"[14] Easton's "authoritative allocation of values and resources,"[15] and Almond's "distribution of advantage and disadvantages," "conflict resolution," and "decision-making,"[16] greatly expanded

an appreciation of administration's political nature. From such a perspective, Harlan Cleveland writes of the government executive as "a political animal" attempting to survive in "a political jungle,"[17] while V. O. Key writes of "administration as politics,"[18] Harold Stein stated it most succinctly: ". . . it can be said that the concept of public administration as politics . . . is designed particularly to refer to the administrator's understanding and pursuit of his objectives and his relations with the social environment outside his agency that affects or is capable of affecting its operations."[19]

3. **Bureaucrats and bureaucracy are driven by agency interests.** In comparison to the other branches of government, administrative agencies are unique in that they lack a constitutional base or grant of power. As Norton Long has emphasized in his thoughtful treatises, as a result of both this lack of guaranteed existence and the inevitable efforts to insure survival of programs and professional values, "the lifeblood of administration is power. Its attainment, maintenance, increase, dissipation, and loss are subjects the practitioner . . . can ill afford to neglect."[20] In this pursuit of power, agencies, those who manage them, and those who do their business are driven by the highly particularized and parochial views, interests, and values of their organization. In Long's words, because of their insecurity, "agencies and bureaus more or less perforce are in the business of building, maintaining, and increasing their political support," "carrying" into the policy process a concept of agency "interests."[21]

4. **Agencies and bureaucracies are involved in an incessant competition, struggling for various stakes and prizes.** A major contribution of the bureaucratic politics approach is to depict bureaucratic and administrative processes as akin to a game of competition, within which participants vie, maneuver, and struggle for various stakes and prizes such as budget resources, personnel slots, morale, access, autonomy, missions, roles; and essence. In other words, agencies and those within them are constantly jockeying for power, position, and prestige, and this behavior has enormous consequences for public policy. This is certainly the conclusion of Graham Allison in *Essence of Decision: Explaining the Cuban Missile Crisis.* To Allison, bureaucratic politics is one of those nonrational factors at work that partially explain decisionmaking during the time of the Cuban missile crisis and the compromises made with the purely rational model that occurred.[22]

Morton Halperin applied the Allison approach to foreign and national security policymaking, arguing that foreign policy is usually the result of the interplay among interests, participants, rules, stakes, prizes, and actions.[23] The net result is a policy process whereby struggles for organizational survival,[24] expansion and growth,[25] and imperialism[26] are inevitable.

5. **Competition produces a common intra-agency bureaucratic culture and patterned role playing.** To students of bureaucratic politics,

the struggle among contending bureaucracies fosters a distinctive internal mindset or perspective within each agency. As Halperin and Kanter note, "we believe that membership in the bureaucracy substantially determines the participants' perceptions and goals and directs their attention away from the international arena to intra-national, and especially intra-bureaucratic concerns."[27] Moreover, these mindsets involve patterned role playing, best captured by the dictum commonly referred to as "Miles's Law"[28] of "where you stand (on a policy issue) depends upon where you sit (in the bureaucracy)." In other words, policy positions are determined by or are a function of an actor's perspective as developed by his or her bureaucratic culture.

6. **Certain resources and strategies are associated with successful bureaucratic politics.** The very occurrence of bureaucratic politics, of course, gives rise to the employment of various strategies and ploys on the part of the contestants. A study of the behavior strategies people employ when adapting to or competing with one another is most productive in revealing how organizations function and how policy is processed.

Francis Rourke has written insightfully about how bureaucrats play the game of politics and which factors they correlate with success.[29] To Rourke, all bureaucracies are endowed with certain resources: policy expertise, longevity and continuity, and responsibility for program implementation. Some bureaucracies, however, are more successful than others in employing their assets. Rourke believes that agencies are mare likely to succeed if they have the following four differentials: 1. a socially appreciated expertise, 2. the support of the bureaucracy's clientele and constituency groups, 3. good leadership, and 4. organizational vitality and energy.[30] To Rourke, the acquisition, maintenance, and expansion of these four characteristics becomes an objective of all organizations engaged in bureaucratic politics.

Aaron Wildavsky has written of the various tactics employed by agencies involved in the politics of the budgetary process. These tell much about the politics of bureaucracy in the U.S. system. According to Wildavsky, agencies playing the game of resource allocation engage in the following: acquiring a clientele, using "end round" plays to supportive congressional committees, cutting the popular programs and less-visible items, and expanding the base.[31]

7. **Policy made in an arena of bureaucratic politics is characterized by bargaining, accommodations, and compromise.** Bureaucratic politics depicts an organizational structure more akin to a confederation than a hierarchy. Decisions are made less through executive fiat and more in a bargaining arena. Allison writes about decisionmaking in systems so configures. Except in time of crisis or emergency, policy hammered out in a marketplace inevitably involves compromise, accommodation, and mutual adjustment—the mush that results from the clanging and banging and give

and take of bureaucratic interests.[32] Charles Lindblom likewise detects a form of muddling-through incrementalism as a predictable consequence of the nonrational factors known as bureaucratic politics.[33]

8. **Bureaucratic politics involves strong political ties to clientele groups.** As Long, Rourke, Wildavsky, and other of the above-mentioned authors have emphasized, bureaucracies look to clientele groups for political security and support. All agencies have both internal and external constituencies; Internal constituencies comprise professional norms and associations; External constituencies are outside clientele groups who are affected by or otherwise have a strong interest in the business of the agency.

Clientele support is sought as part of a presumed symbiotic relationship between agency and clientele. The mutual benefit is that in exchange for the clientele's important political support for the agency, the clientele gets to have a major say in agency policymaking. There are two sides to this process. Phillip Selznick describes cooptation—agency use (if not commandeering) of outside groups ". . . as a means of averting threats to its stability or existence."[34] The other side is clientele capture, whereby through iron triangles of power consisting of agency personnel, relevant congressional committees and subcommittees, and affected outside interests, the clientele exercise inordinate, highly self-serving influence. I would like to emphasize that cooptation and clientele capture are two sides of the same coin. Both highlight the role of and problems with external groups in bureaucratic politics.

9. **Bureaucrats play politics as they interact with political institutions.** Many students of the policy process have argued that, in the main, policy is thrashed out in substantive subgovernments, subsystems, or issue networks comprised of specialists representing different organizations: operating agencies, congressional panels, affected interests, the media, think tank consultants, and the Executive Office of the President (EOP).[35] These actors are the proximate policymakers within each of the programmatic areas of government. They constitute an indigenous power structure: within which policy is hammered out in a give and take, push and pull, shove and haul process. It is here that bureaucrats interact with political institutions and it is here that political roles and relationships are most visible as bureaucrats attempt to defend their interests, influence events, and court favor.

Cronin writes of tugs-of-war between bureaucrats in the departments and agencies represented in the Cabinet on one hand and the White House on the other. This tension stems from conflicting role perspectives, as departments emphasize particularized programs and policies while presidential advisors are concerned with priorities and politics.[36] Wildavsky writes of conflict between advocates of spending (departments and agencies) and the Office of Management and Budget (OMB), which serves as a guardian on behalf of the presidency.[37] Ripley and Franklin illustrate the various and many interactions between bureaucracy and the Congress and the political character of the interactions.[38] In sum, all of these and many other works well-document the case that bureaucracies develop relationships with political institutions and that in the course of these relationships they give information, provide advice, make decisions, and administer programs in a political way. Chris Jeffries details some of the more obvious political ploys used by agencies: "tell the President only what is necessary to persuade him," "present your option with two obvious unworkable alternatives," "never agree to any position which might compromise yours," "always predict the consequences of not adopting your alternative in terms of worst cases," and "keep issues away from the president."[39] Each reveals the political nature of bureaucracy.

10. **Executive processes essentially involve efforts to coordinate, integrate, and synthesize bureaucratic politics.** In the world of bureaucratic politics, as Richard Neustadt has well argued, the position of president or chief executive is unique in that it is the one true centripetal force in the policy process, the one place where issues can be viewed in a comprehensive way and policy can be coordinated.[40] In fact, the distinctive charge and challenge of chief executives is to reconcile contending interests, transforming them into harmonious government.[41] Richard Fenno has stated it well: The presidency faces "the relative difficulty of promoting unity in the face of the basic pluralism of the American political system."[42] The challenge in the White House and its specialized policy shops in the EOP such as the OMB and National Security Council (NSC) is to reconcile the particulars of bureaucratic politics with general presidential programs.

11. **Proposals for organizational charge and reform are politically motivated.** A major precept of bureaucratic politics is that proposals for change and reform are essentially political phenomena. Organizational change is neither a technical nor a neutral exercise—it is the object of intense political pressure, conflict, and turmoil. Reorganizations have political purposes: They are not undertaken simply to conform to abstract principles; they are proposed and adopted not for therapeutic reasons but for political reasons and with political motives. As Harold Seidman states in his *Politics, Position and Power: The Dynamics of Federal Organization*, "Organizational arrangements are not neutral. They are a way of expressing rational commitment, influencing program direction, ordering priorities. Organizational arrangements give some interests, some perspectives more access."[43]

A corollary is that in proposals for reform, organizations are viewed as political objectives and objects—opportunity and boodle. Of course, agencies and departments have their own positions on reorganization issues as well as their own plans for what best serves organizational interests.

12. **By its very nature, bureaucratic politics raised profound questions concerning control, accountability, responsiveness, and responsibility in a democratic society.** Notions of semi-autonomous bureaucratic subsystems and narrow service empires pursing organizational interests inevitably point of a series of fundamental issues and dilemmas concerning the role of bureaucracy in a democracy. Many have invoked serious questions about how to make the diffused sovereignty and expertise of the bureaucracy respond to both executive direction and the popular will. Some have written on an unwieldy and unresponsive technocracy that needs to be brought under control. Others have discussed the representative nature of U.S. bureaucracy and the contributions it makes through its own intense advocacy to pluralistic democracy. No matter how one stands on these issues, they illustrate how a political approach to a bureaucracy requires an interest in political questions previously ignored during the reign of the politics/administration dichotomy.

In sum, these twelve propositions explicate the major concepts and notions of bureaucratic politics as derived from the writings of its best known and classic proponents. They are promises that provide insights into the actual functioning and behavior of modern U.S. governmental bureaucracies. They are insights into how the government works.

★ *Relevance of Bureaucratic Politics to National Security Studies*

Students of the U.S. national security policy process have long employed the bureaucratic politics approach in an effort to understand defense policymaking. For example, Hammond has discussed the synthesizing and integrating challenges to the NSC amidst rampant bureaucratic politics in the national secured community.[44] Perry Smith highlights the political purposes of service doctrine and the use of doctrine in justifying and furthering bureaucratic interests.[45] Bauer and Yoshpe discuss the confederational nature of the Department of Defense (DoD),[46] while Katzenback discusses the difficulties of phasing out the U.S. horse cavalry in the early twentieth century due to the phenomena of bureaucratic politics.[47]

Many case studies also pinpoint the political role of bureaucracy. Ciboski points to competing technological interests and DoD politics in explaining the 1961 U.S. decision to cancel the skybolt missile program, an action with important ramifications for Britain.[48] Art examines the bureaucratic parochialism and rivalry that underlay the development of the TFX aircraft,[49] and Head explains the decisions in the development of the A-7 aircraft as a victory of some bureaucratic interests over others.[50]

In addition to the literature of academe, a bureaucratic politics approach is employed in governmental studies of the operations of the DoD and the national security policy process. For example, the 1986 report of the Packard Commission on Defense Management—*National Security Planning and Budgeting*—proposed expanding the responsibilities of Joint Chiefs of Staff (JCS) and Secretary of Defense in an effort to dilute service parochialism and enhance the generalist perspective in government.[51] Likewise, the staff report to the Senate Armed Services Committee *Defense Organization: The Need for Change* (commonly referred to as the Goldwater-Nunn Report) discusses operational failures and deficiencies, acquisition problems, lack of strategic direction, and poor interservice coordination as inevitable consequences of an imbalance "between service and joint interests."[52] The Tower Commission's report depicts a policy process involving a struggle between the national security advisor and NSC staff on the one hand and the cabinet secretaries and department officials on the other.[53] And, during his testimony before a special congressional inquiry into the Iran/Contra Affair, Lt. Col. Oliver North spoke of bureaucratic gridlock between the Central Intelligence Agency (CIA), the state, and the DoD as the rationale for his ad hoc approach to government policy.[54]

Combining and integrating these disparate insights yields a number of fruitful propositions that will underlie all subsequent pieces in this volume (see Figure 1). It should be emphasized that each proposition is a logical derivative from the tenets of bureaucratic politics.

Conclusion

Bureaucratic politics as an academic approach has much to contribute to an understanding of the U.S. national security policy process. In reaction to the politics/administration dichotomy, the bureaucratic politics model has developed with twelve major propositions, each of which sheds light on the reality of the policy process and decisionmaking in large, complex bureaucracies such as the NSC, DoD, and JCS. Too frequently, the application of the model to national security has been desultory and fragmented. Our purpose in this volume is to employ this model as thoroughly and comprehensively as possible in order to gain the full benefit of treating national security administration as public administration—a form of administration that is particularly amenable to a bureaucratic politics approach.[55]

Figure 1

Characteristics of the National Security Policy Process as Seen from the Bureaucratic Politics Perspective

- The national security policy process is fragmented, nonhierarchical, and nonmonolithic.
- It is best conceived of as a confederation of functional and organizational constituencies and subsystems—a bargaining arena rather than a command structure.
- Decisionmaking requires inter- and intra-agency coordination and the integration of components.
- Bureaucratic professionalism, politics, particularism and parochialism, and outside affected groups color the process. Policy proposals bubbling out of the bureaucracy are influenced by these factors.
- Patterned role playing pervades. Adversarial advocacy is best explained with the dictum "where you stand depends upon where you sit!"
- Policy is hammered out in a political atmosphere with important inputs from the president and Congress. Hence, the name of the game is to influence those external institutions.
- Decisionmaking is constrained by fiscal, organizational, political, and cognitive limitation.
- Decisions are driven by SOPs, incrementalism, muddling through, satisfying, compromise, and accommodation.
- Crises and salience centralize organization to the NSC, Defense Review Board, budget process, and the White House.
- Declaratory policy can steer and guide but is not equivalent to policy programs and actions.
- Budget considerations drive strategy rather than vice versa, producing a strategy/resource mismatch.
- The policy process is personality dependent.
- Policy implementation is not automatic. It requires continuous negotiations and follow-through.
- Reorganization issues are intensely political, raising questions of authority, influence, and access.

Bureaucratic politics as a practice within the government, of course, will continue to be a matter of debate. No attempt will be made here to settle that debate. The reality of bureaucratic politics is both good and bad. The good is policy by compromise, consultation, and consensus; policy made in intense debate and deliberation with a sense of multiple advocacy; policymaking by specialists and experts; and dampers on policy extremism. The bad is problems of coordination, zero sum "dog eat dog" parochialism, and the lack of accountability. Regardless of either benefits or costs, recognizing bureaucratic politics leads to a realistic understanding of the U.S. policy process. Ignoring bureaucratic politics can only lead to ignorance and naïvete.

★ **David C. Kozak** is a *Professor of Political Science at the United States Military Academy.*

Endnotes

[1]The classic statement concerning public administration as both science and art is found in the writings of Dwight Waldo, most notably The *Study of Public Administration* (Random House. 1955).

[2]The term *polymorphic* is first applied to public administration in John C. Buechner, *Public Administration* (Dickerson Publishing, 1968), 18.

[3]Politics/administration dichotomy as a descriptive concept seems to be first coined by Wallace S. Sayre, "Premises of Public Administration: Past and Emerging," *Public Administration Review* 18, no. 2 (1958): 102–105.

[4]Frank Goodnow, *Politics and Administration* (Macmillan, 1900) and W. F. Willoughby, *Principles of Public Administration* (Johns Hopkins Press, 1927).

[5]Woodrow Wilson, "The Study of Administration," *Political Science Quarterly 2* (1887): 197-222. Reprinted in Jay M. Shafratz and Albert C, Hyde (eds.), *Classics of Public Administration* (Moore, 1978), 10.

[6]Wilson, "Study of Administration."

[7]Max Weber, "Politics as a Vocation," in *From Max Weber,* H. S. Garth and C. W. Mills, eds. (Oxford University Press, 1946), 95.

[8]Donald Allensworth Sayre, *Public Administration: The Execution of Public Policy* (J. P. Lippincott Co., 1973), 147.

[9]See, for example, Fritz Monstein Marx, ed. *The Elements of Public Administration* (Prentice-Hall, 1946).

[10]Sayre, *Public Administration,* 1–4.

[11]George H. Appleby, *Policy and Administration* (University of Alabama Press, 1949), 112.

[12]Appleby, *Policy and Administration.* 29-30.

[13]Appleby, *Policy and Administration*. 32.

[14]Harold Lasswell, *Politics: Who Gets What, When, How* (Meridan Books, 1958).

[15]David Easton, *The Political System* (Knopf, Inc., 1953), Chap. 5.

[16]See Gabriel Almond and G. B. Powell, Jr., *Comparative Politics* (Little, Brown, 1966), Chap. 2; and Austin Rammey, *Governing* (Holt, Rinehart & Winston, 1971), Chap. 1.

[17]Harlan Cleveland, "Executives in the Political Jungle," *Annals of the American Association of Political and Social Science* 307 (September 1956): 37-47.

[18]V. O. Key, *Politics, Parties and Pressure Groups,* (Thomas Y. Crowell, 1958).

[19]Harold Stein, *Public Administration and Policy Development* (Harcourt, Brace and World, Inc., 1952), i.

[20]Norton E. Long, "Power and Administration," *Public Administration Review* 9 (Autumn 1949): 257. See also Norton E. Long. "Bureaucracy and Constitutionalism," *American Political Science Review* 46 (Sept. 1952): pp. 808-18 and "Public Policy and Administration: The Goals of Rationality and Responsibility," *Public Administration Review* 14 (1954): 22-31.

[21]Long, "Power and Administration," 258.

[22]Graham T. Allison, *Essence of Decision: Explaining the Cuban Missile Crisis* (Little, Brown 1971), especially 256-257.

[23]See Morton Halperin, *Bureaucratic Politics and Foreign Policy* (Brookings Institute, 1974): Morton Halperin and Arnold Kanter, eds., *Readings in American Foreign Policy: A Bureaucratic Perspective* (Little, Brown, 1973), 1042; and Morton Halperin, "Why Bureaucrats Play Games," *Foreign Policy* 2 (1971), 70-90.

[24]For an elaboration of the concept of survival see Herbert A. Simon, Donald W. Smithberg and Victor A. Thompson, *Public Administration* (Knopf, 1950), 381-401.

[25]For an elaboration of the concept of growth see Anthony Downs, *Inside Bureaucracy* (Little, Brown, 1967), 5-23.

[26]For an illustration of the concept of imperialism see Matthew Holden, Jr., "Imperialism in Bureaucracy," *American Political Science Review* 50 (December 1966): 943-951.

[27]Halperin and Kanter, *American Foreign Policy,* 3.

[28]For the origins of Miles's Law see: Richard E. Neustadt and Ernest May, *Thinking in Time* (Free Press, 1986), 157.

[29]See Francis E. Rourke, *Bureaucracy, Politics, and Public Policy,* 3rd ed. (Little, Brown, 1984).

[30]Rourke, *Bureaucracy, Politics, and Public Policy,* 91.

[31]Aaron Wildavsky, *The Politics of The Budgetary Process,* 3rd ed. (Little, Brown, 1981).

[32]Allison, *Essence of Decision*, 256.

[33]Charles E. Lindbom, "The Science of Muddling Through," *Public Administration Review* 19 (Spring 1959): 79-88.

[34]Philip Selznick, *TVA and the Grass Roots* (University of California Press, 1949), 13.

[35]For the concept of subsystem issue networks see Hugh Heclo, "Issue Networks and the Executive Establishment" in *The New American Political System,* ed. Anthony King (American Enterprise Institute, 1979), 87-124.

[36]Thomas Cronin, *The State of the Presidency,* 2nd ed. (Little, Brown, 1980), Chapters 5, 7, and 8.

[37]Aaron Wilavsky, *Budgeting* (Little, Brown, 1975), 24-25.

[38]Randall B. Ripley and Grace A. Franklin, *Congress, the Bureaucracy, and Public Policy,* 3rd ed. (Dorsey Press, 1984).

[39]Chris L. Jeffries, "Defense Decisionmaking in the Organizational-Bureaucratic Context," in *American Defense Policy,* 4th ed., ed. John E. Endicott and Roy W. Stafford, Jr. (The Johns Hopkins University Press, 1977), 236.

[40]Richard E. Neustadt, *Presidential Power* (Wiley, 1980).

[41]Colin Campbell, *Managing the Presidency: Carter, Reagan, and the Search for Executive Harmony* (University of Pittsburgh Press, 1986).

[42]Richard P. Fenno, Jr., *The President's Cabinet* (Vintage Books, 1959), p. 271.

[43]Harold Seidman, *Politics, Position and Power: The Dynamics of Federal Organization* 2nd ed. (Oxford University Press, 1976).

[44]Paul Y. Hammond, *Organizing for Defense: The American Military Establishment in the Twentieth Century* (Princeton University Press, 1961); *Super Carriers and B-36 Bombers: Appropriations, Strategy and Politics,* Inter-University-case Program, No. 97. (Bobbs Merril Co., Inc., 1963); and "The National Security Council: An Interpretation and Appraisal," *American Political Science Review 54* (December, 1960): 899-910.

[45]Perry M. Smith, *The Air Force Plans for Peace: 1943-45* (The Johns Hopkins University Press, 1970).

[46]Theodore W. Bauer and Harry B. Yoshpe, "Unity or Confederation: Defense Organization and Management," *American Defense Policy* 6th ed., eds. John Endicott and Roy Stafford (The Johns Hopkins University Press, 1977), 258-64.

[47]Edward L. Katzenback Jr., "The Horse Cavalry in the Twentieth Century: A Study in Policy Response," *Public Policy* 7 (1958): 120-49.

[48]Kenneth A. Ciboski, "The Bureaucratic Connection: Explaining the Skybolt Decision," in *American Defense Policy* 4th ed., 374-88.

[49]Robert J. Art, *The TFX Decision: McNamara and the Military* (Little, Brown, 1968).

[50]Richard G. Head, "Doctrinal Innovation and the A-7 Attach Aircraft Decisions," *American Defense Policy,* 3rd ed., eds. Richard Head and Ervin Rokke (The Johns Hopkins University Press, 1973), 431-445.

[51]"National Security Planning and Budgeting," *A Report to the President by the President's Blue Ribbon Commission on Defense Management* (June 1986).

[52]"Defense Organization: The Need for Change," *Staff Report to the Committee on Armed Services, United States Senate* (October 16, 1985), 15, 636.

[53]*The Tower Commission Report, a New York Times Report,* (Bantam Books, 1987), 95.

[54]*Taking the Stand: The Testimony of Lieutenant Colonel Oliver L. North* (Pocket Books, 1987).

[55]For an application of public administration to national security policy see: Chris Jeffries, "Public Administration and the Military," *Public Administration Review* (July/Aug. 1977): 321-333.

★ ★ ★ ★ ★

Questions

1. What is the politics-administration dichotomy?
2. Why was the politics-administration dichotomy so widely respected until World War II?
3. What are the basic principles of the bureaucratic politics model?
4. What are the strengths of the bureaucratic politics model for understanding public administration in general?
5. What are the strengths of the bureaucratic politics model for understanding national security issues in particular?

☆ ☆ ☆

On Liberty (1859)

John Stuart Mill

Under what conditions does the government have a legitimate right to limit liberty? Classical liberals (people who support a free market economy and limited, representative government) want to maximize economic and political liberty because they believe freedom is essential to the health and vitality of society. British philosopher John Stuart Mill, a leading classical liberal, has been called the "Einstein of the nineteenth century." In his essay On Liberty, *the most famous work ever written on this subject, he asserts "that the sole end for which mankind are warranted, individually or collectively in interfering with the liberty of action of any of their number, is self-protection." Mill specifically denies that advancing the welfare of some is sufficient grounds for limiting the freedom of others. Freedom of speech is especially important because only when speech is unrestricted will we be able to discover the truth.*

The subject of this Essay is not the so-called Liberty of the Will, so unfortunately opposed to the misnamed doctrine of Philosophical Necessity; but Civil, or Social Liberty: the nature and limits of the power which can be legitimately exercised by society over the individual. A question seldom stated, and hardly ever discussed, in general terms, but which profoundly influences the practical controversies of the age by its latent presence, and is likely soon to make itself recognized as the vital question of the future. It is so far from being new, that, in a certain sense, it has divided mankind, almost from the remotest ages; but in the stage of progress into which the more civilized portions of the species have now entered, it presents itself under new conditions, and requires a different and more fundamental treatment.

The struggle between Liberty and Authority is the most conspicuous feature in the portions of history with which we are earliest familiar, partic-

☆ ☆ ☆ ☆ ☆ ☆

From John Stuart Mill, *On Liberty* (1859).

ularly in that of Greece, Rome, and England. But in old times this contest was between subjects, or some classes of subjects, and the government. By liberty, was meant protection against the tyranny of the political rulers. The rulers were conceived (except in some of the popular governments of Greece) as in a necessarily antagonistic position to the people whom they ruled. They consisted of a governing One, or a governing tribe or caste, who derived their authority from inheritance or conquest, who, at all events, did not hold it at the pleasure of the governed, and whose supremacy men did not venture, perhaps did not desire, to contest, whatever precautions might be taken against its oppressive exercise. Their power was regarded as necessary, but also as highly dangerous; as a weapon which they would attempt to use against their subjects, no less than against external enemies. To prevent the weaker members of the community from being preyed upon by innumerable vultures, it was needful that there should be an animal of prey stronger than the rest, commissioned to keep them down. But as the king of the vultures would be no less bent upon preying upon the flock than any of the minor harpies, it was indispensable to be in a perpetual attitude of defense against his beak and claws. The aim, therefore, of patriots, was to set limits to the power which the ruler should be suffered to exercise over the community; and this limitation was what they meant by liberty. It was attempted in two ways. First, by obtaining a recognition of certain immunities, called political liberties or rights, (which it was to be regarded as a breach of duty in the ruler to infringe, and which, if he did infringe, specific resistance, or general rebellion, was held to be justifiable). A second, and generally a later expedient, was the establishment of constitutional checks, (by which the consent of the community, or of a body of some sort supposed to represent its interests, was made a necessary condition to some of the more important acts of the governing power). To the first of these modes of limitation, the ruling power, in most European countries, was compelled, more or less, to submit. It was not so with the second; and, to attain this, or when already in some degree possessed, to attain it more completely, became everywhere the principal object of the lovers of liberty. And so long as mankind were content to combat one enemy by another, and to be ruled by a master, on condition of being guaranteed more or less efficaciously against his tyranny, they did not carry their aspirations beyond this point.

A time, however, came in the progress of human affairs, when men ceased to think it a necessity of nature that their governors should be an independent power, opposed in interest to themselves. It appeared to them much better that the various magistrates of the State should be their tenants or delegates, revocable at their pleasure. In that way alone, it seemed, could they have complete security that the powers of government would never be abused to their disadvantage. By degrees, this new demand for elective and temporary rulers became the prominent object of the exertions of the popular party, wherever any such party existed; and superseded, to a considerable extent, the previous efforts to limit the power of rulers. As the struggle proceeded for making the ruling power emanate from the periodical choice of the ruled, some persons began to think that too much importance had been attached to the limitation of the power itself. *That* (it might seem) was a resource against rulers whose interests were habitually opposed to those of the people. What was now wanted was that the rulers should be identified with the people; that their interest and will should be the interest and will of the nation. The nation did not need to be protected against its own will. There was no fear of its tyrannizing over itself. Let the rulers be effectually responsible to it, promptly removable by it, and it could afford to trust them with power of which it could itself dictate the use to be made. Their power was but the nation's own power, concentrated, and in a form convenient for exercise. This mode of thought, or rather perhaps of feeling, was common among the last generation of European liberalism, in the Continental section of which it still apparently predominates. Those who admit any limit to what a government may do, except in the case of such governments as they think ought not to exist, stand out as brilliant exceptions among the political thinkers of the Continent. A similar tone of sentiment might by this time have been prevalent in our own country, if the circumstances which for a time encouraged it, had continued unaltered.

But, in political and philosophical theories, as well as in persons, success discloses faults and infirmities which failure might have concealed from observation. The notion, that the people have no need to limit their power over themselves, might seem axiomatic when popular government was a thing only dreamed about, or read of as having existed at some distant period of the past. Neither was that notion necessarily disturbed by such temporary aberrations as those of the French Revolution, the worst of which were the work of an usurping few, and which, in any case, belonged, not to the permanent working of popular institutions, but to a sudden and convulsive outbreak against monarchical and aristocratic despotism. In time, however, a democratic republic came to occupy a large portion of the earth's surface, and made itself felt as one of the most powerful members of the community of nations; and elective and responsible government became subject to the observations and criticisms which wait upon a great existing fact. It was now perceived that such phrases as "self-government," and "the power of the people over themselves," do not express the true state of the case. The "people" who exercise the power, are not always the same people with those over whom it is exercised; and the "self-government" spoken of is not the government of each by himself, but of each by all the rest. The will of the people, moreover, practically means the will of the most numerous or the most active *part* of the people: the majority, or those who succeed in making themselves accepted as the majority; the people, consequently, *may* desire to oppress a part of their number; and precautions are as much needed against this as against any other abuse of power. The limitation, therefore, of the power of government over individuals loses none of its importance when the holders of power are regularly accountable to the community, that is, to the strongest party therein. This view of things, recommending itself equally to the intelligence of thinkers and to the inclination of those important classes in European society to whose real or supposed interests democracy is adverse, has had no difficulty in establishing itself; and in political speculations "the tyranny of the majority" is now generally included among the evils against which society requires to be on its guard.

Like other tyrannies, the tyranny of the majority was at first, and is still vulgarly, held in dread, chiefly as operating through the acts of the public authorities. But reflecting persons perceived that when society is itself the tyrant—society collectively, over the separate individuals who compose it—its means of tyrannizing are not restricted to the acts which it may do by the hands of its political functionaries. Society can and does execute its own mandates: and if it issues wrong mandates instead of right, or any mandates at all in things with which it ought not to meddle, it practices a social tyranny more formidable than many kinds of political oppression, since, though not usually upheld by such extreme penalties, it leaves fewer means of escape, penetrating much more deeply into the details of life, and enslaving the soul itself. Protection, therefore, against the tyranny of the magistrate is not enough: there needs protection also against the tyranny of the prevailing opinion and feeling; against the tendency of society to impose, by other means than civil penalties, its own ideas and practices as rules of conduct on those who dissent from them; to fetter the development, and, if possible, prevent the formation, of any individuality not in harmony with its ways, and compel all characters to fashion themselves upon the model of its own. There is a limit to the legitimate interference of collective opinion with individual independence: and to find that limit, and maintain it against encroachment, is as indispensable to a good condition of human affairs, as protection against political despotism.

But though this proposition is not likely to be contested in general terms, the practical question, where to place the limit—how to make the fitting adjustment between individual independence and social control—is a subject on which nearly everything remains to be done.

. . .

The object of this Essay is to assert one very simple principle, as entitled to govern absolutely the dealings of society with the individual in the way of compulsion and control, whether the means used be physical force in the form of legal penalties, or the moral coercion of public opinion. That principle is that the sole end for which mankind are warranted, individually or collectively in interfering with the liberty of action of any of their number, is self-protection. That the only purpose for which power can be rightfully exercised over any member of a civilized community, against his will, is to prevent harm to others. His own good, either physical or moral, is not a sufficient warrant. He cannot rightfully be compelled to do or forbear because it will be better for him to do so, because it will make him happier, because, in the opinions of others, to do so would be wise, or even right. These are good reasons for remonstrating with him, or reasoning with him, or persuading him, or entreating him, but not for compelling him, or visiting him with any evil, in case he do otherwise. To justify that, the conduct from which it is desired to deter him, must be calculated to produce evil to some one else. The only part of the conduct of any one, for which he is amenable to society, is that which concerns others. In the part which merely concerns himself, his independence is, of right, absolute. Over himself, over his own body and mind, the individual is sovereign.

It is, perhaps, hardly necessary to say that this doctrine is meant to apply only to human beings in the maturity of their faculties. We are not speaking of children, or of young persons below the age which the law may fix as that of manhood or womanhood. Those who are still in a state to require being taken care of by others, must be protected against their own actions as well as against external injury. For the same reason, we may leave out of consideration those backward states of society in which the race itself may be considered as in its nonage. The early difficulties in the way of spontaneous progress are so great, that there is seldom any choice of means for overcoming them; and a ruler full of the spirit of improvement is warranted in the use of any expedients that will attain an end, perhaps otherwise unattainable. Despotism is a legitimate mode of government in dealing with barbarians, provided the end be their improvement, and the means justified by actually effecting that end. Liberty, as a principle, has no application to any state of things anterior to the time when mankind have become capable of being improved by free and equal discussion. Until then, there is nothing for them but implicit obedience to an Akbar or a Charlemagne, if they are so fortunate as to find one. But as soon as mankind have attained the capacity of being guided to their own improvement by conviction or persuasion (a period long since reached in all nations with whom we need here concern ourselves), compulsion, either in the direct form or in that of pains and penalties for non-compliance, is no longer admissible as a means to their own good, and justifiable only for the security of others.

It is proper to state that I forego any advantage which could be derived to my argument from the idea of abstract right, as a thing independent of utility. I regard utility as the ultimate appeal on all ethical questions; but it must be utility in the largest sense, grounded on the permanent interests of man as a progressive being. Those interests, I contend, authorize the subjection of individual spontaneity to external control, only in respect to those actions of each, which concern the interest of other people. If any one does an act hurtful to others, there is a prima facie case for punishing him, by law, or, where legal penalties are not safely applicable, by general disapprobation. There are also many positive acts for the benefit of others, which he may rightfully be compelled to perform; such as, to give evidence in a court of justice; to bear his fair share in the common defense, or in any other joint work necessary to the interest of the society of which he enjoys the protection; and to perform certain acts of individual beneficence, such as saving a fellow-creature's life, or interposing to protect the defenseless against ill-usage, things which whenever it is obviously a man's duty to do, he may rightfully be made responsible to society for not doing. A person may cause evil to others not only by his actions but by his inaction, and in neither case he is justly accountable to them for the injury. The latter case, it is true, requires a much more cautious exercise of compulsion than the former. To make any one answerable for doing evil to others, is the rule; to make him answerable for not preventing evil, is, comparatively speaking, the exception. Yet there are many cases clear enough and grave enough to justify that exception. In all things which regard the external relations of the individual, he is *de jure* amenable to those whose interests are concerned, and if need be, to society as their protector. There are often good reasons for not holding him to the responsibility; but these reasons must arise from the special expediencies of the case: either because it is a kind of case in which he is on the whole likely to act better, when left to his own discretion, than when controlled in any way in which society have it in their power to control him; or because the attempt to exercise control would produce other evils, greater than those which it would prevent. When such reasons as these preclude the enforcement of responsibility, the conscience of the agent himself should step into the vacant judgment-seat, and protect those interests of others which have no external protection; judging himself all the more rigidly, because the case does not admit of his being made accountable to the judgment of his fellow creatures.

But there is a sphere of action in which society, as distinguished from the individual, has, if any, only an indirect interest: comprehending all that portion of a person's life and conduct which affects only himself, or if it also affects others, only with their free, voluntary, and undeceived consent and participation. When I say only himself, I mean directly, and in the first instance: for whatever affects himself, may affect others through himself; and the objection which may be grounded on this contingency will receive consideration in the sequel. This, then, is the appropriate region of human liberty. It comprises, first, the inward domain of consciousness; demanding liberty of conscience, in the most comprehensive sense; liberty of thought and feeling; absolute freedom of opinion and sentiment on all subjects, practical or speculative, scientific, moral, or theological. The liberty of expressing and publishing opinions may seem to fall under a different principle, since it belongs to that part of the conduct of an individual which concerns other people; but, being almost of as much importance as the liberty of thought itself, and resting in great part on the same reasons, is practically inseparable from it. Secondly, the principle requires liberty of tastes and pursuits; of framing the plan of our life to suit our own character; of doing as we like, subject to such consequences as may follow: without impediment from our fellow-creatures, so long as what we do does not harm them, even though they should think our conduct foolish, perverse, or wrong. Thirdly, from this liberty of each individual, follows the liberty, within the same limits, of combination among individuals; freedom to unite, for any purpose not involving harm to others: the persons combining being supposed to be of full age, and not forced or deceived.

No society in which these liberties are not, on the whole, respected, is free, whatever may be its form of government; and none is completely free in which they do not exist absolute and unqualified. The only freedom which deserves the name, is that of pursuing our own good in our own way, so long as we do not attempt to deprive others of theirs, or impede their efforts to obtain it. Each is the proper guardian of his own health, whether bodily, or mental and spiritual. Mankind are greater gainers by suffering each other to live as seems good to themselves, than by compelling each to live as seems good to the rest.

☆ *Liberty of Thought and Discussion*

The time, it is to be hoped, is gone by when any defense would be necessary of the "liberty of the press" as one of the securities against corrupt or tyrannical government. No argument, we may suppose, can now be needed, against permitting a legislature or an executive, not identified in interest with the people, to prescribe opinions to them, and determine what doctrines or what arguments they shall be allowed to hear. This aspect of the question, besides, has been so often and so triumphantly enforced by preceding writers, that it needs not be specially insisted on in this place. Though the law of England, on the subject of the press, is as servile to this day as it was in the time of the Tudors, there is little danger of its being actually put in force against political discussion, except during some temporary panic, when fear of insurrection drives ministers and judges from their propriety; and, speaking generally, it is not, in constitutional countries, to be apprehended, that the government, whether completely responsible to the people or not, will often attempt to control the expression of opinion, except when in doing so it makes itself the organ of the general intolerance of the public. Let us suppose, therefore, that the government is entirely at one with the people, and never thinks of exerting any power of coercion unless in agreement with what it conceives to be their voice. But I deny the right of the people to exercise such coercion, either by themselves or by their government. The power itself is illegitimate. The best government has no more title to it than the worst. It is as noxious, or more noxious, when exerted in accordance with public opinion, than when in opposition to it. If all mankind minus one, were of one opinion, and only one person were of the contrary opinion, mankind would be no more justified in silencing that one person, than he, if he had the power, would be justified in silencing mankind. Were an opinion a personal possession of no value except to the owner; if to be obstructed in the enjoyment of it were simply a private injury, it would make some difference whether the injury was inflicted only on a few persons or on many. But the peculiar evil of silencing the expression of an opinion is, that it is robbing the human race; posterity as well as the existing generation; those who dissent from the opinion, still more than those who hold it. If the opinion is right, they are deprived of the opportunity of exchanging error for truth: if wrong, they lose, what is almost as great a benefit, the clearer perception and livelier impression of truth, produced by its collision with error.

It is necessary to consider separately these two hypotheses, each of which has a distinct branch of the argument corresponding to it. We can never be sure that the opinion we are endeavouring to stifle is a false opinion; and if we were sure, stifling it would be an evil still.

First: the opinion which it is attempted to suppress by authority may possibly be true. Those who desire to suppress it, of course deny its truth; but they are not infallible. They have no authority to decide the question for all mankind, and exclude every other person from the means of judging. To refuse a hearing to an opinion, because they are sure that it is false, is to assume that *their* certainty is the same thing as *absolute* certainty. All silencing of discussion is an assumption of infallibility. Its condemnation may be allowed to rest on this common argument, not the worse for being common.

Unfortunately for the good sense of mankind, the fact of their fallibility is far from carrying the weight in their practical judgment, which is always allowed to it in theory; for while every one well knows himself to be fallible, few think it necessary to take any precautions against their own fallibility, or admit the supposition that any opinion, of which they feel very certain, may be one of the examples of the error to which they acknowledge themselves to be liable. Absolute princes, or others who are accustomed to unlimited deference, usually feel this complete confidence in their own opinions on nearly all subjects. People more happily situated, who sometimes hear their opinions disputed, and are not wholly unused to be set right when they are wrong, place the same unbounded reliance only on such of their opinions as are shared by all who surround them, or to whom they habitually defer: for in proportion to a man's want of confidence in his own solitary judgment, does he usually repose, with implicit trust, on the infallibility of "the world" in general. And the world, to each individual, means the part of it with which he comes in contact; his party, his sect, his church, his class of society: the man may be called, by comparison, almost liberal and large-minded to whom it means anything so comprehensive as his own country or his own age. Nor is his faith in this collective authority at all shaken by his being aware that other ages, countries, sects, churches, classes, and parties have thought, and even now think, the exact reverse. He devolves upon his own world the responsibility of being in the right against the dissentient worlds of other people; and it never troubles him that mere accident has decided which of these numerous worlds is the object of his reliance, and that the same causes which make him a Churchman in London, would have made him a Buddhist or a Confucian in Peking. Yet it is as evident in itself as any amount of argument can make it, that ages are no more infallible than individuals; every age having held many opinions which subsequent ages have deemed not only false but absurd; and it is as certain that many opinions, now general, will be rejected by future ages, as it is that many, once general, are rejected by the present.

The objection likely to be made to this argument would probably take some such form as the following. There is no greater assumption of infallibility in forbidding the propagation of error, than in any other thing which is done by public authority on its own judgment and responsibility. Judgment is given to men that they may use it. Because it may be used erroneously, are men to be told that they ought not to use it at all? To prohibit what they think pernicious, is not claiming exemption from error, but fulfilling the duty incumbent on them, although fallible, of acting on their conscientious conviction. If we were never to act on our opinions, because those opinions may be wrong, we should leave all our interests uncared for, and all our duties unperformed. An objection which applies to all conduct, can be no valid objection to any conduct in particular. It is the duty of governments, and of individuals, to form the truest opinions they can; to form them carefully, and never impose them upon others unless they are quite sure of being right. But when they are sure (such reasoners may say), it is not conscientiousness but cowardice to shrink from acting on their opinions, and allow doctrines which they honestly think dangerous to the welfare of mankind, either in this life or in another, to be scattered abroad without restraint, because other people, in less enlightened times, have persecuted opinions now believed to be true. Let us take care, it may be said, not to make the same mistake: but governments and nations have made mistakes in other things, which are not denied to be fit subjects for the exercise of authority: they have laid on bad taxes, made unjust wars. Ought we therefore to lay on no taxes, and, under whatever provocation, make no wars? Men, and governments, must act to the best of their ability. There is no such thing as absolute certainty, but there is assurance sufficient for the purposes of human life. We may, and must, assume our opinion to be true for the guidance of our own conduct: and it is assuming no more when we forbid bad men to pervert society by the propagation of opinions which we regard as false and pernicious.

I answer, that it is assuming very much more. There is the greatest difference between presuming an opinion to be true, because, with every opportunity for contesting it, it has not been refuted, and assuming its truth for the purpose of not permitting its refutation. Complete liberty of contradicting and disproving our opinion, is the very condition which justifies us in assuming its truth for purposes of action; and on no other terms can a being with human faculties have any rational assurance of being right.

When we consider either the history of opinion, or the ordinary conduct of human life, to what is it to be ascribed that the one and the other are no worse than they are? Not certainly to the inherent force of the human understanding; for, on any matter not self-evident, there are ninety-nine persons totally incapable of judging of it, for one who is capable; and the capacity of the hundredth person is only comparative; for the majority of the eminent men of every past generation held many opinions now known to be erroneous, and did or approved numerous things which no one will now justify. Why is it, then, that there is on the whole a preponderance among mankind of rational opinions and rational conduct? If there really is this preponderance—which there must be, unless human affairs are, and have always been, in an almost desperate state—it is owing to a quality of the human mind, the source of everything respectable in man either as an intellectual or as a moral being, namely, that his errors are corrigible. He is capable of rectifying his mistakes by discussion and experience. Not by experience alone. There must be discussion, to show how experience is to be interpreted. Wrong opinions and practices gradually yield to fact and argument: but facts and arguments, to produce any effect on the mind, must be brought before it. Very few facts are able to tell their own story, without comments to bring out their meaning. The whole strength and value, then, of human judgment, depending on the one property, that it can be set right when it is wrong, reliance can be placed on it only when the means of setting it right are kept constantly at hand. In the case of any person whose judgment is really deserving of confidence, how has it become so? Because he has kept his mind open to criticism of his opinions and conduct. Because it has been his practice to listen to all that could be said against him; to profit by as much of it as was just, and expound to himself, and upon occasion to others, the fallacy of what was fallacious. Because he has felt, that the only way in which a human being can make some approach to knowing the whole of a subject, is by hearing what can be said about it by persons of every variety of opinion, and studying all modes in which it can be looked at by every character of mind. No wise man ever acquired his wisdom in any mode but this; nor is it in the nature of human intellect to become wise in any other manner. The steady habit of correcting and completing his own opinion by collating it with those of others, so far from causing doubt and hesitation in carrying it into practice, is the only stable foundation for a just reliance on it: for, being cognizant of all that can, at least obviously, be said against him, and having taken up his position against all gainsayers—knowing that he has sought for objections and difficulties, instead of avoiding them, and has shut out no light which can be thrown upon the subject from any quarter—he has a right to think his judgment better than that of any person, or any multitude, who have not gone through a similar process.

It is not too much to require that what the wisest of mankind, those who are best entitled to trust their own judgment, find necessary to warrant their relying on it, should be submitted to by that miscellaneous collection of a few wise and many foolish individuals, called the public. The most intolerant of churches, the Roman Catholic Church, even at the canonization of a saint, admits, and listens patiently to, a "devil's advocate." The holiest of men, it appears, cannot be admitted to posthumous honors, until all that the devil could say against him is known and weighed. If even the Newtonian philosophy were not permitted to be questioned, mankind could not feel as complete assurance of its truth as they now do. The beliefs which we have most warrant for, have no safeguard to rest on, but a standing invitation to the whole world to prove them unfounded. If the challenge is not accepted, or is accepted and the attempt fails, we are far enough from certainty still; but we have done the best that the existing state of human reason admits of; we have neglected nothing that could give the truth a chance of reaching us: if the lists are kept open, we may hope that if there be a better truth, it will be found when the human mind is capable of receiving it; and in the meantime we may rely on having attained such approach to truth, as is possible in our own day. This is the amount of certainty attainable by a fallible being, and this the sole way of attaining it.

Strange it is, that men should admit the validity of the arguments for free discussion, but object to their being "pushed to an extreme"; not seeing that unless the reasons are good for an extreme case, they are not good for any case. Strange that they should imagine that they are not assuming infallibility, when they acknowledge that there should be free discussion on all subjects which can possibly be *doubtful*, but think that some particular principle or doctrine should be forbidden to be questioned because it is so *certain*, that is, because *they are certain* that it is certain. To call any proposition certain, while there is any one who would deny its certainty if permitted, but who is not permitted, is to assume that we ourselves, and those who agree with us, are the judges of certainty, and judges without hearing the other side.

In the present age—which has been described as "destitute of faith, but terrified at scepticism"—in which people feel sure, not so much that their opinions are true, as that they should not know what to do without them—the claims of an opinion to be protected from public attack are rested not so much on its truth, as on its importance to society. There are, it is alleged, certain beliefs, so useful, not to say indispensable to well-being, that it is as much the duty of governments to uphold those beliefs, as to protect any other of the interests of society. In a case of such necessity, and so directly in the line of their duty, something less than infallibility may, it is maintained, warrant, and even bind, governments, to act on their own opinion, confirmed by the general opinion of mankind. It is also often argued, and still oftener thought, that none but bad men would desire to weaken these salutary beliefs; and there can be nothing wrong, it is thought, in restraining bad men, and prohibiting what only such men would wish to practise. This mode of thinking makes the justification of restraints on discussion not a question of the truth of doctrines, but of their usefulness; and flatters itself by that means to escape the responsibility of claiming to be an infallible judge of opinions. But those who thus satisfy themselves, do not perceive that the assumption of infallibility is merely shifted from one point to another. The usefulness of an opinion is itself matter of opinion: as disputable, as open to discussion, and requiring discussion as much, as the opinion itself. There is the same need of an infallible judge of opinions to decide an opinion to be noxious, as to decide it to be false, unless the opinion condemned has full opportunity of defending itself. And it will not do to say that the heretic may be allowed to maintain the utility or harmlessness of his opinion, though forbidden to maintain its truth. The truth of an opinion is part of its utility. If we would know whether or not it is desirable that a proposition should be believed, is it possible to exclude the consideration of whether or not it is true? In the opinion, not of bad men, but of the best men, no belief which is contrary to truth can be really useful: and can you prevent such men from urging that plea, when they are charged with culpability for denying some doctrine which they are told is useful, but which they believe to be false? Those who are on the side of received opinions, never fail to take all possible advantage of this plea; you do not find *them* handling the question of utility as if it could be completely abstracted from that of truth: on the contrary, it is, above all, because their doctrine is "the truth," that the knowledge or the belief of it is held to be so indispensable. There can be no fair discussion of the question of usefulness, when an argument so vital may be employed on one side, but not on the other. And in point of fact, when law or public feeling do not permit the truth of an opinion to be disputed, they are just as little tolerant of a denial of its usefulness. The utmost they allow is an extenuation of its absolute necessity or of the positive guilt of rejecting it.

In order more fully to illustrate the mischief of denying a hearing to opinions because we, in our own judgment, have condemned them, it will be desirable to fix down the discussion to a concrete case; and I choose, by preference, the cases which are least favorable to me—in which the argument against freedom of opinion, both on the score of truth and on that of utility, is considered the strongest. Let the opinions impugned be the belief in a God and in a future state, or any of the commonly received doctrines of morality. To fight the battle on such ground, gives a great advantage to an unfair antagonist; since he will be sure to say (and many who have no desire to be unfair will say it internally), are these the doctrines which you do not deem sufficiently certain to be taken under the protection of law? Is the belief in a God one of the opinions, to feel sure of which, you hold to be assuming infallibility? But I must be permitted to observe, that it is not the feeling sure of a doctrine (be it what it may) which I call an assumption of infallibility. It is the undertaking to decide that question *for others*, without allowing them to hear what can be said on the contrary side. And I denounce and reprobate this pretension not the less, if put forth on the side of my most solemn convictions. However positive any one's persuasion may be, not only of the falsity but of the pernicious consequences—not only of the pernicious consequences, but (to adopt expressions which I altogether condemn) the immorality and impiety of an opinion; yet if, in pursuance of that private judgment, though backed by the public judgment of his country or his cotemporaries, he prevents the opinion from being heard in its defense, he assumes infallibility. And so far from the assumption being less objectionable or less dangerous because the opinion is called immoral or impious, this is the case of all others in which it is most fatal. These are exactly the occasions on which the men of one generation commit those dreadful mistakes, which excite the astonishment and horror of posterity. It is among such that we find the instances memorable in history, when the arm of the law has been employed to root out the best men and the noblest doctrines; with deplorable success as to the men, though some of the doctrines have survived to be (as if in mockery) invoked, in defense of similar conduct towards those who dissent from *them*, or from their received interpretation.

Mankind can hardly be too often reminded, that there was once a man named Socrates, between whom and the legal authorities and public opinion of his time, there took place a memorable collision. Born in an age and country abounding in individual greatness, this man has been handed down to us by those who best knew both him and the age, as the most virtuous man in it; while *we* know him as the head and prototype of all subsequent teachers of virtue, the source equally of the lofty inspiration of Plato and the judicious utilitarianism of Aristotle, *i maestri di color che sanno*, the two headsprings of ethical as of all other philosophy. This acknowledged master of all the eminent thinkers who have since lived—whose fame, still growing after more than two thousand years, all but outweighs the whole remainder of the names which make his native city illustrious—was put to death by his countrymen, after a judicial conviction, for impiety and immorality. Impiety, in denying the gods recognized by the State; indeed his accuser asserted (see the *Apologia*) that he believed in no gods at all. Immorality, in being, by his doctrines and instructions, a "corrupter of youth." Of these charges the tribunal, there is every ground for believing, honestly found him guilty, and condemned the man who probably of all then born had deserved best of mankind, to be put to death as a criminal.

To pass from this to the only other instance of judicial iniquity, the mention of which, after the condemnation of Socrates, would not be an anticlimax: the event which took place on Calvary rather more than eighteen hundred years ago. The man who left on the memory of those who witnessed his life and conversation, such an impression of his moral grandeur, that eighteen subsequent centuries have done homage to him as the Almighty in person, was ignominiously put to death, as what? As a blasphemer. Men did not merely mistake their benefactor; they mistook him for the exact contrary of what he was, and treated him as that prodigy of impiety, which they themselves are now held to be, for their treatment of him. The feelings with which mankind now regard these lamentable transactions, especially the latter of the two, render them extremely unjust in their judgment of the unhappy actors. These were, to all appearance, not bad men—not worse than men most commonly are, but rather the contrary: men who possessed in a full, or somewhat more than a full measure, the religious, moral, and patriotic feelings of their time and people: the very kind of men who, in all times, our own included, have every chance of passing through life blameless and respected. The high-priest who rent his garments when the words were pronounced, which, according to all the ideas of his country, constituted the blackest guilt, was in all probability quite as sincere in his horror and indignation, as the generality of respectable and pious men now are in the religious and moral sentiments they profess; and most of those who now shudder at his conduct, if they had lived in his time, and been born Jews, would have acted precisely as he did. Orthodox Christians who are tempted to think that those who stoned to death the first martyrs must have been worse men than they themselves are, ought to remember that one of those persecutors was Saint Paul.

Let us add one more example, the most striking of all, if the impressiveness of an error is measured by the wisdom and virtue of him who falls into it. If ever any one, possessed of power, had grounds for thinking himself the best and most enlightened among his cotemporaries, it was the Emperor Marcus Aurelius. Absolute monarch of the whole civilized world, he preserved through life not only the most unblemished justice, but what was less to be expected from his Stoical breeding, the tenderest heart. The few failings which are attributed to him, were all on the side of indulgence: while his writings, the highest ethical product of the ancient mind, differ scarcely perceptibly, if they differ at all, from the most characteristic teachings of Christ. This man, a better Christian in all but the dogmatic sense of the word, than almost any of the ostensibly Christian sovereigns who have since reigned, persecuted Christianity. Placed at the summit of all the previous attainments of humanity, with an open, unfettered intellect, and a character which led him of himself to embody in his moral writings the Christian ideal, he yet failed to see that Christianity was to be a good and not an evil to the world, with his duties to which he was so deeply penetrated. Existing society he knew to be in a deplorable state. But such as it was, he saw or thought he saw, that it was held together and prevented from being worse, by belief and reverence of the received divinities. As a ruler of mankind, he deemed it his duty not to suffer society to fall in pieces; and saw not how, if its existing ties were removed, any others could be formed which could again knit it together. The new religion openly aimed at dissolving these ties: unless, therefore, it was his duty to adopt that religion, it seemed to be his duty to put it down. Inasmuch then as the theology of Christianity did not appear to him true or of divine origin; inasmuch as this strange history of a crucified God was not credible to him, and a system which purported to rest entirely upon a foundation to him so wholly unbelievable, could not be foreseen by him to be that renovating agency which, after all abatements, it has in fact proved to be; the gentlest and most amiable of philosophers and rulers, under a solemn sense of duty, authorized the persecution of Christianity. To my mind this is one of the most tragical facts in all history. It is a bitter thought, how different a thing the Christianity of the world might have been, if the Christian faith had been adopted as the religion of the empire under the auspices of Marcus Aurelius instead of those of Constantine. But it would be equally unjust to him and false to truth, to deny, that no one plea which can be urged for punishing anti-Christian teaching, was wanting to Marcus Aurelius for punishing, as he did, the propagation of Christianity. No Christian more firmly believes that Atheism is false, and tends to the dissolution of society, than Marcus Aurelius believed the same things of Christianity; he who, of all men then living, might have been thought the most capable of appreciating it. Unless any one who approves of punishment for the promulgation of opinions, flatters himself that he is a wiser and better man than Marcus Aurelius—more deeply versed in the wisdom of his time, more elevated in his intellect above it—more earnest in his search for truth, or more single-minded in his devotion to it when found;—let him abstain from that assumption of the joint infallibility of himself and the multitude, which the great Antoninus made with so unfortunate a result.

Aware of the impossibility of defending the use of punishment for restraining irreligious opinions, by any argument which will not justify Marcus Antoninus, the enemies of religious freedom, when hard pressed, occasionally accept this consequence, and say, with Dr. Johnson, that the persecutors of Christianity were in the right; that persecution is an ordeal through which truth ought to pass, and always passes successfully, legal penalties being, in the end, powerless against truth, though sometimes beneficially effective against mischievous errors. This is a form of the argument for religious intolerance, sufficiently remarkable not to be passed without notice.

A theory which maintains that truth may justifiably be persecuted because persecution cannot possibly do it any harm, cannot be charged with being intentionally hostile to the reception of new truths; but we cannot commend the generosity of its dealing with the persons to whom mankind are indebted for them. To discover to the world something which deeply concerns it, and of which it was previously ignorant; to prove to it that it had been mistaken on some vital point of temporal or spiritual interest, is as important a service as a human being can render to his fellow-creatures, and in certain cases, as in those of the early Christians and of the Reformers, those who think with Dr. Johnson believe it to have been the most precious gift which could be bestowed on mankind. That the authors of such splendid benefits should be requited by martyrdom; that their reward should be to be dealt with as the vilest of criminals, is not, upon this theory, a deplorable error and misfortune, for which humanity should mourn in sackcloth and ashes, but the normal and justifiable state of things. The propounder of a new truth, according to this doctrine, should stand, as stood, in the legislation of the Locrians, the proposer of a new law, with a halter round his neck, to be instantly tightened if the public assembly did not, on hearing his reasons, then and there adopt his proposition. People who defend this mode of treating benefactors, cannot be supposed to set much value on the benefit; and I believe this view of the subject is mostly confined to the sort of persons who think that new truths may have been desirable once, but that we have had enough of them now.

But, indeed, the dictum that truth always triumphs over persecution, is one of those pleasant falsehoods which men repeat after one another till they pass into commonplaces, but which all experience refutes. History teems with instances of truth put down by persecution. If not suppressed forever, it may be thrown back for centuries. To speak only of religious opinions: the Reformation broke out at least twenty times before Luther, and was put down. Arnold of Brescia was put down. Fra Dolcino was put down. Savonarola was put down. The Albigeois were put down. The Vaudois were put down. The Lollards were put down. The Hussites were put down. Even after the era of Luther, wherever persecution was persisted in, it was successful. In Spain, Italy, Flanders, the Austrian empire, Protestantism was rooted out; and, most likely, would have been so in England, had Queen Mary lived, or Queen Elizabeth died. Persecution has always succeeded, save where the heretics were too strong a party to be effectually persecuted. No reasonable person can doubt that Christianity might have been extirpated in the Roman empire. It spread, and became predominant, because the persecutions were only occasional, lasting but a short time, and separated by long intervals of almost undisturbed propagandism. It is a piece of idle sentimentality that truth, merely as truth, has any inherent power denied to error, of prevailing against the dungeon and the stake. Men are not more zealous for truth than they often are for error, and a sufficient application of legal or even of social penalties will generally succeed in stopping the propagation of either. The real advantage which truth has, consists in this, that when an opinion is true, it may be extinguished once, twice, or many times, but in the course of ages there will generally be found persons to rediscover it, until some one of its reappearances falls on a time when from favourable circumstances it escapes persecution until it has made such head as to withstand all subsequent attempts to suppress it.

What is boasted of at the present time as the revival of religion, is always, in narrow and uncultivated minds, at least as much the revival of bigotry; and where there is the strongest permanent leaven of intolerance in the feelings of a people, which at all times abides in the middle classes of this country, it needs but little to provoke them into actively persecuting those whom they have never ceased to think proper objects of persecution. For it is this—it is the opinions men entertain, and the feelings they cherish, respecting those who disown the beliefs they deem important, which makes this country not a place of mental freedom. For a long time past, the chief mischief of the legal penalties is that they strengthen the social stigma. It is that stigma which is really effective, and so effective is it, that the profession of opinions which are under the ban of society is much less common in England, than is, in many other countries, the avowal of those which incur risk of judicial punishment. In respect to all persons but those whose pecuniary circumstances make them independent of the good will of other people, opinion, on this subject, is as efficacious as law; men might as well be imprisoned, as excluded from the means of earning their bread. Those whose bread is already secured, and who desire no favors from men in power, or from bodies of men, or from the public, have nothing to fear from the open avowal of any opinions, but to be ill-thought of and ill-spoken of, and this it ought not to require a very heroic mould to enable them to bear. There is no room for any appeal *ad misericordiam* in behalf of such persons. But though we do not now inflict so much evil on those who think differently from us, as it was formerly our custom to do, it may be that we do ourselves as much evil as ever by our treatment of them. Socrates was put to death, but the Socratic philosophy rose like the sun in heaven, and spread its illumination over the whole intellectual firmament. Christians were cast to the lions, but the Christian Church grew up a stately and spreading tree, overtopping the older and less vigorous growths, and stifling them by its shade. Our merely social intolerance kills no one, roots out no opinions, but induces men to disguise them, or to abstain from any active effort for their diffusion. With us, heretical opinions do not perceptibly gain or even lose, ground in each decade or generation; they never blaze out far and wide, but continue to smolder in the narrow circles of thinking and studious persons among whom they originate, without ever lighting up the general affairs of mankind with either a true or a deceptive light. And thus is kept up a state of things very satisfactory to some minds, because, without the unpleasant process of fining or imprisoning anybody, it maintains all prevailing opinions outwardly undisturbed, while it does not absolutely interdict the exercise of reason by dissentients afflicted with the malady of thought. A convenient plan for having peace in the intellectual world, and keeping all things going on therein very much as they do already. But the price paid for this sort of intellectual pacification, is the sacrifice of the entire moral courage of the human mind. A state of things in which a large portion of the most active and inquiring intellects find it advisable to keep the genuine principles and grounds of their convictions within their own breasts, and attempt, in what they address to the public, to fit as much as they can of their own conclusions to premises which they have internally renounced, cannot send forth the open, fearless characters, and logical, consistent intellects who once adorned the thinking world. The sort of men who can be looked for under it, are either mere conformers to commonplace, or time-servers for truth whose arguments on all great subjects are meant for their hearers, and are not those which have convinced themselves. Those who avoid this alternative, do so by narrowing their thoughts and interests to things which can be spoken of without venturing within the region of principles, that is, to small practical matters, which would come right of themselves, if but the minds of mankind were strengthened and enlarged, and which will never be made effectually right until then: while that which would strengthen and enlarge men's minds, free and daring speculation on the highest subjects, is abandoned.

Those in whose eyes this reticence on the part of heretics is no evil, should consider in the first place, that in consequence of it there is never any fair and thorough discussion of heretical opinions; and that such of them as could not stand such a discussion, though they may be prevented from spreading, do not disappear. But it is not the minds of heretics that are deteriorated most, by the ban placed on all inquiry which does not end in the orthodox conclusions. The greatest harm done is to those who are not heretics, and whose whole mental development is cramped, and their reason cowed, by the fear of heresy. Who can compute what the world loses in the multitude of promising intellects combined with timid characters, who dare not follow out any bold, vigorous, independent train of thought, lest it should land them in something which would admit of being considered irreligious or immoral? Among them we may occasionally see some man of deep conscientiousness, and subtile and refined understanding, who spends a life in sophisticating with an intellect which he cannot silence, and exhausts the resources of ingenuity in attempting to reconcile the promptings of his conscience and reason with orthodoxy, which yet he does not, perhaps, to the end succeed in doing. No one can be a great thinker who does not recognize, that as a thinker it is his first duty to follow his intellect to whatever conclusions it may lead. Truth gains more even by the errors of one who, with due study and preparation, thinks for himself, than by the true opinions of those who only hold them because they do not suffer themselves to think. Not that it is solely, or chiefly, to form great thinkers, that freedom of thinking is required. On the contrary, it is as much and even more indispensable, to enable average human beings to attain the mental stature which they are capable of. There have been, and may again be, great individual thinkers, in a general atmosphere of mental slavery. But there never has been, nor ever will be, in that atmosphere, an intellectually active people. Where any people has made a temporary approach to such a character, it has been because the dread of heterodox speculation was for a time suspended. Where there is a tacit convention that principles are not to be disputed; where the discussion of the greatest questions which can occupy humanity is considered to be closed, we cannot hope to find that generally high scale of mental activity which has made some periods of history so remarkable. Never when controversy avoided the subjects which are large and important enough to kindle enthusiasm, was the mind of a people stirred up from its foundations, and the impulse given which raised even persons of the most ordinary intellect to something of the dignity of thinking beings. Of such we have had an example in the condition of Europe during the times immediately following the Reformation; another, though limited to the Continent and to a more cultivated class, in the speculative movement of the latter half of the eighteenth century; and a third, of still briefer duration, in the intellectual fermentation of Germany during the Goethian and Fichtean period. These periods differed widely in the particular opinions which they developed; but were alike in this, that during all three the yoke of authority was broken. In each, an old mental despotism had been thrown off, and no new one had yet taken its place. The impulse given at these three periods has made Europe what it now is. Every single improvement which has taken place either in the human mind or in institutions, may be traced distinctly to one or other of them. Appearances have for some time indicated that all three impulses are well-nigh spent; and we can expect no fresh start, until we again assert our mental freedom.

Let us now pass to the second division of the argument, and dismissing the supposition that any of the received opinions may be false, let us assume them to be true, and examine into the worth of the manner in which they are likely to be held, when their truth is not freely and openly canvassed. However unwillingly a person who has a strong opinion may admit the possibility that his opinion may be false, he ought to be moved by the consideration that however true it may be, if it is not fully, frequently, and fearlessly discussed, it will be held as a dead dogma, not a living truth.

There is a class of persons (happily not quite so numerous as formerly) who think it enough if a person assents undoubtingly to what they think true, though he has no knowledge whatever of the grounds of the opinion, and could not make a tenable defense of it against the most superficial objections. Such persons, if they can once get their creed taught from authority, naturally think that no good, and some harm, comes of its being allowed to be questioned. Where their influence prevails, they make it nearly impossible for the received opinion to be rejected wisely and considerately, though it may still be rejected rashly and ignorantly; for to shut out discussion entirely is seldom possible and, when it once gets in, beliefs not grounded on conviction are apt to give way before the slightest semblance of an argument. Waiving, however, this possibility—assuming that the true opinion abides in the mind, but abides as a prejudice, a belief independent of, and proof against, argument—this is not the way in which truth ought to be held by a rational being. This is not knowing the truth. Truth, thus held, is but one superstition the more accidentally clinging to the words which enunciate a truth.

If the intellect and judgment of mankind ought to be cultivated, a thing which Protestants at least do not deny, on what can these faculties be more appropriately exercised by any one, than on the things which concern him so much that it is considered necessary for him to hold opinions on them? If the cultivation of the understanding consists in one thing more than in another, it is surely in learning the grounds of one's own opinions. Whatever people believe, on subjects on which it is of the first importance to believe rightly, they ought to be able to defend against at least the common objections. But, some one may say, "Let them be *taught* the grounds of their opinions. It does not follow that opinions must be merely parroted because they are never heard controverted. Persons who learn geometry do not simply commit the theorems to memory, but understand and learn likewise the demonstrations; and it would be absurd to say that they remain ignorant of the grounds of geometrical truths, because they never hear any one deny, and attempt to disprove them." Undoubtedly, and such teaching suffices on a subject like mathematics, where there is nothing at all to be said on the wrong side of the question. The peculiarity of the evidence of mathematical truths is that all the argument is on one side. There are no objections, and no answers to objections. But on every subject on which difference of opinion is possible, the truth depends on a balance to be struck between two sets of conflicting reasons. Even in natural philosophy, there is always some other explanation possible of the same facts; some geocentric theory instead of heliocentric, some phlogiston instead of oxygen; and it has to be shown why that other theory cannot be the true one: and until this is shown and until we know how it is shown, we do not understand the grounds of our opinion. But when we turn to subjects infinitely more complicated, to morals, religion, politics, social relations, and the business of life, three-fourths of the arguments for every disputed opinion consist in dispelling the appearances which favor some opinion different from it. The greatest orator, save one, of antiquity, has left it on record that he always studied his adversary's case with as great, if not with still greater, intensity than even his own. What Cicero practiced as the means of forensic success, requires to be imitated by all who study any subject in order to arrive at the truth. He who knows only his own side of the case, knows little of that. His reasons may be good, and no one may have been able to refute them. But if he is equally unable to refute the reasons on the opposite side; if he does not so much as know what they are, he has no ground for preferring either opinion. The rational position for him would be suspension of judgment, and unless he contents himself with that, he is either led by authority, or adopts, like the generality of the world, the side to which he feels most inclination. Nor is it enough that he should hear the arguments of adversaries from his own teachers, presented as they state them, and accompanied by what they offer as refutations. This is not the way to do justice to the arguments, or bring them into real contact with his own mind. He must be able to hear them from persons who actually believe them; who defend them in earnest, and do their very utmost for them. He must know them in their most plausible and persuasive form; he must feel the whole force of the difficulty which the true view of the subject has to encounter and dispose of else he will never really possess himself of the portion of truth which meets and removes that difficulty. Ninety-nine in a hundred of what are called educated men are in this condition; even of those who can argue fluently for their opinions. Their conclusion may be true, but it might be false for anything they know: they have never thrown themselves into the mental position of those who think differently from them, and considered what such persons may have to say; and consequently they do not, in any proper sense of the word, know the doctrine which they themselves profess. They do not know those parts of it which explain and justify the remainder; the considerations which show that a fact which seemingly conflicts with another is reconcilable with it, or that, of two apparently strong reasons, one and not the other ought to be preferred. All that part of the truth which turns the scale, and decides the judgment of a completely informed mind, they are strangers to; nor is it ever really known, but to those who have attended equally and impartially to both sides, and endeavored to see the reasons of both in the strongest light. So essential is this discipline to a real understanding of moral and human subjects, that if opponents of all important truths do not exist, it is indispensable to imagine them and supply them with the strongest arguments which the most skillful devil's advocate can conjure up.

To abate the force of these considerations, an enemy of free discussion may be supposed to say, that there is no necessity for mankind in general to know and understand all that can be said against or for their opinions by philosophers and theologians. That it is not needful for common men to be able to expose all the misstatements or fallacies of an ingenious opponent. That it is enough if there is always somebody capable of answering them, so that nothing likely to mislead uninstructed persons remains unrefuted. That simple minds, having been taught the obvious grounds of the truths inculcated on them, may trust to authority for the rest, and being aware that they have neither knowledge nor talent to resolve every difficulty which can be raised, may repose in the assurance that all those which have been raised have been or can be answered, by those who are specially trained to the task.

Conceding to this view of the subject the utmost that can be claimed for it by those most easily satisfied with the amount of understanding of truth which ought to accompany the belief of it; even so, the argument for free discussion is no way weakened. For even this doctrine acknowledges that mankind ought to have a rational assurance that all objections have been satisfactorily answered; and how are they to be answered if that which requires to be answered is not spoken? or how can the answer be known to be satisfactory, if the objectors have no opportunity of showing that it is unsatisfactory? If not the public, at least the philosophers and theologians who are to resolve the difficulties, must make themselves familiar with those difficulties in their most puzzling form; and this cannot be accomplished unless they are freely stated, and placed in the most advantageous light which they admit of. The Catholic Church has its own way of dealing with this embarrassing problem. It makes a broad separation between those who can be permitted to receive its doctrines on conviction, and those who must accept them on trust. Neither, indeed, are allowed any choice as to what they will accept; but the clergy, such at least as can be fully confided in, may admissibly and meritoriously make themselves acquainted with the arguments of opponents, in order to answer them, and may, therefore, read heretical books; the laity, not unless by special permission, hard to be obtained. This discipline recognizes a knowledge of the enemy's case as beneficial to the teachers, but finds means, consistent with this, of denying it to the rest of the world: thus giving to the *élite* more mental culture, though not more mental freedom, than it allows to the mass. By this device it succeeds in obtaining the kind of mental superiority which its purposes require; for though culture without freedom never made a large and liberal mind, it can make a clever *nisi prius* advocate of a cause. But in countries professing Protestantism, this resource is denied; since Protestants hold, at least in theory, that the responsibility for the choice of a religion must be borne by each for himself, and cannot be thrown off upon teachers. Besides, in the present state of the world, it is practically impossible that writings which are read by the instructed can be kept from the uninstructed. If the teachers of mankind are to be cognizant of all that they ought to know, everything must be free to be written and published without restraint.

If, however, the mischievous operation of the absence of free discussion, when the received opinions are true, were confined to leaving men ignorant of the grounds of those opinions, it might be thought that this, if an intellectual, is no moral evil, and does not affect the worth of the opinions, regarded in their influence on the character. The fact, however, is that not only the grounds of the opinion are forgotten in the absence of discussion, but too often the meaning of the opinion itself. The words which convey it cease to suggest ideas, or suggest only a small portion of those they were originally employed to communicate. Instead of a vivid conception and a living belief, there remain only a few phrases retained by rote; or, if any part, the shell and husk only of the meaning is retained, the finer essence being lost. The great chapter in human history which this fact occupies and fills, cannot be too earnestly studied and meditated on.

It is illustrated in the experience of almost all ethical doctrines and religious creeds. They are all full of meaning and vitality to those who originate them, and to the direct disciples of the originators. Their meaning continues to be felt in undiminished strength, and is perhaps brought out into even fuller consciousness, so long as the struggle lasts to give the doctrine or creed an ascendency over other creeds. At last it either prevails, and becomes the general opinion, or its progress stops; it keeps possession of the ground it has gained, but ceases to spread further. When either of these results has become apparent, controversy on the subject flags, and gradually dies away. The doctrine has taken its place, if not as a received opinion, as one of the admitted sects or divisions of opinion: those who hold it have generally inherited, not adopted it; and conversion from one of these doctrines to another, being now an exceptional fact, occupies little place in the thoughts of their professors. Instead of being, as at first, constantly on the alert either to defend themselves against the world, or to bring the world over to them, they have subsided into acquiescence, and neither listen, when they can help it, to arguments against their creed, nor trouble dissentients (if there be such) with arguments in its favor. From this time may usually be dated the decline in the living power of the doctrine. We often hear the teachers of all creeds lamenting the difficulty of keeping up in the minds of believers a lively apprehension of the truth which they nominally recognize, so that it may penetrate the feelings, and acquire a real mastery over the conduct. No such difficulty is complained of while the creed is still fighting for its existence: even the weaker combatants then know and feel what they are fighting for, and the difference between it and other doctrines; and in that period of every creed's existence, not a few persons may be found, who have realized its fundamental principles in all the forms of thought, have weighed and considered them in all their important bearings, and have experienced the full effect on the character, which belief in that creed ought to produce in a mind thoroughly imbued with it. But when it has come to be an hereditary creed, and to be received passively, not actively—when the mind is no longer compelled, in the same degree as at first, to exercise its vital powers on the questions which its belief presents to it, there is a progressive tendency to forget all of the belief except the formularies, or to give it a dull and torpid assent, as if accepting it on trust dispensed with the necessity of realizing it in consciousness, or testing it by personal experience; until it almost ceases to connect itself at all with the inner life of the human being. Then are seen the cases, so frequent in this age of the world as almost to form the majority, in which the creed remains as it were outside the mind, encrusting and petrifying it against all other influences addressed to the higher parts of our nature; manifesting its power by not suffering any fresh and living conviction to get in, but itself doing nothing for the mind or heart, except standing sentinel over them to keep them vacant.

To what an extent doctrines intrinsically fitted to make the deepest impression upon the mind may remain in it as dead beliefs, without being ever realized in the imagination, the feelings, or the understanding, is exemplified by the manner in which the majority of believers hold the doctrines of Christianity. By Christianity I here mean what is accounted such by all churches and sects—the maxims and precepts contained in the New Testament. These are considered sacred, and accepted as laws, by all professing Christians. Yet it is scarcely too much to say that not one Christian in a thousand guides or tests his individual conduct by reference to those laws. The standard to which he does refer it, is the custom of his nation, his class, or his religious profession. He has thus, on the one hand, a collection of ethical maxims, which he believes to have been vouchsafed to him by infallible wisdom as rules for his government; and on the other, a set of every-day judgments and practices, which go a certain length with some of those maxims, not so great a length with others, stand in direct opposition to some, and are, on the whole, a compromise between the Christian creed and the interests and suggestions of worldly life. To the first of these standards he gives his homage; to the other his real allegiance. All Christians believe that the blessed are the poor and humble, and those who are ill-used by the world; that it is easier for a camel to pass through the eye of a needle than for a rich man to enter the kingdom of heaven; that they should judge not, lest they be judged; that they should swear not at all; that they should love their neighbor as themselves; that if one take their cloak, they should give him their coat also; that they should take no thought for the morrow; that if they would be perfect, they should sell all that they have and give it to the poor. They are not insincere when they say that they believe these things. They do believe them, as people believe what they have always heard lauded and never discussed. But in the sense of that living belief which regulates conduct, they believe these doctrines just up to the point to which it is usual to act upon them. The doctrines in their integrity are serviceable to pelt adversaries with; and it is understood that they are to be put forward (when possible) as the reasons for whatever people do that they think laudable. But any one who reminded them that the maxims require an infinity of things which they never even think of doing, would gain nothing but to be classed among those very unpopular characters who affect to be better than other people. The doctrines have no hold on ordinary believers—are not a power in their minds. They have an habitual respect for the sound of them, but no feeling which spreads from the words to the things signified, and forces the mind to take *them* in, and make them conform to the formula. Whenever conduct is concerned, they look round for Mr. A and B to direct them how far to go in obeying Christ.

Now we may be well assured that the case was not thus, but far otherwise, with the early Christians. Had it been thus, Christianity never would have expanded from an obscure sect of the despised Hebrews into the religion of the Roman empire. When their enemies said, "See how these Christians love one another" (a remark not likely to be made by anybody now), they assuredly had a much livelier feeling of the meaning of their creed than they have ever had since. And to this cause, probably, it is chiefly owing that Christianity now makes so little progress in extending its domain, and after eighteen centuries, is still nearly confined to Europeans and the descendants of Europeans. Even with the strictly religious, who are much in earnest about their doctrines, and attach a greater amount of meaning to many of them than people in general, it commonly happens that the part which is thus comparatively active in their minds is that which was made by Calvin, or Knox, or some such person much nearer in character to themselves. The sayings of Christ coexist passively in their minds, producing hardly any effect beyond what is caused by mere listening to words so amiable and bland. There are many reasons, doubtless, why doctrines which are the badge of a sect retain more of their vitality than those common to all recognized sects, and why more pains are taken by teachers to keep their meaning alive; but one reason certainly is, that the peculiar doctrines are more questioned, and have to be oftener defended against open gainsayers. Both teachers and learners go to sleep at their post, as soon as there is no enemy in the field.

The same thing holds true, generally speaking, of all traditional doctrines—those of prudence and knowledge of life, as well as of morals or religion. All languages and literatures are full of general observations on life, both as to what it is, and how to conduct oneself in it; observations which everybody knows, which everybody repeats, or hears with acquiescence, which are received as truisms, yet of which most people first truly learn the meaning, when experience, generally of a painful kind, has made it a reality to them. How often, when smarting under some unforeseen misfortune or disappointment, does a person call to mind some proverb or common saying, familiar to him all his life, the meaning of which, if he had ever before felt it as he does now, would have saved him from the calamity. There are indeed reasons for this, other than the absence of discussion: there are many truths of which the full meaning *cannot* be realized, until personal experience has brought it home. But much more of the meaning even of these would have been understood, and what was understood would have been far more deeply impressed on the mind, if the man had been accustomed to hear it argued *pro* and *con* by people who did understand it. The fatal tendency of mankind to leave off thinking about a thing when it is no longer doubtful, is the cause of half their errors. A contemporary author has well spoken of "the deep slumber of a decided opinion."

But what! (it may be asked) Is the absence of unanimity an indispensable condition of true knowledge? Is it necessary that some part of mankind should persist in error, to enable any to realize the truth? Does a belief cease to be real and vital as soon as it is generally received—and is a proposition never thoroughly understood and felt unless some doubt of it remains? As soon as mankind have unanimously accepted a truth, does the truth perish within them? The highest aim and best result of improved intelligence, it has hitherto been thought, is to unite mankind more and more in the acknowledgment of all important truths: and does the intelligence only last as long as it has not achieved its object? Do the fruits of conquest perish by the very completeness of the victory?

I affirm no such thing. As mankind improve, the number of doctrines which are no longer disputed or doubted will be constantly on the increase: and the well-being of mankind may almost be measured by the number and gravity of the truths which have reached the point of being uncontested. The cessation, on one question after another, of serious controversy, is one of the necessary incidents of the consolidation of opinion; a consolidation as salutary in the case of true opinions, as it is dangerous and noxious when the opinions are erroneous. But though this gradual narrowing of the bounds of diversity of opinion is necessary in both senses of the term, being at once inevitable and indispensable, we are not therefore obliged to conclude that all its consequences must be beneficial. The loss of so important an aid to the intelligent and living apprehension of a truth, as is afforded by the necessity of explaining it to, or defending it against, opponents, though not sufficient to outweigh, is no trifling drawback from, the benefit of its universal recognition. Where this advantage can no longer be had, I confess I should like to see the teachers of mankind endeavoring to provide a substitute for it; some contrivance for making the difficulties of the question as present to the learner's consciousness, as if they were pressed upon him by a dissentient champion, eager for his conversion.

But instead of seeking contrivances for this purpose, they have lost those they formerly had. The Socratic dialectics, so magnificently exemplified in the dialogues of Plato, were a contrivance of this description. They were essentially a negative discussion of the great questions of philosophy and life, directed with consummate skill to the purpose of convincing any one who had merely adopted the commonplaces of received opinion, that he did not understand the subject—that he as yet attached no definite meaning to the doctrines he professed; in order that, becoming aware of his ignorance, he might be put in the way to attain a stable belief, resting on a clear apprehension both of the meaning of doctrines and of their evidence. The school disputations of the Middle Ages had a somewhat similar object. They were intended to make sure that the pupil understood his own opinion, and (by necessary correlation) the opinion opposed to it, and could enforce the grounds of the one and confute those of the other. These last-mentioned contests had indeed the incurable defect, that the premises appealed to were taken from authority, not from reason; and, as a discipline to the mind, they were in every respect inferior to the powerful dialectics which formed the intellects of the "Socratici viri": but the modern mind owes far more to both than it is generally willing to admit, and the present modes of education contain nothing which in the smallest degree supplies the place either of the one or of the other. A person who derives all his instruction from teachers or books, even if he escape the besetting temptation of contenting himself with cram, is under no compulsion to hear both sides; accordingly it is far from a frequent accomplishment, even among thinkers, to know both sides; and the weakest part of what everybody says in defense of his opinion, is what he intends as a reply to antagonists. It is the fashion of the present time to disparage negative logic—that which points out weaknesses in theory or errors in practice, without establishing positive truths. Such negative criticism would indeed be poor enough as an ultimate result; but as a means to attaining any positive knowledge or conviction worthy the name, it cannot be valued too highly; and until people are again systematically trained to it, there will be few great thinkers, and a low general average of intellect, in any but the mathematical and physical departments of speculation. On any other subject no one's opinions deserve the name of knowledge, except so far as he has either had forced upon him by others, or gone through of himself, the same mental process which would have been required of him in carrying on an active controversy with opponents. That, therefore, which when absent, it is so indispensable, but so difficult, to create, how worse than absurd is it to forego, when spontaneously offering itself! If there are any persons who contest a received opinion, or who will do so if law or opinion will let them, let us thank them for it, open our minds to listen to them, and rejoice that there is some one to do for us what we otherwise ought, if we have any regard for either the certainty or the vitality of our convictions, to do with much greater labor for ourselves.

It still remains to speak of one of the principal causes which make diversity of opinion advantageous, and will continue to do so until mankind shall have entered a stage of intellectual advancement which at present seems at an incalculable distance. We have hitherto considered only two possibilities: that the received opinion may be false, and some other opinion, consequently, true; or that, the received opinion being true, a conflict with the opposite error is essential to a clear apprehension and deep feeling of its truth. But there is a commoner case than either of these; when the conflicting doctrines, instead of being one true and the other false, share the truth between them; and the nonconforming opinion is needed to supply the remainder of the truth, of which the received doctrine embodies only a part. Popular opinions, on subjects not palpable to sense, are often true, but seldom or never the whole truth. They are a part of the truth; sometimes a greater, sometimes a smaller part, but exaggerated, distorted, and disjoined from the truths by which they ought to be accompanied and limited. Heretical opinions, on the other hand, are generally some of these suppressed and neglected truths, bursting the bonds which kept them down, and either seeking reconciliation with the truth contained in the common opinion, or fronting it as enemies, and setting themselves up, with similar exclusiveness, as the whole truth. The latter case is hitherto the most frequent, as, in the human mind, one-sidedness has always been the rule, and many-sidedness the exception. Hence, even in revolutions of opinion, one part of the truth usually sets while another rises. Even progress, which ought to superadd, for the most part only substitutes one partial and incomplete truth for another; improvement consisting chiefly in this, that the new fragment of truth is more wanted, more adapted to the needs of the time, than that which it displaces. Such being the partial character of prevailing opinions, even when resting on a true foundation, every opinion which embodies somewhat of the portion of truth which the common opinion omits, ought to be considered precious, with whatever amount of error and confusion that truth may be blended. No sober judge of human affairs will feel bound to be indignant because those who force on our notice truths which we should otherwise have overlooked, overlook some of those which we see. Rather, he will think that so long as popular truth is one-sided, it is more desirable than otherwise that unpopular truth should have one-sided asserters too; such being usually the most energetic, and the most likely to compel reluctant attention to the fragment of wisdom which they proclaim as if it were the whole.

Thus, in the eighteenth century, when nearly all the instructed, and all those of the uninstructed who were led by them, were lost in admiration of what is called civilization, and of the marvels of modern science, literature, and philosophy, and while greatly overrating the amount of unlikeness between the men of modern and those of ancient times, indulged the belief that the whole of the difference was in their own favor; with what a salutary shock did the paradoxes of Rousseau explode like bombshells in the midst, dislocating the compact mass of one-sided opinion, and forcing its elements to recombine in a better form and with additional ingredients. Not that the current opinions were on the whole farther from the truth than Rousseau's were; on the contrary, they were nearer to it; they contained more of positive truth, and very much less of error. Nevertheless there lay in Rousseau's doctrine, and has floated down the stream of opinion along with it, a considerable amount of exactly those truths which the popular opinion wanted; and these are the deposit which was left behind when the flood subsided. The superior worth of simplicity of life, the enervating and demoralizing effect of the trammels and hypocrisies of artificial society, are ideas which have never been entirely absent from cultivated minds since Rousseau wrote; and they will in time produce their due effect, though at present needing to be asserted as much as ever, and to be asserted by deeds, for words, on this subject, have nearly exhausted their power.

In politics, again, it is almost a commonplace, that a party of order or stability, and a party of progress or reform, are both necessary elements of a healthy state of political life; until the one or the other shall have so enlarged its mental grasp as to be a party equally of order and of progress, knowing and distinguishing what is fit to be preserved from what ought to be swept away. Each of these modes of thinking derives its utility from the deficiencies of the other; but it is in a great measure the opposition of the other that keeps each within the limits of reason and sanity. Unless opinions favorable to democracy and to aristocracy, to property and to equality, to co-operation and to competition, to luxury and to abstinence, to sociality and individuality, to liberty and discipline, and all the other standing antagonisms of practical life, are expressed with equal freedom, and enforced and defended with equal talent and energy, there is no chance of both elements obtaining their due; one scale is sure to go up, and the other down. Truth, in the great practical concerns of life, is so much a question of the reconciling and combining of opposites, that very few have minds sufficiently capacious and impartial to make the adjustment with an approach to correctness, and it has to be made by the rough process of a struggle between combatants fighting under hostile banners. On any of the great open questions just enumerated, if either of the two opinions has a better claim than the other, not merely to be tolerated, but to be encouraged and countenanced, it is the one which happens at the particular time and place to be in a minority. That is the opinion which, for the time being, represents the neglected interests, the side of human well-being which is in danger of obtaining less than its share. I am aware that there is not, in this country, any intolerance of differences of opinion on most of these topics. They are adduced to show, by admitted and multiplied examples, the universality of the fact, that only through diversity of opinion is there, in the existing state of human intellect, a chance of fair play to all sides of the truth. When there are persons to be found, who form an exception to the apparent unanimity of the world on any subject, even if the world is in the right, it is always probable that dissentients have something worth hearing to say for themselves, and that truth would lose something by their silence.

It may be objected, "But *some* received principles, especially on the highest and most vital subjects, are more than half-truths. The Christian morality, for instance, is the whole truth on that subject, and if any one teaches a morality which varies from it, he is wholly in error." As this is of all cases the most important in practice, none can be fitter to test the general maxim. But before pronouncing what Christian morality is or is not, it would be desirable to decide what is meant by Christian morality. If it means the morality of the New Testament, I wonder that any one who derives his knowledge of this from the book itself, can suppose that it was announced, or intended, as a complete doctrine of morals. The Gospel always refers to a preexisting morality, and confines its precepts to the particulars in which that morality was to be corrected, or superseded by a wider and higher; expressing itself, moreover, in terms most general, often impossible to be interpreted literally, and possessing rather the impressiveness of poetry or eloquence than the precision of legislation. To extract from it a body of ethical doctrine, has never been possible without eking it out from the Old Testament, that is, from a system elaborate indeed, but in many respects barbarous, and intended only for a barbarous people. St. Paul, a declared enemy to this Judaical mode of interpreting the doctrine and filling up the scheme of his Master, equally assumes a preexisting morality, namely, that of the Greeks and Romans; and his advice to Christians is in a great measure a system of accommodation to that even to the extent of giving an apparent sanction to slavery. What is called Christian, but should rather be termed theological, morality, was not the work of Christ or the Apostles, but is of much later origin, having been gradually built up by the Catholic Church of the first five centuries, and though not implicitly adopted by moderns and Protestants, has been much less modified by them than might have been expected. For the most part, indeed, they have contented themselves with cutting off the additions which had been made to it in the Middle Ages, each sect supplying the place by fresh additions, adapted to its own character and tendencies. That mankind owe a great debt to this morality, and to its early teachers, I should be the last person to deny; but I do not scruple to say of it, that it is, in many important points, incomplete and one-sided, and that unless ideas and feelings, not sanctioned by it, had contributed to the formation of European life and character, human affairs would have been in a worse condition than they now are. Christian morality (so called) has all the characters of a reaction; it is, in great part, a protest against Paganism. Its ideal is negative rather than positive; passive rather than active; Innocence rather than Nobleness; Abstinence from Evil, rather than energetic Pursuit of Good: in its precepts (as has been well said) "thou shalt not" predominates unduly over "thou shalt." In its horror of sensuality, it made an idol of asceticism, which has been gradually compromised away into one of legality. It holds out the hope of heaven and the threat of hell, as the appointed and appropriate motives to a virtuous life: in this falling far below the best of the ancients, and doing what lies in it to give to human morality an essentially selfish character, by disconnecting each man's feelings of duty from the interests of his fellow-creatures, except so far as a self-interested inducement is offered to him for consulting them. It is essentially a doctrine of passive obedience; it inculcates submission to all authorities found established; who indeed are not to be actively obeyed when they command what religion forbids, but who are not to be resisted, far less rebelled against, for any amount of wrong to ourselves. And while, in the morality of the best Pagan nations, duty to the State holds even a disproportionate place, infringing on the just liberty of the individual; in purely Christian ethics that grand department of duty is scarcely noticed or acknowledged. It is in the Koran, not the New Testament, that we read the maxim—"A ruler who appoints any man to an office, when there is in his dominions another man better qualified for it, sins against God and against the State." What little recognition the idea of obligation to the public obtains in modern morality, is derived from Greek and Roman sources, not from Christian; as, even in the morality of private life, whatever exists of magnanimity, high-mindedness, personal dignity, even the sense of honor, is derived from the purely human, not the religious part of our education, and never could have grown out of a standard of ethics in which the only worth, professedly recognized, is that of obedience.

I am as far as any one from pretending that these defects are necessarily inherent in the Christian ethics, in every manner in which it can be conceived, or that the many requisites of a complete moral doctrine which it does not contain, do not admit of being reconciled with it. Far less would I insinuate this of the doctrines and precepts of Christ himself. I believe that the sayings of Christ are all, that I can see any evidence of their having been intended to be; that they are irreconcilable with nothing which a comprehensive morality requires; that everything which is excellent in ethics may be brought within them, with no greater violence to their language than has been done to it by all who have attempted to deduce from them any practical system of conduct whatever. But it is quite consistent with this, to believe that they contain and were meant to contain, only a part of the truth; that many essential elements of the highest morality are among the things which are not provided for, nor intended to be provided for, in the recorded deliverances of the Founder of Christianity, and which have been entirely thrown aside in the system of ethics erected on the basis of those deliverances by the Christian Church. And this being so, I think it a great error to persist in attempting to find in the Christian doctrine that complete rule for our guidance, which its author intended it to sanction and enforce, but only partially to provide. I believe, too, that this narrow theory is becoming a grave practical evil, detracting greatly from the value of the moral training and instruction, which so many well-meaning persons are now at length exerting themselves to promote. I much fear that by attempting to form the mind and feelings on an exclusively religious type, and discarding those secular standards (as for want of a better name they may be called) which heretofore coexisted with and supplemented the Christian ethics, receiving some of its spirit, and infusing into it some of theirs, there will result, and is even now resulting, a low, abject, servile type of character, which, submit itself as it may to what it deems the Supreme Will, is incapable of rising to or sympathizing in the conception of Supreme Goodness. I believe that other ethics than any one which can be evolved from exclusively Christian sources, must exist side by side with Christian ethics to produce the moral regeneration of mankind; and that the Christian system is no exception to the rule that in an imperfect state of the human mind, the interests of truth require a diversity of opinions.

It is not necessary that in ceasing to ignore the moral truths not contained in Christianity, men should ignore any of those which it does contain. Such prejudice, or oversight, when it occurs, is altogether an evil; but it is one from which we cannot hope to be always exempt, and must be regarded as the price paid for an inestimable good. The exclusive pretension made by a part of the truth to be the whole, must and ought to be protested against, and if a reactionary impulse should make the protestors unjust in their turn, this one-sidedness, like the other, may be lamented, but must be tolerated. If Christians would teach infidels to be just to Christianity, they should themselves be just to infidelity. It can do truth no service to blink the fact, known to all who have the most ordinary acquaintance with literary history, that a large portion of the noblest and most valuable moral teaching has been the work, not only of men who did not know, but of men who knew and rejected, the Christian faith.

I do not pretend that the most unlimited use of the freedom of enunciating all possible opinions would put an end to the evils of religious or philosophical sectarianism. Every truth which men of narrow capacity are in earnest about, is sure to be asserted, inculcated, and in many ways even acted on, as if no other truth existed in the world, or at all events none that could limit or qualify the first. I acknowledge that the tendency of all opinions to become sectarian is not cured by the freest discussion, but is often heightened and exacerbated thereby; the truth which ought to have been, but was not, seen, being rejected all the more violently because proclaimed by persons regarded as opponents. But it is not on the impassioned partisan, it is on the calmer and more disinterested bystander, that this collision of opinions works its salutary effect. Not the violent conflict between parts of the truth, but the quiet suppression of half of it, is the formidable evil; there is always hope when people are forced to listen to both sides; it is when they attend only to one that errors harden into prejudices, and truth itself ceases to have the effect of truth, by being exaggerated into falsehood. And since there are few mental attributes more rare than that judicial faculty which can sit in intelligent judgment between two sides of a question, of which only one is represented by an advocate before it, truth has no chance but in proportion as every side of it, every opinion which embodies any fraction of the truth, not only finds advocates, but is so advocated as to be listened to.

We have now recognized the necessity to the mental well-being of mankind (on which all their other well-being depends) of freedom of opinion, and freedom of the expression of opinion, on four distinct grounds, which we will now briefly recapitulate.

First, if any opinion is compelled to silence, that opinion may, for aught we can certainly know, be true. To deny this is to assume our own infallibility.

Secondly, though the silenced opinion be an error, it may, and very commonly does, contain a portion of truth; and since the general or prevailing opinion on any object is rarely or never the whole truth, it is only by the collision of adverse opinions that the remainder of the truth has any chance of being supplied.

Thirdly, even if the received opinion be not only true, but the whole truth, unless it is suffered to be, and actually is, vigorously and earnestly contested, it will, by most of those who receive it, be held in the manner of a prejudice, with little comprehension or feeling of its rational grounds. And not only this, but, fourthly, the meaning of the doctrine itself will be in danger of being lost, or enfeebled, and deprived of its vital effect on the character and conduct: the dogma becoming a mere formal profession, inefficacious for good, but cumbering the ground, and preventing the growth of any real and heartfelt conviction, from reason or personal experience.

. . .

★ **John Stuart Mill** *(1806-1873) was an English philosopher and social reformer. A leading nineteenth-century intellectual, he was leader of the Benthamite utilitarian movement and helped form the Utilitarian Society. His major works include* A System of Logic *(1843),* On Liberty *(1859),* Utilitarianism *(1863) and* Three Essays on Religion *(1874). He was also elected to parliament, where he was a leading advocate for women's suffrage and liberalism.*

★ ★ ★ ★ ★

Questions

1. Is liberty valuable mostly for achieving goals such as peace, individual fulfillment, and wealth, or is liberty a legitimate end in itself?
2. To what extent does open and free expression of ideas guarantee that the truth will emerge in any particular situation?
3. Would Mill agree with highway speed limits?

★ ★ ★

The Scope and Bias of the Pressure System

E. E. Schattschneider

Group theory was a mainstay of 1950s political science. Analysis of the influence of pressure groups and their beneficial role in democracy was a minor academic industry. E.E. Schattschneider offers what is now a classic critique of pressure group analysis by demonstrating the extent to which powerful pressure groups, especially those dominated by the wealthy elite, exclude the participation of others and limit the scope of democracy. Schattschneider insists that pressure group politics is dominated not by the large organizations discussed by political scientists, but by highly effective small groups.

The scope of conflict is an aspect of the scale of political organization and the extent of political competition. The size of the constituencies being mobilized, the inclusiveness or exclusiveness of the conflicts people expect to develop have a bearing on all theories about how politics is or should be organized. In other words, nearly all theories about politics have something to do with the question of who can get into the fight and who is to be excluded.

Every regime is a testing ground for theories of this sort. More than any other system American politics provides the raw materials for testing the organizational assumptions of two contrasting kinds of politics, *pressure politics* and *party politics*. The concepts that underlie these forms of politics constitute the raw stuff of a general theory of political action. The basic issue between the two patterns of organization is one of size and scope of conflict;

* * * * * *

pressure groups are small-scale organizations while political parties are very large-scale organizations. One need not be surprised, therefore, that the partisans of large-scale and small-scale organizations differ passionately, because the outcome of the political game depends on the scale on which it is played.

To understand the controversy about the scale of political organization it is necessary first to take a look at some theories about interest-group politics. Pressure groups have played a remarkable role in American politics, but they have played an even more remarkable role in American political theory. Considering the political condition of the country in the first third of the twentieth century, it was probably inevitable that the discussion of special interest pressure groups should lead to development of "group" theories of politics in which an attempt is made to explain everything in terms of group activity, i.e., an attempt to formulate a universal group theory. Since one of the best ways to test an idea is to ride it into the ground, political theory has unquestionably been improved by the heroic attempt to create a political universe revolving about the group. Now that we have a number of drastic statements of the group theory of politics pushed to a great extreme, we ought to be able to see what the limitations of the idea are. . . .

Nevertheless, in spite of the excellent and provocative scholarly work done by Beard, Latham, Truman, Leiserson, Dahl, Lindbloom, Laski and others, the group theory of politics is beset with difficulties that are theoretical, growing in part out of sheer over-statements of the idea and in part out of some confusion about the nature of modern government.

One difficulty running through the literature of the subject results from the attempt to explain *everything* in terms of the group theory. On general grounds it would be remarkable indeed if a single hypothesis explained everything about so complex a subject as American politics. . . .

As a matter of fact, the distinction between *public* and *private* interests is a thoroughly respectable one; it is one of the oldest known to political theory. In the literature of the subject the public interest refers to general or common interests shared by all or by substantially all members of the community. Presumably no community exists unless there is some kind of community of interests, just as there is no nation without some notion of national interests. If it is really impossible to distinguish between private and public interests the group theorists have produced a revolution in political thought so great that it is impossible to foresee its consequences. For this reason the distinction ought to be explored with great care. . . .

The reality of the common interest is suggested by demonstrated capacity of the community to survive. There must be something that holds people together.

In contrast with the common interests are the special interests. The implication of this term is that these are interests shared by only a few people or a fraction of the community; they *exclude* others and may be *adverse* to them. A special interest is exclusive in about the same way as private property is exclusive. In a complex society it is not surprising that there are some interests that are shared by all or substantially all members of the community and some interests that are not shared so widely. The distinction is useful precisely because conflicting claims are made by people about the nature of their interests in controversial matters. . . .

Since one function of theory is to explain reality, it is reasonable to add that it is a good deal easier to explain what is going on in politics by making a distinction between public and private interests than it is to attempt to explain *everything* in terms of special interests. The attempts to prove that all interests are special forces us into circumlocutions such as those involved in the argument that people have special interests in the common good. The argument can be made, but it seems a long way around to avoid a useful distinction. . . .

All public discussion is addressed to the general community. To describe the conflict of special-interest groups as a form of politics means that the conflict has become generalized, has become a matter involving the broader public. In the nature of things *a political conflict among special interests is never restricted to the groups most immediately interested.* Indeed, it is an appeal (initiated by relatively small numbers of people) for the support of vast numbers of people who are sufficiently remote to have a somewhat different perspective on the controversy. . . .

We can now examine the second distinction, the distinction between organized and unorganized groups. The question here is not whether the distinction can be made but whether or not it is worth making. Organization has been described as "merely a stage or degree of interaction" in the development of a group.

The proposition is a good one, but what conclusions do we draw from it? We do not dispose of the matter by calling the distinction between organized and unorganized groups a "mere" difference of degree because some of the greatest differences in the world are differences of degree. . . . At this point we have a distinction that makes a difference. The distinction between organized and unorganized groups is worth making because it ought to alert us against an analysis which begins as a general group theory of politics but ends with a defense of pressure politics as inherent, universal, permanent and inevitable. This kind of confusion comes from the loosening of categories involved in the universalization of group concepts. . . .

If we are able, therefore, to distinguish between public and private interests and between organized and unorganized groups we have marked out the major boundaries of the subject; *we have given the subject shape and scope.* We are now in a position to attempt to define the area we want to explore. Having cut the pie into four pieces, we can now appropriate the piece we want and leave the rest to someone else. For a multitude of reasons *the most likely field of study is that of the organized, special-interest groups.* The advantage of concentrating on organized groups is that they are known, identifiable and recognizable. The advantage of concentrating on special-interest groups is that they have one important characteristic in common: they are all exclusive. This piece of the pie (the organized special-interest groups) we shall call the *pressure system.* The pressure system has boundaries we can define; we can fix its scope and make an attempt to estimate its bias. . . .

By the time a group has developed the kind of interest that leads it to organize it may be assumed that it has also developed some kind of political bias because *organization is itself a mobilization of bias in preparation for action.* Since these groups can be identified and since they have memberships (i.e., they include and exclude people), it is possible to think of the scope of the system.

When lists of these organizations are examined, the fact that strikes the student most forcibly is that *the system is very small.* The range of organized, identifiable, known groups is amazingly narrow; there is nothing remotely universal about it. . . .

The business or upper-class bias of the pressure system shows up everywhere. Businessmen are four or five times as likely to write to their congressmen as manual laborers are. College graduates are far more apt to write to their congressmen than people in the lowest educational category are. . . .

The bias of the system is shown by the fact *that even nonbusiness organizations reflect an upper-class tendency.* . . .

The class bias of associational activity gives meaning to the limited scope of the pressure system, because *scope and bias are aspects of the same tendency.* The data raise a serious question about the validity of the proposition that special-interest groups are a universal form of political organization reflecting *all* interests. As a matter of fact, to suppose that everyone participates in pressure-group activity and that all interests get themselves organized in the pressure system is to destroy the meaning of this form of politics. The pressure system makes sense only as the political instrument of a segment of the community. It gets results by being selective and biased; *if everybody got into the act the unique advantages of this form of organization would be destroyed, for it is possible that if all interests could be mobilized the result would be a stalemate.*

Special-interest organizations are most easily formed when they deal with small numbers of individuals who are acutely aware of their exclusive interests. To describe the conditions of pressure-group organization in this way is, however, to say that it is primarily a business phenomenon. Aside from a few very large organizations (the churches, organized labor, farm organizations, and veterans' organizations) the residue is a small segment of the population. *Pressure politics is essentially the politics of small groups.*

The vice of the groupist theory is that it conceals the most significant aspects of the system. The flaw in the pluralist heaven is that the heavenly chorus sings with a strong upper-class accent. Probably about 90 percent of the people cannot get into the pressure system.

The notion that the pressure system is automatically representative of the whole community is a myth fostered by the universalizing tendency of modern group theories. *Pressure politics is a selective process* ill designed to serve diffuse interests. The system is skewed, loaded and unbalanced in favor of a fraction of a minority.

★ *Prolific author and theorist,* **E. E. Schattschneider** *taught political science at Wesleyan University from 1930 through 1970.*

★ ★ ★ ★ ★

Questions

1. To what extent do interest groups provide expanded opportunities for participation in government and politics?
2. To what extent do interest groups effectively limit opportunities for participation in government and politics?
3. What groups in society tend to have exceptional influence in the political process?
4. To what extent does the pressure group system create a bias in favor of the rich?
5. What can be done to expand opportunities for citizen participation in a pressure-group dominated system?

★ ★ ★

Interest Group Liberalism

Theodore Lowi

Liberals want more government; conservatives want less. Right? Wrong. Analysis of the budgets of the Reagan administration alone put this myth to rest. What is of interest in this particular article is that careful observers were aware that this liberal-conservative distinction was functionally dead long before the Reagan era. The problem, according to Cornell political scientist Ted Lowi, is that such prevailing myths fill politics with an "empty rhetoric" that "has produced a crisis of public authority." Now (in the 1960s), a new and detrimental public philosophy—"interest group liberalism"—has arisen, which equates the good of the nation with the use of government to promote the advantage of selected interest groups.

In the constitutional epoch immediately preceding our own, ending in 1937, the perennial issue underlying all debate on public policy—and therefore the key to public philosophy in that period—was the question of the nature of government itself and whether expansion or contraction best produced public good. Liberal and conservative regimes derived their principles and rationalizations of governing and policy formulation from their positions on the question. Expansion of government was demanded by liberals as the only means of combating the injustices of a brutal physical and social world that would not change as long as it was taken as natural. Favoring government expansion became the mark of the contemporary liberal. His underlying assumption was that the instruments of government provided the means for conscious induction of social change; without capacity for such change no experimentation with any new institutional norms or means of expanding

★ ★ ★ ★ ★ ★

rights would be possible. Opposition to such means, but not necessarily those forms or those rights, became the mark of the contemporary conservative. . . .

The old dialogue has passed into the graveyard of consensus. Yet it persists. Since it has no real, operable meaning any more, it is almost purely ritualistic. However, its persistence has had its real effects. The persistence of this state of affairs so far beyond its own day, has been responsible for two pathological conditions in the 1960s. The first is that the empty rhetoric has produced a crisis of public authority. Without a basis for meaningful adversary proceedings, there has been little, if any, conflict among political actors at the level where each is forced regularly into formulating general rules, applicable to individual acts of state and at one and the same time ethically plausible to the individual citizen. The tendency of individuals to accept governmental decisions because they are good has probably at no time in this century been less intense and less widely distributed in the United States. This is producing many problems of political cynicism and irresponsibility in everyday political processes; and these problems, in turn, have tended toward the second pathological condition, the emergence of an ersatz public philosophy that seeks to justify power and to end the crisis of public authority by parceling out public authority to private parties. That is, the emerging public philosophy seeks to solve the problem of public authority by defining it away. A most maladaptive "political formula," it will inevitably exacerbate rather than end the crisis, even though its short-run effect is one of consensus and stabilization.

Out of the developing crisis in public authority has developed an ersatz political formula that does, for all its problems, offer the public man some guidance and some justification in his efforts to shape, form and provide for the administration of positive laws in the positive state. There are several possible names for this contemporary replacement of liberalism-conservatism. A strong possibility would be corporatism, but its history as a concept gives it several unwanted connotations, such as conservative Catholicism or Italian fascism, that keep it from being quite suitable. Another is syndicalism, but among many objections is the connotation of anarchy too far removed from American experience or intentions. However, the new American public philosophy is a variant of those two alien philosophies.

The most clinically accurate term to describe the American variant is *interest-group liberalism*. It may be called liberalism because it expects to use government in a positive and expansive role, it is motivated by the highest sentiments, and it possesses strong faith that what is good for government is good for the society. It is "interest-group liberalism" because it sees as both necessary and good that the policy agenda and the public interest be defined in terms of the organized interests in society. In a brief sketch, the working model of the interest-group liberal is a vulgarized version of the pluralist model of modern political science. It assumes: (1) Organized interests are homogeneous and easy to define, sometimes monolithic. Any "duly elected" spokesman for any interest is taken as speaking in close approximation for each and every member. (2) Organized interests pretty much fill up and adequately represent most of the sectors of our lives, so that one organized group can be found effectively answering and checking some other organized group as it seeks to prosecute its claims against society. And (3) the role of government is one of ensuring access particularly to the most effectively organized, and of ratifying the agreements and adjustments worked out among the competing leaders and their claims. This last assumption is supposed to be a statement of how our democracy works and how it ought to work. Taken together, these assumptions constitute the Adam Smith "hidden hand" model applied to groups. Ironically, it is embraced most strongly by the very people most likely to reject the Smith model applied in its original form to firms in the market.

These assumptions are the basis of the new public philosophy. The policy behaviors of old-school liberals and conservatives, of Republicans and Democrats, so inconsistent with liberalism-conservatism criteria, are fully consistent with the criteria drawn from interest-group liberalism: *The most important difference between liberals and conservatives, Republicans and Democrats—however they define themselves—is to be found in the interest groups they identify with. Congressmen are guided in their votes, Presidents in their programs, and administrators in this discretion, by whatever organized interests they have taken for themselves as the most legitimate; and that is the measure of the legitimacy of demands. . . .*

The fact that a doctrine has some support in the realities of power certainly helps to explain its appeal as a doctrine. But there were also several strongly positive reasons for the emergence of this particular doctrine. The first, and once perhaps the only, is that it has helped flank the constitutional problems of federalism. Manifestations of the corporate state were once limited primarily to the Extension Service of the Department of Agriculture, with self-administration by the land grant colleges and the local farmers and commerce associations. Self-administration by organized groups was an attractive technique precisely because it could be justified as so decentralized and permissive as to be hardly federal at all. Here began the ethical and conceptual mingling of the notion of organized private groups with the notions of "local government" and "self-government." Ultimately direct interest group participation in government became synonymous with self-government, first for reasons of strategy, then by belief that the two were indeed synonymous. As a propaganda strategy it eased acceptance in the courts, then among the locals who still believed the farmer was and should be independent. Success as strategy increased usage; usage helped elevate strategy to doctrine. The users began to believe in their own symbols.

A second positive appeal of interest-group liberalism is strongly related to the first. Interest-group liberalism helps solve a problem for the democratic politician in the modern state where the stakes are so high. This is the problem of enhanced conflict and how to avoid it. The politician's contribution to society is his skill in resolving conflict. However, direct confrontations are sought only by the zealous ideologues and "outsiders." The typical American politician displaces and defers and delegates conflict where possible; he squarely faces conflict only when he must. Interest-group liberalism offers a justification for keeping major combatants apart. It provides a theoretical basis for giving to each according to his claim, the price for which is a reduction of concern for what others are claiming. In other words, it transforms logrolling from necessary evil to great good. This is the basis for the "consensus" so often claimed these days. It is also the basis for President Kennedy's faith that in our day ideology has given over to administration. . . .

The third positive appeal of interest-group liberalism is that it is a direct, even if pathological, response to the crisis of public authority. The practice of dealing only with organized claims in formulating policy, and of dealing exclusively through organized claims in implementing programs, helps create the sense that power need not be power at all, nor control. If sovereignty is parceled out among the groups, then who's out anything? . . . *If* the groups to be controlled control the controls, *then* "to administer does not always mean to rule." The inequality of power, ultimately the involvement of coercion in government decisions, is always a gnawing problem in a democratic culture. Rousseau's General Will stopped at the boundary of a Swiss canton. The myth of the group and the group will is becoming the answer to Rousseau in the big democracy. . . .

For all the political advantages interest-group liberals have in their ideology, there are high *costs* involved. Unfortunately, these costs are not strongly apparent at the time of the creation of a group-based program. As Wallace Sayre once observed, the gains of a change tend to be immediate, the costs tend to be cumulative. However, it takes no long-run patience or the spinning of fine webs to capture and assess the consequences of group-based policy solutions. Three major consequences are suggested and assessed here: (1) the atrophy of institutions of popular control; (2) the maintenance of old and creation of new structures of privilege; and (3) conservatism, in several senses of the word.

. . . In his *The Public Philosophy,* Lippmann was rightfully concerned over the "derangement of power" whereby modern democracies tend first toward unchecked elective leadership and then toward drainage of public authority from elective leaders down into their constituencies. However, Lippmann erred if he thought of constituencies only as voting constituencies. Drainage has tended toward "support group constituencies," and with special consequence. Parceling out policy-making power to the most interested parties destroys political responsibility. A program split off with a special imperium to govern itself is not merely an administrative unit. It is a structure of power with impressive capacities to resist central political control.

Besides making conflict-of-interest a principle of government rather than a criminal act, participatory programs shut out the public. To be more precise, programs of this sort tend to cut out all that part of the mass that is not . . . specifically organized around values strongly salient to the goals of the program. They shut out the public, first, at the most creative phase of policy making—the phase where the problem is first defined. Once problems are defined, alliances form accordingly and the outcome is both a policy and a reflection of superior power. If the definition is laid out by groups along lines of established group organization, there is always great difficulty for an amorphous public to be organized in any other terms. The public is shut out, secondly, at the phase of accountability. In programs in which group self-administration is legitimate, the administrators are accountable primarily to the groups, only secondarily to President or Congress as institutions. In brief, to the extent that organized interests legitimately control a program there is functional rather than substantive accountability. This means questions of equity, balance and equilibrium to the exclusion of questions of overall social policy and questions of whether or not the program should be maintained or discontinued. It also means accountability to experts first and amateurs last; and an expert is a man trained and skilled in the mysterious and technologies of the program. . . .

Finally, the public is shut out by tendencies toward conspiracy to shut the public out. One of the assumptions underlying direct group representation is that on the boards and in the staff and among the recognized outside consultants there will be regular countervailing and checks and balances. In Schattschneider's terms, this would be expected to expand the "scope of conflict." But there is nothing inevitable about that, and the safer assumption might well be the converse. . . .

. . . Government by and through interest groups is in impact conservative in almost every sense of that term. Part of its conservatism can be seen in another look at the two foregoing objections: Weakening of popular government and support of privilege are, in other words, two aspects of conservatism. It is beside the point to argue that these consequences are not intended. A third dimension of conservatism, stressed here separately, is the simple conservatism of resistance to change. David Truman, who has not been a strong critic of self-government by interest groups, has, all the same, identified a general tendency of established agency-group relationships to be "highly resistant to disturbance." . . . If there is already a tendency in a pluralistic system, then agency-group relationships must be all the more inflexible to the extent that the relationship is official and legitimate. . . .

No individual interest group can be expected to take fullest account of the consequences of its own claims. This is what Presidents and Congresses are for, and this is what will continue to be delegated away as long as the ideology of interest-group liberalism allows. In effect this means that restoring pluralism as an effective principle of democratic politics requires destroying it as a principle of government. If this is to be accomplished, reform must begin with the replacement of interest-group liberalism with some contemporary version of the rule of law. The program of reform must include at least: debate that centers upon the actual consequences of public policies and of their forms of implementation; a legislative process that regularly treats enabling legislation rather than revision; political brokers that have to deal in substantive as well as functional issues; and adaptation of public controls to loch needs through choice of appropriate level of government rather than through delegations of the choice to the most interested parties.

★ **Theodore Lowi** *is Professor of Political Science at Cornell University.*

★ ★ ★ ★ ★

Questions

1. To what extent do Democrats and Republicans vary in their basic philosophies?
2. To what extent do Democrats and Republicans represent different sets of organized interest groups?
3. If the process is open to all, why is interest group activity detrimental to society?
4. To what extent do elected representatives represent influential groups rather than the unorganized elements of their constituencies?
5. To what extent is interest group liberalism leading to a lack of confidence in government?

★ ★ ★

Political Snipers

Robert Dreyfuss

Moses with a gun . . . the earth as planet of the apes . . . Charlton Heston's presidency of the National Rifle Association conjures some interesting connections. In this article Robert Dreyfuss takes aim at one of the nation's most powerful interest groups in an attempt to understand how such groups operate and how they effectively exert influence in American politics. The NRA's techniques focus on using loopholes in the system to have an effect much greater than the organization's membership would normally exert as a minority of the population. Fundraisers focused on wealthy contributors and enormous campaigns in selected electoral districts explain much of the NRA's success.

. . . This is the story of how the NRA [National Rifle Association] managed to accumulate so much influence over the democratic process. It is an unnerving ride through the loopholes in federal election law, which allow a powerful special interest to bring almost overwhelming force to bear in a single congressional district. It is the story of how the firearms lobby bludgeoned its opponents with slashing, near-anonymous attack commercials and buried them with bulk mailings on hot-button themes unrelated to guns. It is the story of how conservative financiers and the Republican Party used the NRA to do some of their dirty work, and the price the NRA is now extracting for those services.

This story leads to the question of how the NRA gets its money in the first place, and here, too, there is more than first meets the eye. Despite its image as a membership organization subsisting entirely on $35 membership dues, the NRA actually collects much of its money in large donations from upper-middle-class and even wealthy supporters. Big contributors, bequests, fundraising dinners, and backing from the gun industry have combined to

★ ★ ★ ★ ★ ★

"Political Snipes," by Robert Dreyfuss, reprinted by permission from *American Prospect,* Fall 1995.

provide the NRA with a substantial block of funds. The NRA uses that money for direct-mail solicitations, in effect converting large contributions into many smaller ones, which it then channels into political campaigns. . . .

★ *Lawyers, Guns, and Money*

What made the NRA such a useful tool to conservatives, of course, was its ability to raise and spend vast amounts of money. In 1994 the NRA was the nation's single biggest spender on elections. But how did it raise all the cash? Although the NRA's closemouthed tradition makes answering that question somewhat difficult, interviews with many current and former NRA officials, along with experts on the pro-gun movement, provide a fairly detailed picture—a picture that looks somewhat different from the grass roots, middle-American image NRA officials have nurtured for years.

It is true that like most direct-mail operations, the bulk of the NRA's daily operating revenue comes from small contributions, averaging about $18 per donor, and from annual dues of $35. Not surprisingly, most of this money comes from the ranks of American gun owners, who at last count were some 70 million strong. But that is not the entire story. Like the Republican and Democratic parties, which tout the fact that their average giver sends them between $10 and $25, the small average can obscure the presence of large backers. The NRA maintains an additional base of big contributors, who are clearly a few income levels above the typical working-class NRA member. This list includes the nation's 20,000 gun dealers and manufacturers and a small group of wealthy conservative financiers. . . .

The NRA conducts a broad fundraising campaign for several of its organizations, from the NRA itself to the ILA, the NRA Foundation, and the Political Victory Fund PAC. In a column in the *American Rifleman,* the NRA's monthly, NRA President Thomas L. Washington cited a single dinner held in Corpus Christi, Texas, where 907 people donated more than $175,000 to the NRA. And the NRA recently published a list of 214 "Friends of the NRA" fundraising events scheduled between April and October 1995.

The *American Rifleman* routinely lists the names of groups and individuals around the country who give the NRA at least $1,000 at a time; until earlier this year, the magazine listed those who donated special, onetime gifts of $250 or more but dropped that practice because of space limitations. And some NRA members have left the NRA bequests in the hundreds of thousands of dollars—their parting shot, so to speak.

Finally, there is the gun industry . . . the NRA in 1993 earned $8.6 million from advertising income, largely through ads from the gun industry in NRA magazines. And the NRA has arranged with gun dealers around the country to help the NRA solicit contributions from gun buyers. According to Tom Washington's "The President's Column" in the *American Rifleman,* just one dealer—Midway Arms of Columbia, Missouri—raised more than $678,000 for the NRA in four years. "It isn't just individual volunteers who benefit our Association," wrote Washington. "Many businesses donate their time and efforts as well."

Thanks to the Federal Election Commission [FEC], those millions raised by the NRA cannot be spent on federal campaigns. The FEC carefully regulates how a PAC, in this case the Political Victory Fund (PVF) of the NRA, raises or spends its cash.

Or does it?

The answer is: It does, but not very well. There are so many loopholes in the FEC rules that an organization like the NRA can do just about anything it wants to do for political objectives. Here's how.

A glance at the NRA's PAC records on file at the FEC, provided by the Center for Responsive Politics, shows that the overwhelming bulk of the NRA's PAC money comes into the PVF in donations of less than $200. Anything more than $200 must be reported to the FEC on an itemized basis. Yet over the six-year period ending December 31, 1994, the PVF reported itemized donations of only $278,631. During the same period, the PVF raised a total of $16,499,000.

One might conclude that large donors stay away from the PVF. But the FEC is not required to verify the accuracy of the NRA's filing. The forms that the NRA fills out simply list the itemized gifts as a line item, then present a lump-sum total for the bulk of the PVF income under the nonitemized heading. Even if the FEC suspects that there is something fishy about the lopsided nature of the PVF's income, it cannot investigate on its own without evidence of wrongdoing. The FEC takes the NRA's report on faith, just as it does with every other PAC.

More important, though, the FEC does not regulate the so-called "administrative and fundraising" costs associated with a PAC. That means that the NRA can spend unlimited sums, millions of dollars, to raise PAC funds, paying for repeated mailings to the NRA's 3.4 million members—and it does not have to report a single cent of those fundraising costs to the FEC. (That is also true for all other PACs, but it is particularly important for a large organization that can harvest small contributions, as opposed to, say, a trade association with a few dozen members whose executives kick in big bucks.)

And that is exactly what the NRA does. Using its corporate treasury, which is "soft money," that is, not regulated by the FEC, the NRA in 1994 spent at least $2 million—and probably much more—asking NRA members to contribute to the PVF. That, in turn, is what raised the PVF's $6.83 million during 1993-94. Through the science of direct mail, the NRA can estimate how much each dollar spent on soliciting donations to the PVF will bring in. So, while the FEC rules prevent a wealthy donor from giving more than $1,000 to a PAC, nothing prevents that donor from giving the NRA $5,000 in soft money, which the NRA then plows into PVF fundraising. A direct donation of $5,000 in soft money suddenly becomes $5,000, $10,000, or more in "hard money"—in other words, legally usable, reportable PAC cash. . . .

★ *Not-So-Independent Expenditures*

Those who have found themselves in the NRA's sights, however, are generally more familiar with the organization's use of another legal loophole that allows the NRA to support candidates well beyond the limits on direct donations to campaigns.

Because the FEC cannot regulate free speech (thank goodness), the NRA—like any individual, corporation, or group—can spend unlimited amounts of money to promote its cause, even during an election, as long as the NRA does not engage in what is called "express advocacy." Express advocacy means that the NRA must cross a fuzzy line by explicit, campaign-style promotion of a particular candidate. If a promotion crosses that line, the thinking goes, the money spent on it ought to count as a direct political contribution, thus subject to the limits set by the FEC.

But the line is so fuzzy that the NRA can run television commercials criticizing a candidate and supporting the NRA's laissez-faire attitude toward semiautomatic weapons without falling under FEC regulations at all. In the 1992 Synar race, the NRA liberally took advantage of this loophole, running one attack advertisement with "hard" PVF money blasting Synar and then, sandwiched around another commercial, following up with a second spot that used the same spokesman, Charlton Heston, yet did not mention Synar by name. That second commercial was paid for by the NRA's corporate account, not by its PAC—thus giving the NRA a double bang for its buck.

All of these loopholes, including the biggest one of all, the use of independent expenditures, were used expertly by the NRA in 1994. To put the NRA's use of independent expenditures in perspective, consider this: In 1993-94, the NRA accounted for fully one-third of all independent expenditures by all groups during the election. . . .

★ *Self-Inflicted Wounds*

Stricter campaign finance law or tougher FEC regulation of the NRA seems an unlikely possibility as long as Republicans control Congress. But the NRA's coziness with the Republican Party may yet cost the organization some loyalty among its many lower and middle-class members, many of whom find the Republican stances on economics less appealing than the party's opposition to gun control.

In the past the NRA has been able to whip-saw organized labor, many of whose members oppose gun control. But the trade union rank-and-file is only beginning to appreciate that the NRA is an ally of bitterly anti-union legislators. Already, the AFL-CIO is launching a labor counteroffensive against the NRA. That movement is starting in the West, where key AFL-CIO state presidents and affiliates studying the NRA's role in the 1994 elections. Don Judge, president of the Montana AFL-CIO, in a state where the NRA and the militia movement are powerful side-by-side forces, says that his organization is trying to educate union members that the candidates supported by the NRA are precisely the ones who, once in office, vote against labor on every issue from the minimum wage to right-to-work to safety and health provisions. "Many of us have decided, what have we got to lose in confronting this?" asks Judge. "The kind of people being promoted by the NRA, with rare exceptions, typically do not support the kinds of things that are important to working people, beyond the issue of gun ownership."

In Pennsylvania, the AFL-CIO was rocked by the Democrats' rout in 1994, and Rick Bloomingdale, president of the AFL-CIO there, is ready to confront the NRA. Bloomingdale points out that the NRA backed the victorious Republican Representative Tom Ridge in Pennsylvania's governor's race last year, even though Ridge had voted for the assault weapon ban in Congress in 1994. Says Bloomingdale, "We finally know what the NRA-PAC stands for: the National Republican Association." When the Pennsylvania AFL-CIO began running ads last year featuring a union member and the slogan, "I'm the NRA and I'm supporting Harris Wofford," the NRA's lawyers hit them with a cease and desist order because "I'm the NRA" is copyrighted by the organization. Adds Bloomingdale, "The same people who support the NRA are the people trying to bust unions."

A study by Professor Paul Clark of Pennsylvania State University shows that the NRA consistently backs candidates whose positions on economic issues are far to the right. "While [the NRA] claims not to take positions on overtly economic issues, the candidates they support clearly do," he says. "Significantly, they have had some success at convincing union members to support their organizations and their candidates."

Warren Cassidy, a former NRA executive vice president, worries openly that the NRA's lurch to the right may involve a quid pro quo to support the Republicans on issues that have nothing to do with guns. "When does that quid pro quo begin to hurt your organization?" he asks. "With all the connections to a strong conservative movement, NRA got caught up in that tide and they might not be able to extricate themselves." He warns: "It isn't necessarily true that all those chits should fall to one party, the Republican Party, because we have always had a strong, strong blue-collar element, both rural and urban, in the NRA. And many, many, many of these people are union members." . . .

In the meantime, NRA officials have more immediate concerns. In its single-minded favor to defeat even the most hesitant supporters of gun control, the NRA may have recklessly stretched its spending to the breaking point. The direct-mail scheme upon which the NRA has built its empire has been costly, and the organization recently traded a sizeable chunk of its inheritance for a posh new headquarters building. All of this has led many former NRA officials to say that the organization will crash in the near future. Reports of financial difficulties have attracted the scrutiny of the Internal Revenue Service.

Still, on Capitol Hill a healthy symbiosis between the Republicans and the NRA continues to thrive. While a good number of mainstream Republicans see the NRA as a loose cannon and an organization of zealots flirting with the far right, these Republicans still want the NRA's money and grassroots army at election time, and they still worry that any misstep—even in the course of the routine give-and-take that occurs in a legislative session—could bring the NRA down on their heads. . . .

★ **Robert Dreyfuss** *contributes articles on politics to many journals and is a senior correspondent for* The American Prospect.

★ ★ ★ ★ ★

Questions

1. What tactics does the NRA employ in its war against gun control?
2. How does the NRA raise funds?
3. How does the NRA influence legislation?
4. If the tactics used by the NRA are legal, and available to all citizens, can they still be unfair?
5. Should interest groups be more strictly regulated?

☆ ☆ ☆

The Miscast Institution

Thomas E. Patterson

Meet the Press has engaged television viewers for years—indeed, decades—but in politics a much more popular activity unfolds during every presidential campaign season that might better be called "Blame the Press." During every major election the public blames the news media for unappreciated outcomes. Objective observers, like political scientists, enjoy asking questions, like, "To what extent are the news media actually responsible for election outcomes?" In this thoughtful essay Thomas Patterson finds that although the news media are simply not equipped to run or decide the success of political campaigns, American voters depend entirely too much on news reports for the incisive analysis needed to make good decisions.

The United States is the only democracy that organizes its national election campaign around the news media. Even if the media did not want the responsibility for organizing the campaign, it is theirs by virtue of an election system built upon entrepreneurial candidacies, floating voters, freewheeling interest groups, and weak political parties.

It is an unworkable arrangement: the press is not equipped to give order and direction to a presidential campaign. And when we expect it to do so, we set ourselves up for yet another turbulent election.

The campaign is chaotic largely because the press is not a political institution and has no capacity for organizing the election in a coherent manner. The news can always be made better. Election coverage in 1992 was a marked improvement over 1988, and in a few respects the best coverage ever. The journalist Carl Bernstein, reflecting a widely shared opinion among

☆ ☆ ☆ ☆ ☆ ☆

members of the press, declared that 1992 coverage closely approximated "the ideal of what good reporting has always been: the best obtainable version of the truth."

Yet news and truth are not the same thing. The news is a highly refracted version of reality. The press magnifies certain aspects of politics and downplays others, which are often more central to issues of governing. During the last six weeks of the 1992 campaign, the economy got a lot of attention from the press, but it still received less coverage than campaign-trail controversies, including disputes over Clinton's draft record, Perot's on-again, off-again candidacy and spats with the press, and Bush's wild charges ("the Ozone Man," "bozos").

The attention that Clinton's trip to the Soviet Union while a graduate student at Oxford received in the closing weeks of the campaign was in itself revealing of the gap between news value and the nation's real concerns. When Bush questioned Clinton's trip on CNN's "Larry King Live," it exploded into the headlines in a way that policy issues seldom do. News of Clinton's Moscow visit overshadowed such October issues as developments on the North American Free Trade Agreement, CIA revelations on the U.S. government's role in the arming of Iraq, and a change in Clinton's healthcare proposal.

The press's restless search for the riveting story works against its intention to provide the voters with a reliable picture of the campaign. It is a formidable job to present society's problems in ways that voters can understand and act upon. The news media cannot do the job consistently well. Walter Lippmann put it plainly when he said that a press-based politics "is not workable. And when you consider the nature of news, it is not even thinkable."

Lippmann's point was not that news organizations are somehow inferior to political organizations but that each has a different role and responsibility in society. Democracy cannot operate successfully without a free press that is acting effectively within its sphere. The problem arises when the press is expected to perform the job of political institutions as well. . . .

The belief that the press can substitute for political institutions is widespread. Many journalists, perhaps most of them, assume they can do it effectively. Scholars who study the media also accept the idea that the press can organize elections. Every four years, they suggest that the campaign could be made coherent *if* the media would only report it differently.

However, the press merely appears to have the capacity to organize the voters' alternatives in a coherent way. . . . The press is in the news business, not the business of politics, and because of this, its norms and imperatives are not those required for the effective organization of electoral coalitions and debate. Journalistic values and political values are at odds with each other.

The proper organization of electoral opinion requires an institution with certain characteristics. It must be capable of seeing the larger picture—of looking at the world as a whole and not in small pieces. It must have incentives that cause it to identify and organize those interests that are making demands for policy representation. And it must be accountable for its choices, so that the public can reward it when satisfied and force amendments when dissatisfied.

The press has none of these characteristics. The media has its special strengths, but they do not include these strengths.

The press is a very different kind of organization from the political party, whose role it acquired. A party is driven by the steady force of its traditions and constituent interests, which is why the Democratic leadership in 1952 chose Stevenson, a New Deal liberal, over Kefauver, a border-state populist. The press, in contrast, is "a restless beacon." Its concern is the new, the unusual, and the sensational. Its agenda shifts abruptly when a new development breaks.

The party has the incentive—the possibility of acquiring political power—to give order and voice to society values. Its *raison d'etre* is to articulate interests and to forge them into a winning coalition. The press has no such incentive and no such purpose. Its objective is the discovery and development of good stories. Television-news executive Richard Salant once said that his reporters covered stories from "nobody's point of view." What he was saying, in effect, was that journalists are driven by news opportunities, not by political values.

The press is also not politically accountable. The political party is made accountable by a formal mechanism—elections. The vote gives office-holders a reason to act in the majority's interest, and it offers citizens an opportunity to boot from office anyone they feel has failed them. Thousands of elected officials have lost their jobs this way. The public has no comparable hold on the press. Journalists are neither chosen by the people nor removable by them. . . .

Other democracies have recognized the inappropriateness of press-based elections. Although national voting in all Western democracies is media-centered in the sense that candidates depend primarily on mass communication to reach the voters, no other democracy has a system in which the press fills the role traditionally played by the political party. Journalists in other democracies actively participate in the campaign process, but their efforts take place within an electoral structure built around political institutions. In the United States, however, national elections are referendums in which the candidates stand alone before the electorate and have no choice but to filter their appeals through the lens of the news media.

★ **Thomas E. Patterson** *is Bradlee Professor of Government and the Press at Harvard University.*

★ ★ ★ ★ ★

Questions

1. How much information do voters get from television and newspapers, as opposed to their political parties and elected officials?
2. What is the quality level of most political reporting?
3. What does a voter need to read in order to be well informed?
4. To what extent is news reporting overly focused on sensational stories?
5. To what extent are citizens responsible for the sensationalism of the press?

★ ★ ★

The Military's War with the Media: Causes and Consequences

Bernard E. Trainor

Just like the military officers he is concerned about, journalist Bernard Trainor pulls no punches when it comes to military-press relations: "It is clear that today's officer corps carries as part of its cultural baggage a loathing for the press." What is the root of this animosity? Trainor admits that the previous generation of officers, those who served in Vietnam, had good reason to abhor the treatment they received from certain members of the press, but he can find no good reason for the fact that the bitterness of the Vietnam experience persists among officers not yet born at that war's conclusion. Trainor concludes that today's hostility is due to an inability on the part of the military to accept the fact that most journalists currently have a favorable opinion of the officer corps

At first they are polite, respectfully prefacing each question with "sir." But when faced with their own prejudices, the veneer of civility evaporates, hostility surfaces, and the questions give way to a feeding frenzy of accusations. I have experienced this phenomenon repeatedly when discussing relations between the military and the media with young officers and cadets at service academies and professional military schools. It is clear that today's officer corps carries as part of its cultural baggage a loathing for the press.

★ ★ ★ ★ ★ ★

Indeed relations with the press—a term applied to both print and television media—are probably worse now than at any other period in the history of the republic. I say this recognizing that Vietnam is usually cited as the nadir in military-media relations. At least during the Vietnam War, military men actually experienced what they judged to be unfair treatment at the hands of the fourth estate, and the issue was out in the open.

The majority of today's career officers, however, have had no association with the press. Most of them were children during the war. But all of them suffer this institutional form of posttraumatic syndrome. It is a legacy of the war, and it takes root soon after they enter service. Like racism, anti-Semitism, and all other forms of bigotry, it is irrational but nonetheless real. The credo of the military seems to be "duty, honor, country, and hate the media."

Although most officers no longer say the media stabbed them in the back in Vietnam, the military still smarts over the nation's humiliation in Indochina and subconsciously still blames television and the press for loss of public support for the war. Today the hostility manifests itself in complaints that the press will not keep a secret and that it endangers lives by revealing details of sensitive operations. The myth of the media as an unpatriotic, left-wing anti-military establishment is thus perpetuated.

Having spent most of my adult life in the military and very little of it as a journalist, I am more qualified to comment on military culture than that of the media, and I must admit that in the post-Vietnam years, I too was biased against the media. But having feet in both camps now gives me a unique perspective, which I try to share with each, particularly the military.

Did the press stab the military in the back during Vietnam? Hardly. The press initially supported the war, but as casualties mounted and the Johnson administration failed to develop a coherent strategy to bring it to a satisfactory conclusion, the press became critical. Whether it influenced public opinion or simply reflected it will be argued for years to come. But it was a misguided policy that was primarily at fault for the debacle, not the media.

The media, however, were guilty of instances of unfair and sensational reporting that veterans of that war still resent. This was particularly true in the latter stages when the nation was weary of nightly war news and cub newspaper and television journalists tried to make headlines out of thin gruel. More supervision over them should have been exercised by editors, but it was not, and many in the military, already frustrated by the war, felt that the press was deliberately trying to humiliate them.

The legacy of the war sharpened the tension that exists between the media and the military, but it is not its cause. The roots of tension are in the very nature of the institutions. The military is hierarchical, with great inner pride and loyalties. It is the antithesis of a democracy and must be so if it is to be effective. It is action oriented and impatient with outside interference. Many things it legitimately does make little sense to civilians, who have little knowledge of military matters. The military wants only to be left alone to carry out its assigned mission. A free press, on the other hand, is one of the great virtues of a democracy, wherein the concentration of power is viewed as a danger.

The press is a watchdog over institutions of power—military, political, economic, and social. Its job is to inform the people about the doings of its institutions. By its very nature, it is skeptical and intrusive. As a result, there will always be a divergence of interests between the two. That both are essential to the well-being of the nation is beyond question, but the problem of minimizing the natural friction between the two is a daunting one.

I have found striking similarities between my colleagues in both camps. Both are idealistic, bright, totally dedicated to their professions, and technically proficient. They willingly work long hours under arduous conditions, crave recognition, and feel that they are underpaid. The strain on family life is equally severe in both professions. But there are notable differences. A journalist tends to be creative; a soldier is more practical. Reporters are independent; military men are team players. The former tend to be liberal and skeptical; the latter are conservative and obedient.

The all-volunteer force in a subtle way has contributed to this friction. At the height of the cold war and throughout the Vietnam War, the military was at the forefront of American consciousness. Scarcely a family had no son or other loved one liable to the draft. As a result, the shadow of national service cast itself over the family dinner table and generated a personal interest in the armed forces in all Americans. The experience of fathers and older brothers who had fought in World War II and Korea maintained a lively interest in soldiering. With the end of the draft and the advent of a professional army, this awareness disappeared along with the pertinence of the older generation of warriors. Only the families of those who volunteered for the service kept touch with the modern army.

The military, which for so long was part of society, drifted away from it. Military bases are now few and far between and located in remote areas, unseen by most Americans. A large percentage of volunteer servicemen marry early and settle down to a life where their base and service friends are the focal point of their lives. No longer do uniformed soldiers rush home on three-day passes whenever they can get them. When servicemen do go home, they do so wearing civilian clothes. They are no longer given the tolerant attitude of the public toward the military in eccentricity of dress and hair style; they are no longer marked by short haircuts and shiny shoes. Off post, they are indistinguishable in appearance from the civilian cohort.

To the average civilian, the term military has come to be equated with the Pentagon, intercontinental missiles, $600 toilet seats, and other manifestations of waste, fraud, and abuse. The flesh-and-blood association the public formerly had with the armed forces has atrophied; the military has become just another bureaucracy in the public's mind. For its part, the military, in the relative isolation of self-contained ghettos, has lost touch with a changing America. It focuses on warlike things and implicitly rejects the amorality of the outside world it has sworn to defend. In an age of selfishness, the professional soldier takes pride in selflessness. A sense of moral elitism has emerged within the armed forces, which is apparent today to any civilian who deals with the military. The all-volunteer force not only has created a highly competent military force; it has also created a version of Cromwell's Ironside Army, contemptuous of those with less noble visions. It is no wonder that those who choose the profession of arms look with suspicion upon those of the press who pry into their sacred rituals.

There is another big difference that bears directly on the relationship between the media and the military; the military is hostile toward journalists, while journalists are indifferent toward the military. To journalists, the military is just another huge bureaucracy to report on, no different from Exxon or Congress. But whereas business people and politicians try to enlist journalists for their own purposes, those in the military try to avoid journalists and when they cannot face the prospect defensively with a mixture of fear, dread, and contempt.

Most of my military brethren would be surprised to know that when asked for an opinion about the military, professional young journalists with no association with the military rate career officers highly. They view officers as bright, well educated, dedicated, and competent, although they wonder why anyone would make the service a career. Their prejudgment of enlisted personnel is far less flattering. Most journalists view enlisted men and women as disadvantaged, not-too-bright, high school dropouts who come from broken homes and cannot fit into civilian society.

But after journalists have first reported on the military, their views are radically different. They will lavishly praise the enlisted personnel they met and relate how enthusiastic they were, how well they knew their jobs, how proud they were of what they were doing, and how eager they were to explain their duties. Genuine admiration and enthusiasm come through in the reporter's retelling of experiences. "But what of the officers?" "The officers? . . . Oh, they're a bunch of horses' asses."

To know why such a critical assessment of officers is made, one has only to take a hypothetical, though typical, walk in the journalist's shoes on his or her first interview with a senior officer. In this interview, it happens to be a general.

After an endless round of telephone calls to set up the interview, the well-disposed journalist, notebook and tape recorder in hand, arrives at headquarters and is met by a smiling public affairs officer who signs the journalist in and provides a pass. The officer walks the visitor through a series of offices under the baleful stare of staff factotums; the escort confirms the legitimacy of the stranger's presence. At last the journalist arrives at a well-appointed anteroom where everyone speaks in hushed tones.

After a wait, the door to a better-appointed office opens, and the journalist is ushered in with the announcement, "THE general will see you now." Not knowing whether to genuflect, our visitor enters the sanctum sanctorum vaguely aware of others entering also. Graciously received by the general, this outsider is invited to sit down THERE, while the general resumes his place behind his imposing desk backed by flags and military memorabilia. Besides the general and the public affairs officer, several other officers of varied ranks are present; they are not introduced. All take seats at the nod of the general; one places himself facing the general but slightly to the rear at the outer edge of the reporter's peripheral vision.

Following introductory pleasantries, the interview gets underway with the journalist setting the tape recorder on the coffee table and opening a notebook. This triggers a similar action on the part of the others. The visitor's tape recorder is immediately trumped by at least two others, and the general's entourage poises with pencils and yellow legal pads to take note of the proceedings. Throughout the interview, marked by elliptical responses to questions, the journalist is aware of knowing looks, nods, and shrugs being exchanged among the others. More disconcerting is the series of hand and arm signals being given to the general by the officer sitting to the rear and acting like an operatic prompter. The journalist is given his or her allotted time to the second and then escorted out of the office as the general busies himself with the papers on his desk.

After turning in the badge and being wished "Good day!" the journalist is back out on the street wondering what it was all about. Why all the lackeys? Were they hiding something?. Why the signals? Didn't the general know enough about the subject to discuss it without a prompter? Puzzled, the representative of the press walks away wondering whether the host was a charlatan or a fool.

Obviously this illustration is an exaggeration, but those who have been through the process know that it is barely an exaggeration. Military officers raise suspicions because they appear defensive and protective.

The attitude of the military when meeting with the press is bound to affect that of the press, and vice versa. If it is one of mutual suspicion and antagonism, the relationship will never improve, and, in the end, it is the American public who will be the loser.

There is nothing more refreshing than an open relationship. Senior officers know their business and can talk about it sensibly without a bunch of flacks around, and they should do so. Journalists know that there are some topics that are off-limits in any meeting with the press and respect the obligation of a military officer not to disclose information he or she should not. It is a poor journalist indeed who tries to trap an officer into a disclosure that is legitimately classified. In many cases, the tape recorders and legions of witnesses are protective devices in case a journalist does a hatchet job on the person being interviewed. This is useless protection because a reporter who is out to paint a deliberately unfair picture of a person or institution will do it regardless of recorded safeguards of accuracy. The best protection against the unscrupulous is not to deal with them.

Each of the services has expended great effort at improving military-media relations. Public affairs officers are trained at Fort Benjamin Harrison, and all major commands have graduates of the school to act as a bridge between the warrior and the scribe. Installations and war colleges sponsor symposia, seminars, and workshops to improve relations with the media. Special tours of military installations and activities are conducted for the press by the Defense Department and the services, and some components of the fourth estate even reciprocate. But these efforts have little effect on military attitudes and make few military converts because most of them end up on focusing on the mechanics of the relationship rather than its nature.

What is frequently overlooked by the military is that journalism is as professional as the military, with pride in its integrity and strict norms of conduct for its members. For example, it is absolutely forbidden on the *New York Times* to tape an interview secretly by telephone or in person or to mislead as to the identity of the reporter. Most other newspapers have similar restrictions. As a result, there are few instances of yellow journalism today. The journalistic world knows who the unscrupulous are within its ranks and gives them short shrift. An unscrupulous journalist will never last on a reputable paper, and advertisers upon which a newspaper depends for its existence are not inclined to place ads in papers with a reputation for unfair reporting.

This is not to say that journalists will not use every legitimate means to dig out a story. The reputation of government agencies, including the military, for overclassifying, withholding the truth, or putting a spin on events is well known, and good reporters will never take things at face value. The tendency of journalists to disbelieve half of what they are told also adds to the military's paranoia.

There is no question, however, that some journalists go too far in reporting a story, and so do some newspapers. Journalism is a profession, but it is also a business, and businesses must show profit, a situation that leads to fierce competition among the media. A scoop means sales, and sales mean profit. For a reporter, a scoop also means reputation; and if a journalist's editors were not pushing for exclusive stories, he or she would do so to enhance his or her reputation and maybe win a Pulitzer prize.

Thus, a journalist may uncover a story relating to national security that would jeopardize that security if it was made public. This is particularly true if it is on operational matters, the favorite complaint of today's officer corps. Eager to be on the front page, the journalist may disregard the security sensitivity of a story and file it to the newspaper. But that is where editors come in. They are mature professionals with long years in the business and good judgment on the implications of a story. In truly critical instances, an editor will withhold a damaging story.

The record of the American press is good, despite unsubstantiated claims made by military officers that the press leaks operational information. Two examples will illustrate the point. Newsrooms knew beforehand of the planned airstrikes on Libya in 1986 and held the news until the raids had taken place so as not to endanger the air crews. And every Washington journalist knew that the late Col. Richard Higgins had held a sensitive job in the Office of the Secretary of Defense immediately prior to his U.N. assignment in Lebanon, where he was kidnapped. Yet in hopes that his captors did not know of Higgins's unique background, no mention was made of it in the American press until after it appeared in a Lebanese newspaper.

Whether the press acted responsibly during the Panama invasion when it reported the air movement of troops on the night of the operation is the latest subject of debate. News of the airlift was on television prior to H hour, but nothing was said of a planned airborne assault. Whether anyone in the press knew for certain one was about to take place is unknown, but if it was known, nothing was disclosed publicly. The air activity was alternately reported as a buildup for military action or part of the war of nerves against the Noriega regime. The government itself actually contributed to the leak the night before when it said the unusual air movements about which they were being questioned were routine readiness exercises unrelated to Panama, only to withdraw the "unrelated to Panama" part of their statement prior to the assault the following day.

On the whole, the military was satisfied with the press coverage of its Panama intervention. Certainly it received more favorable reporting than the Grenada operation in 1983. However, the one vehicle designed to improve military-media relations during military operations, the press pool, was a failure.

The idea of a press pool emerged as the result of the exclusion of journalists from the Grenada operation. The press had howled that the people had the right to know what their armed forces were doing and the press should not be denied entry to a war zone. They concluded that they were shut out more to cover up military incompetence than to preserve operational security and more convinced of that interpretation when stories of incompetence surfaced. Press pools were established to allow selected journalists from the various journalistic media to represent the press as a whole during future operations. The pool reporters were rotated periodically and were told to be ready on short notice to accompany military units. A list of names was held at the Pentagon for that purpose. Individuals were not to be told where they were going or what was about to happen.

The system was tested in some peacetime readiness exercises, to everybody's satisfaction. But in its first real test during tanker escort operations in the Persian Gulf, reporters complained that they were isolated from the action and kept ignorant of events. Many charged that their military hosts were more interested in brainwashing them than exposing them to the news.

Panama was the second test, and again the pool concept failed. Reporters were flown to Panama but kept at Howard Air Force base and given briefings during the high points of the operation. When they were taken into Panama City, it was to view events and locations of little news value. Meanwhile, journalists not in the pool were streaming into Panama on their own and providing vivid firsthand accounts of the action. Pool reporters cried "Foul!" For their part, the military complained that the journalists made unreasonable demands for transportation and communications facilities, as well as being unmindful of the dangers involved in taking them to the fighting. Nobody was or is happy with the pool arrangement.

The pool concept suffers three fatal flaws. The first is that the military will always want to put on its best face in hopes of influencing the reporters it is hosting. When faced with the choice of taking a reporter to the scene of a confused and uncertain firelight or to the location of a success story, it is not difficult to guess which will be chosen, regardless of its relative newsworthiness. Second, because the military brought pool reporters to the scene of action, it also feels responsible for transporting them, and this may not be logistically convenient at certain times. Third, the military is protective and feels responsible for the safety of civilians they are sponsoring. Keeping the press pool isolated at an air base in Panama was a genuine reflection of military concern for the reporters' safety. It is only during long campaigns like Vietnam that the protective cloak wears thin, and then usually because journalists find ways of getting out from under the wing of the military.

Implicit in the military attitude is not only its institutional sense of responsibility but also its lack of understanding of journalists. If the pool is to work better, the services must recognize that they have no obligation to the pool other than to get them to the scene of the action and brief them on the situation. Beyond that, reporters are on their own. They are resourceful and can take care of themselves. Any additional assistance rendered to them is appreciated but unnecessary, and lack of it is certainly no grounds for restricting coverage of the story.

The press, on the other hand, should be selective in who they send to war. Pool membership should require a fit, versatile journalist who knows something about the military. Few reporters have previous military experience, and few editors can afford the luxury of a military specialist on their payrolls. But the Defense Department would be happy to provide pool members with orientations and primers on military matters so that reporters could learn some military jargon and the difference between a smoke grenade and a fragmentation grenade.

Oldtimers long for the days of Ernie Pyle and Drew Middleton, when the military and the press saw events as one and there was a love bond between the two. In those days the military could do no wrong, and when it did, a censor saw to it that the public remained ignorant. Those were the days when the nation was on a holy crusade against the evil pomps and works of fascism and nazism. In the desperate struggle, propaganda was more important than truth. Had it been otherwise, many of the World War II heroes we revere today would have been pilloried by the press as butchers and bunglers.

Today's generals have none of the protection of a Mark Clark or Eisenhower. Moral crusades are no longer the order of the day, and unquestioned allegiance to government policy died with Vietnam. The government lied too often to the American people and lost their confidence. Today the press does what Thomas Jefferson envisaged for it when he rated it more important than the army as a defender of democratic principles: it keeps a sharp eye on the military and on the government it serves.

This should not dismay the professional soldier. After all, parents have a right to know what they are doing to and with their sons and daughters and their tax money. If it is done honestly, even with mistakes, there is little to fear from the press.

This is the challenge to today and tomorrow's military leaders: they must regain the respect and confidence of the media that they once had in the dark days of a long-ago war. The press is not going to go away, but the anti-media attitude that has been fostered in young officers must be exorcised if both institutions are to serve the republic.

★ *Retired Marine Corps Lt. General* **Bernard E. Trainor** *is currently an Adjunct Senior Fellow at the Council on Foreign Relations and an Adjunct Associate at the Center for Science and International Affairs at the John F. Kennedy School of Government at Harvard University.*

★ ★ ★ ★ ★

Questions

1. What happened in Vietnam that made military officers bitter towards the news media?
2. Why has the bitterness continued long after the war is over?
3. What is the proper relationship between the press and the military?
4. Is most media coverage of the military today unfavorable?
5. Is most media coverage of the military today unfair?

☆ ☆ ☆

The Structural Constant: The Conservative Constitution versus Civilian Control

Samuel Huntington

Common knowledge is sometimes wrong. Harvard Political Scientist Samuel Huntington provides a case in point. Although most college teachers of American government probably tell their students that the U.S. Constitution provides for civilian control of the military, Huntington insists that civilian control is limited and "has emerged despite rather than because of constitutional provisions." Civilian control does not automatically follow from making the president the commander in chief. The president must share his military power with the states, with Congress, and with various departments of government. This dispersion of power makes military management susceptible to politics.

☆ The Constitutional Absence of Objective Civilian Control

The United States Constitution, despite the widespread belief to the contrary, does not provide for civilian control. That is, it does not permit the objective civilian control compatible with a high level of military professionalism. The

☆ ☆ ☆ ☆ ☆ ☆

essence of civilian control in this sense is a clear distinction between political and military responsibilities and the institutional subordination of the latter to the former. These are unknown to the Constitution, which mixes political and military functions, interjecting politics into military affairs and military affairs into politics. Present in the minds of the Framers when they wrote it and perpetuated in its provisions was an essentially subjective approach to civil-military relations. Civilian control has at times existed in the United States, but it has emerged despite rather than because of constitutional provisions.

The very aspects of the Constitution which are frequently cited as establishing civilian control are those which make it difficult to achieve. Civilian control would be maximized if the military were limited in scope and relegated to a subordinate position in a pyramid of authority culminating in a single civilian head. The military clauses of the Constitution, however, provide for almost exactly the opposite. They divide civilian responsibility for military affairs and foster the direct access of the military authorities to the highest levels of government:

(1) Within the total federal system of government, the militia clauses divide control over the militia between the state and national government.

(2) Within the national government, the separation of powers divides control of the national military forces between Congress and the President.

(3) Within the executive branch of the national government, the Commander in Chief clause tends to divide control over the military between the President and departmental secretaries.

These latter two previsions reflect the distribution of military powers in the British government in the eighteenth century The similarity, however, turned into a fundamental difference in the course of a century and a half. The evolution of British government centralized all authority over the military in the Cabinet, and the British constitution today provides for extremely effective civilian control. The American Constitution, however, remains frozen in the eighteenth-century pattern. The centrifugal politics of this country and the written, inflexible character of the Constitution combined to obstruct changes similar to those in Great Britain. American lack of concern with military affairs, furthermore, left the constitutional structure almost unsupplemented by statutory enactments. Prior to the twentieth century the only significant additions were the office of the Secretary of War created in 1789 and the office of the Secretary of the Navy created in 1798. For most of American history, the Constitution and little else determined the legal structure of American civil-military relations.

★ *The Framers and Civilian Control*

The speeches and writings of the Framers of the Constitution abound with statements that the military should be subordinated to the civil power. If this is the case, how is it that they apparently failed so completely to carry out their intention? The answer is, of course, that military professionalism and civilian control as the subordination of that profession to political institutions were simply unknown to the eighteenth century. In terms of providing for civilian control, the Constitution was drafted at just the wrong time in history. It was a product of the last years of preprofessional officership. If it had been framed twenty-five years later, its clauses with respect to military power might well have been significantly different. But, as it was, for all their political wisdom and insight, the Framers did not, with a few exceptions, foresee the emergence of military professionalism and objective civilian control. It is no criticism of them that they did not provide for something which did not exist when they were drafting the Constitution. Their approach to civilian control was reflected in their ideas on military officership, military forces, and governmental organization.

Military Officership. The Constitution does not envisage a separate class of persons exclusively devoted to military leadership. "I am not acquainted with the military profession," George Mason proclaimed at the Virginia convention and, except for Hamilton, Pinckney, and a few others, he spoke for all the Framers. They knew neither military profession nor separate military skills. Military officership was the attribute of any man of affairs. Many members of the Federal Convention had held military rank during the Revolution; Washington was only the most obvious of the soldier-statesmen. They combined in their own persons military and political talents much as the samurai founders of modern Japan also combined them a hundred years later. Following Blackstone, they believed that in a free state the citizen did not cease to be a citizen when he became a soldier but rather became a soldier because he was a citizen.[1]

Such views were clearly revealed in the ineligibility and incompatibility clauses of Article I, Section 6:

> No Senator or Representative shall, during the Time for which he was elected, be appointed to any civil office under the Authority of the United States, which shall have been created, or the Emoluments whereof shall have been increased during such time; and no person holding any Office under the United States shall be a Member of either House during his Continuance in Office.

The Convention almost unanimously supported the second clause of this paragraph making legislative office incompatible with judicial or executive (including military) office. This was required by the separation of powers. It reflected the necessity of keeping the legislature distinct from the executive rather than the desirability of keeping the political distinct from the military. Attention at the Convention centered on the first clause of the paragraph. As reported from the Committee of Detail, this clause proposed to make members of the legislature ineligible for appointment to any national office during the time for which they were elected. Opinions on the desirability of permitting legislators to assume civil office varied and were finally resolved by compromise. There was, however, a universal belief that Senators and Representatives should be eligible for appointment to a military office. "Exclude the officers of the army & navy," said Gouveneur Morris, "and you form a band having a different interest from & opposed to the civil power: you stimulate them to despise & reproach those 'talking Lords who dare not face the foe.'" What would occur, he inquired, in the

> . . . case of a war, and the Citizen the most capable of conducting it, happening to be a member of the Legislature. What might have been the consequence of such a regulation at the commencement, or even in the Course of the late contest for our liberties?

Others, such as Edmund Randolph, who favored the general ineligibility of legislators for executive office also recognized that military talent might well exist in Congress and supported an exception with respect to military office. Consequently, the final draft applied incompatibility to both civil and military office but the eligibility limitations only to civil office. Subsequently, in the Virginia convention Madison defended the eligibility provisions concerning civil office by citing the absence of any such restrictions upon appointment to military office. His argument plus the lack of any opposition to legislative eligibility to military office in the ratification debates indicates how widespread was the acceptance of this Cincinnatus theory of military leadership.[2]

Military Forces. The Framers' concept of nonprofessional officership could have been embodied in either of the two forms of military organization familiar to eighteenth-century America: the standing army and the citizen militia. These forms, however, were essentially the extension into the military realm of different political beliefs. The standing army with its upper-class officers and lower-class enlisted men was basically an aristocratic institution. It was associated with the British Crown and the European despotism. It was also quite unnecessary in the eyes of many Americans. The distance of the United States from Europe meant that it required no permanent military force with the possible exception of small frontier garrisons to deal with the Indians. Consequently, it was generally agreed that primary reliance must be put upon a citizen militia composed of part-time officers and enlisted men.

This was the only form of military force suitable for the new republic. The militia embodied the democratic principle that defense of the nation was the responsibility of every citizen. The distinction between officers and enlisted men was minimized, and the line between them did not correspond to any sharp cleavage in the social structure.

Preference for the militia was almost universal throughout the states. "There was not a member in the federal Convention," Edmund Randolph remarked with only slight exaggeration, "who did not feel indignation" at the prospect of a standing army. The ratifying conventions were even more strongly opposed to regular military forces. Nonetheless, they approved a Constitution which, while barring standing armies to the states, gave the national government unlimited power to maintain a military force, the only restriction being that no appropriations for this purpose could be made for more than two years. The reasons for this apparent anomaly were twofold. First, it was generally recognized that the national government would have to maintain some sort of permanent force along the frontier. Secondly, there was always the possibility that a standing army might be necessary in an emergency. But the hope and expectation were that this emergency would never occur and that the power would never be utilized. Few provisions in the Constitution were agreed to with more reluctance, and some delegates most vehemently opposed to standing forces refused to sign the Constitution. Criticism of this unrestricted congressional power was wide spread in the state conventions. A number of states proposed requiring an extraordinary majority in Congress for the maintenance of such a force or suggested amendments declaring the militia to be "the natural defence of a free state" and standing armies in peace "dangerous to liberty."[3]

Preference for the militia had two important results for future civilian control. First, it assigned a major place in the American military scheme to a force which could never be professionally officered or subjected to civilian control. At the time, of course, professional officers were just as rare in standing armies as they were in citizen militias. The former, however, because they were composed of full-time soldiers, could eventually evolve into a disciplined body of professionals. This was impossible in a part-time militia force. Secondly, the expectation that the militia would be the main reliance for defense made the framers relatively unconcerned with devising institutional techniques to control military forces in being. In part, this was the result of the feeling that such devices could never be successful. To a larger extent, it reflected the view that such devices were unnecessary. The republic would be defended by its loyal citizen-soldiers. Civilian supremacy would be maintained by eliminating a distinct military force.

Governmental Organization. The Framers' concept of civilian control was to control the uses to which civilians might put military force rather than to control the military themselves. They were more afraid of military power in the hands of political officials than of political power in the hands of military officers. Unable to visualize a distinct military class, they could not fear such a class. But there was need to fear the concentration of authority over the military in any single governmental institution. As conservatives, they wanted to divide power, including power over the armed forces. The national government if it monopolized military power would be a threat to the states; the president if he had sole control over the armed forces would be a threat to the Congress. Consequently, the Framers identified civilian control with the fragmentation of authority over the military. Concern for the independence of Congress from executive control, rather than in understanding of the distinct nature of the political and military functions, caused them to make legislative and military office incompatible. The issue of the relative desirability of a militia versus a standing army was subordinate to the issues of the relative power of the states and the nation, the executive and the legislature, over the military forces, whatever their character. Those who wished a strong national government had no hesitancy in arguing: (1) that continuation of the Articles of Confederation would mean standing armies in every state; (2) that the proposed national government necessarily had to have the power to raise a standing army; and (3) that to avoid the necessity of exercising this power, the national government should also organize and discipline the militia. Supporters of states rights, on the other hand, argued that it was unnecessary for the national government to have a standing army and that, in any case, the states ought to have exclusive control over the militia in order to protect themselves against the standing army of the national government.[4]

★ *The Militia Clauses and Military Federalism: The Empire Within an Empire*

The militia clauses of the Constitution hamper civilian control in two ways. First, they give constitutional sanction to a semi-military force which can never be completely subordinated to military discipline nor completely removed from political entanglements. Secondly, they give constitutional sanction to a division of control over the militia between state and national governments which necessarily involves the militia in the conflicting interest of the federal system. This unique combination of characteristics—part civilian and part military, part state and part national—tends to make the militia independent of the policy-making institutions of government.

The Framers had good reasons to prefer a militia force to a regular army. But there was little rational justification for splitting up the control of this force. As Madison said, this control "did not seem in its nature to be divisible between two distinct authorities." Politics if not logic, however, forced the Framers, Madison included, to support dual control. Some, such as Hamilton, wanted complete control in the United States. Others wished the national government to be completely excluded from authority over the militia. The clash of these viewpoints produced a variety of compromise suggestions. In the end, the balance of political forces resulted in the following militia clauses:

> The congress shall have Power . . .
> To provide for calling forth the Militia to execute the Laws of the Union, suppress Insurrections and repel Invasions;
> To provide for organizing, arming, and disciplining the Militia, and for governing such part of them as may be employed in the Service of the United States, reserving to the States respectively, the Appointment of Officers, and the Authority of training the Militia according to the discipline prescribed by Congress . . . The President shall be Commander-in-Chief . . . of the Militia of the several States, when called into the actual service of the United States . . .

In addition, of course, Congress also has the authority to "raise and support armies" under the army clause.[5] The exercise of these authorities can be divided into two periods. From 1792 to 1903, the militia was under state control in time of peace and dual control in time of war. After 1903 the militia was under dual control in time of peace and national control in time of war.*

State control existed in peacetime throughout the nineteenth century because Congress, in the Militia Act of 1792, which was the basic legislation in this field until 1903, refused to exercise its powers under the militia clauses and provided for neither effective federal supervision nor effective federal support. Consequently, the militia remained exclusively state forces when not in the active service of the United States. When they were in such service, however, the dual control under the militia clauses resulted in constant confusion and bickering over the purposes for which the militia might be used and the appointment of officers. In 1812, for instance, when the President called out the militia, the governors of Massachusetts and Connecticut

*The problems raised by the militia clauses have not changed fundamentally in more recent years, and this discussion of the militia will include events after 1940. In contrast, the discussion of the separation of powers and the Commander in Chief clause in this chapter will be limited to the period previous to 1940; the special problems arising after 1940 will be treated separately in Part III.

asserted that they and not he had the right to decide whether the circumstances justified the call. Later in the war militia on the Niagara frontier refused on constitutional grounds to enter Canada to support regular American troops fighting there. In the Spanish-American War, militia units likewise refused to serve outside the United States. The president was constitutional Commander in Chief of the militia while it was in federal service. Yet how could he function in this capacity when his officers in war as well as peace were appointed by state governors? In the War of 1812 state governors challenged the authority of the President to subordinate militia units to the command of Regular Army general offices. State officials removed their troops from national service as they saw fit and upset the lines of command by appointing militia officers to higher rank than the regular officers to whom the militia units were theoretically subordinate. In the Civil War, also, the states appointed the regimental officer of the militia and the national volunteers assigned to the states, while the President appointed the general officers. The Act of April 22, 1898 providing for the Volunteer Army for the Spanish-American War reproduced this division of authority.[6]

Dual control in war did not survive the nineteenth century. The militia has fought twentieth-century wars as an exclusively national force under the army clause. Nor did the system of state control in time of peace extend past 1903. Dual control under the militia clauses became a reality when Congress passed the Dick Act of that year. The effects of these changes were twofold. The military importance of the militia in time of war was enhanced because it now had the wherewithal to become an effective military body. The political power of the militia in time of peace was enhanced because it was placed between two competing authorities. Civilian control of the militia—difficult in time of war in the nineteenth century—became in the twentieth century difficult in time of peace. Thus, the militia clauses are the constitutional base for a potent political organization—the National Guard, and its spokesman, the National Guard Association. It is generally recognized that constitutions are created by political forces. It is also true, however, that constitutions may themselves create or impel the creation of political interests. This is the case with the militia clauses and the National Guard. Were it not for these clauses, the Guard and the National Guard Association would not exist with the influence which they have today.

The National Guard Association was formed in 1878 by a group of militia officers for the primary purpose of getting Congress to exercise its responsibilities under the militia clauses. It was designed to "present a united front" for joint control.[7] Its founders wished the national government to supply money, instruction, standards, and a certain measure of supervision to the state militia. The Regular Army was opposed because it did not think the militia could be an effective national force. The dual control advocates, however, won their first victory in 1903 and subsequently strengthened and maintained their position despite the continuing hostility of the Regular Army. Throughout its existence the Guard has recognized its dependence upon the militia clauses and has stoutly defended its dual status. Guard officers maintain that these clauses embody the true sentiments of the Framers on military policy. Constitutional "dual control" is opposed to central control and to exclusive state control. The latter is impossible because it is not economically feasible for the states to carry the entire cost of the Guard; the former is unconstitutional because, according to the Guard, the army clause gives Congress the power only to maintain a standing army not to keep a federal militia. For the Guard, dual control in peace means that the national government should supply the funds and the know-how while the states supply the command and direction. The Association has consistently sought more federal money for Guard activities but resolutely opposed any extension of federal control. In 1949, for instance, it demanded increased federal aid for armories and construction, a uniform clothing allowance for National Guard officers, and the franking privilege for National Guard mail. At the same time it vigorously condemned further federal control over the Guard, describing the 1948 Gray Board recommendation for a single national reserve force as "unconstitutional, un-American . . . contrary to our concept and philosophy of life . . . ill-advised and illegal." Upon the constitutional base of the militia clauses, the National Guard has created a political force of formidable proportion. As the president of the Association frankly and accurately proclaimed, the Guard is an "empire within an empire."[8] Within its sphere of interest its word is law, or becomes law very quickly. The extent of this power, and the ways in which the militia clauses contribute to it, may be seen in: (1) its legal status; (2) its constitutional symbolism; (3) its official representation in state and national governments; (4) the peculiar position of the National Guard Association; and (5) the influence of the Guard with Congress.

Legal Status. The efforts of the Association to enhance the Guard's dual status have put the latter in a unique legal position. The National Guard is a single organization with a double existence. As the "National Guard of the several states and territories," it is organized under the militia clause and has the mission of preserving law and order within the states under the orders of the authorities. In this capacity it may be "called forth" by the President under the appropriate authority of Congress for the limited constitutional purposes of executing the laws of the United States, suppressing insurrection, and repelling invasions. If this were its only status, the Guard would be constitutionally incapable of participating, as an organization, in foreign war. In 1917, without authority permitting overseas service, its members went into the national army as groups of individuals, and Guard organization was disrupted. As a result, the Association in 1933 secured the passage of an act which makes the Guard as the "National Guard of the United States" a reserve component of the Army of the United States under the army clause. In this capacity, its mission is to furnish units for all types of military operations anywhere in the world. As the National Guard of the United States, it may be "ordered" to active service by the President after Congress has declared the existence of a national emergency. The Guard has the best of two worlds. Its status under the militia clause protects it against federal control in peacetime. Its status under the army clause insures it of a prominent role in wartime.

Constitutional Symbolism. As a militia under dual control, the Guard identifies itself with two venerated constitutional symbols: the citizen-soldier and states' rights. Guardsmen are "amateur soldiers," citizens first and soldiers second in the Minute Man tradition. "In the future as in the past," the Association declared in 1944, "and based upon sound tradition, long experience, and this Nation's fundamental law, the citizen-soldier must be the major dependence of the Nation in time of war." The federal reserves, however, can likewise claim to be citizen-soldiers. But only the Guard can also invoke the banner of states' rights. Our "organizations," claimed President Walsh, "belong to the States and are merely loaned to the Federal Government in wartime." The Guard wants the "Federal system adhered to" in the military establishment. The Guard can thus expect the support of the state governments against the national government. In 1943, for instance, the Conference of Governors urged continued dual status for the Guard in the postwar period, and in 1948 the Executive Committee of the conference joined the Guard in denouncing the Gray Board report. Its state affiliations enhance the political influence of the Guard relative to that of the reserve associations of the national forces. In 1954 the Reserve Officers Association had 60,000 members and the NGA had 34,000. The ROA normally has had more money and a larger staff than the NGA. Nonetheless, without a secure base of operations in the states, the ROA has not equaled the NGA in political influence. In 1946 the president of the ROA described his organization as the "younger brother" of the National Guard Association and admitted that "The National Guard has much of what we the Reserves have not had."[9]

State and National Representation. The position of the Guard is strengthened by its official foothold in both the state and national governments. The heads of the Guard in the states are the adjutants general appointed by the governors. These officials represent the Guard within the state governments and are linked nationally through the Adjutants General Association which is a "corollary" organization of the NGA. The Guard is represented in the Department of the Army by the Chief of the National Guard Bureau, who under the National Defense Act of 1920 must be a Guardsman, and by the National Guard members of the joint General Staff committees which, under the same act, must consider all policies affecting the Guard. These national representatives keep the NGA well informed of what transpires within the Army and the War Department. The Guard has regularly insisted that it be included at an early stage in the preparation of War Department policies which might affect it. Exclusion of the Guard in the development of policy generally means opposition by the NGA when the programs are submitted to Congress.[10]

The National Guard Association. The NGA, like so many other powerful groups, occupies an ambiguous position on the borderline between a private association and a public body. Legally it is simply a voluntary organization of National Guard officers. Nonetheless, it considers itself to be "the authorized Representative of the National Guard of the United States." It is also closely tied in with the official state and national representation of the Guard. In 1948, when only 42 percent of Guard officers belonged to the NGA, the Association declared it to be the responsibility of the adjutants general "to insist that every National Guard Officer be a member of the National Guard Association." To this end it urged the states to require each new Guard officer to fill out an NGA membership application prior to appearing before the official examining board. Through such techniques, the NGA by 1953 achieved a 99 percent membership among Guard officers. As a private association the NGA carries on public relations activities, publishes the monthly *National Guardsman,* and represents the Guard with respect to a wide variety of legislation. At one point in the debate over the Selective Service Act of 1948, for example, when it looked as if the Guard viewpoint would not prevail, the Association brought members from thirty-four states to Washington to lobby with their congressmen. In two days they were eminently successful in getting Congress to adopt the National Guard position. In President Walsh's words, the great virtue of the NGA is that it is

> . . . the only agency on which the National Guard can rely to protect its interest, for the Association is free and untrammeled and it does not have to conform to any particular pattern nor is it bound within the narrow limits of channels of communication or the chain of command.[11]

Influence with Congress. In the final analysis the influence of the Guard boils down to its influence with Congress. The fate of the militia is in the hands of Congress. Conceivably, Congress could destroy the dual status of the Guard and undermine its political power by refusing to exercise its functions under the militia clause and by returning to the pre-1903 situation. Conversely, Congress could federalize the Guard and make it an exclusively national instrumentality under the army clause. NGA officers, however, assert that "We should settle the future of the National Guard." If the NGA is going to "settle" the fate of the Guard, it must settle the actions of Congress on National Guard affairs. For half a century it has been astoundingly successful in doing exactly this. The local roots of the Guard, its appeals to states' rights and the citizen-soldier, its support from the state governments, its lobbying and pressure tactics, have made it a power on Capitol Hill. "Congress," in the words of President Walsh, "has ever been our refuge and our strength."

The record of National Guard success with Congress begins with the Dick Act of 1903. Representative Dick himself was a former president of the National Guard Association. In 1908 the Association secured the passage of the second Dick Act strengthening federal support of the Guard. In 1916 the Guard "threw every ounce of its energy to an effort to defeat" the Continental Army plan of the General Staff. It was successful, and the National Defense Act of that year was in line with its views. The position of the Guard was greatly strengthened four years later by the National Defense Act of 1920, which the Guard described as "a great achievement and a great victory." In passing the 1933 act making the Guard a reserve component of the Army in peace as well as war "Congress saw eye to eye with the proposals submitted by the National Guard." Throughout the twenties and thirties, the NGA successfully devoted its efforts to increasing the appropriations of the Guard from $13,000,000 in 1920 to $72,000,000 in 1941. In 1940 when the original Selective Training and Service Bill as proposed in Congress did not secure the interests of the Guard, the Association had inserted into it the "National Guard protective clause" which declared it to be "essential that the strength and organization of the National Guard as an integral part of the first line of defense of this nation be at all times maintained and assured." In 1946 the Guard fought efforts by the War Department to set up a large Organized Reserve Corps which the Guard viewed as a "competing" and "parallel" organization. A War Department recommendation for a $40,000,000 appropriation for the ORC was eliminated by Congress at the insistence of the National Guard. The Guard had no difficulty, however, in getting funds for itself. For Fiscal Year 1949 the Budget Bureau recommended $195,000,000 for the Guard. The NGA did not think this enough and got the economy minded Eightieth Congress to appropriate $290,000,000. In 1948 the Association was also successful in getting its views written into the Selective Service Act and in blocking the legislative recommendations of the Gray Board. In 1954 when an Assistant Secretary of Defense suggested that the Guard should be used only for Home Guard and civil defense functions, President Walsh confidently picked up the challenge: "If they want war, let it begin here."[12]

The record shows that Congress has indeed given, in Walsh's words, "generous support" to the Guard. Continuing his reflections on the Eightieth Congress, the president went on to wonder if

> . . . any organization has been so successful in the legislative field in so brief a period as the National Guard Association. It is indeed a great accomplishment to have attained all the major legislative objectives of this Association.

Two years later the NGA Legislative committee reported that the Association had "been phenomenally successful in obtaining the enactment of legislation essential to its well-being and development."[13] So long as the Guard retains its jealously protected dual status, this will continue to be the situation. Ensconced behind the militia clauses as an "empire within an empire," this premier military lobby effectively dominates those congressional proceedings which interest it. It is a Frankenstein monster created by the Constitution of the United States. That document underwrites its slogan that "There will always be a National Guard."

★ *The Separation of Powers: Dual Control over the National Forces*

In many respects the most significant aspect of the separation of powers is not the relative division of power between President and Congress, but the effects which this division has upon the power of other groups. The existence of two coordinate bodies means that the power of each of these bodies vis-à-vis other groups is less than it would be if either possessed full sovereign authority. The principal beneficiaries of this spreading of power have been organized interest groups, bureaucratic agencies, and the military services. The separation of powers is a perpetual invitation, if not an irresistible force, drawing military leaders into political conflicts. Consequently, it has been a major hindrance to the development of military professionalism and civilian control in the United States.

With only minor modifications the Framers reproduced in the Constitution the division of authority over the military which prevailed in England and the colonies in the middle of the eighteenth century. "The purse & the sword," said George Mason, "ought never to get into the same hands [whether legislative or executive]." The President inherited the powers of the English king, Congress the powers of the English Parliament. The executive authority of the President, Hamilton stated in *The Federalist,* "will resemble equally that of the king of Great Britain and of the governor of New York." The Framers did, however, make one major adjustment in favor of the legislature. In giving Congress the war power, they altered British practice and established a significant precedent in the evolution of representative government. The result was that congress was given the power

> To declare war, grant Letters of Marque and Reprisal, and make Rules concerning Captures on Land and Water;
>
> To raise and support Armies, but no Appropriation of Money to that Use shall be for a longer Term than two Years;
>
> To provide and maintain a Navy;
>
> To make Rules for the Government and Regulation of the land and naval Forces . . . And
>
> To make all laws which shall be necessary and proper for carrying into Execution the foregoing Powers, and all other Powers vested by this Constitution in the Government of the United States, or in any Department or Officer thereof.

And the President was made "Commander in Chief of the Army and Navy of the United States."[14]

The general intent of this division of power is clear. Further problems arise, however, from the nature of the grant of presidential power. This clause is unique in the Constitution in that it grants authority in the form of an *office* rather than in the form of a *function*. The President is not given the function "to command the Army and Navy"; he is given the office of "Commander in Chief." This difference in form is of considerable importance. By defining the presidential power as an office, the Framers left undefined its specific powers and functions. This eased the approval of the Constitution in the ratifying conventions, but it gave subsequent generations something to cogitate about and argue about. What, after all, are the powers of the Commander in Chief? They might range from the extremely broad power to conduct war to a narrowly restricted power of military command. They certainly exclude all powers specifically assigned to Congress or the states, and they probably include all purely military powers not so assigned. But does the office possess nonmilitary powers as well? The Framers themselves seemed to hold conflicting opinion on this point. The Supreme Court in 1850, however, declared that the duty and power of the President as Commander in Chief were "purely military," and denied the similarity between the presidential authority and the royal prerogative.[15] So long as the Commander in Chief power is interpreted as purely military, it really adds little authority to the presidential office. Indeed, down to the Civil War it was, in Professor Corwin's phrase, "the forgotten clause" of the Constitution. In the Civil War and in World War II, however, Lincoln and Roosevelt used the clause to justify an extraordinarily broad range of nonmilitary presidential actions largely legislative in nature. The justification of these actions by the Commander in Chief clause was persuasive, however, only because John Rutledge defined that power as an office rather than a function. It may be argued that the office of Commander in Chief possesses authority to seize a strike-bound war plant. It would be impossible to argue that the function of commanding the Army and Navy implied such authority. In other words, the clause has been of relatively little direct use in securing civilian control over the military. Indeed, in one respect it has been directly detrimental to such control. But because it was phrased as an office rather than a function, it has been of great use to the President in expanding his power at the expense of Congress. This, in turn, has broadened the area of conflict between these two institutions and, consequently, has indirectly further impeded civilian control by increasing the likelihood that military leaders will be drawn into this political controversy.[16]

The means through which the President has exercised his powers with respect to military affairs include the appointment of military personnel, the issuance of executive orders and commands, and reliance upon the instrumentality of the civilian secretary. Congressional weapons include statutes, appropriations, and investigations. These weapons have normally been wielded on behalf of Congress by the military and naval affairs committees, the appropriations committees, and special wartime investigating committees. On occasion both sides have found it necessary or expedient to appeal to the military for support of their plans or to seize upon and push military plans for purposes of their own. The involvement of the national officer corps in politics has, consequently, been less consistent and more sporadic in nature than the involvement of the militia officer corps. The division of authority between two separate governments demanded a permanent political spokesman for the interests of the militia. The division of authority between two branches of the same government led to the transitory involvement of individuals and cliques of officers in controversies over military strength, military strategy, military organization, and military appointments. Until 1940, these issues generally were not of great importance in national politics. Consequently, the separation of powers was primarily a passive, latent obstacle to the emergence of military professionalism. Its implications for civilian control were not clearly obvious because military policy was of relatively minor concern to both Congress and President.

Military Strength. The pattern of national politics respecting the strength of military forces tend to obscure the extent of military participation in politics. Prior to 1940 the executive was generally more favorably inclined towards a larger military establishment than was Congress. Congress had less immediate contact with foreign dangers and was under greater popular pressure to cut spending. In addition, the easiest way to assert congressional authority in the budget process was simply to reduce executive requests. Thus, the institutional jealousy of the two branches, even apart from constituent pressure, tended to make Congress less favorable to military appropriations. The result was that military leaders were generally on the side of the President; they appeared before congressional committees to support his program. Military involvement in politics on the side of Congress tends to be conspicuous and dramatic. Military involvement in politics on the side of the President tends to be subtle and less obvious. Undoubtedly, some administrations did use popular officers to rally congressional support for their military proposals. But it is extremely difficult to draw the line between the soldier giving professional advice to Congress as to what the country needs for its defense and the soldier lobbying with Congress for the administration. The two roles are distinct in theory but blended in practice. In the period following World War II on the other hand, a number of significant variations from this pattern have occurred, with Congress taking a more sympathetic view to military request than the President.

Military Strategy. It is more difficult to identify continuing executive and legislative positions on strategy than on military strength. To the extent that there were persistent patterns, Congress generally favored a more aggressive and offensively minded strategy, while the President supported caution and restraint. When the issue was joined, both have been able to find elements in the officer corps favorable to their positions. Officers who did not find support for their strategic views in the top levels of the executive branch had no trouble in locating congressmen willing to push their strategy. Similarly, congressmen who wanted to attack the administration with respect to its strategy were usually able to find officers willing to lend an air of professional respectability to their criticism.

The most extreme example of the mixing of politics and strategy occurred in the Civil War. The purpose of the congressional Committee on the Conduct of the War was defined by one of its founders as "to keep an anxious, watchful eye over all the executive agents who are carrying on the war at the direction of the people . . . We are not under the command of the military of this country. They are under ours as a Congress."[17] The Committee favored a "radical" policy involving stringent opposition to slavery and an aggressive "On to Richmond" strategy. The President and General McClellan were for going slow on both counts. Consequently, the Committee had little hesitancy in using its power to undermine McClellan and force his withdrawal from command. Its members were certain that their own capabilities with respect to military strategy made them at least the equal of the generals. In opposing McClellan, they were assisted by many Army officers who shared their views and who actively subverted "Little Mac's" authority. On the other hand, generals such as Hooker and Burnside, who were sympathetic to the Committee's position, were hamstrung by the conspiratorial activities of more conservative subordinates.

Military Organization. With respect to military organization a natural coincidence of viewpoints led military soldiers to side with Congress against the President. Congress normally tried to enhance its own power against the executive by detailed legislative prescription of military organization. Military officers generally supported this as tending to strengthen their position against the President and civilian secretaries. Consequently, military organization issues present many more obvious examples of military involvement in politics than do those with respect to strategy.

During the Civil War, Congress undertook to lay out the details of military organization, and forced Lincoln to divide the army into corps so as to reduce the number of troops under McClellan's command. After the war, the Army Appropriation Act in 1867 directed the President to issue all orders and instructions relative to military operations through the General of the Army (Grant). It also provided that the General of the Army should not be removed or assigned to command elsewhere than at Washington, except at his own request or with the approval of the Senate. This effort to transfer some of the President's authority as Commander in Chief to a military subordinate was undoubtedly unconstitutional, but it is not the only instance in American history where it has been attempted.

Congress has generally supported military offices in the War Department opposed to the centralization of authority in the Secretary of War or in the General Staff. The independent position of the Corps of Engineers with respect to its civil functions is only the most extreme example of this tendency to combine military and legislative power against executive power. In 1901, four staff chiefs—the quartermaster general, the surgeon general, the paymaster general, and the chief of engineers—got Congress to strengthen their position despite the opposition of the Secretary of War. Subsequently, in the controversy over the relative powers of the Chief of Staff and the adjutant general, the Secretary of War successfully backed the former, but the latter received vindication at the hands of a congressional committee. In the army organization act of 1920, Congress required the Secretary of War to submit the comments of the General Staff, pro and con, with any proposed legislation unless this was "incompatible with the public interest." The effect of this provision was to invite general staff officers "to try their controversy with their chief before a Congressional committee." In 1914 and 1915 naval officers under the leadership of Admiral Fiske worked with congressional sympathizers to secure the creation of the office of the Chief of Naval Operations despite the opposition of the President and Secretary Daniels.[18]

Military Appointments. No single pattern of military involvement in politics prevails with respect to personnel appointments. The extent to which individuals become involved and the side they choose are functions of their views on policy and their political affiliations. Both Congress and the President, however, usually tried to maximize their own influence by securing the appointment of officers generally sympathetic to their views on military affairs and by blocking the appointment of those who were hostile. In the Mexican War, for instance, the two senior generals in the Army, Major Generals Scott and Taylor, were Whigs. President Polk, a Democrat, feared that he could not trust these officers and did not wish them to become popular military idols. Hence he asked Congress to create the position of lieutenant general whose occupant would outrank Scott and Taylor. To this position he planned to appoint a Democratic senator, Thomas Hart Benton. But Congress refused to go along with the idea, and in 1848 Taylor was elected president. During the Civil War, the Committee on the conduct of the War actively tried to advance its favorite generals and to get rid of those who opposed its policies. A routine, if unusually important, exercise of congressional influence occurred in the appointment of Dewey to the command of the Asiatic Squadron prior to the outbreak of the Spanish-American War. Secretary of the Navy Long was opposed to Dewey; Assistant Secretary Theodore Roosevelt supported him. T. R. called in Dewey and asked him if he knew any Senators. When the naval officer admitted to knowing Senator Proctor of Vermont, that legislator was induced to approach President McKinley, and the appointment went through.[19]

The differing interests of Congress and the President thus determined the side which military officers supported. On issues of military strength they were normally with the President, on organizational issues they were with Congress, on strategy they were divided, and on personnel issues they followed their own best interests. Whenever significant questions of military policy arose, the national officers were drawn into the legislative-executive struggle on one side or the other. The separation of powers made it impossible for American officers ever to be at ease in their professionalism.

★ The Commander in Chief Clause: The Political-Military Hierarchy

One major function of the Commander in Chief clause has been to justify the exercise of broad presidential powers in times of national emergency. A second principal function has been to complicate the achievement of civilian control in the executive branch. Just as the separation of powers is a standing invitation to military leaders to bypass the President and go directly to Congress, the Commander in Chief clause is a standing invitation to bypass the civilian secretary and go to the President.

The Commander in Chief clause is the outstanding example of the Framers' mixing of political and military functions. The same thinking which permitted them to envision Senators becoming generals in war also permitted them to accept a civilian President as military commander in chief. In most societies, from primitive nomadic tribes down to their own time, it had been customary for the chief of state also to be the chief military commander. This had been true of the Greek city state, the Roman republic, and the European national monarchies; it was to be true of Napoleonic France. Virtually all the state constitutions at the time made the governor commander in chief of the militia. Military command was as much a function of the chief executive as the appointment of administrative officials or the negotiation of alliances. It was only natural for this role to be assigned to the President. He was to be a republican Soldier-President patterned upon the Royal Warrior of the European states.

The extent to which the Framers expected the President to exercise military functions may be seen in their failure to curb his authority personally to lead troops on the field of battle. Such a restriction was contained in the New Jersey plan and had the support of Hamilton. The convention, however, explicitly rejected these attempts to limit his authority to command in person. Some criticisms of this power were voiced in state conventions but there, too, efforts to curtail it were unsuccessful. The intention and the expectation of the Framers and of the people was that the President could, if he so desired, assume personal command in the field. Early presidents did not hesitate to do this. Washington personally commanded the militia called out to suppress the Whiskey Rebellion. James Madison took a direct hand in organizing the ineffectual defense of Washington in 1814. During the Mexican War, President Polk, although he did not command the army in the field, nonetheless personally formulated the military strategy of the war and participated in a wide range of exclusively military matters. The last instance of a President directly exercising military functions was Lincoln's participation in the direction of the Union armies in the spring of 1862. The President personally determined the plan of operations, and, through his War Orders, directed the movement of troop units. It was not until Grant took over in Virginia that presidential participation in military affairs came to an end. No subsequent President essayed the direction of military operations, although Theodore Roosevelt in World War I argued conversely that his previous experience as Commander in Chief proved his competence to command a division in France.[20]

Until the middle of the nineteenth century, no real distinction existed between political and military competence. Any man of affairs was capable of command, and the exercise by the President of his military functions created no difficulties. There was a single, clear political-military hierarchy running from the President through the Secretaries of War and the Navy to the uniformed commanders. Political and military responsibilities and abilities were mixed all along the line. The President frequently had previous military experience; the Secretary of War almost always had. The top generals, on the other hand, were usually involved in politics. The organization of the service departments, consequently, was little different from that of any other department.

This unified hierarchy began to break up as the military function became professionalized. The President was no longer qualified to exercise military command. And even if he were qualified by previous training, he could not devote time to this function without abandoning his political responsibilities. The political functions of the Presidency became incompatible with the military functions of the Commander in Chief. Nor were the civilian politicians appointed Secretaries of War and the Navy competent to exercise military command. On the other hand, the emergence of the military profession produced officers whose experience had been exclusively military, who were quite different types from the politician secretaries, and who were technically qualified to command. The constitutional presumption that the President exercised command still remained, however, and complicated the relations among President, secretary, and military chief. Under the Constitution the military chief was military, the secretary political, and the President political and military. Normally, one would assume that the secretary, with his duty to represent the interests of his department, would be more military in outlook, if not in capability, than the President with his broader interests and responsibilities. The Constitution, however, reversed this relationship, and obscured the clearness of the hierarchy. Did the chain of command go up through the secretary, a civilian politician, to the President? Or were there two lines of authority emanating from the Presidency: a political-administrative line to the secretary and a military command line directly to the highest professional officer? These issues have befogged American military organization down to the present day.

★ The Balanced, Coordinate, and Vertical Types of Executive Civil-Military Relations

It is possible to conceive of three different types of executive civil-military relations among the President, secretary, and military chief.* The *balanced pattern* assigns to the President a purely political function: the decision of the highest policy issues and the general supervision of the military establishment. Beneath him is the secretary, also a purely political figure, responsible for the entire military organization. Below the secretary, the hierarchy divides into military and administrative components. The highest professional officer is the leading military adviser to the secretary and normally has command of the military forces. The military chief is subordinate to the secretary who is subordinate to the President, but neither of the two civilian officials exercise military command. Military command stops at the level of the military chief. Also subordinate to the secretary and administrative officials (civilian or military) who direct the nonmilitary supply, logistical, and financial activities of the department.

This balance pattern of organization tends to maximize military professionalism and civilian control.[21] Civilian and military responsibilities are clearly distinguished, and the latter are subordinated to the former. The President and the secretary handle political matters; the military chief military matters; and the staff or bureau chiefs administrative matters. The scope of the authority of the professional military chief is limited to the military realm by the administrative bureaus, and the level of his authority, subordinate to the secretary, does not involve him in political decisions. Administrative and military interests are balanced by the secretary under the authority of the President. English civil-military relations have been organized along comparable lines since the last half of the nineteenth century. Between 1794 and

*There are, of course, other possible structures of executive civil-military relations, such as one making a military officer departmental secretary. This analysis, however, will be confined to the three ideal types relevant to American experience. Although professional military men have occasionally been appointed Secretary of War, this is unusual and contrary to accepted practice. The only plan seriously advanced to put military men in the place of the secretary was the unsuccessful 1815 proposal to substitute a board of three naval officers for the Secretary of the Navy.

1870 the War Office administered the civilian affairs of the army, and the Commander in Chief, directly under the sovereign, was responsible for military command and discipline. In 1870, however, the Cabinet insisted that the military chief be subordinated to the Secretary of State for War. A fully balanced scheme was achieved with the abolition of the post of Commander in Chief in 1895 and the subsequent creation of the office of Chief of the Imperial General Staff. The same system also existed at the Admiralty. This organization was possible only because the sovereign consented, however reluctantly, to have his role as first general and admiral become, in Bagehot's phrase, a "dignified" part of the constitution. The "efficient" hierarchy of control ran from Parliament to Cabinet to Prime Minister to Secretary of State for War and then to the military chief and the administrative bureaus of the War Office. In the United States, however, no President has permitted his constitutional functions as Commander in Chief to atrophy. These remain efficient and not dignified. Consequently, the balanced pattern of organization has been difficult to achieve and even more difficult to maintain. American civil-military relations almost inevitably gravitate in the direction of other arrangements which tend to weaken military professionalism and civilian control.

The *coordinate scheme* involves the separation of military and administrative functions immediately below the President. The secretary is limited to nonmilitary administrative duties, and the military chief discharges his military functions directly under the President. The chain of administration goes from President to Secretary to bureau chiefs; the chain of command from President to military chief to the military forces. This accords with constitutional theory and keeps civilians, except the President, out of the military hierarchy. It tends, however, to undermine civilian control. The scope of the authority of the military chief is limited to military matters, but the level of his authority with direct access to the President involves him in political issues. The President is normally too busy with other affairs to devote sufficient attention to the interrelation of political and military policies, and the military chief consequently has to make political decisions. His direct access to the President also encourages the latter to try his hand at military affairs and to intervene in professional military planning and command where he has no special competence.

The *vertical pattern* solves the problem of the Commander in Chief clause in a different manner, but one which is equally inconsistent with civilian control. In this scheme the secretary and the military chief have identical responsibilities. The administrative bureau heads are subordinated to the professional military chief, and the professional military chief is subordinated to the secretary who is in turn responsible to the President. Since the President is still Commander in Chief, and some connection must exist between him and the rest of the military hierarchy, the secretary is given a place in the military chain of command and is described as the President's deputy commander in chief or in some similar terms. The military chief, however, is given control over all the activities of the department under the secretary, the specifically military command and planning functions being delegated down the hierarchy to a subordinate of the military chief's on the same level as the administrative chiefs of bureaus. This prevents the military chief from achieving direct access to the President because his responsibilities are identical with those of the secretary. Consequently, he can claim no peculiar relation to the President and must be subordinate to the secretary. On the other hand, he supervises all the activities of the department below the secretary and, consequently, may be able to reduce the secretary to a figurehead. By combining in his own person political and administrative responsibilities, as well as functions of military command, the military chief transgresses his competence. He sacrifices higher level for broader scope, which is equally damaging to his professional status. Also, the extension of the constitutional myth so that not only the President but also the secretary is assumed to exercise military command violates the facts of reality.

The American constitutional system thus does not facilitate the stable existence of a balanced pattern of executive civil-military relations. The President's power as Commander in Chief inevitably tends to push the executive structure in the direction of either the coordinate or the vertical pattern. The interests of the military chief leads him to seek both direct access to the President and over-all supervision of both the military and administrative aspects of his department. The secretary, on the other hand, attempts both to maintain exclusive access to the President and to have a multiplicity of subordinates reporting to him. Neither secretary nor military chief ever completely achieve their two objectives. The level and scope of military authority tend to be inversely related. Inevitably, the secretary tends to get cut off from his department by a military head who oversees both military and administrative aspects, or he tends to surrender the military aspect to the professional chief who maintains a direct command relationship with the President.

★ *Civilian Control and Constitutional Government*

Objective civilian control has existed in the United States but it has been the product of geographical isolation and the international balance of power, which permitted the virtual elimination of standing military forces and the exclusion of the military from political power. Civilian control in this sense has been so effective that Americans have called it a fundamental principle of their system of government. But they have been deluding themselves. They have ascribed to the Constitution a virtue of geography. Objective civilian control has been extraconstitutional, a part of our political tradition but not of our constitutional tradition. Civilian control has, in a sense, been like the party system. The Framers did not foresee the rise of popular democracy; consequently, they did not provide for political parties. They did not foresee the rise of the military profession; consequently, they did not provide for civilian control. Neither is contemplated in the Constitution, yet both have been called into existence by nonconstitutional forces. The Constitution has contributed its share to obstructing the growth of a strong party system such as exists in Great Britain. It has also contributed its share to obstructing effective civilian control such as exists in Great Britain. The restraints of a written constitution have proved effective against some of the most powerful functional imperatives.

The question thus arises: to what extent is it possible, short of amending the Constitution, to provide for civilian control in the existing framework? The difficulties are constant but they are not all of equal strength. The extent to which the Commander in Chief clause operates to damage civilian control depends largely upon the individuals who occupy that office. It adds nothing and detracts much from military professionalism and civilian control. The British Prime Minister who is not commander in chief and has no military functions has more effective control over his military forces than does the American President. The principal positive use of the clause has been to expand presidential power against Congress in nonmilitary areas. If the clause can come to be viewed primarily in this nonmilitary sense, and if the presidents can exercise constitutional self-restraint so as to make their military command of the armed forces as honorific as that of the king of England, this obstacle of civilian control would be removed, and a balanced pattern of executive organization be made workable.

The militia clauses only directly hamper the development of military professionalism in one segment of the armed forces. Conceivably, of course, Congress could abolish dual control over the militia. But in the face of the political strength of the National Guard this hardly seems possible. And, given the existing situation, it probably would not even be desirable. The more appropriate course is to make the best of the situation of military federalism. The existence of the Guard will necessarily prevent the development of a strong and ready national reserve organization. The Constitution has made the Guard into a powerful political force, and it is not inconceivable that this political strength may make the Guard into an effective military organization. At the end of 1954, the Army and Air National Guard has almost 400,000 men on drill pay status—twice the number of the Army and Air Force Reserves. At the beginning of 1956 Guard ground forces consisted of 21 infantry divisions, 6 armored division, 9 regimental combat teams, 9 armored cavalry regiments, 123 antiaircraft battalions, 74 field artillery battalions, and miscellaneous other units. The Air National Guard was organized into 27 combat wings. The readiness of the Guard was at a higher level than ever before in its history. Many of the antiaircraft units and interceptor squadrons were participating in the air defense of the nation on a semiactive alert status.[22] By its very nature the National Guard can never be brought fully within objective civilian control. But it may still be possible to create a respectable reserve force within the existing constitutional and political framework.

The real constitutional stumbling block to objective civilian control is the separation of powers. This is the essence of the American system of government, and its impact is felt throughout the armed forces. Short of fundamental constitutional change, the separation of powers cannot be altered. Indeed, it is highly questionable whether, even if such change were possible, it would be worth the price. There are values other than civilian control and military professionalism and these were the values the Framers had in mind when they wrote the Constitution. Foreign countries may have more effective systems of civilian control but no country has as effective a system of restraints upon arbitrary political power or such a unique balance of executive unity and legislative diversity. Inevitably, both military officers attempting to adhere to professional standards and civilian secretaries attempting to exercise civilian control look with envy to the cabinet system. Such a system, however, is not for the United States. Within the framework of the separation of powers, institutional adjustments can be made which will reduce its deleterious effects upon civilian control. But it will never be possible to eliminate these effects completely. A lessor measure of civilian control and lower standards of military professionalism are the continuing prices the American people will have to pay for the other benefits of their constitutional system.

★ **Samuel Huntington** *is the Eaton Professor of the Science of Government and Director of the John M. Olin Institute for Strategic Studies at Harvard University.*

Endnotes

[1]William Blackstone, *Commentaries on the Laws of England* (Oxford, 3rd ed., 4 vols., 1768), I, 407, 413–44.

[2]For the discussion of this clause, see Max Farrand (ed.), *The Records of the Federal Convention of 1787* (New Haven, 4 vols., 1911–1937), I, 380, II, 286–290; Jonathan Elliot (ed.), *The Debates in the Several Conventions* (Washington, 4 vols., 1836), III 372–373. For the few instances in which the clause has been invoked in practice, see *Hind's Precedents of the House of Representatives* (Washington, 1907), ch. XVI, and *Cannon's Precedents* (Washingtion, 1935), ch. 16.

[3]Farrand, *Records,* II, 326, 329–330, 563, 640, III, 207; Elliot, *Debates* I, 326, 328, 335, II, 77–80, 136–137, III, 381, 660, IV, 244; Charles Warren, *The Making of the Constitution* (Cambridge, 1947), pp. 474, 483; James Madison, No. 41, *The Federalist* (Modern Library ed.), pp. 262–263.

[4]Farrand, *Records,* I, 465, II, 385; No. 8, *The Federalist,* pp. 42–43; Elliot, *Debates,* II, 520–521, III, 169, 378, 410–411, Patrick Henry commented with respect to the nationalist claim: "This argument destroys itself. It demands a power, and denies the probability of its exercise."

[5]Farrand, *Records,* II, 136, 168, 182, 330, 385, II, 332; Elliot, *Debates,* III, 382, IV, 422–424.

[6]See Emory Upton, T*he Military Policy of the United States* (Washington, 1912), pp. 100-103; F. B. Wiener, "The Militia Clause of the Constitution," *Harvard Law Review,* LIV (December 1940), 192-193; Leonard D. White, *The Jeffersonians* (New York, 1951), pp. 540–541. Compare Washington's revolutionary difficulties. James B. Scott, *The Militia* (S. Doc. 695, 64th Cong., 2d Sess., 1917), pp. 25–26.

[7]F. P. Todd, "Our National Guard: An Intoduction to Its History," *Military Affairs,* V (Summer, Fall 1941), 73–86, 152–170, at pp. 162–163. Aside from these brief articles and a few law review pieces, little scholarly work has been done on the National Guard and the National Guard Assoication. There is a gold mine here for an enterprising student of American political history.

[8]*Official Proceedings of the Natl. Guard Assoc., 6th Annual Convention,* 1944, pp. 28–29, 44; *1948,* pp. 111, 242–244, 254–255; *1949,* pp. 202–210. For the Gray Board recommendations, see Committee on Civilian Components, *Reserve Forces for National Security* (Washingtion, 1948), pp. 9–24.

[9]*Statement of Policy Adopted by the Natl. Guard Assn. and the Adjutants General Assn. in Joint Convention,* Baltimore, May 4, 1944, pp. 1, 4; *Proceedings, NGA Convention, 1944,* p. 100; *1945,* pp. 65–66; *1946,* pp. 114–115; *1948,* p. 65; Public Administration Clearing House, *Public Administration Organizations, 1954* (Chicago, 1954), pp. 102, 119.

[10]*Proceedings, NGA Convention, 1943,* pp. 89, 93–96; *1945,* pp. 50–55.

[11]*Proceedings, NGA Convention, 1945,* p. 47; *1946,* p. 43; *1948,* pp. 34, 66, 80–81; *1950,* pp. 264–265; *1953,* pp. 299–290.

[12]*Proceedings, NGA Convention, 1943,* pp. 56, 67, 88; *1944,* pp. 44, 53, 55, 58, 65, 69, 73, 74; *1945,* p. 56; *1946,* pp. 28–32; *1948,* pp. 47–49, 57, 91–92; *1953,* p. 28; *Time,* LXIII (Mar. 1, 1954), 18.

[13]*Proceedings, NGA Convention, 1948,* pp. 33–34; *1950,* p. 245.

[14]For discussion of royal and parliamentary authority, see Blackstone, *Commentaries,* I, 257–258, 262, 412–413; J. S. Omond, *Parliament and the Army, 1642–1904* (Cambridge, 1933), pp. 7–8; John W. Fortescue, *A History of the British Army* (London, 13 vols., 1899–1930), II, 568. The Framers at first adopted *in toto* the language of the basic English statute, 13 Car. II, c. 6 (1661), but then realized that they could not make the President, like the king, commander in chief of the militia in peace as well as war. See Farrand, *Records,* I, 139–140, II, 185, 426–427; No. 69, *The Federalist,* p. 448. For the continuing debate as to whether the war power was properly legislative or executive, see Farrand, *Records,* I, 64–66; Alexander Hamilton, *Works* (New York, 12 vols., ed., by H. C. Lodge, 1904), IV, 145–146; James Madison, *Writings* (New York, 9 vols., 1900–1910), VI, 145; Clarence A. Berdahl, *War Powers of the Executive in the United States* (Urbana, Ill., 1921), p. 79. Compare W. W. Crosskey, *Politics and the Constitution* (Chicago, 2 vols., 1953), I, 422–428.

[15]Fleming v. Page, 9 How. 603, 615, 618 (1850). The powers of the British king as general of the kingdom extended to many nonmilitary areas. Blackstone, *Commentaries,* I, 262ff. For the views of the Framers on the Commander in Chief power, see Farrand, *Records,* I, 244, 292, II, 145, 319, 426-427, III, 624; Elliot, *Debates,* IV, 114; *The Federalist,* pp. 448, 482.

[16]For the boundaries between presidential and congressional military powers, see Edward S. Corwin, *The President: Office and Powers* (New York, 1948), ch. vi; Ex Parte Milligan, 4 Wall. 2 (1866); Berdahl, *War Powers, passim;* Howard White, *Executive Influence in Determining Military Policy in the United States* (Urbana, Ill., 1924), ch. iii; and R. G. Albion's interesting, in unconvincing, views, "The Naval Affairs Committee, 1816–1947," U.S. Naval Institute *Proceedings,* LXXVIII (November 1952), 1929.

[17]Quoted in T. H. Williams, "The Committee on the Conduct of the War: An Experiment in Civilian Control," *Jour. Amer. Mil. Institute,* III (Fall 1939), 141.

[18]Lloyd M. Short, *The Development of National Administrative Organization in the United States* (Baltimore, 1923), p. 119; Berdahl, *War Powers,* pp. 111–114; Upton, *Military Policy,* pp. 250–251; Pendleton Herring, *The Impact of War* (New York, 1941), pp. 141–142; Arthur A. Maass, *Muddy Waters: The Army Engineers and the Nation's Rivers* (Cambridge, Mass., 1951), *passim;* White, *Executive Influence,* pp. 237–238, 263; Otto L. Nelson, Jr., *National Security and the General Staff* (Washington, 1946), pp. 130–166; John Dickinson, *The Building of an Army* (New York, 1922), p. 320; Bradley A. Fiske, *From Midshipman to Rear Admiral* (New York, 1919), pp. 563–571.

[19]Donald W. Mitchell, *History of the Modern Ameican Navy from 1883 through Pearl Harbor* (New York, 1946), pp. 62–63.

[20]Farrand, *Records,* I, 244, III, 217–218, 624, IV, 53; Elliot, *Debates,* II, 408, 412, 522–523, III, 59–60, 496–498; Leonard D. white, *The Jeffersonians,* p. 220, and *The Jacksonians* (New York, 1954), pp. 51–57; Herring, *Impact of War,* pp. 146-147.

[21]The theoretical rationale of the balanced pattern was developed in A. T. Mahan, "The Princilpls of Naval Administration," *Naval Administration and Warfare* (Boston, 1908), pp. 3–48, and Spenser Wilkinson, Preface to the 2d edition of *The Brain of an Army* (London, 1913). Mahan's essay and Wilkinson's preface are brilliant analyses of executive military organization and are basic to an understanding of the subject.

[22]Secreatary of Defense, *Semiannual Report, July 1 to December 31, 1954,* p. 58; *New York Times,* January 13, 1956, p. 6; *New York Herald Tribune,* November 22, 1953, p. 1, Novemer 20, 1955, Sec. 2, p. 3.

★ ★ ★ ★ ★

Questions

1. What constitutional provisions involve the military?
2. What constitutional provisions disperse control of the military?
3. What constitutional provisions make the military susceptible to political pressure?
4. What constitutional provisions help military leaders to evade civilian control?
5. To what extent does civilian control hamper sound professional military practice?

★ ★ ★

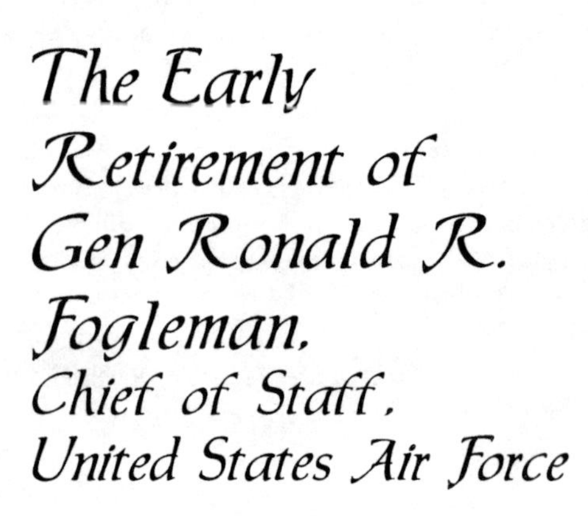

The Early Retirement of Gen Ronald R. Fogleman, Chief of Staff, United States Air Force

Edited by Dr. Richard H. Kohn*

Editorial Abstract: Air Force chief of staff Gen Ronald Fogleman's early retirement in 1997 has caused great speculation. Was this a "resignation in protest"? Here for the first time, in an interview with former Air Force historian Richard H. Kohn, General Fogleman explains his thinking and his reasons for choosing this unprecedented course of action.

On Monday, 28 July 1997, Gen Ronald R. Fogleman asked Secretary of the Air Force Sheila Widnall to be relieved of his duties as chief of staff of the Air Force and retired as soon as possible, a year before the end of his four-year term. At the time, the press and electronic media overwhelmingly

★ ★ ★ ★ ★ ★

*The editor thanks Jacqueline Gorman (University of North Carolina at Chapel Hill) for transcription of the interview tape; Jonathan Phillips (University of North Carolina at Chapel Hill) for research assistance with the introduction and annotation; and, for help in locating documents and specific items of information, Yvonne Kinkaid and Perry Jamieson (United States Air Force History Support Office), Elizabeth Muenger (Air Force Academy historian), Duane Reed and his staff (Air Force Academy Cadet Library Special Collections Department), and Barbara Levergood (Electronics Documents librarian, Davis Library, University of North Carolina at Chapel Hill).

Reprinted by permission from *Aerospace Power Journal*, Spring 2001.

interpreted General Fogleman's act as a resignation in protest over the secretary of defense's intention to block the promotion of Brig Gen Terryl "Terry" Schwalier to major general. Schwalier had commanded the 4404th Composite Wing in Saudi Arabia the previous year when a terrorist bomb had destroyed the Air Force housing complex known as Khobar Towers outside Dhahran Air Base, killing 19 airmen and wounding a total of some three hundred Americans. After one Department of Defense (DOD) and two Air Force investigations, Fogleman had concluded that Schwalier had done everything that could be expected of a commander and had no culpability in the tragedy; punishing him would have a chilling effect on commanders around the world who might then infer that protecting their forces outweighed accomplishing their missions.

Reports had circulated some weeks earlier that General Fogleman would resign if the secretary blocked Schwalier's promotion. But the truth of the matter was that General Fogleman's decision to leave was neither a resignation nor an act of protest; it was a retirement. Had he resigned in protest, he would have waited until after the secretary of defense announced his decision in the Schwalier case and explained publicly and unambiguously that the request for retirement was the product of disagreements over specific decisions and policies. Instead, General Fogleman chose to leave quietly. In a brief public statement written and issued the same day, the chief stated, "My values and sense of loyalty to our soldiers, sailors, Marines and especially our airmen led me to the conclusion that I may be out of step with the times and some of the thinking of the establishment. This puts me in an awkward position. If I were to continue to serve as chief of staff of the Air Force and speak out, I could be seen as a divisive force and not a team player. I do not want the Air Force to suffer for my judgment and convictions."

Until now, General Fogleman has not elaborated on or clarified that brief public statement he issued at the end of July 1997. His public statement at the time stated specifically that he "was driven by the desire to defuse the perceived confrontation between myself and the secretary of defense over his impending decision on the Khobar Towers terrorist attack." As he explains below, it "was a request for retirement versus a resignation.... My request was very carefully worded and consistent with historical practice and precedent.... I wanted to take that off the table and give him [the secretary of defense] one last opportunity to act on the Schwalier case on the merit and facts of the case, rather than the issue of the secretary of defense's power vis-à-vis some service chief." In leaving, General Fogleman recognized that a resignation in protest over policy would encroach on civilian control of the military, one of the foundations of American government and national defense, by setting a precedent that military leaders might resign instead of accepting a decision they opposed. Fogleman knew that there was no tradition or practice of resignation in protest in the United States military.

Indeed, the causes of General Fogleman's action were complex and lay rooted in a series of issues that went back many months. He had contemplated early retirement for at least a year and a half. "I said publicly from the beginning that Miss Jane [Mrs. Fogleman] and I considered being chief a four-year tour, not a sentence.... There were certain things that I intended to accomplish, and when they were done, I felt that I might want to leave rather than hang on. I had watched people hang on into that fourth year and just did not think it was value gained for them or the organization." Fundamentally, he believed that his continued service depended on his effectiveness as an adviser to the national leadership and as an advocate for, and leader of, his service. While he had good relationships with the other chiefs and the chairman and vice chairman of the joint chiefs, he was disappointed in some of the discussions and some of the positions taken by the group. There had been disagreements over the modernization of the tactical aircraft inventory of the Air Force, Navy, and Marines; he disagreed with the determination of the Quadrennial Defense Review in early 1997 to reduce the number of F-22 airplanes to be purchased and, worse, was disgusted by the process which produced the decision. There were other conflicts: "Some serious resource allocation decisions were being made on the basis of superficial, often mistaken, thinking." In the summer of 1997, General Fogleman clashed with Secretary Widnall over the punishment of 1st Lt Kelly Flinn, the first woman B-52 pilot, whose impending court-martial for adultery, disobeying orders, and lying to an investigating officer led to national headlines, much criticism of the Air Force, and her separation with a general rather than an honorable discharge.

Then came the Schwalier decision. "As chief of staff of the United States Air Force, charged with providing military advice to the civilian leadership that the civilian leadership did not value for whatever reason, I had become ineffective as a spokesman." "When you sense that you have lost the confidence of the folks you're dealing with—almost to the extent where the service will be punished—that's one reason to leave." Another was that General Fogleman had "simply lost respect and confidence in the leadership that I was supposed to be following." General Fogleman "watched the way the United States Air Force as an institution was treated, for purely political reasons, and the way an individual was treated and came to the conclusion that it was fundamentally wrong." He remembered, "You really do have to get up and look at yourself in the mirror every day and ask, 'Do I feel honorable and clean?' I just could not begin to imagine facing the Air Force after Secretary [William S.] Cohen made the decision to cancel General Schwalier's promotion. It wasn't only Cohen. It was the Washington scene, the pressure from the Hill—from people who were uninformed—it was the way DOD treated this man and the Air Force. To merely shrug this off and say, 'Hey, it's okay, guys, we'll do better next time....' "

General Fogleman had also recently read H. R. McMaster's *Dereliction of Duty: Lyndon Johnson, Robert McNamara, the Joint Chiefs of Staff, and the Lies That Led to Vietnam,* a book detailing how the joint chiefs in 1964–65 had failed to insist on giving their advice directly to the president and had gone along with having their views misrepresented, thus contributing to the decision to intervene in Vietnam and pursue a strategy of gradual escalation. "There was the incredible performance of the joint chiefs at that time and then seeing some of the things that were going on in the tank and now, maybe not on the same scale, but the same sickness...service parochialism, the willingness to collectively go along with something because there was at least some payoff for your service somewhere in there...a slippery slope."

Thus, as General Fogleman makes clear below, he had come to believe that he could no longer serve effectively as chief of staff. "I felt out of step—the [Quadrennial Defense Review], discussions, and decisions that I saw being made in the tank, problems with the Air Force leadership over the Kelly Flinn affair. A whole series of things convinced me that perhaps I was riding the wrong horse here. After a while, you look around and experience some serious doubts about whether you can be right and everybody else is wrong." As he concluded, "We also serve on a personal level. Unless you really believe, and see, that you are continuing to contribute..., when you begin to believe that your continued service is detrimental," then "the pressure" is to leave. "In my heart, I concluded that my continued service was not in the best interest of the Air Force."

In December 1997, some four-and-a-half months after his decision, the editor interviewed General Fogleman by telephone. What follows is a transcript of that conversation, transcribed by Ms. Jacqueline Gorman of the Curriculum in Peace, War, and Defense of the University of North Carolina at Chapel Hill. The transcript was then edited, reviewed by General Fogleman, annotated by the editor, and returned to General Fogleman for final approval. The purpose of publishing it is to clarify why he took the unprecedented step of asking for early retirement and doing so with so little explanation at the time—not resigning in protest but leaving out of a sense of obligation that the Air Force and the nation would be served more effectively if a new chief of staff were to take his place.

★ *Interview*

11 December 1997

Richard H. Kohn: General Fogleman, why did you decide to ask for early retirement?

Ronald R. Fogleman: The answer to that question is complex: on one level, simple, but on another, more complicated. Let me begin on one level. When I became the chief, I received a number of letters from people like you who essentially said that they thought the chief needed to restore the soul of the Air Force. That caught me somewhat by surprise because I was not sure exactly what the soul of the Air Force was, or what was required to fix it. But my conclusion was that somehow we had found ourselves, or allowed ourselves, through a series of decisions and actions, to lose sight of our values. The trouble came not from some overriding set of principles, but more from employing situational ethics (i.e., cronyism and other things) that made it seem as though the institution lacked integrity. So in the back of my mind, there seemed a necessity, or charge if you will, to work this issue on my watch.

Another factor grew out of a meeting in the fall of 1994 with all the other four-stars, before I became the chief, in which we discussed what we thought the Air Force needed more than anything else in the near term.[1] We concluded generally that the Air Force had been through an extraordinary period of change, most of it necessary in the altered world where we were heading. The change was both externally and internally driven. But it would be extremely valuable if we could give the Air Force some stability for a period of time from internal turbulence.

These two elements lay in the background as I began my tenure—my tour, if you will. I looked very carefully at the law specifying my duties as chief of staff: the responsibilities relative to organizing, training, and equipping the force and the separation of duties between the secretary of the Air Force and the chief.[2] So as I began the job, I thought I had a good understanding of what needed to be done in the Air Force. I did not have any special agenda. As we kicked off the tour, we ran into a series of things that we had to deal with: changing the uniform and a lack of confidence in the personnel system, promotions, and the evaluation system.[3] I think our decisions in these areas were generally very well received.

I had also inherited two pieces of unfinished business. One was the F-15 shoot-down of the Black Hawk helicopter over Iraq.[4] The other one was the B-52 crash up at Fairchild.[5] The F-15 shoot-down was making its way through the legal process, and there wasn't much I could do about it until the process called for my action.

As I dealt with day-to-day business, stabilizing the Air Force (in terms of internal changes), I continued to think about the soul of the Air Force as an issue. As I dealt with these issues, the stress on accountability emerged—without my intending at the beginning of my watch to focus on accountability. At the completion of the court-martial of the AWACS captain at Tinker (I had been reading all the background investigation material), I was satisfied that the outcome was appropriate and just: no one was court-martialed who should not have been, or vice-versa, or issued letters of reprimand, Article 15s, and so forth.[6] But I was appalled when I asked the question, "Let me see the evaluation reports on the people." I discovered that none of what they had done was reflected in those reports, and from that, I then began to see the connectivity to standards, values, and core beliefs.[7] That's when I made the tape[8] in which I talked about Air Force values and accountability—not because I was some zealot, but because I have always believed that if you want people, or an institution, to do something, you must explain what you expect of their behavior. The rules and standards for the behavior of any individual, group, or unit must be universally known and uniformly applied. That tape was designed for an internal audience, but it got much more play than that, and from then on, I believe we began to see a change all through the chain of command on the issue of accountability. If anything, it may have started to go too far. Commanders were deferring to lawyers rather than taking action, short of legal action, to correct the shortcomings of people. As I continued to work on other things that I thought were very important—the long-range planning effort for one—this issue of accountability and standards took on a kind of life of its own. The secretary of the Air Force and I emphasized very strongly the ideas of core values: excellence in all we do, service before self, and integrity.[9] These became identified with me and with the secretary, but largely with me. This is important background leading up to the events of 1997.

On another level—viewing the Air Force from the outside as a military historian,[10] as someone who has tried to stay involved in academic affairs as well as national security affairs—I sincerely believed that the nation was at a unique crossroads, that the country had a tremendous number of internal needs, that the external threats were lower than we had faced in half a century, and that we had an opportunity—if we could have a serious discussion about national security strategy and defense issues—to restructure our military into a smaller, better focused institution to respond to the kinds of challenges coming in the next 10 to 15 years. It was not a military that was going to be shaped by some force-structure slogan like two MRCs,[11] and it had to include a fundamental understanding of whether there really was a "revolution in military affairs" and how we could and should fight future wars. So I had begun to speak out about the Quadrennial Defense Review,[12] and I was hopeful that the QDR would start us down that path.

In this regard, in "the tank"[13] I began to question some of the things that we were doing, or that we were planning to do, based on old paradigms—but not very successfully. As we began talking more and more about the QDR, an event occurred in September of 1996 which kind of put the QDR in a context that struck me as all wrong. An Army two-star from the JCS came by to see all the chiefs, and when he came to see me, he sat on that couch in the chief's office and said, "I have a message from the chairman,[14] and the message is, that in the QDR we want to work hard to try and maintain as close to the status quo as we can. In fact, the chairman says we don't need any Billy Mitchells during this process." That shocked me a little bit. I replied, "Well, that's an unfortunate use of a term, but I understand the message." From that point on, I really did not have much hope for the QDR. I guess I lost all hope when Bill Perry[15] left because he had the stature to have given the services the blueprint, and I think the services would have fallen in line.

Kohn: Did you or the other chiefs ask Secretary Perry to stay or to press for that?

Fogleman: I did. I went to see him in early November of 1996, after completing my second year in office. I had a policy of visiting him to talk about the year in review and the future. There were strong rumors that he would go. I told him, "Mr. Secretary, you have the stature and you have the confidence and the vote; if the QDR is going to go anywhere, you need to come down to the tank, and you need to give us your vision." Short of that, I said I didn't have much hope. A week later, he announced his retirement.

Secretary Cohen faced a very difficult challenge in the QDR and was, quite frankly, not as well grounded in real military issues as one might have thought, given his time on the Senate Armed

Services Committee.[16] He worked hard but was at the mercy, like all of us, of his advisers, and particularly what I thought was a rather close circle of people who lacked much experience in the issues. Once Bill Perry left, work on the QDR went into suspended animation until Cohen arrived because no one wanted to get out in front of the new boss. He arrived with a very limited amount of time to deliver the QDR to the Hill, a difficult challenge. I came to believe that the QDR could not be completed in three months, or even six. To an extent, he tried to solicit the advice of his military people, but it became clear that this QDR was to be more a political response than a sincere effort to reshape our military. It was driven by the consideration to come up with $60 billion in savings to apply to the procurement of new weapons. From an Air Force perspective, we had no problem with procurement reform; our modernization program was fully funded, fully budgeted, so it was interesting to watch this unfold. The major issue that concerned me was TACAIR modernization.[17] This issue had been inflamed by Bill Owens,[18] who had incorrectly quoted some statistics that got over onto the Hill and into the public about how large a part of the budget the TACAIR program would consume vis-à-vis other things. This line of argument took on a life of its own. If you look at the history of TACAIR, anytime the amateurs mess with it, it gets screwed up; and when the pros put together a program and follow through, the result is a pretty solid program.

Kohn: Do you mean the design of the aircraft, its requirements, its role, and its mission?

Fogleman: Exactly. After the Second World War, the Navy, in its battles internally over carrier air, essentially allowed their program to atrophy. The Air Force, on the impetus from Arnold[19] and the others who came after him, worked very hard to achieve a balanced program. When Korea[20] came along, the Air Force had an air superiority fighter, a fighter-bomber, bomber forces coming on stream. In the air superiority realm, there are many similar experiences in the past. In Korea, who had the aces? Who did the daytime patrolling? It wasn't that there weren't great naval aviators or great Marine aviators, but the Navy did not have equipment since they had been diverted to thinking about things other than the core issue of airpower. Who thinks about airpower full-time for the nation? The Air Force.

After Korea, TACAIR lost to the domination of nukes. So the Air Force began building fighter-bombers like F-105s. The Navy studied airplanes like Vigilantes that could deliver tactical nukes off of carriers. The US did not possess an air superiority fighter when Vietnam began.[21] We did a dismal job in Vietnam in the air-to-air business and used not an air-to-air fighter but a missile platform, the F-4, and it became the backbone of the forces. But it was never a great air superiority fighter.

Kohn: Was the issue at this time (1996 and 1997) the F-22?

Fogleman: No, the whole TACAIR program, not just a single aircraft. But eventually it came down to that, and so we took a fully funded program, the F-22, into the QDR, whereupon the folks at OSD [Office of the Secretary of Defense] decided to make major disruptions in this program for no good reason at all.[22] On the one hand you have somebody who is fairly well grounded in the airpower business giving advice to the senior leadership, and on the other side a bunch of number crunchers, and in the end, the decision gets made, I think, on political grounds more than anything else.

Kohn: How did this differ from most major aircraft programs or even most major defense issues, historically and in the last 20 years? Isn't what you describe the nature of the business—in "the building" [the Pentagon], in the budget process, and in programming?

Fogleman: Yes, in the macro sense. But in the micro sense, I'm not so sure because of the internal nature of the debate. If somebody can show me that something makes sense from a resource allocation or budgetary standpoint, or similarly reasonable measures, I'm more than willing to lose the argument—and have lost lots of those arguments, walked away none the worse for wear. But this was an issue in which the nature of the presentation, the nature of the discussion, and the rationale for the changes, were basically going to upset an integrated tactical air modernization program that included the F-18, the Joint Strike Fighter, and the F-22. I think just fundamentally, OSD ignored the military rationale.

Kohn: Is it inconsistent to speak about a fundamental restructuring of the armed forces, in part to prepare for a possible revolution in warfare and a lower threat than at any time since the 1920s, while advocating a modernization program that looks to many on the outside as incremental: that is, purchasing some old technologies, even purchasing the newest technology (the F-22), which could, perhaps, be skipped? How would you respond to that criticism?

Fogleman: If this was argued by someone in OSD, I would ask if they knew the true capability of this airplane. In the "black world" [very highly classified programs], the F-22 is a truly revolutionary airplane. On the surface, it looks conventional, like an F-15 with some stealth capabilities. But the combination of stealth, supercruise, and integrated avionics is a quantum jump. It will allow the United States to cease worrying about air superiority for the first 35 years of the next century. With air superiority so critical to everything we do and considering the double-digit SAMs [surface-to-air missiles] of the next 10 to 15 years, it looks like a program we must have. One of the side benefits of the end of the cold war was our gaining access to foreign weapons; we discovered that the SA-10s, -11s, and -12s are much better than we thought. In planning for asymmetrical warfare—people's ability to deny us things we need in such situations as the Taiwan Strait crisis, when we sent two carriers in and watched the Chinese move their SA-10s up—we need that airplane.[23] Those two carriers did nothing more than make a political statement, which is fine as long as that is all that's necessary. So one understands why a service chief begins saying he will try and be as balanced in his tour as he possibly can be, as joint, but then a weapon system comes along that truly is revolutionary. There are only two revolutionary weapon systems in the entire DOD budget: the F-22 and the airborne laser.[24] There are no others. I will acknowledge that I may be wrong on this, but I don't think so. I guess my problem was arguing from facts and knowledge and finding decisions being made by people without a fundamental understanding of what the weapon system contributed. Somehow that just didn't strike me as right.

Kohn: In the past, some of your predecessors and some other service chiefs would have taken this fight into the bureaucratic world of beltway and national politics. They would have leaked, they would have struggled, they would have made allies, they would have gone to the Congress....

Fogleman: I think I did a lot of fighting in that arena. That's how we were able to get a lot of the funds restored. And the fight is not over. We will get the F-22, but the issue from my perspective was this: you pay me to give you military advice, and I'm giving you military advice; I'm watching not just whether or not you take it but how the advice is considered, part of a larger web of what became my relationship with Secretary Cohen and OSD.

Kohn: Can you translate this background into the decision to retire early?

Fogleman: Let me draw one more thread, one more part of the equation: Khobar Towers.[25] My side of that story has not been well told. I watched with great interest as that event happened and subsequent events unfolded. I watched people in Washington make statements on the basis of no factual knowledge whatsoever. I waited for about a week until after all the high-profile people had gone through Dhahran and then went to Saudi Arabia myself. I sat down with the commander,[26] listened to what he had to say—to include his offering to retire to remove any kind of a target for people to attack both the institution and individuals. I told him at that time that I did not want him to retire but to get the facts out. "This goes beyond you. This is an important issue having to do with whether we support our troops in the field when we send them out there, and if you have screwed up, you can expect to be held accountable. If you haven't, then I will support you." I then watched the way the investigations unfolded.[27] I watched the way the United States Air Force as an institution was treated, for purely political reasons, and the way an individual was treated and came to the conclusion that it was fundamentally wrong. I think a hell of a lot of other people came to that same conclusion.

As chief of staff of the United States Air Force, charged with providing military advice to the civilian leadership that the civilian leadership did not value for whatever reason, I had become ineffective as a spokesman. This was a crowd that took any kind of military advice that ran counter to administration policy or desires as a sign of disloyalty on the part of the person providing the advice. That was one element; the other was based on what I had seen and the way the Khobar Towers tragedy had been handled. I simply lost respect and confidence in the leadership that I was supposed to be following.

Kohn: By this do you mean OSD?

Fogleman: Yes.

Kohn: JCS, too?

Fogleman: Not so much the JCS, although I was disappointed in the JCS. There were some discussions and decisions in the tank that I thought were just absolutely absurd, some at fairly high levels of classification. More and more in the tank I found myself being the one who was raising the b- - - - - - - flag, and it resulted in a couple of fairly high-profile articles on arms control—things of that nature—that made some of the civilian leadership uncomfortable.[28]

Kohn: Relative to theater ballistic missile and strategic nuclear defense?

Fogleman: Yes, both.

Kohn: Did your disenchantment with the leadership extend to the president, the NSC [National Security Council], or Congress?

Fogleman: I don't think so. I had one confidant within the NSC with whom I would talk occasionally. This really did not involve the president; frankly, my dealings with the president, both as a CINC[29] and as a service chief, led me to conclude that he executed his commander-in-chief responsibilities pretty well, at least his interface with the military. As a service chief, your primary responsibility is to advocate for your service, and when you sense that you have lost the confidence of the folks you're dealing with—almost to the extent where the service will be punished—that's one reason to leave. Then there was the internal pressure which says: here's a guy who has talked about integrity, talked about doing what's right, talked about taking care of the troops and all of these things, and you realize that the secretary of defense is going to make a decision that is just fundamentally wrong.

Kohn: Many people believed that perhaps General Schwalier should not be punished, but promoting him after such a disaster seemed to fly in the face of any sense of accountability. How would you respond to that point, and who, if anyone, should be held accountable for the Khobar Towers disaster?

Fogleman: Well, I recognized, and I think General Schwalier recognized, everybody recognized, that no matter what happened, his career was over. This was a man who had, at the tactical and operational levels, done everything reasonable (and beyond) to protect his troops. Have you seen an article by Matt Labash in the November 24, 1997 issue of The Weekly Standard?

Kohn: No.

Fogleman: Labash has done as fine a job of researching and reporting on Khobar Towers as I have seen anywhere.

Kohn: Does that article explain your view of what really happened and who should be held accountable, if anyone?

Fogleman: Yes.[30]

Kohn: When did you first consider the idea of leaving office early?

Fogleman: First of all, I said publicly from the very beginning that Miss Jane and I considered being chief a four-year tour, not a sentence. I had not been the choice of the Air Force to become chief. Frankly, that had a sort of liberating effect on me because I felt I could deal on a different level with the secretary. There were certain things that I intended to accomplish, and when they were done, I felt that I might want to leave rather than hang on. I had watched people hang on into that fourth year and just did not think it was value gained for them or the organization.

Kohn: That they had ceased to be effective?

Fogleman: Yes. They were going through the motions rather than working for the good of the institution.

Kohn: Were some other items involved in your decision to leave early? Perhaps one was personnel issues, such as the pilot shortage, the lower retention of airmen, the promotion system, the dominance of below-the-zone promotions, and the difficulties of the OER [Officer Efficiency Report] system, a lot of which were related to the ops tempo of the force. Were frustrations in those areas at all involved?

Fogleman: No. In fact, those were what I considered unfinished business and really argued against leaving because early on in the tour, we addressed the issues of confidence in the OER and personnel system.[31] We did that very openly, and we seemed to put that stuff to rest.

The real challenges that I saw facing us as I got ready to step over the side was pilot retention, and we put into place nine months before I left, some of the actions that are starting to bear fruit now, specifically the ops tempo problem.[32] We have worked that in several ways. We went to the chairman and got relief from the responsibility for some weapon systems.[33] One of the ideas that I was disappointed did not succeed (although I knew it could) was the Air Expeditionary Force. We wanted to demonstrate to the CINCs that because of technology and logistics—mobility—forces did not have to be stationed in deserts to be responsive within 36 or 48 hours. We could demonstrate that the Air Force had the capability to deploy very rapidly and had several times. We were just on the verge of getting to that next step.

But what frustrated me was that some serious resource-allocation decisions were being made on the basis of superficial, often mistaken, thinking.

Kohn: Was your relationship with Secretary Widnall involved in the decision?

Fogleman: I think we generally had a good relationship right up to the Kelly Flinn controversy.[34] Until then, I thought the Air Force senior leadership, both civilian and military, understood the issue of accountability and how important it was to apply the UCMJ [Uniform Code of Military Justice] universally. I don't know what pressure Secretary Widnall was getting, but I came into work one morning, and she indicated that she was contemplating an honorable discharge for Kelly Flinn. I said, "Madam Secretary, if you give her an honorable discharge, you can also select a new chief of staff." That was the only time I ever talked that way to any direct supervisor or leader because I felt so strongly about it.

Kohn: The Flinn case sounds like one more drip on the forehead, moving you towards something that you had been thinking about increasingly for six months or so previous to the decision.

Fogleman: Yes. The Flinn case was a cut-and-dried thing as far as I was concerned, and I had studied the facts intensively.

Kohn: Was Gen Joseph Ralston's failure to be appointed chairman of the JCS part of the decision at all?[35]

Fogleman: No, not really, although it was a great personal and professional disappointment because we had worked for a long time to give him an opportunity. First of all, he was the right person for the job. Secretary Cohen was more a victim of circumstance than anything else. I don't have harsh feelings about this.

Kohn: What historical precedents guided you in the decision? Did Vietnam, and particularly H. R. McMaster's book *Dereliction of Duty,* influence you?[36]

Fogleman: Yes, I did read that book, as you know, and I must say that it did play a part. History is a series of events, and when you analyze major crises and reconstruct chains of events, asking, what could someone have done at one point or another that might have changed the outcome, you are encouraged to act. There was the incredible performance of the joint chiefs at that time, and then seeing some of the things that were going on in the tank and now, maybe not on the same scale, but the same sickness...service parochialism, the willingness to collectively go along with something because there was at least some payoff for your service somewhere in there.

Kohn: In other words, horse-trading and being bought off.

Fogleman: Yes, and it is a slippery slope.

Kohn: How would your leaving alter that equation?

Fogleman: In two ways. One is personal; you really do have to get up and look at yourself in the mirror every day and ask, "Do I feel honorable and clean?" I just could not begin to imagine facing the Air Force after Secretary Cohen made the decision to cancel General Schwalier's promotion. It wasn't only Cohen. It was the Washington scene, the pressure from the Hill—from people who were uninformed—it was the way DOD treated this man and the Air Force. To merely shrug this off and say, "Hey, it's okay guys, we'll do better next time...." It wasn't just the Air Force. The other services' commanders—lieutenant commanders, Marines, Army types—were really watching this case. People who are or will be out there as tactical commanders are a lot less comfortable today than they were before this decision. They may not have read the detailed reports, but I think they've read the articles. There was an incredibly large number of people at Dhahran, and what is interesting is the number of letters I received from various locations around the world, from people who were there sometime during that year, who watched the kinds of actions and preparations that were being taken. These people exist almost as emissaries within other organizations. In the same way morale is established and affected—you know, the whisper factor, not a major force but they are there—this will affect our military forces.

You asked a larger question: what difference will it make? No one has told me this, but as I have sat and observed what has occurred in Washington since my departure, I can give one example of how my leaving may have made a major difference or had some influence, and that is the big debate about whether the United States would sign the land-mine treaty.[37] This was an item that the service chiefs cared very deeply about. We said, "Look, these things are critical to us in Korea, and while we are committed to working for some replacement, to allow some very altruistic motive to put our forces in the field at risk is wrong." And so we had consistently opposed signing the treaty. But about the time I made my decision to leave, tremendous pressure was being exerted by people within the NSC and elsewhere, and it began to have a telling effect, I think, on the chiefs because we were about to get beat up worldwide in the media over the US not going to Ottawa to sign the big treaty. My departure may have alerted people to remember to pay attention, every now and then, to the military judgment of the chiefs because those guys over there have other options than to sit still and take their licks. I can't prove that, but I suspect it very strongly. I think the politicians were reluctant to take on the chiefs because they didn't want somebody else to step over the side.

Kohn: Whom did you consult about your decision and when? What, in general, did your advisers say?

Fogleman: I really did not consult. To the extent that I talked to anybody, I corresponded with you by e-mail and with Perry Smith.[38] This was a very personal decision. When I left home that morning, I had not made the decision to submit my request for early retirement. When I went to work that morning, Miss Jane and I had talked about it over the weekend. It was Monday, the 28th of July (I had recently returned from a trip overseas). I don't think there was any one thing that day that triggered it. It was just that when I went in, and sat there, and thought about events—saw what was coming up, looking down the road—I decided I was going to preempt the decision on the Khobar Towers so that my leaving would not be in response to the decision on General Schwalier, to defuse that conflict.

Kohn: You did not want your request to be seen as a reaction to Khobar Towers?

Fogleman: Correct. And, in fact, the reason it was a request for retirement versus a resignation is that it was consistent with everything that I had said up to that date—which was, this is a tour and not a sentence. My request was very carefully worded and consistent with historical practice and precedent.[39]

Kohn: So you do not view your departure as a resignation in protest?

Fogleman: No.

Kohn: You wrote specifically about stepping aside to avoid a perceived conflict with the secretary of defense. What, exactly, did you mean and have in mind?

Fogleman: There had been stories in the media that I had gone to the secretary of defense and threatened to resign if he canceled Schwalier's promotion.[40] That was simply untrue, but the secretary being a political animal and having watched him respond more to press stories than to the intel briefings, the perception of a conflict was clearly going to affect his decision. So I wanted to take that off the table and give him one last opportunity to act on the Schwalier case on the merit and facts of the case, rather than the issue of the secretary of defense's power vis-à-vis some service chief.

Kohn: Was there anything further that you hoped to accomplish by stepping down, beyond what you have said previously about losing your effectiveness with the civilian leadership and timing the request to avoid a confrontation?

Fogleman: My statement to the troops captured my perspective in very general terms.[41] I felt out of step—the QDR, discussions and decisions that I saw being made in the tank, problems with the Air Force leadership over the Kelly Flinn affair. A whole series of things convinced me that perhaps I was riding the wrong horse here. After a while, you look around and experience some serious doubts about whether you can be right and everybody else is wrong.

Kohn: Are there guidelines under which military leaders working directly for the highest civilians can—appropriately—request early retirement? Did you consider the precedent you might be setting and try to think through what is proper and what is improper in our system of government?

Fogleman: I thought it through to this extent: when you reach that level, you are a product of all your years, and hopefully one of the reasons you are appointed is that people recognize that you possess some kind of internal moral compass and some expertise in the profession of arms in a democracy. I was not thinking about trying to establish some future norm; I was thinking about it more in terms of my own personal views and perspectives on the substance of my service as chief of staff. I think I was selected because folks thought I knew something about the business and that I stood for certain values. When you reach a point in your tenure where (1) you think you've accomplished most of the things that you set out to do and (2) you begin to see evidence that your values and your advice, your expertise, are not valued by those in charge.... Having spent three tours in Washington, I have watched how people can be gracefully continued in a position but just frozen out of any kind of effective participation. Knowing how bad that is for an institution, it is better to step aside and let the leadership appoint someone who they are more comfortable with, who will be able to represent the institution and play in the arena.

Kohn: Why did you choose a retirement ceremony in Colorado rather than in Washington, D.C.?

Fogleman: Well, first, I was in Colorado [establishing residence after leaving Washington on terminal leave] and, second, I was the first Air Force chief of staff to graduate from the Academy. It seemed to complete a circle for me.

Kohn: The location was not a statement about not wanting the Washington establishment to be present at your retirement?

Fogleman: No, it really wasn't.

Kohn: Why have you remained silent about leaving until now? Do you plan to write anything or grant other interviews?

Fogleman: No I don't, particularly, and I have grave misgivings about this interview. Perhaps, some day, I may want to write something, but I am not sure that (1) I would be able to present this in a way that made any sense, and (2) I do not consider myself to be bearing any particular cross. I don't believe anybody out there is breathlessly awaiting the Ron Fogleman story. That's just sort of my take on all of this. This may be a story that does not need to be told.

Kohn: Reflect on the pressures in the Office of Chief of Staff in general. Would you do anything differently in your approach, style, or relationships in the office as you look back upon it now?

Fogleman: It's kind of interesting. I don't know if I would categorize this as the pressures of the office, but I had never really thought about the fact that the senior military guy in a service finds himself in a unique position. As you come up through the ranks, if you are the A Flight commander and somebody screws up in A Flight, you are responsible for that. But you are also in a position to take some direct action to try to fix that; the squadron is not necessarily harmed by what happened in A Flight, nor the wing or higher echelons. Think of it at every level. If you are the squadron commander, or the wing commander, the responsibility is finite, and the impact of decisions or disciplinary actions or whatever is always finite, all the way up through and including commanding a major command. In other words, as you look at the institution, if you happen to be in C

Flight and someone messed up in A Flight, you felt a little sorry for the A Flight commander, but there was never any blow to you personally, or to your beliefs. When I was the Air Mobility Command commander and I read something about an event in Air Combat Command or Materiel Command, I thought, "I'm sure glad that's not happening in my command; I wonder what I can do to help them." The problem is for that commander. But for the chief of staff of the Air Force, no matter where something happens within your institution, it's a personal blow for you. When you see both accurate and inaccurate representations of events in the media, it's a different kind of feeling.

The Washington routine never pressured me greatly. I knew when I went there that my job was to deal with the Washington scene. That was my job. As I moved from one position to another in my career, I tried to read the job description, bring to bear all the expertise that I developed through the years, and apply it to the current job and not worry about the fact that I'm no longer wearing a G suit, or in the case of the chief of staff, no longer in command. And so Miss Jane and I, I don't think, found it onerous from that perspective.

Kohn: You felt you were prepared for the job? Three tours in Washington, having the historical perspective, ready both by experience and personality.

Fogleman: I never felt any trepidation from that perspective. I remember a social occasion when General Piotrowski was the Ninth Air Force commander.[42] Someone was flattering him and asked, "Well, General Pete, what did you do to prepare yourself to be the Ninth Air Force commander? How did you do that?" General Piotrowski thought for a moment and then replied, "I did it one day at a time." I think that's how you find yourself in whatever job you are in; you prepare yourself one day at a time.

Kohn: My last question is a tough one, Ron. You have been a very respected and popular chief. But there are people in the force who are unhappy with your decision to step down. They disagree with you, feel a sense of loss and in some very few cases, perhaps, even a sense of betrayal. They—officer and enlisted—identified with you, believed that you were in step. If you think you were out of step, then they think they are out of step also. How are they supposed to carry on? Do you have any thoughts for them?

Fogleman: I may not have a good answer. But I go back to our ethic that says we serve on two levels. First, we serve as part of a profession: service before self, integrity, strive for excellence in all that you do. From this perspective, the answer is that it doesn't matter what happens. You ignore it. You keep soldiering on, you just keep slugging away. But we also serve on a personal level. Unless you really believe, and feel, that you are continuing to contribute to the Air Force and thus to the country and to the national defense, when you begin to believe that your continued service is detrimental to the Air Force, the pressure is in the opposite direction. Then the institution becomes more important than the individual, and, looking at the core value of service before self, the choice becomes staying another year and going through the motions or stepping down. In my heart, on the personal level and on the professional level, I concluded that my continued service was not in the best interest of the Air Force, in Washington where I was serving, given my beliefs, and considering the advice I was offering to our national leadership.

Notes

[1]The day before taking office, General Fogleman met in the secretary of the Air Force's conference room in the Pentagon with the other Air Force four-stars, who were in Washington to attend the retirement of his predecessor.

[2]The duties of the Air Force chief of staff are specified in *U.S. Code,* Title 10, chap. 805, sec. 8033 (1996).

[3]General Fogleman's predecessor, Gen Merrill "Tony" McPeak, had overseen what many considered a radical change in the style and insignia of the Air Force uniform. A uniform board review in January 1995 reduced over twenty-five hundred suggestions to 363 proposals, 55 of which General Fogleman approved, including restoring the traditional shoulder insignia instead of sleeve rings to identify officer rank. See Suzann Chapman, "Last Uniform Changes?" *Air Force Magazine* 78 (May 1995): 24; and "Air Force Announces Uniform Changes," *Air Force News,* on-line, Internet, 11 September 2000, available from "http://www.af.mil/news/Mar1995/n19950313_208.html".

[4]On 14 April 1994, two F-15Cs of the 53d Fighter Squadron enforcing the "no fly" zone over northern Iraq mistakenly shot down two Army Black Hawk helicopters engaged in UN humanitarian missions for the Kurds, killing all 26 passengers, including 15 Americans; five Kurdish civilians; and British, French, and Turkish military officers. John F. Harris, "Four May Receive Court-Martial for Copter Mishap," Washington Post, 30 August 1994, 2; and Eric Schmitt, "Inquiry Urges Crew Stand Trial in Downing of Copters over Iraq," *New York Times,* 30 August 1994, A2.

[5]On 24 June 1994, a B-52H of the 325th Bomb Squadron, 92d Bomb Wing at Fairchild Air Force Base (AFB), Wash., crashed while preparing to land after practicing maneuvers for an air show, killing all four crewmen. The pilot in command had over a long period of time demonstrated a disregard for Air Force flying rules and regulations, and this was known by the senior commanders in the wing. No appropriate action had been taken to discipline him or rein in his noncompliant behavior.

[6]Investigations by the Air Force resulted in charges of dereliction of duty against Capt James Wang, a crew member of the airborne warning and control system (AWACS) aircraft from the 963d Airborne Control Squadron controlling the airspace at the time, and charges of negligent homicide and dereliction of duty against one of the F-15 pilots and four other AWACS crew members. Captain Wang was acquitted, and charges against the others were dropped following Article 32 (the equivalent to grand jury) investigations. Altogether, eight officers were reprimanded, counseled, or admonished, and one punished nonjudicially. See news briefing, Maj Gen Nolan Sklute, Office of the Assistant Secretary of Defense (Public Affairs), 15 August 1995, on-line, Internet, 26 November 2000, available from http://www.defenselink.mil/news/Aug1995/t081795_tsklu-81.html; Susanne M. Schafer, "U.S. Pilot Charged for Downing Copters," *Chicago Sun Times,* 8 September 1994, 3; Owen Canfield, "Air Force Closes Case on 26 Deaths," *Chicago Sun Times,* 21 June 1995, 26; Frank Oliveri, "USAF Accuses Six in Iraq Shootdown," *Air Force Magazine* 77 (November 1994): 15; and Bruce B. Auster, "Strange Justice, Air Force Style," *U.S. News & World Report* 118 (15 May 1995): 42, 44. Article 15 of the *Uniform Code of Military Justice* outlines the punishments commanders can impose on the men and women under their command without resort to court-martial or other judicial proceedings.

[7]In August 1995, General Fogleman (in the words of the Air Force judge advocate general) "concluded that the failures of certain officers to meet Air Force standards were not appropriately reflected in their performance evaluations" and "therefore, personally issued letters of evaluation...describing their failure" that became "a permanent part of each individual's record." For the two F-15 pilots, three officers on the AWACS aircraft, and two generals in the chain of command, this action effectively ended their careers in the Air Force. The chief of staff also grounded the pilots and AWACS crew members and disqualified them from duties in flying operations for three years. Sklute; Eric Schmitt, "Chief of Air Force Grounds 5 Pilots," *New York Times,* 15 August 1995, A1; and Chris Black, "Shifts in Air Force Policy Are Seen after Reprimands," *Boston Globe,* 16 August 1995, 3.

[8]In a short videotape released in mid-August 1995, required to be viewed by every Air Force officer, Senior Executive Service civilian, and noncommissioned officer in the top three grades, General Fogleman reviewed the Black Hawk accident, as well as the actions taken against the individuals involved and the officers who wrote their performance evaluations. He used the affair to emphasize Air Force standards; personal accountability; and the necessity for officers to lead, to pursue excellence in the performance of their duties, to act always with integrity, and to

place service before self. See transcript, on-line, Internet, 13 September 2000, available from http://www.usafa.af.mil/core-value/accountability.html. For background, see Sklute.

[9]Sheila E. Widnall, previously professor of aeronautics and astronautics, director of the Fluid Dynamics Research Laboratory, and associate provost at the Massachusetts Institute of Technology, was secretary of the Air Force from August 1993 to October 1997.

[10]General Fogleman earned a master's degree in history at Duke University and taught military history at the Air Force Academy from December 1970 to November 1972, when he went back to combat-crew training for his second flying tour in Southeast Asia.

[11]MRCs were *major regional conflicts,* a term for large conventional wars in a limited geographical area, such as the Persian Gulf War of 1990–1991 or an invasion of South Korea by North Korea which would involve American forces. The shift in defense policy, planning, and force structure from deterring and preparing for a world war against the Soviet Union to focusing on regional conflicts began with the reconsideration that resulted in the Bush administration's base force policy of 1990. Lorna S. Jaffe, *The Development of the Base Force* (Washington, D.C.: Joint History Office, Office of the Chairman of the Joint Chiefs of Staff, July 1993), 2-9, 11-13, 16, 18, 21-22, 25-26, 29, 33, 36, 45; and *National Security Strategy of the United States* (Washington, D.C.: White House, August 1991), 7-11, 27-29, 31. The ability to fight nearly simultaneously two MRCs (now called major theater wars) became the chief planning factor shaping the size and configuration of the American armed forces after the "Bottom-Up Review" of defense policy and force structure undertaken by the Clinton administration in 1993. Defense Department briefing, Gen Colin Powell and Les Aspin, subject: DOD Bottom-Up Review, 1 September 1993, Federal Information Systems Corporation, Federal News Service, accessed through Academic Universe, "bottom up review" Search Terms, 13 December 2000; and Les Aspin, *Report on the Bottom-Up Review,* October 1993, sec. 2, "Addressing Regional Dangers and Seizing Opportunities," on-line, Internet, 15 December 2000, available from http://stinet.dtic.mil/str/index.html (search "Les Aspin").

[12]The Quadrennial Defense Review (QDR)—a comprehensive reconsideration of American national security policy, defense strategy, and force structure expected to be repeated every four years at the beginning of a presidential administration—originated in a recommendation by DOD's 1995 Commission on the Roles and Missions of the Armed Forces. DOD undertook its first QDR in 1996–1997; the report in the spring of 1997 listed a number of reductions, adjustments, realignments, and planned changes in defense posture. See *Directions for Defense, Roles and Missions Commission of the Armed Forces, Report to Congress, the Secretary of Defense, and the Chairman of the Joint Chiefs of Staff,* 24 May 1995, executive summary, on-line, Internet, 26 November 2000, available from http://www.fas.org/man/docs/ corm95/di1062.html; William S. Cohen, *Report of the Quadrennial Defense Review,* May 1997, on-line, Internet, 26 November 2000, available from http://www.defenselink.mil/pubs/qdr/index.html; and

Background on the Quadrennial Defense Review, May 1997, H.R. 3230 National Defense Authorization Act for Fiscal Year 1997, Title IX, subtitle B sec. 923, Quadrennial Defense Review/Force Structure Review, on-line Internet, 16 January 2001, available from http://www.comw.org/qdr/backgrd.htm. General Fogleman discussed the QDR at greater length with reporter George Wilson. See Wilson, *This War Really Matters: Inside the Fight for Defense Dollars* (Washington, D.C.: Congressional Quarterly Press, 2000), 38-44.

[13]The "tank" is the conference room in the Pentagon where the Joint Chiefs of Staff (JCS) meet, so named, according to popular lore, because "access to the entrance used by staff officers was down a flight of stairs through an arched portal, supposedly giving the impression of entering a tank." Ronald H. Cole et al., *The Chairmanship of the Joint Chiefs of Staff* (Washington, D.C.: Office of the Chairman of the Joint Chiefs of Staff, 1995), 177.

[14]Gen John M. D. Shalikashvili, US Army, was chairman of the JCS from October 1993 to September 1997.

[15]William J. Perry, who had worked in the defense and financial industries in technical and executive capacities and served on the Stanford University faculty in engineering and international security, was secretary of defense from February 1994 to January 1997. He had been undersecretary of defense for research and engineering from 1977 to 1981 and deputy secretary of defense in 1993–1994 Roger R. Trask and Alfred Goldberg, *The Department of Defense, 1947–1997 Organization and Leaders* (Washington, D.C.: Historical Office, Office of the Secretary of Defense, 1997), 121, 141.

[16]William S. Cohen became secretary of defense on 24 January 1997. A lawyer and former elected official in Bangor, Maine, he served in the US House of Representatives (1973–1979) and US Senate (1979–1997), where he was a member of the Armed Services and Governmental Affairs Committees. Trask and Goldberg, 127. For a more personal profile, see John Donnelly, "The Evolution of William Cohen," *Boston Globe Magazine,* 22 October 2000, 14-15, 28-36.

[17]The 1997 DOD tactical air (TACAIR) modernization program proposed to replace completely by the year 2030 the A-10, F-15, F-16, and F-117 aircraft of the Air Force and the F-14, F/A-18, and AV-8B aircraft of the Navy and Marine Corps with F/A-18E/F, F-22, and Joint Strike Fighter aircraft, for the air superiority anti-air-warfare, suppression of enemy air defenses, fleet air defense, interdiction short- and long-range attack, reconnaissance, and close air support missions. The overall purpose was to secure "overwhelming air domination for US forces" for the next generation. See *Statement of Dr. Paul G. Kaminski, Undersecretary of Defense for Acquisition and Technology before the Subcommittee on Research and Development and the Subcommittee on Procurement of the House Committee on National Security on the DOD Tactical Aviation Modernization Program,* Committee on National Security Military Research and Development Subcommittee meeting jointly with the Military Procurement Committee, US House of Representatives, 105th Cong. 1st sess., 5 March 1997, 242-66, on-line, Internet, 16 January 2001, available from "http://www.acq.osd.mil/ousda/kaminski/aviation_modernization.html".

[18]Adm William A. Owens was vice chairman of the JCS, March 1994–February 1996.

[19]General of the Air Force Henry H. "Hap" Arnold was chief of the Army Air Corps and commanding general of the Army Air Forces from September 1938 to his retirement in June 1946. His five-star rank was awarded by act of Congress in 1949, the year before his death.

[20]The Korean War began in June 1950.

[21]The United States intervened with its own ground-force units and Americanized the Vietnam War during the first half of 1965.

[22]The QDR reduced the total planned procurement of F-22s from 438 to 339, to provide three wings of the aircraft. Ramp-up to full production was to be slowed, and the maximum production rate reduced from 48 aircraft per year to 36. However, DOD promised in the future to consider other F-22 variants to replace F-15E and F-117 long-range interdiction aircraft "when they reach the end of their service lives beyond 2015." Cohen, sec. 7, 45. For an analysis of the QDR, see Wilson, 25ff.

[23]In March 1996, prior to the election for president on Taiwan, the People's Republic of China moved military forces to its coast on the Straits of Taiwan and fired missiles over the island in an apparent attempt to intimidate Taiwan into voting against Lee Teng-hui, who had taken steps that appeared to move the island toward independence. In response, the United States repositioned into the area the aircraft carriers *Independence* and *Nimitz* with their support vessels, implying that any attempt to invade or harass Taiwan with military force would be opposed by the use of US forces. News briefing, Kenneth H. Bacon, Office of the Assistant Secretary of Defense (Public Affairs), 19 March 1996, on-line, Internet, 16 January 2001, available from http://www.defenselink.mil/news/Mar1996/ t031996_t0319asd.html; Geoffrey Crothall and Dennis Engbarth, "US Sends Second Carrier, Support Ships to Strait," *South China Morning Post,* 12 March 1996, 1; Geoffrey Crothall, "Li Warns US against Show of Force in Strait," *South China Morning Post,* 18 March 1996, 1; and Michael Dobbs, "Chinese Revert to Mao Formula in New War of Nerves on Taiwan," *Washington Post,* 16 March 1996, A20.

[24]For a more extended discussion of the F-22 program, see Michael J. Costigan, *The F-22: The Right Fighter for the Twenty-first Century?* Air War College Maxwell Paper no. 9 (Maxwell AFB, Ala.: Air University Press, August 1997). The airborne laser (ABL) program originated in the aftermath of the Gulf War to find a defense against theater ballistic missiles. Transferred from the Strategic Defense Initiative Office to the Air Force in 1992, the program has been developing a high-energy laser mounted in a Boeing 747 designed to destroy missiles during their boost phase. In 1995 General Fogleman listened to a briefing on the program at Kirtland AFB, N. Mex., and threw his full support behind the effort. "The Airborne Laser is going to be to directed-energy weapons what the F-117 was to stealth and precision munitions," he told an interviewer. John A. Tirpak, "First Force: The USAF Chief of Staff Talks about Airpower, the Air Force, and the Future," *Air Force Magazine* 79 (September 1996): 41. "Given the nature of

this revolutionary weapon system, the ABL will be studied in other roles…, other uses will be found." Johan Benson, "Conversations…with Gen. Ronald Fogleman," *Aerospace America* 34 (July 1996): 15. See also Suzann Chapman, "The Airborne Laser," *Air Force Magazine* 79 (January 1996): 54-55; Airborne Laser History, on line, Internet, 26 November 2000, available from http://www.airbornelaser.com/special/abl/history; and Capt Gilles Van Nederveen, "A Light Dawns: The Airborne Laser," *Aerospace Power Journal* (PIREP, Spring 2001).

[25]On 25 June 1996, terrorists exploded a large truck bomb outside the American air base at Dhahran, Saudi Arabia, killing 19 airmen and wounding some three hundred Americans in the high-rise housing complex named Khobar Towers.

[26]The commander of the 4404th Composite Wing (Provisional) was Brig Gen Terryl J. Schwalier, USAF.

[27]The bombing was investigated by Congress (hearings before the Senate Armed Services and House National Security Committees); a task force appointed by the secretary of defense and headed by Gen Wayne A. Downing, USA, Retired, the most recent former commander of US Special Operations Command; and by two separate Air Force groups, the first headed by Lt Gen James Record and the second by Lt Gen Richard Swope (Air Force inspector general) and Maj Gen Bryan Hawley (Air Force judge advocate general). Matt Labash, "The Scapegoat: How the Secretary of Defense Ended the Career of an Exemplary Air Force General," *The Weekly Standard* 3 (24 November 1997): 20-29.

[28]In an interview with Bill Gertz of the *Washington Times,* described on 10 March 1997 ("Service Chiefs Fear Missile Defense Deal with Russia Could Blunt U.S. Edge, General Says"), General Fogleman was reported as saying that "the military service chiefs are worried that an agreement being negotiated with Russia could impose harmful restrictions on future U.S. missile defenses as part of a side agreement to a U.S.-Russian defense treaty." "All the chiefs have great concerns about this," Gen. Fogleman told The Washington Times. "I would hate to see us negotiate away any kind of advantage we might have in space-based sensors, or in the airborne laser or anything like that.' " The previous week, there had been discussions in Moscow over a possible side agreement between the two countries "expanding the…1972 Anti-Ballistic Missile treaty to cover short-range missile defenses."

[29]General Fogleman was commander in chief (CINC) of US Transportation Command, August 1992–October 1994.

[30]In "The Scapegoat," Labash, a staff writer at *The Weekly Standard,* used numerous interviews with (and public statements by) people involved in the incident and the investigations afterward, as well as the conclusions of the investigation reports, to argue that General Schwalier had been extremely aggressive and had done everything in his power to protect the people under his command, and that political pressures to hold someone accountable for the deaths led the secretary of defense to deny Schwalier promotion to major general.

[31]The changes in the officer promotion and assignment systems in 1995 were outlined in Bruce D. Callander, "A New Shot at the Officer Promotion System," and "The New Way of Officer Assignments," *Air Force Magazine* 78 (July 1995): 70-73, and 78 (September 1995): 90-93, respectively. A quality-of-life survey (answered by 356,409 Air Force uniformed and civilian members) in 1995 revealed that 50 and 53 percent of enlisted and officers, respectively, did not think their promotion systems were fair. See Peter Grier, "The Quality of Military Life," *Air Force Magazine* 79 (December 1996): 33-34. Dissatisfaction with the evaluation and assignment systems diminished in the 1996 survey. See Suzann Chapman, "USAF Survey Shows Positive Trends," *Air Force Magazine* 79 (October 1996): 12.

[32]Predictions about a pilot shortage and retention problems were detailed in Bruce D. Callander, "And Now, the Pilot Shortage," *Air Force Magazine* 79 (March 1996): 70-74.

[33]General Shalikashvili permitted General Fogleman for a period of time to set the level of tasking for certain weapon systems like the AWACS and airborne battlefield command and control center—which were small in numbers of aircraft but in almost continuous use—for the purposes of training crews and expanding their numbers.

[34]1st Lt Kelly Flinn, the first female B-52 line pilot in the Air Force, graduated from the Air Force Academy in 1993 and joined the 23d Bomb Squadron, Minot AFB, N. Dak., in October 1995. At the base, she had a brief affair with an enlisted man and then with the husband of an enlisted woman in her wing. She was ordered to break off the affair and allegedly told investigators first that she was not involved with the man and then that she had ended the relationship when she was at the time living with him. Her case became national news when she asked the secretary of the Air Force for permission to resign from the service with an honorable discharge rather than face court-martial. See Frank Spinner, attorney, "Military Career of Lt Kelly Flinn," 20 May 1997, on-line, Internet, 26 November 2000, available from http://www.kellyflinnfoundation.org/military.htm; David Van Biema, "Sex in the Military: The Rules of Engagement," *Time* 149 (2 June 1997): 36-37; Elaine Sciolino, "Air Force Chief Has Harsh Words for Pilot Facing Adultery Charge," *New York Times*, 22 May 1997, A1, B12; and editorial, "The Discharge of Kelly Flinn," *New York Times*, 23 May 1997, A30.

[35]Gen Joseph Ralston, USAF, the vice chairman of the JCS, was named by the secretary of defense to succeed General Shalikashvili, but in June 1997, in the wake of the controversy over Kelly Flinn, General Ralston withdrew from consideration because of involvement in an extramarital affair some 13 years earlier, when he was a student at the National War College. "Ralston: Uproar Ends Bid," The NewsHour with Jim Lehrer, 9 June 1997, on-line, Internet, 16 January 2001, available from http://www.pbs.org/newshour/bb/military/jan–jun97/ralston_6–9.html.

[36]H. R. McMaster argues in *Dereliction of Duty: Lyndon Johnson, Robert McNamara, the Joint Chiefs of Staff, and the Lies That Led to Vietnam* (New York: HarperCollins 1997) that the joint chiefs contributed to the American failure in the Vietnam War by not expressing their disagreements—with the policy of gradual escalation—directly to the president, and by allowing their views to be misrepresented to Congress and the public by the Johnson administration in 1964-1965 According to McMaster, the chiefs went along with a policy they opposed in part out of loyalty to their civilian superiors, in part because of benefits each gained for their service in bargains with the secretary of defense, and in part because they expected later to be able to negotiate changes in the policy and strategy. The editor was McMaster's primary adviser at the University of North Carolina at Chapel Hill for the MA and PhD theses on which the book was based.

[37]The treaty to ban the development, production, acquisition, and use of antipersonnel land mines in war, and to remove those in use and eliminate stockpiles, was signed in Ottawa, Canada, in December 1997. Some 133 countries signed the treaty. Because of opposition from the Pentagon, but after much consultation and last-minute diplomacy, the United States refused to be a signatory. Raymond Bonner, "U.S. Seeks Compromise to Save Treaty Banning Land Mines," "Land Mine Treaty Takes Final Form over U.S. Dissent," *New York Times,* 17 September 1997, A6, and 18 September 1997, A1, respectively; Dana Priest and Charles Trueheart, "U.S. Makes One Last Pitch on Mine Treaty," Dana Priest "Mine Decision Boosts Clinton-Military Relations," Howard Schneider "Dozens of Nations, but Not U.S., Sign Land-Mine Treaty," *Washington Post,* 16 September 1997, A14, 21 September 1997, A22, 4 December 1997, A33, respectively; editorial, "Land Mine Foe Wins Peace Prize," *San Francisco Chronicle,* 11 October 1997, A20; and "Land Mine Treaty Goes into Effect—Without the U.S.," *Chicago Sun-Times,* 2 March 1999, 18.

[38]Maj Gen Perry McCoy Smith, who retired from the Air Force in 1986, served with General Fogleman in the F-15 fighter wing in Bitburg, Germany, in 1977. A PhD in political science from Columbia University and the author of numerous books (most recently a biography of the hero Jimmie Dyess), General Smith is also a television analyst and teacher of leadership, ethics, and strategic thinking to corporations and nonprofit and government organizations. He lives in Augusta Georgia.

[39]General Fogleman's handwritten note, misdated "27 Jul 97," read in its entirety "Secretary Widnall[,] I request that I be retired from active duty at the earliest possible date, but not later than 1 Sep 1997, the fifth anniversary of my promotion to my current grade/rank. Very Respectfully[,] Ron Fogleman [signature] [,] Ronald R. Fogleman[,] General, USAF[.]"

[40]In June, reports reached the press that General Fogleman was telling associates privately that he might seek early retirement if General Schwalier's promotion was withdrawn. See Bradley Graham, "Cohen Near Decision on Fatal Saudi Blast," *Washington Post,* 29 June 1997, A4; Michael Hedges, "Air Force Chie

Decides to Quit," *The Detroit News,* 29 July 1997, on-line, Internet, 27 November 2000, available from http://www.detnews.com/1997/nation/9707/29/07290078.htm; and Susanne M. Schafer, "Head of Air Force Asks to Step Down," *Las Vegas Review-Journal,* 29 July 1997, on-line, Internet, 27 November 2000, available from http://lvrj.com/lvrj_home/1997/Jul-29-Tue-1997/news/5796823.html.

[41]The entire statement, written personally by General Fogleman and dated 30 July 1997 but released on 28 July, was published in *Air Force Times,* 11 August 1997, 15:

As my tenure as your chief of staff ends, I want to tell you what an honor and a privilege it has been to represent everyone in the United States Air Force.

The timing of my announcement was driven by the desire to defuse the perceived confrontation between myself and the secretary of defense over his impending decision on the Khobar Towers terrorist attack. The decision to retire was made after considerable deliberation over the past several weeks.

On one level, I've always said that my serving as the chief of staff was a "tour" not a "sentence" and that I would leave when I made all the contributions that I could. After I accepted this position in 1994, I met with other senior leaders of the Air Force to discuss our goals for my tenure. We wanted to take care of the troops and their families, to stabilize the force, to set a course for modernization and to develop a new strategic vision. During some difficult and challenging times we have worked hard to accomplish that and more. Certainly there is more to be done, but the framework of the plan and the leadership [are] in place to move forward with the support and efforts of the magnificent men and women of our Air Force.

On another level, military service is the only life I have ever known. My stock in trade after 34 years of service is my military judgment and advice. After serving as chief of staff for almost three years, my values and sense of loyalty to our soldiers, sailors, Marines and especially our airmen led me to the conclusion that I may be out of step with the times and some of the thinking of the establishment.

This puts me in an awkward position. If I were to continue to serve as chief of staff of the Air Force and speak out, I could be seen as a divisive force and not a team player. I do not want the Air Force to suffer for my judgment and convictions. In my view this would happen if I continue as your chief. For these reasons I have decided to retire and devote more time to personal interests and my family...but the Air Force will always be in my thoughts.

Miss Jane and I have met a lot of wonderful American service men and women—active duty, Guard, Reserve, civilians and family members—and they will continue to be a part of our lives. We have been proud to represent the men and women of the United States Air Force around the globe and to serve in the finest Air Force in the world. God bless and keep you all as you continue to serve this great nation.

[42]Gen John L. Piotrowski commanded Ninth Air Force from October 1982 to July 1985 as a lieutenant general and then was promoted to four stars to serve as vice chief of staff of the Air Force and commander of US Space Command. He retired in March 1990.

★ ★ ★ ★ ★

Contributor

- **Dr. Richard H. Kohn** *(AB, Harvard; MS, PhD, University of Wisconsin at Madison) is professor of history and chair of the Curriculum in Peace, War, and Defense at the University of North Carolina at Chapel Hill. He has served as executive secretary of the Triangle Institute for Security Studies, a consortium of faculty at Duke University, University of North Carolina, and North Carolina State University interested in national and international security studies. He has also served on the faculties of several universities and was chief of Air Force History and chief historian for the United States Air Force from 1981 to 1991. He currently serves on the Air University Board of Visitors and the editorial board of* Aerospace Power Journal. *The author or editor of a number of books and journal articles, Dr. Kohn presently is working on a book about presidential war leadership in American history and is codirecting a project investigating the gap between military and civilian attitudes and culture in the United States today.*

Disclaimer

☆ ☆ ☆

Generals Versus The President: Eisenhower and the Army, 1953–1955
A Case in Civil Military Relations

A. J. Bacevich and Lawrence F. Kaplan

☆ 1

Between the autumn of 1953 and the summer of 1955, the leaders of the United States Army struggled against a national security policy they thought flawed, dangerous, and even immoral. Ironically, in opposing the strategy of massive retaliation, senior Army leaders placed themselves at cross purposes with a former five-star general who had been elected President of the United States, Dwight D. Eisenhower. This case is the story of that conflict. It describes the basis of the Army's opposition to Eisenhower's policies and the means that Army leaders chose to advance their position. It also

☆ ☆ ☆ ☆ ☆ ☆

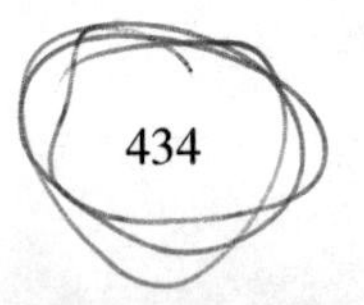

describes the response by civilian leaders determined to prevail in a controversy that in their view touched on core issues of civilian control.

Elected by a landslide in November 1952, Eisenhower brought to the presidency clear-cut views regarding American national security policy. In the near term, ending the Korean War stood out as his first priority. Beyond that was the challenge of preserving the American commitment to the policy of containment. The West's struggle to resist the forces of global communism was likely to continue indefinitely. Without American leadership, that struggle would surely fail. Moreover, Eisenhower believed that the moral, political, and economic—not military—dimensions of the struggle against communism were preeminent. As a candidate, he had vowed to put the nation on course to "achieve both security and solvency."[1] A confident society firmly wedded to its political ideals and sustained by a vigorous economy was fundamental to the new President's conception of grand strategy. Eisenhower accepted his party's time-honored insistence that the twin keys to a healthy economy were a balanced budget and low taxes.

The economy that the new Republican team inherited was not being managed in accordance with these principles. The final budget submitted by the Truman administration projected a federal deficit of $9.9 billion on outlays totaling less than $80 billion. Such profligacy, in Eisenhower's eyes, courted ruin. But with defense-related spending comprising 62% of overall federal spending for fiscal year 1953, eliminating that deficit (without raising taxes) would be possible only by targeting defense for major cuts.[2]

A reduced defense budget and a smaller military establishment made sense for other reasons as well. Were the country to maintain a huge peacetime defense establishment, Eisenhower feared that it might become a "garrison state." If insecurity induced Americans to trade their democratic traditions for a semi-authoritarian order and an economy organized to service military needs, the United States might become indistinguishable from its adversaries. Thus, it was imperative to craft military policies that would neither corrupt America politically nor inhibit the working of the nation's market economy.

For the Department of Defense, the implications of this line of thinking were profound. Once in office, Eisenhower and his National Security Council (NSC) wasted no time in spelling out those implications. By April 1953 the new administration had already signaled its intentions, declaring in NSC 149/2, "Basic National Security Policies and Programs in Relation to Their Costs," that a strong American economy was "a vital factor in the long-term survival of the free world" and warning that deficit spending and high taxes would "weaken and might eventually destroy that economy." Although short on specifics NSC 149/2 committed the administration to a program of economizing on defense, expanding and modernizing the United States Ai Force while reducing the size of the Army and the Navy.[3]

In singling out the Air Force for favored treatment, NSC 149/2 was harbinger of things to come. In spelling out the details of what would becom known as his "New Look" military policy, the president did not procee arbitrarily. He was committed to consulting the Joint Chiefs of Staff (JCS prior to rendering a decision. But the new President fully intended that the be *his* chiefs. Accepting frequently expressed Republican complaints that th Joint Chiefs inherited from Truman had been tainted by their support fo Truman's controversial Korean War policies, Eisenhower purged the JC soon after taking office. Admiral Arthur W. Radford replaced Omar Bradle as JCS Chairman. Admiral Robert B. Carney and General Nathan F. Twinin became Navy Chief of Naval Operations and Air Force Chief of Staff respec tively. For the Army, Eisenhower chose General Matthew B. Ridgway.

Knowing that the rush of day-to-day Pentagon business made it difficul to make long-range in-depth planning, the President directed his new tean of military advisers to undertake a broad-gauged study of overall defens policy *before* taking office. Eisenhower asked for "a fresh view" of strategi concepts, roles and missions, force structure, readiness, and weapons technol ogy, a view that would also take into account the budgetary limitation implied by NSC 149/2. Eisenhower hoped that such a perspective from hi top military advisers would aid the NSC "in developing policies for the mos effective employment of national resources to insure the defense of our coun try for the long pull."[4]

Preparing this analysis took the incoming chiefs the better part of month. Even so, the report that they rendered on August 8 was disappoint ing. In large part, it was a brief for the status quo. The President's new tean of uniformed advisers assessed overall U. S. military planning as "sound an adequate." They avoided prickly questions related to roles and missions an refused to contemplate any cuts in defense spending, warning that any suc reduction "would result in an almost equal reduction in overall security. Only with regard to U. S. commitments overseas did they offer a concret suggestion. "We are overextended," the incoming chiefs declared. Thei solution to this predicament was to draw down forward-deployed garrison and to devote greater attention to continental defense, proposals that wer largely irrelevant to the emerging outlines of Eisenhower's national securit policy.[5]

★ 11

One week later, on August 15, 1953, Ridgway was sworn in as Chief of Staff, U. S. Army. By any measure, the new Army chief was one of the outstanding soldiers of his generation. Son of a career officer, Ridgway had graduated from West Point with the Class of 1917. He first achieved distinction as a leader of airborne troops in the European theater during World War II. But Ridgway's finest hour had come in Korea. Assuming command during the desperate days following the Chinese intervention in the fall of 1950, he revitalized a badly demoralized 8th U.S. Army, energized the UN defensive effort, and turned the tide of battle. It was a superlative demonstration of generalship. Subsequently, Ridgway had replaced Douglas MacArthur as Supreme Commander Allied Powers in the Pacific and, once Eisenhower decided to enter politics, he had succeeded Ike as NATO military commander.[6]

Ridgway's public persona was that of the no-nonsense fighting general. It was an image that he carefully cultivated, posing for official photographs in "steel pot" with chin strap dangling while affecting hand grenades as essential to his field uniform. To a large extent, image provided an apt reflection of the man. Ridgway the soldier was tough, competent, and personally courageous.

Less evident to the casual observer were a deeply-felt moral sensibility and an almost mystical devotion to the ideal of the warrior professional. To Ridgway, preserving the ethos of authentic professionalism was something akin to a religious obligation. Officership was a calling. Although that calling imposed heavy obligations, it granted soldiers distinctive privileges and responsibilities and endowed them with a status apart from—and in some respects above—their fellow citizens.

Thus, in remarks made upon taking the oath of chief of staff, Ridgway addressed two related themes: "the maintenance of democratic institutions and the protection of the integrity of the military profession." True professionalism, he reminded an audience that included Secretary of Defense Charles E. Wilson and other senior civilian officials, requires "the fearless, forthright expression of honest, objective professional views ... up to the moment of decision by proper civilian authority. It means completely loyal execution of those decisions once announced." But it also means "the giving by civilian authorities to their military services of the same unqualified loyalty they receive." It was, therefore, incumbent upon civilians to "scrupulously respect" the "honestly expressed views of responsible officers," foregoing any temptation "to force unanimity of view," or "to compel adherence to some politico-military 'party line'." In short, "loyalty and complete trust cut both ways. They must flow just as strongly from the top down as from the bottom up."

These were not idle reflections. Ridgway's forceful statement of the mutual obligations inherent in the civil-military compact was both warning and opening gambit in the Army's efforts to forestall a forthcoming shift in national security policy.

★ *III*

The magnitude of that shift soon became apparent. Eisenhower's New Look exacted draconian cuts of the American defense establishment, with the Army especially hard hit. But for Ridgway, the flaws in the new defense policy went beyond simply reductions in troop strength or defense spending, however painful those might be. The *manner* in which civilian leaders exacted those cuts violated the civil-military compact and presumed a radical change in terms. Furthermore, in Ridgway's interpretation, if left unchallenged that revision threatened the very viability of the military profession.

In the fall of 1953, the National Security Council turned to the task of translating Eisenhower's promise of "security with solvency" into concrete policy. Providing the vehicle for this process was NSC 162, initially drafted in September 1953 as a "Review of Basic National Security Policy." In considering this document throughout the following month, the NSC wrestled with the question of how best to resolve the tension between military requirements and fiscal constraints. Should security or solvency receive first priority in administration programs? Exceedingly reluctant to commit itself to an either/or proposition, the NSC sought alternatives that would obviate the need to make any such choice, allowing the administration to persuade itself that it was indeed delivering an effective defense at reduced cost.

Grasping for an economical alternative to a military establishment that it saw as too large and too expensive, the NSC found its solution in nuclear weapons. By placing primary reliance on "the capability of inflicting massive retaliatory damage by offensive striking power," the United States would be able to deter Soviet aggression while also accruing substantial savings. The idea, said Eisenhower, was "to keep the minimum respectable posture of defense while emphasizing this particular offensive capability." Ike knew that a general war fought with nuclear weapons was madness. In such a conflict there would be no winners. The proper aim of U. S. military policy was not to win World War III nor to waste American strength in bloody sideshows but to avoid war altogether.

That individual members of the JCS might find this formula difficult to digest, Ike viewed as simply too bad. Responding to a suggestion that the NSC proceedings might make note of certain Pentagon reservations, the President "replied, with considerable warmth, that he would tolerate no notice of a JCS dissent in the record of action. The Joint Chiefs of Staff were his military advisers; he made the decisions."[7]

★ *IV*

Under the tutelage of Admiral Radford, the JCS was soon hard at work translating the New Look into budget share and force levels. But the resulting squeeze did not affect each of the services equally. Rather, it produced clear winners and clear losers. The biggest winner was the Air Force, in particular the Strategic Air Command. During the lean years of the New Look, the Air Force grew fat. By 1957, for example, the Air Force budget alone fell just one billion dollars short of the Army and Navy budgets combined.

For Ridgway's Army, the New Look was an unmitigated disaster. In December 1953, JCS 2101/113 "Military Strategy and Posture" slashed the Army's budget for fiscal year 1955 from $13 to $10.2 billion and reduced the size of the Army from 1,540,000 to 1,164,000. This was only the beginning. The Army's end strength continued to spiral downward, bottoming out at 859,000. In terms of budget, the news was worse still. While Eisenhower remained in office, the Army's budget never again reached even $10 billion. The regiments and divisions providing the backbone of the fighting army absorbed the brunt of these cuts. In the field, readiness suffered. Reenlistments dropped. Morale plummeted.[8]

In the closing days of 1953, of course, much of this lay in the future. But to Ridgway, that future was clearly visible. By enshrining massive retaliation as the centerpiece of American strategy, the United States in Ridgway's view was effectively abandoning traditional conceptions regarding the nature and purpose of warfare. Implicit in massive retaliation was the notion that the *use* of force had lost its value as an instrument of statecraft. That the administration was implicating senior military leaders in discussions leading to the adoption of such a policy violated Ridgway's sense of civil-military propriety. Worse, this new reliance on nuclear weapons, in Ridgway's view, seemed to legitimize the targeting of civilians. Given the evidence that the Soviets were embarked upon a program of acquiring their own nuclear arsenal, the logic of retaliation could provide a rationale for preventive war waged against civilians, a prospect that Ridgway viewed as unconscionable.

As early as October 13, Ridgway insisted that the administration's reevaluation of basic policy had inadvertently raised fundamental questions about the soldier's role and relationship to civilian authority. The Defense Department as a whole, he complained, was "living in a vacuum created by the absence of national policy." That vacuum was drawing the military into precincts that had hitherto been off-limits. As a result, the distinction between soldier and his civilian masters was becoming blurred in ways that struck Ridgway as dangerous. "The soldier should never have to state what the policy should be. He should stand in his role of saying to the statesman: what is it you want. The statesman should say: this is what we want—what are the military requirements for the reasonable assurance of the attainment of such objectives? We are capable of stating requirements to meet stated objectives. We have not yet [received] the objectives."[9] By venturing into the murky world of high policy, Ridgway feared that soldiers would forfeit the role that had been exclusively theirs: offering professional judgment based solely on the military considerations that justified their claim to a unique status.

Even as soldiers were venturing beyond the traditional military sphere, civilian officials were intruding into the military's business with consequences that in Ridgway's view were likely to produce a calamity. "There are segments of highly placed, very influential people in our Government, who are playing with the idea that because of this tremendous atomic and nuclear capability we are evolving, the time will soon come ... when we can scrap our conventional weapons, and rely on knocking out any opponent by unrestricted use of the unconventional weapons. That too will lead us to disaster." Committing the nation to a strategy based on an explicit threat of killing civilians was something that Ridgway found repugnant. Comparing the prospect of "fiscal bankruptcy" to that of "spiritual bankruptcy" of waging war against noncombatants, the latter would unquestionably "be the worse tragedy of the two."[10]

Like Eisenhower, Ridgway's concern was corruption: the compromise of moral values and the sacrifice of principle. Whereas the President feared corruption in the guise of a garrison state, Ridgway believed that it would follow from a conception of war that violated the tenets of traditional military professionalism. For Ike, discarding military orthodoxy seemed a small price to pay if it allowed the nation to achieve security while also preserving its political birthright. Ridgway believed just the reverse: adhering to the standards of professional orthodoxy was the best guarantee against corruption; to abandon those standards was to invite ruin.

☆ V

In *The Soldier and the State*, Samuel P. Huntington poses this question: "What does the military officer do when he is ordered by a statesman to take a measure which is militarily absurd when judged by professional standards and which is strictly within the military realm without political implications?" In Huntington's view, the answer is clear: given such a "clear invasion of the professional realm by extraneous considerations ... the existence of professional standards justifies military disobedience."[11]

Although not conforming precisely to the conditions specified by Huntington, this was the dilemma that the Army confronted at the end of 1953. In Ridgway's view, massive retaliation *was* a military absurdity. He responded not with disobedience but by organizing a campaign of resistance. Viewed in retrospect, that resistance proceeded on three distinct tiers. First, there was direct opposition: Ridgway's exertions within the JCS and the NSC to overturn massive retaliation. As those efforts failed, Ridgway and other senior Army officers took their case to the media and civilian elites outside of the administration. Superseding both of these efforts was a reaffirmation of basic service doctrine that tacitly repudiated massive retaliation and restated the Army's adherence to a theory of warfare based on two abiding principles: first, that force retained political utility even in an atomic age; second, that the proper objective of military force was the destruction not of civilian populations but of the enemy's armed forces.

First in line as a target for direct opposition were the Joint Chiefs themselves. Ridgway argued that for the JCS to incorporate non-military factors into their deliberations was itself professionally irresponsible. He urged his colleagues to formulate their recommendations strictly according to military criteria unconstrained by extraneous considerations. This meant, in particular, that in offering advice on military policy, the JCS should disregard budgetary constraints. Ridgway complained that JCS 2101/111 had been anything but the product of objective military analysis. Rather, it was a "directed verdict," the product of arbitrary fiscal limitations imposed by political authorities.[12] As such, it was a document to which the JCS should never have been party. Ridgway insisted that the Joint Chiefs should "recommend strategy based on a military estimate of the situation and not on limitations which are unrelated to the threat to our national security."[13]

Such a military estimate, in Ridgway's view, would focus on one crucial fact: that the Soviet Union was acquiring its own nuclear arsenal, the existence of which would negate whatever *military* logic the policy of massive retaliation currently possessed. If the United States failed to anticipate this development, argued Ridgway, Americans would soon awake to a situation in which the nation's chief adversary had achieved parity with the United States in nuclear striking power while already commanding superior conventional strength. Facing this predicament, Ridgway feared that the Joint Chiefs would find themselves being backed into a situation of advocating preventive war as "the only course left open to the United States." For Ridgway, such a prospect represented the ultimate abdication of professional responsibility. Preventive war, he wrote, "must emphatically be rejected." Yet to forestall that prospect required that the United States first recover from its infatuation with massive retaliation.[14]

Ridgway's JCS colleagues were unmoved. Radford remained steadfast in his support of the administration. With the Air Force as chief beneficiary of Eisenhower's shift in national security policy, Twining had little cause for complaint. Although Admiral Carney sympathized with elements of Ridgway's critique, he offered little practical support, preferring to focus the Navy's energies on capturing its own share of the strategic retaliatory mission.

Thus stymied in the JCS, Ridgway turned next to the National Security Council. Long after the Council had turned its attention to other matters Ridgway continued to lobby aggressively against massive retaliation. As it was, Secretary of Defense Wilson and JCS Chairman Radford purported to represent the Pentagon's corporate view within the NSC. From the Army's perspective, neither of these officials was an acceptable spokesman. Wilson made no effort to conceal the fact that he had no sympathy for the Army's complaints about administration policies. Meanwhile, Army leaders accused Radford of playing a double game, posing as disinterested agent of the President while actually using his position to advance key Navy interests.

On December 3, 1954—more than a year after Eisenhower had approved NSC 162/2 and announced that he would brook no further military dissent—the President let Ridgway present his case directly to the NSC. At a meeting convened specifically for the purpose of hearing him out Ridgway attacked massive retaliation head on. He warned of the consequences of Soviet American nuclear parity, a condition that he portrayed as imminent. If in the face of this Soviet nuclear capability the U. S. simply continued on its present course, it would soon "find itself isolated from the rest of the free world" and in a position of overall military inferiority. To forestall this prospect, Ridgway urged the NSC to adopt a strategy based on the requirements of fighting rather than simply deterring war. According to Ridgway, such a war could occur at any time, in any quarter of the globe and it could be fought either "with or without resort to nuclear weapons." Yet even if nuclear weapons were employed, there was no guarantee that they would achieve a decision. Ridgway argued that only a force possessing the clear capability of prevailing in a wide range of contingencies could claim real credibility as a deterrent.[15]

In advocating the creation of a "balanced force," Ridgway also urged the NSC to give up its preoccupation with fiscal constraints. Strategy, he argued should derive from the premise that "national security is the primary consideration in determining military programs, and cost secondary." Assigning primacy to a robust military capability rather than scrimping on defense would save Americans from the temptation of preventive war as an answer to Soviet nuclear parity—a prospect that Ridgway denounced as "devoid of moral prin ciple and ... foreign to the precepts on which the nation was founded." Reiterating a familiar theme, he concluded by insisting that "national fiscal bankruptcy would be far preferable to national spiritual bankruptcy."[16]

Once Ridgway completed his presentation, Eisenhower asked if there were any questions. There being none, Ridgway was dismissed. Once he had departed, members of the NSC took turns critiquing his presentation. Although Eisenhower spoke briefly on Ridgway's behalf—he thought that the general was "not merely presenting a 'parochial' Army viewpoint"—others present made no effort to be kind.[17]

Having given Ridgway his day in court, Eisenhower expected that he and the Army would now fall into line. To prevent any misunderstanding on this point, the President on December 22 summoned Secretary Wilson and the Joint Chiefs to the Oval Office. Eisenhower used this occasion to reaffirm his support for massive retaliation as the centerpiece of U. S. national security policy. He restated his belief that "a major war will be an atomic war." If and when that war occurred, SAC would deliver the American retaliatory response. The Army's job would simply be to "maintain order" following a nuclear exchange. These roles dictated budgetary priorities that the President viewed as no longer subject to debate. Eisenhower emphasized that this was his personal decision. As commander-in-chief, he reminded them, he was "entitled to the loyal support" of his subordinates. He demanded that the Joint Chiefs conduct themselves accordingly.[18]

Yet far from diminishing, the Army's resistance escalated with the coming of the new year. Having failed to budge either the JCS or the NSC, Ridgway and his subordinates took the Army's case to the public. Press reports of the Army's continuing opposition to administration policy began to appear with increasing frequency. Service journals welcomed expressions of dissent. Senior Army officers launched a concerted effort to cultivate civilian elites for potential allies.

The New York Times that landed on the stoop of the White House on January 1, 1955 served notice that the Army's unhappiness with the New Look had not abated. The New Year's Day edition of the *Times* gave prominent coverage to reports of Ridgway's objections to the next round of money-saving personnel cuts.[19] This was only the beginning.

In appearances before military audiences, Ridgway became increasingly candid in upholding the Army's view of warfare. A speech prepared for service school audiences in early 1955 is representative. In a reference to Bernard Brodie's famous book and the school of thought that it had inspired, Ridgway insisted that "the only absolute weapon is man." Despite "remarkable developments in military technology," the outcome of future conflicts would be decided precisely as they had been in the past—through the clash of opposing armies in battle. When it came to thinking about wars to come, "no

concept could be more potentially dangerous, perhaps even fatal" than t
assume that nuclear weapons alone would be decisive. Rather, "only whe
we close with the enemy on the ground—as only armies can do—can w
finally defeat his armed forces, and only by defeating enemy armed forces ca
we win victory over an enemy nation." Implicitly rejecting the legitimacy o
attacks on civilian populations, Ridgway hewed to tradition in asserting tha
"the military objective in war is the defeat of the enemy's armed forces."[20]

At one level, such appearances were simply exercises in telling the troop
what they wanted to hear: offering assurances that they had not yet becom
entirely redundant, that SAC was not going to put them completely out o
business. But the effect of such remarks rippled far beyond the auditoriums o
Fort Benning and Fort Knox. Thus, by early 1955, Army journals wer
featuring articles such as one submitted by a pseudonymous "Colone
Shillelagh" deploring the way that nuclear weapons had corrupted America
thinking about war. As a result of the New Look, wrote Shillelagh,

> We have accepted civil destruction as an object of war and a means of war where formerly it was an incident of war. The question raised is not of humanity but of reality—whether we have forgotten that war is still a political instrument which must have political objectives and methods. This delusion may prove the ultimate irrationality.
>
> We have rejected the precept that indecisive brutality and destruction which advantages neither side will be outlawed by mutual consent or forbearance. We expect war to take the form of tremendous destruction on both sides, though we find no purpose in it. We have surrendered to the idea that a capability will be exercised merely because we possess it.
>
> We have lost sight of our objective of defeating the enemy armed forces as a means to victory and have substituted for it the intangible will of the enemy to resist.... This error leads to the brutalization of war without purpose, to a preoccupation with mass destruction, to the neglect of the political realities.[21]

Shillelagh was by no means alone. Major General James M. Gavin, th
Army's G3, agreed that the New Look was fundamentally flawed. Gavi
began inviting disaffected officers from the Army staff to his Pentagon offic
on Saturday mornings, there to refine the Army's critique of massive retaliation. Gavin insisted that the purpose of this "Coordinating Group" was no
to orchestrate "a revolt against DOD's policies." According to Gavin, th
group sought ways of bringing "to the attention of everyone concerned th
intellectual implications of the bombing policy." The intent was "to hel
people think through the implications of such a national policy," somethin
that Gavin insisted "the American people were entitled to."[22]

Nor did Army dissenters limit themselves to internal audiences. For example, at a meeting of the Council on Foreign Relations on February 14, 1955, Ridgway attacked the notion of assigning primacy to deterrence, insisting that the Army which he led existed "for the single purpose of victory in battle and success in war." For such an Army, deterrence could never be more than a "subsidiary purpose." Despite the availability of nuclear weapons, the ultimate "object of war" remained what it had been since time immemorial: gaining "control of land and the people on it." This, of course, was ineluctably the business of ground forces. Nuclear weapons would have a role to play in future campaigns—Ridgway declared it "inconceivable that a nation would not use every weapon at its disposal"—but it did not follow that such weapons would be decisive.[23]

Gavin's participation in a Council study group convened to examine "Nuclear Weapons and Foreign Policy" offered a similar critique of administration policy. At a study group meeting on May 4, 1955, Gavin warned that even if an American attack "atomized" the entire Soviet Union, "the Red Army would still be rolling." Furthermore, with Western Europeans developing a bad case of "nuclear neurosis" as they contemplated the prospect of a war fought with nuclear weapons on their territory, it was imperative that the U. S. retain the means "to attack the USSR without reducing the allies to ashes." The point was not to ignore nuclear weapons, but to avoid becoming overly dependent upon them. Gavin illustrated his point with an analogy. "The patrolman may have a tommy gun back at the station house as his ultimate weapon, but he uses his night stick to subdue the criminal without punching holes in the local populace." Similarly, he concluded, "the United States has got to demonstrate that it has the power and the discretion to win local scraps without destroying European civilization."[24]

Spanning this direct and indirect opposition was a concerted program of doctrinal dissent. In effect, the Army opted out of massive retaliation, declaring its belief in a theory of warfare consistent with traditional concepts of military professionalism.

A highlight of Ridgway's tenure as Chief of Staff was the revision of Army Field Manual 100-5, *Field Service Regulations: Operations*.[25] FM 100-5 is the bible of Army doctrine, specifying basic operational principles and providing an institutional template for matters ranging from tactics to training to organization. When Ridgway became Chief of Staff, the Army was still using an edition of FM 100-5 published in 1949. It badly needed overhaul.

The revised *Field Service Regulations* promulgated over Ridgway's signature in September 1954 responded to that requirement. The new manual incorporated lessons of the Korean War and reflected the latest thinking about how to adapt to a nuclear battlefield.

Beyond such operational matters, the new FM 100-5 also incorporated three broad themes. The first theme was an insistence that the *use* of force retained political legitimacy, in other words, that the role of American military forces extended beyond deterrence. The second theme was that a policy resting on a willingness to wage war against civilians was both politically ill-advised and morally unacceptable. The third theme was that the clash of land armies remained the inescapable medium through which wars were decided—this notwithstanding the advent of new technologies.

Thus, for example, Chapter 1 of Ridgway's new FM 100-5 returned to the very taproot of military orthodoxy, restating the principle that "war is a political act." Viewed in this context, military forces were "instruments of national policy" employed to achieve objectives that were themselves inherently political. "If the policy objectives are to be realized, policy and not interim expediency must govern the application of military power." Since the single-minded pursuit of military success could produce results that were politically absurd, "victory alone as an aim in war" was unacceptable. To make the point more plainly, FM 100-5 stated flatly that as far as the Army was concerned "indiscriminate destruction is unjustifiable in a military sense." As a result, for its part, the Army did not "deliberately make or invite war upon civilian populations." Instead, the Army sought "the defeat of an enemy by application of military power directly or indirectly against the armed forces which support his political structure." In the final analysis, decision over those enemy forces was gained through ground combat, a fact that affirmed the Army's preeminence as "the decisive component of the military structure."[26]

Although published in September 1954, it was January 4, 1955 before the manual came to public attention, courtesy of a front page story in *The New York Times*. One day later, an irritated Eisenhower felt compelled yet again to explain—and defend—his views on national security, this time in the form of a public letter to Secretary of Defense Wilson in which he reiterated the major themes of his national security policies.

According to the President, the proper basis for "true security" was a "strong and expanding economy." With regard to defense, Eisenhower emphasized that the "first objective" was "to deter an enemy from attack." Given the influence of "scientific progress" on the "character and conduct of war," it made sense for the United States to "base our security on military formations which make maximum use of science and technology in order to minimize numbers of men." By reducing the total number of military personnel, the U. S. would avoid having defense become "an intolerable burden" and would be better positioned to compete with the Soviets over the long haul. Just as the Army's new FM 100-5 never referred explicitly to any specific administration policy, so too the President's letter of January 5 studiously avoided any reference to Ridgway's critique.[27]

★ VI

By early February, even Republican Senate leaders were complaining to Eisenhower of Ridgway's opposition to administration policies long after the time for debate and discussion had passed. The complaint lodged by Senate leaders provoked Eisenhower to explain his differences with Ridgway in the plainest possible terms. As Ridgway correctly understood, those differences were rooted in contradictory visions of the future of war and of the relevance of the military profession. "You see," the President explained,

> the only thing we fear is an atomic attack delivered by air on our cities. Suppose that attack were to occur tomorrow on fifteen of our cities. God damn it. It would be perfect rot to talk about shipping troops abroad when fifteen of our cities were in ruins. You would have disorder and almost complete chaos in the cities and in the roads around them. You would have to restore order and who is going to restore it? Do you think the police and fire departments of those cities could restore order? Nuts! That order is going to have to be restored by disciplined armed forces. ...That's what our military is going to be doing in the first days of an all-out atomic attack. ...Anyone who thinks we are going to immediately ship out of this country division after division is just talking through his hat. It couldn't be done and if I tried to do it, you would want to impeach me. That's the trouble with Ridgway. He's talking theory—I'm trying to talk sound sense.[28]

Yet the "theory" that Ridgway espoused was nothing less than the insistence that force retained utility as a continuation of politics, notwithstanding the introduction of nuclear weapons. Whatever the "sound sense" of Eisenhower's thinking as a basis for national security policy in the particular circumstances of the mid-1950s, Ridgway viewed those policies as a direct threat to the military profession that he cherished and of which he viewed himself as a custodian.

In January, published reports had indicated that Ridgway would be appointed to a second two-year term. By March, the administration had reversed course, announcing that the general would retire at the end of June, citing age as the ostensible reason. The truth was that Ridgway had made himself persona non grata and that Eisenhower was determined to replace him with someone more accommodating. In effect, Ridgway was being fired.[29]

He would not go quietly. If anything, the announcement that he was being eased into retirement freed Ridgway from any need to exercise restraint. Fresh salvos of protest accompanied his departure from active duty. Eisenhower, the revered national hero, remained off-limits to direct attack.

The same could not be said for Secretary Wilson, the President's chief agen in inflicting the New Look on the Army.

On June 27, 1955—just three days before his retirement—Ridgway sen Wilson a final report that was a catalogue of his disagreements with th administration over the previous two years: questions about the efficacy o massive retaliation in an era of atomic plenty; the concern that policies base on the possibility of all-out nuclear war were inconsistent with America' traditional "religious and moral principles"; the warning against allowin military advisers to become politicized and coopted by civilian officials wit little appreciation of the soldier's role; the refusal to abandon the Army' traditional conception of warfare "in order to accommodate enthusiasti theorists having little or no responsibility for the consequences of followin the courses of action they advocate."[30] The report soon leaked to the pres where it attracted the widespread attention.

Attracting much less publicity and yet arguably of greater significance wa Ridgway's testimonial to his fellow soldiers, released on the very eve of hi retirement ceremony. In DA Pamphlet 21-70 published over his signature o June 29, Ridgway made one final effort to prescribe "The Role of th Army." Whatever the changes in warfare brought about by modern technol ogy, DA Pam 21-70 declared that the Army remained "the Decisiv Instrument." As in the past so in the future, wars would be decided by "th trained fighting man who, with his feet on the ground, defeats the enemy' ground fighters, seizes his land, and holds it." Directly contradicting one o the abiding principles of Eisenhower's national securing policy, DA Pam 21 70 declared that "We need more men not less."[31]

Having rid himself of one general who epitomized traditional militar professionalism, Ike chose as his replacement an officer who personified th new model soldier, the polished, and politically-astute Maxwell D. Taylor. I offering Taylor the job of Army Chief of Staff, the President established tw preconditions: he wanted Taylor to give first priority to his duties as member of the JCS rather than to his responsibilities as service chief; and h demanded Taylor's pledge that he would "hold views as to doctrine, basi principles, and relationships which are in accord with those of th President."[32]

Taylor acceded to both preconditions—and in short order proceeded t disregard them both. Taylor's own tenure as Chief of Staff was marked b more friction as Army opposition to the Eisenhower administration's policie persisted. Yet Taylor achieved no greater success at modifying those policie than had his predecessor. Like Ridgway, his departure from active dut would be an angry one, accompanied by his famous indictment *The Uncertai Trumpet*, a book that signified the end of the era of massive retaliation an marked the beginning of the era of "Flexible Response."[33]

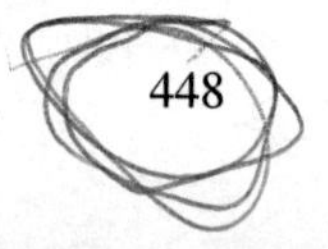

Notes

[1]*New York Times*, 26 September 1952, 12.

[2]Federal spending for fiscal year 1953 totaled $74.1 billion. Of that, $44 billion was for defense and another $2.4 billion for veterans affairs. U.S. Bureau of the Census, *Historical Statistics of the United States, Colonial Times to 1970*, Part 2 (Washington: GPO, 1975), 1114.

[3]Department of State, *Foreign Relations of the United States, 1952–1954: National Security Affairs*, Part I (Washington: GPO, 1984), 307, 310. Hereafter cited as *FRUS.*

[4]Eisenhower to Secretary of Defense Charles E. Wilson, 1 July 1953, cited in Robert J. Watson, *The Joint Chiefs of Staff and National Policy, 1953–1954.* (Washington: GPO, 1986), 14-15.

[5]Cited Ibid., 18-19.

[6]There is no adequate biography of Ridgway. The most complete account of his life and career remains his own memoir, *Soldier* (New York: Harper and Brothers, 1956).

[7]*FRUS, 1952–1954: National Security Affairs*, Part 1, 574. The final document approved by the Council as NSC 162/2 "Basic National Security Policy" is reprinted on pp. 578-97.

[8]A. J. Bacevich, *The Pentomic Era.* (Washington, DC: National Defense University Press, 1986), 15-21.

[9]Ridgway, "Memorandum for the Record," 19 October 1953, Box 28, The Papers of Matthew B. Ridgway, U.S. Army Military History Institute, Carlisle Barracks, Pennsylvania. Hereafter cited as Ridgway Papers.

[10]Ibid.

[11]Samuel P. Huntington, *The Soldier and the State: The Theory and Politics of Civil-Military Relations* (Cambridge, MA: Harvard University Press, 1957), 77.

[12]Memorandum for the Secretary of the Army, Subject: Military Strategy and Policy (JCS 2102/111), 9 December 1953, Box 825, Army Chief of Staff Decimal File, 1953, Records of the Army Staff (Record Group 319), National Archives and Records Administration, Washington, DC.

[13]Memorandum by the Chief of Staff, U.S. Army, Subject: Joint Strategic Objective Plan for an Assumed D-Date of 1 July 1956, 10 March 1954, CCS 381 (11-29-49), Sec. 12, Box 115, Records of the Joint Chiefs of Staff (Record Group 218), NA. Hereafter cited as RG 218.

[14]Memorandum by the Chief of Staff, U.S. Army, Subject: Basic National Security Policy, undated [October 1954], CCS 381 U.S. (1-31-50), Sec. 47, Box 37, RG 218, NA. Section 47 of this file contains two identically titled but substantively different memoranda from Ridgway. The first was drafted sometime after 20 October, the second after 26 October.

[15]Memorandum for the Special Assistant to the President for National Security Affairs, Subject: Review of Basic National Security Policy (NSC 162/2 and NSC 5422/2), 22 November 1954, Box 30, Ridgway Papers.

[16]Ibid.

[17]*FRUS, 1952–1954: National Security Affairs*, Part 1, 804-6.

[18]Andrew J. Goodpaster, Memorandum of Conference with the President, 22 December 1954, Box 3, Ann Whitman File (Ann Whitman Diary), Papers of Dwight D. Eisenhower, Eisenhower Library, Abilene, Kansas.

[19]*New York Times*, 1 January 1955, 5.

[20]Ridgway, "Man: The Virtual Weapon," *Army Combat Forces Journal 5* (March 1955): 16, 19.

[21]Colonel Shillelagh, "...trouble with cavalry is...," *Army Combat Forces Journal 5* (February 1955): 16, 18.

[22]James Gavin, "Beyond the Stars," 187-90, the Papers of James M. Gavin, U.S. Army Military History Institute, Carlisle Barracks, Pennsylvania.

[23]Ridgway, "The Soldier and National Policy," 14 February 1955, vol. 21, Records of Meetings, Archives of the Council on Foreign Relations, New York. Hereafter cited as CFR.

[24]"Nuclear Weapons and Foreign Policy," 4 May 1955, vol. 60, Records of Groups CFR; in addition, see the remarks by Lieutenant General Lyman L. Lemnitzer at the study group meeting of 21 February 1955, also filed in volume 60.

[25]Department of the Army, FM 105-5 *Field Service Regulations: Operations* (September 1954).

[26]Ibid., 4-7.

[27]Eisenhower to Wilson, 5 January 1955, Box 27, Ridgway Papers.

[28]Robert C. Ferrell, ed. *The Diary of James C. Haggerty* (Bloomington: Indiana University Press, 1981), 181-84.

[29]*New York Times*, 21 January 1955, 1; 26 March 1955, 6. See also Stephen E. Ambrose, *Eisenhower: The President* (New York: Simon and Schuster, 1984), 234.

[30]Ridgway's final report to Wilson reprinted in *Soldier*, 323-32.

[31]DA Pamphlet 21-70, "The Role of the Army" (29 June 1955), 7, 9, 14; copy filed in Box 28, Ridgway Papers.

[32]E. Bruce Geelhoed. *Charles E. Wilson and Controversy at the Pentagon, 1953–1957* (Detroit: Wayne State University Press, 1979), 136-38.

[33]Douglas Kinnard, "Civil-Military Relations: The President and the General," *The National Security: Its Theory and Practice, 1945–1960*, Norman A. Graebner, ed. (New York: Oxford University Press, 1986), 204.

☆ ☆ ☆

9/11: A Mega Historical Event

David C. Kozak, Ph.D.

In this thoughtful essay David C. Kozak, Professor of Political Science at the United States Military Academy, reflects on the effects of 9/11/01, observing that for him the attacks of that day are of equal emotional importance to the other most important single events of his lifetime, the assassinations of John F. Kennedy and Martin Luther King, Jr. Kozak notes several exceptional effects of 9/11. One is the sense of national unity that has been felt infrequently, especially since the Vietnam years. Another is the end of the optimism that filled the 90s, when stocks were high and our vulnerability was not a part of day-to-day consciousness. One result of the events of 9/11 is that we now live in an era preoccupied with homeland security.

Beginning in July 2001, my time here at West Point has been one of both great historical significance as well as national sorrow. The historical significance is that throughout 2002 the U.S. Military Academy celebrated its two-hundredth anniversary—200 years of stellar service to the nation. The sorrow, of course, is that during our stay here the attacks of September 11th occurred, with a terrifying immediacy given that here we are located a mere fifty miles north of ground zero.

"9/11" as we have come to know it was a true "mega historical event," ranking in the popular psyche along side the 1941 Japanese attack on Pearl Harbor and the 1963 assassination of President Kennedy as days that traumatized America. Dr. David Goldstein of the Graduate School of Public and International Affairs (GSPIA) at the University of Pittsburgh and renowned expert on World War II and best selling author of the definitive Pearl Harbor book *At Dawn We Slept*[1] refers to 9/11 as "Pearl Harbor plus!"

☆ ☆ ☆ ☆ ☆ ☆

Although the country was not as fully mobilized as in the aftermath of Pearl Harbor and 9/11did not transform the nation to the extent of Pearl Harbor day, 9/11 is Pearl Harbor plus because it was an attack on the continental U.S., it sadly surpasses the casualties of the 1941 attack, and the dead and wounded were mainly civilians and non-combatants. Regardless, for sure, all of us will always remember where we were when we heard the shocking news of the attacks of 9/11 in New York, Washington, D.C., and Pennsylvania.

Professionally, for me, 9/11 is the most stunning single day event to occur in my thirty year career as a political science professor, eclipsing in shock value events such as the assassination attempt on President Ronald Reagan, the resignation of President Nixon, President Ford's pardon of Nixon, and the impeachment trial of President Clinton. Personally, it is one of the most shocking political developments in my lifetime—on an emotional par with the murders of John and Robert Kennedy and Reverend King.

After this year of shock, sorrow, careful watching and reflection, it is obvious that 9/11 has profound impact on American politics, governing processes, and policy priorities. A quick review illustrates the historical implications of that sad day last year.

★ *Political Impacts*

The most obvious impact was a remarkable—though temporary—political unity and bipartisanship. This was particularly striking in the partisan, polarized and poisonous post-impeachment policy environment.

Beginning in the 1980's and into the 1990's and the new century, analysts described American politics as one of "coalitions made of sand," "governing without majorities," and "the collapse of consensus." Such divisions became most punctuated during the Clinton years. President Clinton came into office with only 43 percent of the popular vote. The 1994 midterm elections produced the first Republican Congress in forty years—the assertive "Gingrich Congress"—leaving Clinton the first Democrat President since Truman to face both houses of Congress controlled by Republicans. Things deteriorated in gridlock and bare fisted politics, culminating in Clinton's impeachment trial and further worsening with the divisive 2002 Presidential elections.

As the nation coped with the terrorist disasters of 9/11, the reaction for Democrats as much as Republicans was to rally around the flag which historically has meant to rally around the President as well. There is no greater testimony to this than the words of Democrat Senate Leader Tom Daschle during the traditional "out party" response to President Bush's historic speech to the nation concerning generational responsibility at a joint session of Congress. "On these issues of counter terrorism" the Senator said, "there is no opposition party!" Prior to 9/11 American politics and indeed society were described in terms of divisions. Sociologists Robert Putnam reflected this as a time of "bowling alone"—where people withdrew onto themselves and many felt "disconnected" from the nation's political life. Following 9/11 Putnam referred to a "bowling together" syndrome, where many became reconnected to family, neighborhood, community and co-workers.[2]

Another tangible political consequence was the increase in both stature and approval rating of President George W. Bush. "Bush 43," as he came to be known in comparison with his father "Bush 41," had a presidency begotten of an extremely contentious election: the first contested presidential election in 125 years and the first time since 1888 that the winner of the popular vote did not win the presidency. Accordingly, he began his presidency with strong national divisions, further widened by a Democratic takeover of the Senate in the aftermath of the defection of Republican Senator Jeffords of Vermont. Prior to September 11, Bush's public support and approval rating in Gallup polls hovered slightly above 50 percent. In the aftermath of 9/11 George W's rating soared to a record ninety percent. It was as if he was transformed before our eyes. The events of 9/11 and the nation's response to them obliged us to look at the new President differently. Many Presidency watchers compared his transformation to that of Truman, Ford or Reagan—a leader who at first was dismissed by many as a "light weight or a shadow of predecessors" now rising to the occasion of the mighty majesty of the Presidential office and job! And along the way, a grand irony was that this President who was not particularly known for gifted oratory gave some memorable talks. Though his approval rating has now slipped to the mid-seventies a year after, it is much stronger than was the case prior to 9/11.

☆ *Impacts on Governing Processes*

Historical mega events usually usher in new eras in public policy. In addition to providing an all new national security envelope, 9/11 profoundly impacts the American processes of governance. Prior to the events, American Presidential-Congressional politics were best described in the early George W. administration as a time of "surplus distribution politics." Due to a deal struck in the late 1990's between President Clinton and Speaker Gingrich, the decades-long fight to erase Federal budgetary deficits finally succeeded

The fight in American politics was no longer how to balance the budget but how to distribute a projected multi-trillion dollar surplus over the next decade. Republicans proposed tax cuts for reinvesting in the economy; Democrats offered a shoring up of social programs. Of course, 9/11 put an end to the debate! Now, for as far as we can see, the country is back into deficit spending, not just because of tax cuts but because of the many new counter-terrorism initiatives and military responses.

Two other considerations are relevant here with regards to governance: "the two Presidencies Theory" and "the issue-attention cycle." Both provide important insights here. The two Presidencies theory is the notion that Presidential-Congressional relations are very different in the foreign policy and domestic policy realms.[3] In foreign/defense/national security policy Presidents have much more leeway, latitude and leadership potential. Due to the tradition of a bipartisan foreign policy and the notion that partisanship should stop at the water's edge, to the President's constitutional authority and policy tools as Commander-in-Chief and chief diplomat, and the relative absence of strong constituent and interest group pressures on members of Congress, the President has a much stronger hand to shape policy and to lead in international affairs. Not so in domestic policy where intense interest group and constituency pressures leave presidents as only one of several competitors attempting to put their imprint on legislation. This pattern can be seen even in the early period following 9/11. The President exercised sort of a free rein, except on those issues that go to the heart of the core differences between the two parties such as federalization of airport security personnel (the President opposed nationalization), economic stimulus (Republicans proposing tax cuts in contrast to Democrats proposing spending programs) and Attorney General Ashcroft's policy on detaining suspected terrorists (with many civil liberty minded Democrats and some Republicans opposed).

The concept of the "issue-attention cycle" also accounts for what we are currently experiencing with regard to governing processes[4] Basically, policy makers are victims of their own success. This was especially true of the environmental policy sector. With relative improvements—noxious substances not as readily visible in the air and water—many Americans have backed off their strong environmental stands, presuming often wrongly that the improvements they see signify complete success. Certainly this seems to be the case now with counter-terrorism. The further we get away from 9/11, the more people lapse back into "business as usual," complaining about increased airport security, etc. though the menace is still there!

★ Consequences for Governmental Policies and Priorities

Prior to 9/11, the term "Homeland Security" was an esoteric one usually used simultaneously with cyber security and asymmetric warfare, often reflected on only at highly specialized conferences by only a handful of experts. Since 9/11, it is *the* hot "buzzword" made all the more relevant to Pennsylvanians with our own favorite son Tom Ridge tasked with the awesome and daunting responsibilities of coordinating all U.S. efforts towards that all important end.

After 9/11 we realized there was a vast array of U.S. public (and private for that matter) bureaucracies with homeland security functions, far flung and isolated from each other by bureaucratic culture and resource rivalry. At first, Ridge tried through sheer force of personality to coordinate the some 46 federal departments and agencies that had major homeland security functions (actually 72 where an officer has a badge and carries a gun). Soon it became readily apparent that no matter how skillful the Governor personal brokering was insufficient for these tasks and by June 2002 the President proposed the most far-reaching reorganization of the federal government for reasons of national security since 1947. When finally established, the new Federal Department of Homeland Security will be the second largest Federal department, second only to the Department of Defense in terms of both budget and personnel, and housing under a single departmental roof the Coast Guard, FEEMA, Secret Service, INS, and Customs, as well as several other agencies. This new department and strategies for "first responders" and other new Homeland Security initiatives constitute another tangible consequence of 9/11.

As a major historical event, 9/11 truly ushered in a new era of American politics, government, and public policy. More than a year later we realize that we are in unchartered territory, making it up as we go along, "doing without knowing" and hoping for the best. The story is still unfolding! It is a work in progress! With an American incursion into Afghanistan and Congressional authorization of a preemptive strike against Iraq, as some have said, we may not yet be at the end of the beginning.

★ **David C. Kozak** is a *Professor of Political Science at the United States Military Academy.*

Endnotes

[1]Gordon W. Prange and Donald M. Goldstein, *At Dawn We Slept: The Untold Story of Pearl Harbor*, (New York, N.Y., Penguin Putnam, Inc., December, 1991).

[2]See Robert D. Putnam, "*Bowling Together,*" *The American Prospect*, Vol. 13, no. 3 (February 11, 2002).

[3]See Aaron Wildavsky, "The Two Presidencies," *Transaction*, Vol. 4, No. 2 (Dec. 1966) and Steven A. Shull, ed. *The Two Presidencies: A Quarter Century Assessment* (Chicago: Nelson Hall, 1991).

[4]See Anthony Downs, "Up and Down with Ecology—the 'Issue-Attention Cycle,'" *The Public Interest,* 28 (Summer, 1972), 38-50.

★ ★ ★ ★ ★

Questions

1. In what ways is daily life now different from what it was before 9/11?

2. In what ways is the way we make public policy different from what it was before 9/11?

3. In what ways are our national priorities different from what they were before 9/11?

4. How important was 9/11 when compared with the major events of the twentieth century?

5. After 9/11 are Americans more realistic or simply more depressed?